Digital Anthro

Digital Anthropology

Edited by Heather A. Horst and Daniel Miller

London • New York

English edition
First published in 2012 by
Berg
Editorial offices:
50 Bedford Square, London WC1B 3DP, UK
175 Fifth Avenue, New York, NY 10010, USA

Berg is an imprint of Bloomsbury Publishing Plc.

Library of Congress Cataloging-in-Publication Data

A catalogue record for this book is available from the Library of Congress.

British Library Cataloguing-in-Publication Data

A catalogue record for this book is available from the British Library.

ISBN 978 0 85785 291 5 (Cloth)
978 0 85785 290 8 (Paper)
e-ISBN 978 0 85785 292 2 (institutional)
978 0 85785 293 9 (individual)

Typeset by Apex CoVantage, LLC, Madison, WI, USA.
Printed in the UK by the MPG Books Group

www.bergpublishers.com

Contents

Notes on Contributors

Bart Barendregt is an anthropologist who lectures at the Institute of Social and Cultural Studies at Leiden University in the Netherlands. He is coordinating a four-year research project (Articulation of Modernity) funded by the Netherlands Organization for Scientific Research (NWO) that deals with popular music, modernity and social chance in South East Asia. As a senior researcher, he is also affiliated with an NWO project titled The Future is Elsewhere: Towards a Comparative History of Digital Futurities, which examines Islamic ideas of the information society, halal software and appropriation and localization of digital technology in an overt religious context. Barendregt has done extensive fieldwork in Java, Sumatra, Malaysia and the Philippines and has published on South East Asian performing arts, new and mobile media and popular culture.

Tom Boellstorff is professor in the Department of Anthropology at the University of California, Irvine. From 2007 to 2012 he was editor-in-chief of *American Anthropologist*, the flagship journal of the American Anthropological Association. He is the author of many articles and books, including *The Gay Archipelago: Sexuality and Nation in Indonesia* (Princeton University Press, 2005); *A Coincidence of Desires: Anthropology, Queer Studies, Indonesia* (Duke University Press, 2007); *Coming of Age in Second Life: An Anthropologist Explores the Virtually Human* (Princeton University Press, 2008); and *Ethnography and Virtual Worlds: A Handbook of Method*, with Bonnie Nardi, Celia Pearce and T. L. Taylor (Princeton University Press, 2012).

Stefana Broadbent is currently a teaching fellow in digital anthropology at University College London. Since 1990 she has been studying the evolution of digital practices at home and in the workplace and has recently published a book on the blurring of the boundaries between the two: *L'Intimite au Travail* (FYP Editions, 2011). Previously, she was research director and member of the Strategy Board of Swisscom, where she started the Observatory of Digital Life. The Observatory studied longitudinally the evolution of digital activities in Swiss households. She has been a lecturer in ethnography and design in the Faculty of Architecture at the Politecnico di Milano, and the Ecole Superieur des Art Decoratifs in Paris.

Lane DeNicola is a lecturer in digital anthropology at University College London. His research interests include culture and design; spatial information technology and geomedia; the social and political dimensions of open design; space industrialization in the developing world; scientific visualization; immersive systems and gaming. Prior to his doctoral training in science and technology studies, he worked as a programmer and simulation designer at the Johns Hopkins Applied Physics Laboratory, the MIT Lincoln Laboratory and the Center for Space Research at MIT.

Adam Drazin is coordinator of the MA degree programme in culture, materials and design at the Department of Anthropology, University College London. He lectured previously at Trinity College Dublin. Drazin works principally in the fields of material culture, design anthropology and the Romanian home. He has conducted design anthropology work with HP Labs, the Technical University of Eindhoven and Intel Ireland, mostly exploring material culture with a view to critical design approaches. Prior to lecturing at Trinity College Dublin, he ran his own sole-trader consultancy business. His current research interest is on the cultures of openness and home-making for people who have moved from Romania to Ireland. Other interests include the material culture of intentionality, cultures of design and the more appropriate use of ethnography in innovation. He recently guest-edited a joint special edition of *Anthropology in Action* and the *Irish Journal of Anthropology* on 'Anthropology, Design and Technology in Ireland' and has published in *Ethnos* and *Home Cultures*, among other places.

Haidy Geismar is assistant professor of anthropology and museum studies at New York University. Her research focuses on issues surrounding value and materiality, using museums as a filter. Her research interests are intellectual and cultural property, the formation of digital objects and most broadly the ways in which museums and markets influence and engender relations between persons and things. Since 2000 she has worked as a researcher and curator in Vanuatu and Aotearoa, New Zealand, England and the United States.

Faye Ginsburg is founder and ongoing director of the Center for Media, Culture and History at New York University, where she is also the David Kriser Professor of Anthropology, and codirector of the Center for Religion and Media and of the NYU Council for the Study of Disability. She is an award-winning editor/author of four books, including *Media Worlds: Anthropology on New Terrain* and *Mediating Culture: Indigenous Media in the Digital Age*, which is still in press. She is currently carrying out research on cultural innovation and learning differences with Rayna Rapp.

Heather A. Horst is a Vice Chancellor's Senior Research Fellow in the School of Media and Communication at RMIT University and the co-director of the Digital Ethnography Research Centre. She is the coauthor (with Daniel Miller) of *The Cell Phone: An Anthropology of Communication* (Berg, 2006) and (with Ito et al.) of

Hanging Out, Messing Around and Geeking Out: Kids Living and Learning with New Media (MIT Press, 2010). She is currently writing an ethnography focused on digital media and family life in Silicon Valley. Her current research examines communicative and monetary ecologies in the Caribbean and Pacific.

Jelena Karanović is adjunct assistant professor in the Department of Media, Culture and Communication at New York University. Trained in cultural anthropology, French studies and computer science, Karanović pursues research on new media activism, information rights, media ethnography, media and globalization, France and Europe. Her book manuscript, in preparation, explores the experiences and dilemmas of French free software advocates as they reinvent civic engagement around digital media. By drawing on twenty months of fieldwork conducted online and offline in 2004 and 2005, she analyses how prime vehicles of free-market globalization—intellectual property law and digital media technologies—have invigorated public debates about European integration and the transnational political economy. Her work brings anthropology into dialogue with media studies, science and technology studies and European studies. Her 2010 article, 'Contentious Europeanization: The Paradox of Becoming European through Anti-Patent Activism', appeared in *Ethnos: Journal of Anthropology*.

Thomas M. Malaby is professor and chair in the Department of Anthropology at the University of Wisconsin-Milwaukee and has published numerous works on games, practice and indeterminacy. He is continually interested in the ever-changing relationships among institutions, unpredictability and technology—especially as they are realized through games and gamelike processes. His most recent book, *Making Virtual Worlds: Linden Lab and Second Life* (Cornell University Press, 2009), is an ethnographic examination of Linden Lab and its relationship to its creation, Second Life. He is also a featured author at the blog Terra Nova.

Daniel Miller is professor of material culture in the Department of Anthropology, University College London, where he recently established a programme in digital anthropology. Relevant publications include *Tales from Facebook* (Polity Press, 2011), *Migration and New Media: Transnationalism and Polymedia* (with M. Madianou, Routledge, 2011), *The Cell Phone: An Anthropology of Communication* (with H. Horst, Berg, 2006) and *The Internet: An Ethnographic Approach* (with Don Slater, Berg, 2000). Other recent books include *Blue Jeans* (with S. Woodward, University of California Press, 2011) and *Consumption and Its Consequences* (Polity Press, 2012).

John Postill is an anthropologist (PhD University College London) who specializes in the study of digital media. A senior lecturer in media at Sheffield Hallam University, he is the author of *Localizing the Internet* (2011) and *Media and Nation Building*

(2006) and the co-editor of *Theorising Media and Practice* (2010). He has conducted fieldwork in Malaysia and Spain and is currently writing a book about digital media and the indignados movement. In addition, he is the founder and convener of the Media Anthropology Network, European Association of Social Anthropologists.

Jo Tacchi is deputy dean of research and innovation in the School of Media and Communications at RMIT University. Research and its application in the area of communication for development have been a focus of Tacchi's research since 1999. Her work in this area has been centrally concerned with issues around culture and social change, and in developing suitable methodologies for investigating this. Since 2002 she has led research and research teams spread across Australian universities and a range of national and international organizations, including the United Nations Educational, Scientific and Cultural Organization, the United Nations Development Programme, Intel Corporation, international nongovernmental organizations and Australian government departments and agencies to develop and test innovative methodologies for monitoring and evaluation, for developing and researching approaches to participatory content creation and for research in communication, media and information and communication technology for development.

Part I
Introduction

–1–

The Digital and the Human: A Prospectus for Digital Anthropology

Daniel Miller and Heather A. Horst

This introduction will propose six basic principles as the foundation for a new subdiscipline: digital anthropology.[1] While the principles will be used to integrate the chapters that follow, its larger purpose is to spread the widest possible canvas upon which to begin the creative work of new research and thinking. The intention is not simply to study and reflect on new developments but to use these to further our understanding of what we are and have always been. The digital should and can be a highly effective means for reflecting upon what it means to be human, the ultimate task of anthropology as a discipline.

While we cannot claim to be comprehensive, we will try to cover a good deal of ground, because we feel that to launch a book of this kind means taking responsibility for asking and answering some significant questions. For example, we need to be clear as to what we mean by words such as *digital*, *culture* and *anthropology* and what we believe represents practices that are new and unprecedented and what remains the same or merely slightly changed. We need to find a way to ensure that the vast generalizations required in such tasks do not obscure differences, distinctions and relativism, which we view as remaining amongst the most important contributions of an anthropological perspective to understanding human life and culture. We have responded partly through imposing a common structure to this volume. Each of the contributors was asked to provide a general survey of work in their field, followed by two more detailed (usually ethnographic) case studies, concluded by a discussion of potential new developments.

In this introduction we use the findings of these individual contributions as the foundation for building six principles that we believe constitute the key questions and concerns of digital anthropology as a subdiscipline. The first principle is that the digital itself intensifies the dialectical nature of culture. The term *digital* will be defined as all that which can be ultimately reduced to binary code but which produces a further proliferation of particularity and difference. The dialectic refers to the relationship between this growth in universality and particularity and the intrinsic connections between their positive and negative effects. Our second principle suggests that humanity is not one iota more mediated by the rise of the digital. Rather, we suggest that digital anthropology will progress to the degree that the digital enables us to understand and exposes the framed nature of analogue or predigital life as culture and fails when we fall victim to a broader and romanticized discourse that presupposes a greater authenticity or reality to the predigital. The commitment to holism, the foundation of anthropological perspectives on humanity, represents a third principle. Where some disciplines prioritize collectives, minds, individuals and other fragments of life, anthropologists focus upon life as lived and all the (mess of) relevant factors that comes with that. Anthropological approaches to ethnography focus upon the world constituted within the frame of a particular ethnographic project but also the still wider world that both impacts upon and transcends that frame. The fourth principle reasserts the importance of cultural relativism and the global nature of our encounter with the digital, negating assumptions that the digital is necessarily homogenizing and also giving voice and visibility to those who are peripheralized by modernist and similar perspectives. The fifth principle is concerned with the essential ambiguity of digital culture with regard to its increasing openness and closure, which emerge in matters ranging from politics and privacy to the authenticity of ambivalence.

Our final principle acknowledges the materiality of digital worlds, which are neither more nor less material than the worlds that preceded them. Material culture approaches have shown how materiality is also the mechanism behind our final observation, which is also our primary justification for an anthropological approach. This concerns humanity's remarkable capacity to reimpose normativity just as quickly as digital technologies create conditions for change. We shall argue that it is this drive to the normative that that makes attempts to understand the impact of the digital in the absence of anthropology unviable. As many of the chapters in this volume will demonstrate, the digital, as all material culture, is more than a substrate; it is becoming a constitutive part of what makes us human. The primary point of this introduction, and the emergence of digital anthropology as a subfield more generally, is in resolute opposition to all approaches that imply that becoming digital has either rendered us less human, less authentic or more mediated. Not only are we just as human within the digital world, the digital also provides many new opportunities for anthropology to help us understand what it means to be human.

Defining the Digital through the Dialectic

Some time ago Daniel Miller and Haidy Geismar were discussing the launch of the new master's programme in digital anthropology at University College London. Reflecting upon similar initiatives in museum studies at New York University, Geismar mentioned that one of the challenges of creating such programs revolved around the fact that everyone had different ideas of what the digital implied. Some scholars looked to three-dimensional visualizations of museum objects. For others, the digital referred to virtual displays, the development of websites and virtual exhibitions. Some colleagues looked to innovations in research methodology, while others focused on the digitalization of collections and archives. Still others focused upon new media and digital communication, such as smartphones. Alongside novelty, the word *digital* has come to be associated with a much wider and older meta-discourse of modernism, from science fiction to various versions of technoliberalism. At the end of the day, however, the word seems to have become a discursive catchall for novelty.

For the purposes of this book, we feel it may therefore be helpful to start with a clear and unambiguous definition of the digital. Rather than a general distinction between the digital and the analogue, we define the digital as everything that has been developed by, or can be reduced to, the binary—that is bits consisting of 0s and 1s. The development of binary code radically simplified information and communication, creating new possibilities of convergence between what were previously disparate technologies or content. We will use this basic definition, but we are aware that the term *digital* has been associated with many other developments. For example systems theory and the cybernetics of Norbert Wiener (Turner 2006: 20–8; Wiener 1948) developed from observations of self-regulatory feedback mechanisms in living organisms that have nothing to do with binary code but can be applied to engineering. We also acknowledge that the use of term *digital* in colloquial discourse is clearly wider than our specific usage; we suggest that having such an unambiguous definition has heuristic benefits that will become evident below.

One advantage of defining the digital as binary is that this definition also helps us identify a possible historical precedent. If the digital is defined as our ability to reduce so much of the world to the commonality of a binary, a sort of baseline 2, then we can also reflect upon humanity's ability to previously reduce much of the world to baseline 10, the decimal foundation for systems of modern money. There is a prior and established anthropological debate about the consequences of money for humanity that may help us to conceptualize the consequences of the digital. Just like the digital, money represented a new phase in human abstraction where, for the first time, practically anything could be reduced to the same common element. This reduction of quality to quantity was in turn the foundation for an explosion of differentiated things, especially the huge expansion of commoditization linked to industrialization. In both cases, the more we reduce to the same, the more we can thereby create difference. This is what makes money the best precedent for understanding digital culture and leads to our first principle of the dialectic.

Dialectical thinking, as developed by Hegel, theorized this relationship between the simultaneous growth of the universal and of the particular as dependent upon each other rather than in opposition to each other. This is the case both with money and with the digital. For social science much of the concern was with the way money meant that everything that we hold dear can now be reduced to the quantitative. This reduction to baseline 10 seemed at least as much a threat as a promise to our general humanity. Generalized from Marx and Simmel's original arguments with regard to capitalism by the Frankfurt School and others, money threatens humanity both as universalized abstraction and as differentiated particularity. As an abstraction, money gives rise to various forms of capital and their inherent tendency to aggrandizement. As particularity, money threatens our humanity through the sheer scale and diversity of commoditized culture. We take such arguments to be sufficiently well established as to not require further elucidation here.

Keith Hart (2000, 2005, 2007) was the first to suggest that money might be a useful precedent to the digital, because money provides the basis for a specifically anthropological response to the challenges which the digital in turn poses to our humanity.[2] Money was always virtual to the degree that it extended the possibilities of abstraction. Exchange became more distant from face-to-face transaction and focused on equivalence, calculation and the quantitative as opposed to human and social consequence. Hart recognized that digital technologies align with these virtual properties; indeed, they make money itself still more abstract, more deterritorialized, cheaper, more efficient and closer to the nature of information or communication.

Hart previously argued that if money was itself responsible for such effects, then perhaps humanity's best response was to tackle this problem at its source. He saw a potential for human liberation in various schemes that reunite money with social relations, such as local exchange trading schemes (Hart 2000: 280–7). For Hart, the digital not only exacerbates the problems of money but also can form part of the solution since new money-like schemes based on the Internet may allow us to create more democratized and personalized systems of exchange outside of mainstream capitalism. PayPal and eBay hint at these emancipatory possibilities in digital money and trade. Certainly, as Zelizer (1994) has shown, there are many ways we domesticate and resocialize money. For example many people use the money they earn from side jobs for personal treats, ignoring the apparent homogeneity of money as money.

By contrast Simmel's (1978) masterpiece, *The Philosophy of Money*, includes the first detailed analysis of what was happening at the other end of this dialectical equation. Money was also behind the commodification that led to a vast quantitative increase in material culture. This also created a potential source of alienation as we are deluged by the vast mass of differentiated stuff that surpasses our capacity to appropriate it as culture. Similarly, in our new clichés of the digital we are told that humanity is being swamped by the scale of information and the sheer number of different things we are expected to attend to. Much of the debate about the digital and the human is premised on the threat that the former poses for the latter. We are told that our humanity is beset both by the digital as virtual abstraction *and* its opposite form as the sheer quantity of heterogenized things that are thereby produced. In effect, the digital is producing too much culture, which, because we cannot manage and engage with it, renders us thereby superficial or shallow or alienated.

If Hart argued that our response should be to tackle money at the source, an alternative is presented in *Material Culture and Mass Consumption* (Miller 1987). Miller suggested that people struggle against this feeling of alienation and superficiality not by resocializing money, in the ways described by Zelizer, but through their consumption of commodities in their specificity. The everyday act of shopping, in which we designate most goods as not 'us' before finding one we will buy, is (in a small way) an attempt to reassert our cultural specificity. We use goods as possessions to try and turn the alienable back into the inalienable. Often this fails, but there are many ways in which everyday domestic consumption utilizes commodities to facilitate meaningful relationships between persons (Miller 2007).

If we agree to regard money as the precedent for the digital, Hart and Miller then provide two distinct positions on the consequences of the digital for our sense of our own humanity. Do we address the problems posed by the digital at the point of its production as abstract code or in our relationship to the mass of new cultural forms that have been created using digital technologies? What does seem clear is that the digital is indeed a further twist to the dialectical screw. At the level of abstraction, there are grounds for thinking we have reached rock bottom; there can be nothing more basic and abstract than binary bits, the difference between 0 and 1. At the other end of the scale, it is already clear that the digital far outstrips mere commoditization in its ability to proliferate difference. Digital processes can reproduce and communicate exact copies prodigiously and cheaply. They can both extend commoditization, but equally, in fields such as communication and music, we have seen a remarkable trend towards decommoditization as people find ways to get things for free. Whether commodified (or not), what is clear is that digital technologies are proliferating a vastly increased field of cultural forms, and what we have seen so far may be just the beginning.

To date, most of the literature on the revolutionary impact and potential of the digital has tended to follow Hart in focusing upon the abstract end of the equation. This point of view is represented in this volume by Karanović's discussion of free software and sharing. For example, Kelty (2008) uses historical and ethnographic methods to retrace the work of those who founded and created the free software movement that lies behind many developments in digital culture (see also Karanović 2008), including instruments such as Linux, UNIX and distributed free software such as Napster and Firefox. There are many reasons why these developments have been celebrated. As Karanović notes, they derive from long-standing political debates which include ideals of free access and ideals of distributed invention, both of which seemed to betoken an escape from the endless increase in commoditization, and, in certain areas such as music, have led to a quite effective decommodification. Software that was shared and not sold seemed to realize the new efficiencies and relative costlessness of digital creation and communication. It also expressed a freedom from control and governance, which seemed to realize various forms of anarchist—or more specifically the idealized—links between new technology and liberalism that are discussed by Barendregt and Malaby. It is also a trend continued by the hacker groups discussed by Karanović, leading to the more anarchist aims of organizations such as Anonymous, which is studied by Coleman (2009).

What is clear in Karanović's and others' contributions is that, just as Simmel saw that money was not just a new medium but one that allowed humanity to advance in conceptualization and philosophy towards a new imagination of itself, so open source does not simply change coding. The very ideal and experience of free software and open source leads to analogous ideals of what Kelty (2008) calls recursive publics, a committed and involved population that could create fields ranging from free publishing to the collective creation of Wikipedia modelled on the ideal of open source. At a time when the left-leaning student idealism that had lasted since the 1960s seemed exhausted, digital activism became a plausible substitute. This trend has been a major component of digital anthropology to date, including the impact of mainstream politics discussed by Postill. The enthusiasm is reflected in Hart's contribution to anthropology, which included the establishment of the Open Anthropology Cooperative, a social networking forum for the purpose of democratizing anthropological discussion. Many students also first encounter the idea of a digital anthropology through 'An Anthropological Introduction to YouTube' by Michael Wesch, a professor at the University of Kansas, which celebrates this sense of equality of participation and creation (Wesch 2008).

There are, however, some cracks in this wall of idealism. Kelty (2008) documents the disputes amongst activists over what could become seen as heretical or alternative ideals (see also Juris 2008). Two people's coding technique could diverge to such an extent that people have to take sides. The ideal was of a new arena in which anyone can participate. Companies such as Apple and Microsoft retain their dominance over open source alternatives partly because such ideals flourish more in the initial creative process than in more tedious areas of the management and repair infrastructure, which all platforms require, whether open or closed. But the reality is that only extremely technically knowledgeable 'geeks' have the ability and time to create such open-source developments. This is less true for businesses, and patent controversies and hardware tie-ins can stack the deck against free software.

Curiously Nafus, Leach and Krieger's (2006) study of free/libre/open-source development found that only 1.5 per cent of the geeks involved in open source activities were women, making it one of the most extreme examples of gender discrepancy in this day and age. Even in less technical areas, a report suggests that only 13 per cent of those who contribute to Wikipedia are women (Glott, Schmidt and Ghosh 2010). Women seemed less likely to embrace what was perceived as a rather antisocial commitment of time to technology required of radical activism and activists (though see Coleman 2009). This is precisely the problematic area addressed by Karanović in her analysis of GeekGirlfriend, a campaign that clearly acknowledges, although not necessarily resolves, these issues of gender discrepancy. Such interventions rest in part on what Karanović and Coleman have revealed to be quite an extensive sociality that contrasts with stereotypes of geeks.

As Karanović discusses, there remain regional distinctions in these developments partly because they articulate with different local political traditions. For example French free software activists are mostly oriented towards French and European

Union interlocutors. One problem in these discussions is that the term *liberal* is seen in the United States as a position in opposition to conservative forces, while in Europe the word *liberal* is used to describe the extreme individualism of US right-wing politics and capitalism. In Brazil, the government support of open-source software and free culture more broadly was tied to a culture of resistance to hegemonic global culture, the global order and traditional patterns of production and ownership with the aim of providing social, cultural and financial inclusion for all Brazilian citizens (Horst 2011). Following Hegel, European political traditions tend to see individual freedom as a contradiction in terms; ultimately freedom can only derive from law and governance. Anarchism suits wide-eyed students with little responsibility, but social-democratic egalitarianism requires systems of regulation and bureaucracy, high taxation and redistribution to actually work as human welfare.

The dialectical contradictions involved are especially clear in the impact of the digital upon money itself. There are many welcome technological advances that range from the sheer availability and efficiency of automated teller machines, new finance, the way migrants can remit money via Western Union to the emergence of calling cards (Vertovec 2004), airtime minutes, micropayments and related services in the payments space (Maurer forthcoming). Inspired by the success of M-Pesa in Kenya, the Grameen Bank in Bangladesh and other model projects, throughout the developing world the promise of mobile banking (m-banking) has led to a number of initiatives focused on banking the so-called 'unbanked' (Donner 2008; Donner and Tellez 2008; Morawczynski 2007). This latter area is subject of a major anthropological programme led by Bill Maurer and his Institute for Money, Technology and Financial Inclusion. Preliminary work on the emergence of mobile money in post-earthquake Haiti by Espelencia Baptiste, Heather Horst and Erin Taylor (2010) reveals modifications of the original visioning of mobile money; in addition to the peer-to-peer (P2P) transactions imagined by the services' designers, early adopters of the service are using me-to-me (M2M) transactions to store money on their mobile accounts for safety and security. The cost associated with sending and saving money on ones' own account is perceived as worth the risk of loss of the sum total of the amount saved (Baptiste, Horst and Taylor 2010; Taylor, Baptiste and Horst 2011).

This situation is not quite so positive when we turn to the world of virtual money. In his research, Julian Dibbell (2006) used the classic ethnographic method of participant observation and set himself the task of making some real money via investing and playing with virtual money. He noted that, at the time, in games such as World of Warcraft, 'merely getting yourself off to a respectable start might entail buying a level 60 Alliance warrior account from a departing player ($1,999 on eBay)' (Dibbell 2006: 12). Taken as a whole, in 2005 these games were 'generating a quantity of real wealth on the order of $20 billion each year' (Dibbell 2006: 13). His ethnography revealed that the virtual world of digital money was subject to pretty much every kind of scam and entrepreneurial trick that one finds in offline business—and then some. Furthermore,

Dibbell (2007) also provides one of the first discussions of gold farming, where it was claimed players in wealthy countries farmed out the repetitive, boring keystrokes required to obtain virtual advances in these games to low-income workers in places such as China, though the idea may have become something of a discursive trope (Nardi and Kow 2010). More clearly documented by anthropologist Xiang (2007) is body shopping, where digital labour for mundane tasks such as debugging is imported from low-income countries to Australia or the United States but at lower wages.

The example of money shows that we can find clear positives in new accessibility and banking for the poor but also negatives such as body shopping or new possibilities of financial chicanery found in high finance (Lewis 1989), which contributed to the dot-com debacle (Cassidy 2002) and the more recent banking crisis. This suggests that the new political economy of the digital world is really not that different from the older political economy. The digital extends the possibilities previously unleashed by money, equally the positive and the negative. All this follows from Hart's argument that we need to find emancipation through taming money or expanding open source that is at the point of abstraction. The alternative argument made by Miller looked to the other end of the dialectical equation—at the mass of highly differentiated goods that were being created by these technologies.

Following that logic, we want to suggest an alternative front line for the anthropology of the digital age. The exact opposite of the technophiles of California might be the main informants for a recent study of mothering, whose typical participant was a middle-aged, Filipina domestic worker in London who tended to regard new technologies as either male, foreign, oppressive, or all three (Madianou and Miller 2011). Madianou and Miller's informants may have been deeply suspicious of, and quite possibly detested, much of this new digital technology and only purchased their first computer or started to learn to type within the last two years. Yet Filipina domestics could be the real vanguard troops in marching towards the digital future as they effectively accomplish that which these other studies are in some ways searching for. They may not impact on the creation of digital technologies, but they are at the forefront of developing their social uses and consequences. They use the latest communicative technologies not for reasons of vision, or ideology, or ability, but for reasons of necessity. They live in London and Cambridge, but in most cases their children still live in the Philippines. In an earlier study, Parrenas's (2005) participants saw their children for only twenty-four weeks out of the last eleven years. Such cases exemplify the wider point noted by Panagakos and Horst (2006) regarding the centrality of new communication media for transnational migrants. The degree to which these mothers could effectively remain mothers depended almost entirely upon the degree to which they could use these new media to remain in some sort of contact with their children. In short, it was hard to think of any population for whom the prospects granted by digital technologies would matter more. It was in observing the usage by domestics that Madianou and Miller formulated their concept of polymedia, extending earlier ideas on media and communicative ecologies to consider the interactivity between different media and their importance to the emotional repertoire that these mothers required in dealing with their children.

But transnational mothering through polymedia was not the first time the Philippines appeared at the vanguard of digital media and technology. As has been chronicled by Pertierra and colleagues (2002), the Philippines is globally recognized as the capital of phone texting. From its early introduction through today, more texts are sent per person in the Philippines than anywhere else in the world. Texting soon became central to the formation and maintenance of relationships and was claimed (with some exaggeration) to have played a key role in overthrowing governments. The point of this illustration is that texting is a prime case of a technology intended only as a minor add-on, whose impact was created through the collectivity of consumers. It was poverty and need that drove these innovations in usage, not merely the affordances of the technology.

In the case of the disabled activists discussed by Ginsburg, necessity is paired with explicit ideology. The activists are well aware that digital technologies have the potential to transform their relationship to the very notion of being human—a vision driven by long years in which they knew they were equally human, but other people did not. This is not to presume that such realizations, when accomplished, are always entirely positive. In general, the mothers studied by Madianou and Miller claimed that the new media had allowed them to act and feel more like real mothers again. When Madianou and Miller spoke to the children of these same domestics in the Philippines, some of them felt that their relationships had deteriorated as a result of this constant contact that amounted to surveillance. As Tacchi notes in her contribution, the use of digital media and technology for giving voice involves far more than merely transplanting digital technologies and assuming they provide positive affordances. The subsequent consequences are created in the context of each place, not given in the technology.

The point is not to choose between Hart's emphases upon the point of abstraction and Miller's on the point of differentiation. The principle of the dialectic is that it is an intrinsic condition of digital technologies to expand both, and the impact is also intrinsically contradictory, producing both positive and negative effects. This was already evident in the anthropological study of money and commodities. A critical contribution of digital technologies is the way they exacerbate but also reveal those contradictions. Anthropologists need to be involved right across this spectrum, from Karanović's analysis of those involved in the creation of digital technology to Ginsburg's work on those who place emphasis upon their consequences.

Culture and the Principle of False Authenticity

Having made clear what exactly we mean by the term *digital*, we also need to address what is implied by the term *culture*. For this we assert as our second principle something that may seem to contradict much of what has been written about digital technologies: people are not one iota more mediated by the rise of digital technologies. The problem is clearly illustrated in a recent book by Sherry Turkle (2011) which is infused with a nostalgic lament for certain kinds of sociality or humanity deemed lost as a result of new digital technologies ranging from robots to Facebook. The implication of her book is that prior forms of sociality were somehow more natural or authentic by virtue of being less mediated. For example, Turkle bemoans people coming home from work and going on Facebook instead of watching TV. In fact, when it was first introduced, TV was subject to similar claims as to its lack of authenticity and the end of true sociality (Spiegel 1992); yet TV is in no way more natural and, depending on the context, could be argued to be a good deal less sociable than Facebook. Turkle reflects a more general tendency towards nostalgia widespread in journalism and a range of work focusing on the effects of media that view new technology as a loss of authentic sociality. This often exploits anthropological writing on small-scale societies, which are taken to be a vision of authentic humanity in its more natural and less-mediated state.

This is entirely antithetical to what anthropological theory actually stands for. In the discipline of anthropology, all people are equally cultural—that is, they are the products of objectification. Australian aboriginal tribes may not have much material culture, but instead they use their landscape to create extraordinary and complex cosmologies that then become the order of society and the structures guiding social engagement (e.g. Munn 1973; Myers 1986). In anthropology there is no such thing as pure human immediacy; interacting face-to-face is just as culturally inflected as digitally mediated communication, but, as Goffman (1959, 1975) pointed out again and again, we fail to see the framed nature of face-to-face interaction because these frames work so effectively. The impact of digital technologies, such as webcams, are sometimes unsettling largely because they makes us aware and newly self-conscious about those taken-for-granted frames around direct face-to-face encounters.

Potentially one of the major contributions of a digital anthropology would be the degree to which it finally explodes the illusions we retain of a nonmediated, noncultural, predigital world. A good example would be Van Dijck (2007), who uses new digital memorialization such as photography to show that memory was always a cultural rather than individual construction. Photography as a normative material mediation (Drazin and Frohlich 2007) reveals how memory is not an individual psychological mechanism but consists largely of that which it is appropriate for us to recall. The foundation of anthropology, in its separation from psychology, came with our insistence that the subjective is culturally constructed. To return to a previous example, Miller and Madianou's research on Filipina mothers depended on much more than understanding the new communication technologies; at least as much effort was expended upon trying to understand the Filipina concept of motherhood because being a mother is just as much a form of mediation as being on the Internet. Using a more general theory of kinship (Miller 2008), Miller and Madianou argue that the concept of a mother should be understood in terms of a triangle: our normative concept of what mothers in general are supposed to be like, our experience of the particular person who is our mother, and the discrepancy between these two. Filipina mothers were working simultaneously with regional, national and transnational models of how mothers are supposed to act. By the end of the book (Madianou and Miller 2011), the emphasis is not on new media mediating mother–child relationships; rather, it is far more about how the struggle over the concept of being a proper mother mediates how we choose and use polymedia. Tacchi's contribution further illustrates this point. Those involved in development around new media and communication technologies have come to realize that what is required is not so much the local appropriation of a technology but the importance of listening to the differences in culture which determine what a particular technology becomes. Similarly, Ginsburg demonstrates that the issue of what we mean by the word *human* is what determines the impact of these technologies for the disabled. Unless technology can shift the meaning of humanity, technology alone will not make the rest of us more humane.

To spell out this second principle, then, digital anthropology will be insightful to the degree that it reveals the mediated and framed nature of the nondigital world. Digital anthropology fails to the degree it makes the nondigital world appear in retrospect as unmediated and unframed. We are not more mediated simply because we are not more cultural than we were before. One of the reasons digital studies have often taken quite the opposite course has been the continued use of the term *virtual*, with its implied contrast with the *real*. As Boellstorff makes clear, online worlds are simply another arena, alongside offline worlds, for expressive practice, and there is no reason to privilege one over the other. Every time we use the word *real* analytically, as opposed to colloquially, we undermine the project of digital anthropology, fetishizing predigital culture as a site of retained authenticity.

This point has been nuanced recently by some important writing on the theory of mediation (Eisenlohr 2011; Engelke 2010). As consistent with Bourdieu's (1977) concept of habitus, we may imagine that a person born in medieval Europe would see his or her Christianity objectified in countless media and their intertextuality. But in those days, the media would have been buildings, writings, clothing accessories, preaching, and so forth. Meyer (2011) notes that the critical debate over the role of media in Christianity took place during the Reformation. Catholics fostered a culture of materiality in which images proliferated but retained a sense of mediation such that these stood for the greater mystery of Christ. Protestants, by contrast, tried to abolish both the mediation of objects and of wider cultural processes and instead fostered an ideal based on the immediacy of a subjective experience of the divine. In some respects the current negative response to digital technologies stems from this Protestant desire to create an ideal of unmediated authenticity and subjectivity. In short, anthropologists may not believe in the unmediated, but Protestant theology clearly does.

As Eisenlohr (2011) notes, the modern anthropology of media starts with works such as Anderson's (1983), which showed how many key terms, such as *nationalism* and *ethnicity*, developed in large measure through changes in the media by which culture circulates. There are excellent works on the ways, for example, cassette tapes impact upon religion as a form of public circulation prior to digital forms (Hirschkind 2006; Manuel 1993). But in all these cases, it is not that media simply mediates a fixed element called religion. Religion itself is a highly committed form of mediation that remains very concerned with controlling the use and consequences of specific media.

This is evident when we think about the relationship between Protestantism and digital media. At first we see a paradox. It seems very strange that we have several centuries during which Protestants try to eliminate all objects that stand in the way of an unmediated relationship with the divine while Catholics embrace a proliferation of images. Yet when it comes to modern digital media, the position is almost reversed. It is not Catholics, but evangelical Protestants, that seem to embrace with alacrity every kind of new media, from television to Facebook. They are amongst the most enthusiastic adopters of such new technologies. This makes sense once we recognize that, for evangelical Christians, the media does not mediate. Otherwise they would surely oppose it. Rather, Protestants have seen media, unlike images, as a conduit to a more direct, unmediated relationship with the divine (Hancock and Gordon 2005). As Meyer (2008) demonstrates, evangelical Christianity embraces every type of new digital media but does so to create experiences that are ever more full-blooded in their sensuality and emotionality. The Apostolics that Miller studied in Trinidad asked only one question about the Internet: Why did God invent the Internet at this moment in time? The answer was that God intended them to become *the* Global Church, and the Internet was the media for abolishing mere localized religion such as an ordinary church service and instead become globally connected (Miller and Slater 2000: 187–92). More recently the same church has been using Facebook and other new media forms to express the very latest in God's vision for what they should be (Miller 2011: 88–98). This is also why, as Meyer (2011: 33) notes, the less digitally minded religions, as in some versions of Catholicism, try to protect a sense of mystery they see as not fully captured by new media.

In summary, an anthropological perspective on mediation is largely concerned to understand why some media are perceived as mediating and others are not. Rather than seeing predigital worlds as less mediated, we need to study how the rise of digital technologies has created the illusion that they were. For example when the Internet first developed, Steven Jones (1998) and others writing about its social impact saw the Internet as a mode for the reconstruction of community. Yet much of these writings seemed to assume an illusionary notion of community as a natural collectivity that existed in the predigital age (Parks 2011: 105–9; for a sceptical view, see Postill 2008; Woolgar 2002). They became so concerned with the issue of whether the Internet was bringing us back to community that they radically simplified the concept of community itself as something entirely positive (compare Miller 2011: 16–27). In this volume, we follow Ginsburg and Tacchi in asserting that any and every social fraction or marginal community has an equal right to be seen as the exemplification of digital culture, but this is because, for anthropology, a New York accountant or a Korean games player is no more and no less authentic than a contemporary tribal priest in East Africa. We are all the result of culture as mediation, whether through the rules of kinship and religion or the rules of netiquette and game play. The problem is with the concept of authenticity (Lindholm 2007).

Curiously the earlier writings of Turkle (1984) were amongst the most potent in refuting these presumptions of prior authenticity. The context was the emergence of the idea of the virtual and the avatar in role-playing games. As she pointed out, issues of role-play and presentation were just as much the basis of predigital life, something very evident from even a cursory reading of Goffman (1959, 1975). Social science had demonstrated how the real world was virtual long before we came to realize how the virtual world is real. One of the most insightful anthropological discussions of this notion of authenticity is Humphrey's (2009) study of Russian chat rooms. The avatar does not merely reproduce the offline person; it is on the Internet that these Russian players feel able, perhaps for the first time, to more fully express their soul and passion. Online they can bring out the person they feel they really are, which was previously constrained in offline worlds. For these players, just as for the disabled discussed by Ginsburg, it is only on the Internet that a person can finally become real.

Such discussion depends on our acknowledgment that the term *real* must be regarded as colloquial and not epistemological. Bringing together these ideas of mediation (and religion), Goffman, Turkle's early work, Humphrey and the contributions here of Boellstorff and Ginsburg, it should be clear that we are not more mediated. We are equally human in each of the different and diverse arenas of framed behaviour within which we live. Each may, however, bring out different aspects of our humanity and thereby finesse our appreciation of what being human is. Digital anthropology and its core concerns thereby enhance conventional anthropology.

Transcending Method through the Principle of Holism

The next two principles are largely a reiteration of two of the basic conditions of anthropological apprehensions of the world, but both require a certain caution before being embraced. There are several entirely different grounds for retaining a holistic approach within anthropology, one of which has been largely debunked within anthropology itself. Many of the theoretical arguments for holism[3] came from either the organic analogies of functionalism or a culture concept that emphasized internal homogeneity and external exclusivity. Both have been subject to trenchant criticism, and today there are no grounds for anthropology to assert an ideological commitment to holism.

While theoretically suspect, there are, however, other reasons to retain a commitment to holism which are closely connected to anthropological methodology, especially (but not only) ethnography. We will divide these motivations to retain a commitment to holism into three categories: the reasons that pertain to the individual, those that pertain to the ethnographic and those that pertain to the global. The first is simply the observation that no one lives an entirely digital life and that no digital media or technology exists outside of networks that include analogue and other media technologies. While heuristically anthropologists will focus upon particular aspects of life—a chapter on museums, another on social networking, another on politics—we recognize that the person working at the museum builds social networks and gets involved in politics and that the specifics of any of these three may depend on understanding the other two. What Horst conveys in her chapter is precisely this feeling of easy integration of digital technologies within the lives of her participants.

The concept of polymedia developed by Madianou and Miller (2011) exemplifies internal connectivity in relation to personal communications. We cannot easily treat each new media independently since they form part of a wider media ecology in which the meaning and usage of any one depends on its relationship to others (Horst, Herr-Stephenson and Robinson 2010); using e-mail may be a choice against texting and using a social network site; posting comments may be a choice between private messaging and a voice call. Today, when the issues of cost and access have in many places of the world fallen into the background, people are held responsible for which media they choose. In Gershon's (2010) ethnography of US college students, being dumped by boyfriends with an inappropriate media adds much insult to the injury of being dumped. In Madianou and Miller's (2011) work, polymedia are exploited to increase the range of emotional fields of power and communication between parents and their left-behind children.

But this internal holism for the individual and media ecology is complemented by a wider holism that cuts across different domains. For Broadbent (2011), the choice of media is only understood by reference to other contexts. Instead of one ethnography of the workplace and another of home, we see how usage depends on the relationship between work and home and between very close relationships set against weaker relational ties. This second level of holism is implicit in the method of ethnography. In reading Coleman's (2010) review of the anthropology of online worlds (which provides a much more extensive bibliography than the one provided here), it is apparent that there is almost no topic of conventional anthropology that would not today have a digital inflection. Her references range from news broadcasting, mail-order brides, medical services, aspects of identity, finance, linguistics, politics and pretty much every other aspect of life. In essence, the issue of holism relates not just to the way an individual brings together all the dispersed aspects of his or her life as an individual but also how anthropology transcends the myriad foci of research to recognize the co-presence of all these topics within our larger understanding of society. Another point illustrated clearly in Coleman's survey is that there are now more sites to be considered, because digital technologies have created their own worlds. Her most extended example is the ethnography of spamming, a topic that exists only by virtue of the digital, as would be the case of the online worlds represented here by Boellstorff and in our enhanced perception of relative space in offline worlds described by DeNicola.

The holistic sense of ethnography is brought out clearly by the combination of Boellstorff's and Ginsburg's reflections on the ethnography of Second Life. Granting Second Life its own integrity matters for people who feel disabled and disadvantaged in other worlds; it is a site where, for example, they can live a full religious life, carrying out rituals they would be unable to perform otherwise. Boellstorff points out that the holistic ideal of ethnography is increasingly honoured in the breach. This is well illustrated by Drazin who reveals how in design, as in many other commercial contexts, the very terms *anthropological* and *ethnographic* are commonly used these days as tokenistic emblems of such holism often reduced to a few interviews. He argues that we can only understand design practice within the much wider context of more traditional extended ethnography found in anthropology and, increasingly, in other disciplines.

But if proper ethnography were the sole criteria for holism, it would itself become something of a liability. This is why we require a third holistic commitment. There are not just the connections that matter because they are all part of an individual's life or because they are all encountered within an ethnography. Things may also connect up on a much larger canvass, such as the political economy. Every time we make a debit card payment, we exploit a vast network that exists aside from any particular individual or social group, whose connections would not be apparent within any version of ethnography. These connections are closer to the kinds of networks discussed by Castells and Latour or to older traditions such as Wallerstein's (1980) world systems theory. Anthropology and ethnography are more than method. A commitment to ethnography that fails to engage with the wider study of political economy and global institutions would see the wider holistic intention betrayed by mere method. This problem is exacerbated by digital technologies that have created a radical rewiring of the infrastructure of our world. As a result we see even less and understand less of these vast networks than previously. For this bigger picture, we are committed to travel those wires and wireless connections and make them explicit in our studies. Anthropology has to develop its own relationship with what has been called Big Data (boyd and Crawford 2011)—vast amounts of information that are increasingly networked with each other. If we ignore these new forms of knowledge and inquiry, we succumb to yet another version of the digital divide.

Although Broadbent and her associates conducted long-term and intensive studies of media use in Switzerland, she does not limit her evidence to this. There is also a considerable body of statistical and other meta data and a good deal of more systematic recording and mapping that formed part of her project. She thereby juxtaposes data from specifically anthropological methods with data from other disciplines in order to reach her conclusion. In this introduction we are arguing for the necessity of an anthropological approach to the digital, but not through exclusivity or purity that presumes it has nothing to learn from media studies, commercial studies, geography, sociology and the natural sciences. In addition, we do not have a separate discussion of ethnography and anthropological method here since this is well covered by Boellstorff's contribution. We affirm his conclusion that holism should never mean a collapse of the various terrains of humanity, which are often also our specific domains of enquiry into each other. Online worlds have their own integrity and their own intertextuality, taking their genres from each other, as was evident in Boellstorff's (2008: 60–5) monograph on Second Life, which includes a spirited defence of the autonomous nature of online worlds as the subject of ethnography. Both we and Boellstorff think that this integrity is compatible with our preference for including the offline context of Internet usage, where possible, depending upon the actual research question (Miller and Slater 2000). For example, it is instructive that when Horst (2009), in an investigation of teenagers in California, pulls back the lens for a moment to include the bedrooms in which these teenagers are located while on their computers, one suddenly has a better sense of the ambience they are trying to create as a relationship between online and offline worlds (Horst 2010). In his contribution Boellstorff argues that theories of indexicality derived from Pierce can help relate evidence from different domains at a higher level. Digital worlds create new domains, but also, as Broadbent shows, they can effectively collapse established differences, as between work and nonwork, despite all the efforts of commerce to resist this.

There is a final aspect of holism that anthropologists cannot lose sight of. While anthropologists may repudiate holism as ideology, we still have to deal with the way others embrace holism as an ideal. Postill's discussion of the digital citizen reveals how, while democracy is officially secured by an occasional vote, mobile digital governance is imagined as creating conditions for a much more integrated and constant relationship between governance and an active participatory or community citizenship that deals with embracing much wider aspects of people's lives. Often this is based on assuming that previously it was only the lack of appropriate technology that prevented the realization of such political ideals, ignoring the possibility that people may not actually want to be bothered with this degree of political involvement. Political holism thereby approximates what Postill calls a normative ideal. He shows that the actual impact of the digital is an expansion of involvement but is still, for most people, largely contained within familiar points of participation such as elections or communication amongst established activists.

Voice and the Principle of Relativism

Cultural relativism has always been another vertebra within the spine of anthropology; indeed, holism and cultural relativism are closely connected. It is worth reiterating with respect to digital anthropology that much debate and representation of the digital is derived from the imagination of science fiction and modernism that predicts a tightly homogenized global world that has lost its prior expression of cultural difference (Ginsburg 2008). As with holism, there is a version of relativism that anthropologists have repudiated (at least since World War II) associated with a plural concept of cultures that implied pure internal homogeneity and pure external heterogeneity. These perspectives took cultural differences as essentially historical and a priori based on the independent evolution of societies. By contrast, more contemporary anthropology recognizes that, within our political economy, one region remains linked to low-income agriculture and conservatism precisely because that suits the interests of a wealthier and dominant region. That is to say, differences are often constructed rather than merely given by history.

For this reason, Miller (1995) argued that we should complement the concept of a priori difference with one of a posteriori difference. In their ethnography of Internet use, Miller and Slater (2000) refused to accept that the Internet in Trinidad was simply a version or a clone of 'The Internet'; the Internet is always a local invention by its users. Miller makes a similar argument here with respect to Facebook in Trinidad, where the potential for gossip and scandal (and generally being nosy) is taken as showing the intrinsic 'Trinidadianess' of Facebook (Miller 2011). Within this volume, Barendregt provides the most explicit analysis of relativism. He shows that even quite mundane uses of digital communication such as chatting, flirting or complaining about the government become genres quite specific to Indonesia rather than cloned from elsewhere. While in Trinidad the emphasis is more on retained cultural difference, in Indonesia this is overlain by a very deliberate attempt to create a new normativity: the use of digital technologies based on explicit criteria such as their acceptability to Islamic strictures. This may be a response to concerns that if digital technologies are Western, then they are likely to be the Trojan horse that brings in unacceptable cultural practices such as pornography. This produces a highly conscious filtering and transformation to remake these technologies into processes that actually promote rather than detract from Islamic values.

Similarly, in Geismar's contribution we find the conscious attempt to retain cultural difference. The problem for museums is that homogenization can be imposed most effectively at a level we generally fail to appreciate or apprehend because it occurs within basic infrastructure: the catalogue systems that are used to label and order museum acquisitions. If aboriginal societies are going to find indigenously appropriate forms (Thorner 2010), then it may be through control over things such as the structure of archives, modes of viewing and similar logistical fundamentals that need to properly reflect concepts such as the Vanuatu notion of Kastom, which is quite distinct from Western historiography.

The cliché of anthropology is that we assert relativism in order to develop comparative studies. In reality, comparison is more usually an aspiration than a practice. Yet comparison is essential if we want to understand what can be explained by regional and parochial factors and what stands as higher-level generalization. For example, in his contribution Postill directly compars middle-class political engagement in Australia and Malaysia. Horst and Miller's (2006) study of mobile phones and poverty in Jamaica showed that generalizations about the use of phones for entrepreneurship and finding jobs in other regions may not work for Jamaica, where they found a rather different pattern of economic impact. Karanović shows that national differences may remain important even in projects of global conception such as free software. Her work also demonstrates that such practices can have powerful transnational effects—sometimes indirectly, such as conforming to the dominance of the English language, a relatively neglected aspect of digital anthropology.

In practice, the legacy of anthropological relativism continues through the commitment to regions and cultures otherwise neglected and the concern for the peoples and values of those regions. For Barendregt the exploitation of raw materials, the dumping of e-waste, exploitative employment practices such as body shopping, racist stereotypes within role-playing games and new forms of digital inequality are all aspects of our diverse digital worlds. More specifically, many anthropologists have become increasingly concerned with how to give voice to small-scale or marginalized groups that tend to be ignored in academic generalization centred on the metropolitan West. With a few exceptions (Ito, Okabe and Matsuda 2005; Pertierra et al. 2002), most of the early work on digital media and technology privileged economically advantaged areas of North America and Europe. Ignoring a global demography where most people actually live in rural India and China rather than in New York and Paris, the theoretical insights and developments emerging from this empirical base then reflect North American and Northern European imaginations about the world and, if perpetuated, become a form of cultural dominance. As digital anthropology becomes more established, we hope to see studies and ethnographies that are more aligned with the actual demographics and realities of our world.

As Tacchi notes, it is fine to pontificate about giving voice, but dominant groups often failed to engage with the very concept of voice and, as a result, failed to appreciate that voice was as much about people being prepared to listen and change as a result of what they heard as about giving people the technologies to speak. It is only through others' listening that voice acquires value, and this requires a radical shift from vertical to horizontal relationships, as exemplified by the case studies that Tacchi has been involved in over many years. The meaning of the word *voice* is even more literally a point of engagement for Ginsburg. In some cases, digital technologies are what enables physical actions to be turned into audible voice. For some who have autism, the conventional frame of voice in face-to-face interaction is itself debilitating in its distractions. Here digital technologies can be used to find a more constrained medium, within which individuals feel that others can hear them and they can finally come to have a sense of their own voice.

Tacchi provides several examples that echo Amartya Sen's insistence that a cornerstone to welfare is a people's right to determine for themselves what their own welfare should be. This may demand advocacy and pushing into the groups, such as women migrants who, as noted above, matter because of their dependence upon technologies (Madianou and Miller 2011; Panagakos and Horst 2006; Wallis 2008). One version of these discussions has pivoted around the concept of indigeneity (Ginsburg 2008; Landzelius 2006; for an important precedent, see Turner 1992). Where indigenous signified merely unchanging tradition, then the digital would have to be regarded as destructive and inauthentic. But today we recognize that to be termed indigenous is a modern construction and is constantly subject to change. We are then able to recognize the creative usage by all groups, however marginal or deprived. At the other end of the scale are anthropologists such as DeNicola, who recognize that today it may be science in China or South Asia that represents the cutting edge in, for example, the interpretation of digital satellite imagery or the design and development of software (DeNicola 2006).

This leads to the question of the voice of the (digital) anthropologist. Drazin shows how ethnographers involved in design are also used to give voice to the wider public, such as Irish bus passengers, and increasingly that public finds ways of being more directly involved. The problem, however, is that this is quite often used more as a form of social legitimacy than to actually redirect design. As part of the digital anthropology master's programme at University College London, we have had a series of talks by design practitioners. Many report how they are recruited to undertake qualitative and comparative research, but then they see the results of their studies reduced by more powerful forces trained in economics, psychology and business studies to five token personality types or three consumer scenarios, from which all the initial cultural difference has been eliminated. Ultimately many design anthropologists report that they have been used merely to legitimate what the corporation has decided to do on quite other grounds. Others have used these spaces for other ends.

Ambivalence and the Principle of Openness and Closure

The contradictions of openness and closure that arise in digital domains were clearly exposed in William Dibbell's (1993) seminal article, 'A Rape in Cyberspace'. The article explores one of the earliest virtual worlds where users could create avatars, then often imagined as gentler, better people than the figures they represented offline. Into this idyll steps Bungle, whose superior technical skills allows him to take over these avatars, who then engaged in unspeakable sexual practices both with themselves and others. Immediately, the participants whose avatars had been violated switched from seeing cyberspace as a kind of post-Woodstock land of the liberated to desperately searching for some version of the cyberpolice to confront this abhorrent violation of their online selves.

A theorization of this dilemma also appeared in 'The Dynamics of Normative Freedom', one of four generalizations about the Internet in Trinidad (Miller and Slater 2000). The Internet constantly promises new forms of openness, which are almost immediately followed by calls for new constraints and controls, expressing our more general ambivalence towards the experience of freedom. Perhaps the most sustained debate has been with regard to the fears of parents over their children's exposure to such unrestricted worlds, reflected in the title of boyd's (2006) 'Facebook's "Privacy Trainwreck"', and the work of Sonia Livingstone (2009) on children's use of the Internet (Horst 2010). As DeNicola notes, the location broadcasting functions of Foursquare, Latitude and Facebook Places have been spectacularly highlighted by sites such as PleaseRobMe.com and ICanStalkU.com.

The digital came into its own at the tail end of a fashion in academia for the term *postmodern*, which celebrated resistance to authority of all kinds but especially the authority of discourse. Geismar concisely reveals the problems raised by such idealism. Just opening up the museum space tended to lead to confusion amongst those not well informed and to dominant colonization by the cognoscenti. Museums envisage democratic republics of participants, crowd curation and radical archives. This may work in small expert communities, but otherwise, as in most anarchistic practices, those with power and knowledge can quickly come to dominate. Utopian visions were rarely effective in getting people to actually engage with collections. Furthermore, concerns for the indigenous usually require complex restrictions that are in direct opposition to ideals of pure public access. An equally vast and irreconcilable debate has followed the evident tendency of digital technologies to create conditions for decommodification, which may give us free music downloads but start to erode the viability of careers based on creative work. Barendregt discusses the way digital technologies can exacerbate inequalities of global power, leading to exploitation. It is precisely the openness of the digital that creates fear amongst the Indonesians that this will leave them vulnerable to further colonization by the more open West. On the other hand, Barendregt also shows how digital cultures are used to create visions of new Islamic and Indonesian futures with their own versions of techno-utopias.

The contradictory nature of digital openness is especially clear within Postill's chapter on politics, where there is as much evidence for the way Twitter, Facebook, WikiLeaks and Al Jazeera helped facilitate the Arab Spring as there is for the way oppressive regimes in Iran and Syria use digital technologies for the identification of activists and their subsequent suppression (Morozov 2011). By contrast, Postill's ethnographic work in Malaysia is one of the clearest demonstrations of the value of an anthropological approach, not just as long-term ethnography but also its more holistic conceptualization. Instead of labelling the political impact as good or bad, Postill gives a nuanced and plausible account of the contradictory effects of digital technology on politics. Instead of idealized communities, we find cross-cutting affiliations of groups using the Internet to think through new possibilities.

This ambivalence between openness and closure becomes even more significant when we appreciate its centrality to the initial processes of design and conception in creating digital technologies, especially those related to gaming. For Malaby, the essence of gaming is that, unlike bureaucratic control which seeks to diminish or extinguish contingency, gaming creates a structure that encourages contingency in its usage. He sees this realized through his ethnography of the workers at Linden Lab who developed Second Life (Malaby 2009). They retained much of the influence of 1960s idealism found in books such as the *Whole Earth Catalog* (Brand 1968; Coleman 2004; Turner 2006) and similar movements that view technology as a tool of liberation. They remain deeply interested in the unexpected and unintended appropriations by users of their designs. By setting limits upon what they would construct, they hoped to engage in a kind of co-construction with users, who themselves then became as much producers as consumers of the game. Many of the early adopters are technically savvy and more inclined to do the kind of wild adventurous and proficient things the people at Linden Lab would approve of. However, as the game becomes more popular, consumption becomes rather less creative; 'for most of them this seems to involve buying clothes and other items that thousands of others have bought as well' (Malaby 2009: 114). The end point is very evident in Boellstorff's (2008) ethnography of Second Life, which constantly experienced the reintroduction of such mundane everyday life issues as worrying about property prices and the impact on this of one's neighbours.

Not all designers retain these aspirations. Gambling can also be carefully designed to create a precise balance between contingency and attention—we might win, but we need to keep on playing. Malaby quotes the rather exquisite study by Natasha Schull of the digitization of slot machines, where 'digitization enables engineers to mathematically adjust games' pay-out tables or reward schedules to select for specific player profiles within a diverse market' (Schull 2005: 70). Video poker can be tuned into a kind of personalized reward machinery that maximizes the amount of time a payer is likely to remain on the machine. Again, this is not necessity. Malaby's own example of the Greek state-sponsored gambling game Pro-Po returns us to some sort of collusion with Greek people's own sense of the place of contingency in their lives.

An analogous and extensive literature arises around the concept of the 'prosumer' (Beer and Burrows 2010), where traditional distinctions between producers and consumers break down as the creative potentials of consumers are drawn directly into design. For example, digital facilities encourage us to make our own websites and blogs, populate eBay or transform MySpace. When students first encounter the idea of digital anthropology through Wesch's (2008) infectious enthusiasm for YouTube, the appeal is to the consumer as the force that also largely created this same phenomenon (see also Lange 2007). This suggests a more complex digital world where producers deliberately delegate creative work to consumers and designers have little choice but to follow trends created in consumption. This ideal of a 'prosumption' that includes consumers is becoming something of a trend in contemporary capitalism (Ritzer and Jurgenson 2010). Consumers appropriate commercial ideas and are quickly incorporated in their turn (Thrift 2005) and so on. Related to prosumption is the rapid growth of an online feedback culture, such as Trip Advisor for researching holidays, Rotten Tomatoes for reviewing films and a thousand similar popular sources of assessment and criticism that flourished as soon as digital technologies allowed them to. These have so far received far less academic attention than, for example, blogging, although they may have more far-reaching consequences.

The tensions and cross-appropriations between new openness and closure reaffirm our first principle that the digital is dialectical, that it retains those contradictions analysed by Simmel (1978) with regard to the impact of money. But as stated in our second principle, this has always been the case. We are not more mediated or contradictory than we used to be. Mediation and contradiction are the defining conditions of what we call culture. The main impact of the digital has often been to make these contradictions more explicit or to expose contextual issues of power, as in political control for Postill, parent–child relationships for Horst and empowerment and disempowerment in Ginsburg and Tacchi. As Karanović notes, positive developments such as free software work best when they grow beyond mere utopianism and recognize that they require many of the same forms of copyright protection and legal infrastructure as the corporate owners they oppose. After a certain point, many would settle for successful reformation rather than failed revolution.

Yet, curiously, contemporary mass societies often seem no more ready than small-scale societies to accept culture as intrinsically contradictory. Just as Evans-Pritchard (1937) understood the response in terms of witchcraft, so today we still find that most people prefer to resort to blame and assume there is human intentionality behind the negative side of these digital coins. It is much easier to talk of patriarchy or capitalism or resistance and assume these have done the job of analysis than to appreciate that a digital technology is dialectical and intrinsically contradictory; often what we adjudicate as its good and bad implications are inseparable consequences of the same developments, although this is not intended to detract from appropriate political intervention and discernment.

Normativity and the Principle of Materiality

The final principle of materiality cycles back to the first principle concerning the dialectic. A dialectical approach is premised upon a concept of culture that can only exist through objectification (Miller 1987). Several of the authors in this volume have been trained originally in material culture studies and have engaged with digital anthropology as an extension of such studies. As has been argued in various ways by Bourdieu, Latour, Miller and others, rather than privilege a social anthropology that reduces the world to social relations, social order is itself premised on a material order. It is impossible to become human other than through socializing within a material world of cultural artefacts that include the order, agency and relationships between things themselves and not just their relationship to persons. Artefacts do far more than just express human intention.

Materiality is thus bedrock for digital anthropology, and this is true in several distinct ways, of which three are of prime importance. First, there is the materiality of digital infrastructure and technology. Second, there is the materiality of digital content, and, third, there is the materiality of digital context. We started by defining the term *digital* as a state of material being, the binary switch of on or off, 0 and 1. Kelty's (2008) detailed account of the development of open source clearly illustrates how the ideal of freely creating new forms of code was constantly stymied by the materiality of code itself. Once one potential development of code became incompatible with another, choices had to be made which constrained the premise of entirely free and equal participation. The recent work by Blanchette (2011) is promising to emerge as a sustained enquiry into the wider materiality of some of our most basic digital technologies, especially the computer. Blanchette explicitly rejects what he calls the trope of immateriality found from Negroponte's *Being Digital* (1995) through to *Blown to Bits* (Abelson, Lewis and Ledeen 2008). His work builds, instead, upon Kirschenbaum's (2008) detailed analysis of the computer hard disk. Kirschenbaum points out the huge gulf between meta-theorists, who think of the digital as a new kind of ephemerality, and a group called computer forensics, whose job it is to extract data from old or broken hard disks and who rely on the very opposite property—that it is actually quite difficult to erase digital information.

Blanchette proposes a more sustained approach to digital materiality focusing on issues such as layering and modularity in the basic structure of the computer. What is notable is that at this most micro level, dissecting the bowels of a central processing unit, we see the same trade-off between specificity and abstraction that characterized our first principle of the dialectic at the most macro level—what Miller (1987) called the humility of things. The more effective the digital technology, the more we tend to lose our consciousness of the digital as a material and mechanical process, evidenced in the degree to which we become almost violently aware of such background mechanics only when they break down and fail us. Kirschenbaum states, 'computers are unique in the history of writing technologies in that they present a premeditated material environment built and engineered to propagate an illusion of immateriality' (2008: 135). Objects such as hard disks constantly produce errors but are designed to eliminate these before they impact on what we do with them. We delegate such knowledge as the syntax of a UNIX file to those we term 'geeks', who we characterize as antisocial, thereby exiling this knowledge from our ordinary social world, where we find it obtrusive (Coleman 2009).

Another example of this exclusion from consciousness is evident in the topic of e-waste. As with almost every other domain, the digital has contradictory implications for environmental issues. On the one hand, it increases the potential for less tangible information so that music and text can circulate without CDs and books, thereby removing a source of waste. Similarly, the high carbon footprint of long-haul business-class fights can potentially be replaced by video or webcam conferencing. On the other hand, we are becoming aware of a vast detritus of e-waste that often contains problematic or toxic materials that are difficult to dispose of. These are of particular concern to anthropology since e-waste disposal tends to follow the inequalities of global political economy, being dumped onto vulnerable and out-of-sight areas, such as in Africa (Grossman 2006; Park and Pellow 2002; Schmidt 2006)

While Kelty, Kirschenbaum and Blanchette deal with the forensics of material infrastructure, chapters by Drazin, Geismar and Malaby reveal how design itself is a means of systematically embodying and often imposing ideology. Malaby shows how, at Linden Lab, this included explicit consideration of how to incorporate the creativity of future users. As Drazin illustrates, it has taken a while for those involved to move from seeing the social and cultural as merely the context to technology, and instead acknowledge that they themselves are actually the agents who attempt to realize social and cultural values as technology. In a similar way, Geismar shows how attention is moving from the representational implication of museum displays to the way the catalogue often encodes ideas about social relations. Such issues remain pertinent to everyday digital goods, such as Barendregt's discussion of how Islam tries to ensure that the mobile phone itself is rendered halal or religiously appropriate. This is part of a wider field of technology performed as part of a system of informal cannibalization favoured by the street market reengineering of phones found in such peripheral economies as Indonesia.

The second aspect of digital materiality refers not to digital technology but to the content it thereby creates, reproduces and transmits. Dourish and Mazmanian (2011) point out that virtual worlds have made us increasingly, rather than decreasingly, aware of the materiality of information itself as a major component of such content. Coleman (2010) has several references to anthropological and other examinations of the impact of digital technologies upon language and text (Jones, Schiefllin and Smith 2011; Lange 2007, 2009). The chapter by Broadbent on the specific technologies of personal communication is clearly relevant. There are also obvious domains of visual materiality. For example Miller (2000) used Gell's theory of art to show how websites, just as art works, are systematically designed to seduce and entrap some passing Internet surfers while repelling those they have no reason to attract. Similarly Horst shows how online worlds are aesthetically integrated with the bedrooms of young people going online in California, while Geismar explores the impact of digital technologies on museum display. In general, digital, and especially online, worlds have greatly expanded the scope of visual as well as material culture studies.

Materiality applies just as much to persons as to that which they create. Rowland's (2005) ethnography of power in the Cameroon grasslands is a study of such relative materiality. A chief is a highly substantial and visible body, while a commoner may be only ever able to be a partially realized, insubstantial and often rather invisible body. A similar problem arises for the disabled individuals given voice here by Ginsburg. A person can be present, but that doesn't necessarily mean that he or she is particularly visible. The critical feature of digital technologies here is not technical;

it is the degree to which they impact upon power. Being material in the sense of being merely visible can be transformed into material in the sense of being acknowledged and finally respected. If you will forgive the pun, fundamentally being material means coming to matter.

Third, in addition to the materiality of technology and the materiality of content, there is also the materiality of context. Issues of space and place are the central concern of DeNicola's chapter and his discussion of 'spimes', which imply objects', and not just people's, awareness of space. This leads to a kind of Internet of things, where the digital results not just in enhanced use of absolute space, as in the Global Positioning System, but increasing awareness of relative proximity. This may refer to people, such as gay men making contact through Grindr, but also objects sensing their own relative proximity. As DeNicola notes, digital location awareness is not the death of space but rather its further inscription as indelible material position. Similarly several chapters demonstrate how what has been termed the virtual is more a new kind of place rather than a form of placelessness; for example Boellstorff's work on Second Life, Horst's discussion of a fan fiction writer navigating parents, teachers, friends and her fan fiction community of followers and Miller's suggestion at the end of his chapter that in some ways people make their home inside social networks rather than just communicate through them are examples of this.

There is no chapter on time to complement that on space, but this volume is replete with references to speed, which suggests how important digital technologies have been in shifting our experience of time, and that, instead of creating a timelessness, we seem to be becoming constantly more time aware. We might also note a truism within the digitization of contemporary finance. Here digital technologies are used to create complex instruments intended to resolve issues of risk, which simply seem to increase the experience of and exposure to risk. The example of finance supports DeNicola's contention following Gupta and Ferguson (1997) that one of the consequences of these changing forms of materialization may be the transference, or more often the consolidation, of power.

Context refers not just to space and time but also to the various parameters of human interaction with digital technologies, which form part of material practice. Suchman's (2007) studies have led to a greater emphasis upon human–machine reconfigurations that are complemented by the whole development of human–computer interaction as an academic discipline (e.g. Dix 2004; Dourish 2004), an area discussed within Drazin's contribution. Several chapters deal with another aspect of interaction that Broadbent calls attention. A good deal of contemporary digital technologies are, in essence, attention-seeking mechanisms, partly because one of the most common clichés about the digital world is that it proliferates the amount of things competing for our attention so any given medium must, as it were, try still harder. Broadbent notes that some personal media such as the telephone require immediate attention, while others such as Facebook are less demanding. Malaby's chapter has many references to the attention-attracting and -maintaining capacity of games.

Finally, although this section has concentrated on the principle of materiality, it also started with Blanchette's and Kirschenbaum's observations of how digital forms are used to propagate an illusion of the immaterial, a point central to Boellstorff's discussion of the concept of the virtual but evident in fields as diverse as politics and communication. But then, as MacKenzie notes in his excellent book on the materiality of modern finance with regard to new financial instruments, 'we should not simply be fascinated by the virtual quality of derivatives, but need to investigate how that virtuality is materially produced' (MacKenzie 2009: 84). It is because technologies are constantly finding new ways to construct illusions of immateriality that a material culture perspective becomes ever more important. Of all the consequences of this illusion of immateriality, the most important remains the way objects and technologies obfuscate their own role in our socialization. From the infrastructure behind computers to that behind finance, games, design or museum catalogues, we seem less and less aware of how our environment is materially structured and that creates us as human beings. The reason this matters is that it extends Bourdieu's (1977) critical argument about the role of practical taxonomies in making us the particular kinds of people we are, who subsequently take for granted most of what we call culture. Bourdieu showed how a major part of what makes us human is what he called practice—a conjuncture of the material with the socialization of habit, which makes the cultural world appear as second nature, which is natural. This is best captured by the academic concept of normativity.

To end this introduction on the topic of normativity is to expose the single most profound and fundamental reason why attempts to understand the digital world in the absence of anthropology are likely to be lacking. On the one hand, we can be left slack-jawed at the sheer dynamics of change. Every day we share our amazement at the new: a smarter smartphone, the clear webcam chat to our friend in China, the uses of feedback culture, the creativity of 4chan, which gave rise to the more anarchist idealism of Anonymous in the political sphere. Put together we have the impression of being immersed in some Brave New World that washed over us within a couple of decades. All these developments are well covered by other disciplines. Yet, perhaps the most astonishing feature of digital culture is not this speed of technical innovation but rather the speed by which society takes all of these for granted and creates normative conditions for their use. Within months, a new capacity becomes assumed to such a degree that, when it breaks down, we feel we have lost both a basic human right and a valued prosthetic arm of who we now are as humans.

Central to normativity is not just acceptance but moral incorporation (Silverstone, Hirsch and Morley 1992). Again the speed can seem breathtaking. Somehow in those few months we know what is proper and not proper in posting online, writing in an e-mail, appearing on webcam. There may be a short moment of uncertainty. Gershon (2010) suggests this with regard to the issue of what media within polymedia we are supposed to use to dump a boyfriend or girlfriend. But in the Philippines, Madianou and Miller (2011) found that this more collective society tended to impose normativity upon new forms of communication almost instantly. In her case studies of new media technologies in the home, Horst also shows how quickly and easily digital technologies are literally domesticated as normative. One of the main impacts then of digital anthropology is to retain the insights of Bourdieu as to the way material culture socializes into habitus. But instead of assuming this only occurs within long-term customary orders of things given by history, we recognize that the same processes can be remarkably effective when telescoped into a couple of years.

We would therefore suggest that the key to digital anthropology, and perhaps to the future of anthropology itself, is, in part, the study of how things become rapidly mundane. What we experience is not a technology per se but an immediately cultural inflected genre of usage. A laptop, an archive, a process of design, a Facebook page, an agreement to share locational information—none of these can be disaggregated into their material as against their cultural aspects. They are integral combinations based on an emergent aesthetic that is a normative consensus around how a particular form should be used, which in turn constitutes what that then is—what we will recognize as an e-mail, what we agree constitutes design, what have become the two accepted ways of using webcam. The word *genre* implies a combination of acceptability that is simultaneously moral, aesthetic and practical (see also Ito et al. 2010).

Normativity can be oppressive. In Ginsburg's powerful opening example, the disabled activist Amanda Baggs makes clear that digital technologies have the capacity to make someone appear vastly more human than before, but the catch is that this is only to the degree that the disabled use these technologies to conform to what we regard as normatively human, for example performing that key process of attention in what are seen as appropriate ways. This direct confrontation between the digital and the human is what helps us understand the task of digital anthropology. Anthropology stands in direct repudiation of the claims of psychologists and digital gurus that any of these digital transformations represents a change in either our cognitive capacities or the essence of being human—thus the title of this introductory chapter. Being human is a cultural and normative concept. As our second principle showed, it is our definition of being human that mediates what the technology is, not the other way around. Technology may in turn be employed to help shift our conceptualization of being human, which is what Ginsburg's digital activist is trying to accomplish.

The anthropological apprehension is to refuse to allow the digital to be viewed as a gimmick or, indeed, as mere technology. A key moment in the recent history of anthropology came with Terence Turner's (1992) report on the powerful appropriation of video by an Amazonian Indian group, the Kayapo, in their resistance to foreign infiltration (see also Boyer 2006). It was the moment when anthropology had to drop its presumption that tribal societies were intrinsically slow or passive, what Lévi-Strauss called cold. Under the right conditions, they could transform within the space of a few years into canny, worldly and technically proficient activists, just as people in other kinds of society.

Prior to this moment, anthropology remained in the thrall of associations of custom and tradition, which presumed that anthropology would become less relevant as the speed of change in our material environment grew apace with the advent of the digital. But with this last point regarding the pace of normative impositions, we see why the very opposite is true. The faster the trajectory of cultural change, the more relevant the anthropologist, because there is absolutely no sign that the changes in technology are outstripping the human capacity to regard things as normative. Anthropology is one of the few disciplines equipped to immerse itself in the process by which digital culture becomes normative culture and to understand what this tells us about being human. The lesson of the digital for anthropology is that, far from making us obsolete, the story that is anthropology has barely begun.

Acknowledgements

Thanks to Stefana Broadbent, Haidy Geismar, Keith Hart, Webb Keane, Wallis Motta, Dan Perkel, Kathleen Richardson, Christo Sims and Richard Wilk for comments on a draft of this chapter.

Notes

1. All references to authors within this book are to their contribution within this volume unless stated otherwise.
2. See also Keith Hart's website: http://thememorybank.co.uk/papers/.
3. At the methodological level, holism represents a commitment to understanding the broader context and the integration of the various institutions into an analysis. Theoretically, holism is associated with structural functionalism, which held that certain phenomenon in society (e.g. kinship or houses) represent the whole.

References

Abelson, H., H. Lewis and K. Ledeen. 2008. *Blown to Bits: Your Life, Liberty and Happiness After the Digital Explosion.* Boston: Addison Wesley.

Anderson, B. 1983. *Imagined Communities.* London: Verso.

Baptiste, E., H. Horst and E. Taylor. 2010. *Haitian Monetary Ecologies and Repertoires: A Qualitative Snapshot of Money Transfer and Savings.* Report from the Institute for Money, Technology and Financial Inclusion, 16 November. http://www.imtfi.uci.edu/imtfi_haiti_money_transfer_project.

Beer, D., and R. Burrows. 2010. Consumption, Prosumption and Participatory Web Cultures: An Introduction. *Journal of Consumer Culture* 10: 3–12.

Blanchette, J.-F. 2011. A Material History of Bits. *Journal of the American Association for Information Science and Technology* 62(6): 1042–57.

Boellstorff, T. 2008. *Coming of Age in Second Life.* Princeton, NJ: Princeton University Press.

Bourdieu, P. 1977. *Outline of a Theory of Practice.* Cambridge: Cambridge University Press.

boyd, d. 2006. Facebook's 'Privacy Trainwreck': Exposure, Invasion, and Drama. *Apophenia Blog*, 8 September. http://www.danah.org/papers/FacebookAndPrivacy.html.

boyd, d., and K. Crawford. 2011. *Six Provocations for Big Data.* Paper presented at the Oxford Internet Institute Decade in Internet Time Symposium, 22 September. http://www.scribd.com/doc/65215137/6-Provocations-for-Big-Data.

Boyer, D. 2006. Turner's Anthropology of Media and Its Legacies. *Critique of Anthropology* 26: 47–60.

Brand, S. 1968. *Whole Earth Catalog.* Published by S. Brand.

Broadbent, S. 2011. *L'Intimité au Travail.* Paris: Fyp Editions.

Cassidy, J. 2002. *Dot.con.* London: Allen Lane.

Coleman, G. 2004. The Political Agnosticism of Free and Open Source Software and the Inadvertent Politics of Contrast. *Anthropological Quarterly* 77: 507–19.

Coleman, G. 2009. The Hacker Conference: A Ritual Condensation and Celebration of a Lifeworld. *Anthropological Quarterly* 83(1): 42–72.

Coleman, G. 2010. Ethnographic Approaches to Digital Media. *Annual Review of Anthropology* 39: 487–505.

DeNicola, L. 2006. The Bundling of Geospatial Information with Everyday Experience. In *Surveillance and Security: Technological Politics and Power in Everyday Life*, ed. T. Monahan, 243–64. London: Routledge.

Dibbell, J. 1993. A Rape in Cyberspace. *The Village Voice*, 21 December, 36–42.

Dibbell, J. 2006. *Play Money.* New York: Basic Books.

Dibbell, J. 2007. The Life of a Chinese Gold Farmer. *New York Times Magazine*, 17 June, 200.

Dix, A. 2004. *Human Computer Interaction.* Harlow: Pearson Education.

Donner, J. 2008. Research Approaches to Mobile Use in the Developing World: A Review of the Literature. *The Information Society* 24(3): 140–59.

Donner, J., and C. A. Tellez. 2008. Mobile Banking and Economic Development: Linking Adoption, Impact, and Use. *Asian Journal of Communication* 18(4): 318–32.

Dourish, P. 2004. *Where the Action Is: The Foundations of Embodied Interaction.* Cambridge, MA: MIT Press.

Dourish, P., and M. Mazmanian. 2011. *Media as Material: Information Representations as Material Foundations for Organizational Practice.* Working Paper for the Third International Symposium on Process Organization Studies Corfu, Greece, June. http://www.dourish.com/publications/2011/materiality-process.pdf.

Drazin, A., and D. Frohlich. 2007. Good Intentions: Remembering Through Framing Photographs in English Homes. *Ethnos* 72(1): 51–76.

Eisenlohr, P., ed. 2011. What Is Medium? Theologies, Technologies and Aspirations. *Social Anthropology* 19: 1.

Engelke, M. 2010. Religion and the Media Turn: A Review Essay. *American Ethnologist* 37: 371–9.

Evans-Pritchard, E. 1937. *Witchcraft, Oracles and Magic Among the Azande*. Oxford: Oxford University Press.

Gershon, I. 2010. *The Breakup 2.0.* Ithaca, NY: Cornell University Press.

Ginsburg, F. 2008. Rethinking the Digital Age. In *The Media and Social Theory*, ed. D. Hesmondhalgh and J. Toynbee, 127–44. London: Routledge.

Glott, R., P. Schmidt and R. Ghosh. 2010. Wikipedia Survey—Overview of Results: United Nations University. http://www.wikipediasurvey.org/docs/Wikipedia_Overview_15March2010-FINAL.pdf.

Goffman, E. 1959. *The Presentation of Self in Everyday Life.* Garden City, NY: Anchor Books.

Goffman, E. 1975. *Frame Analysis.* Harmondsworth: Penguin.

Grossman, E. 2006. *High Tech Trash: Digital Devices, Hidden Toxics, and Human Health.* Washington, DC: Island Press.

Gupta, A., and J. Ferguson. 1997. *Culture, Power, Place: Explorations in Critical Anthropology.* Durham, NC: Duke University Press.

Hancock, M., and T. Gordon. 2005. 'The Crusade Is the Vision': Branding Charisma in a Global Pentecostal Ministry. *Material Religion* 1: 386–403.

Hart, K. 2000. *The Memory Bank: Money in an Unequal World.* London: Profile Books.

Hart, K. 2005. *The Hit Man's Dilemma: Or Business, Personal and Impersonal.* Chicago: University of Chicago Press for Prickly Paradigm Press.

Hart, K. 2007. Money Is Always Personal and Impersonal. *Anthropology Today* 23(5): 16–20.

Hirschkind, C. 2006. *The Ethical Soundscape; Cassette Sermons and Islamic Counterpublics.* New York: Columbia University Press.

Horst, H. 2009. Aesthetics of the Self Digital Mediations. In *Anthropology and the Individual*, ed. D. Miller, 99–113. Oxford: Berg.

Horst, H. 2010. Families. In *Hanging Out, Messing Around, Geeking Out: Living and Learning with New Media*, ed. M. Ito, S. Baumer, M. Bittanti, d. boyd, R. Cody, B. Herr, H. Horst, P. Lange, D. Mahendran, K. Martinez, C. Pascoe, D. Perkel, L. Robinson, C. Sims and L. Tripp, 149–94. Cambridge, MA: MIT Press.

Horst, H. 2011. Free, Social and Inclusive: Appropriation and Resistance of New Media Technologies in Brazil. *International Journal of Communication* 5: 437–62.

Horst, H., B. Herr-Stephenson and L. Robinson. 2010. Media Ecologies. In *Hanging Out, Messing Around, and Geeking Out: Kids Living and Learning with New Media*, ed. Mizuko Ito, Baumer, M. Bittanti, d. boyd, R. Cody, B. Herr, H. Horst, P. Lange, D. Mahendran, K. Martinez, C. Pascoe, D. Perkel, L. Robinson, C. Sims and L. Tripp, 29–78. Cambridge, MA: MIT Press.

Horst, H., and D. Miller. 2006. *The Cell Phone: An Anthropology of Communication.* Oxford: Berg.

Humphrey, C. 2009. The Mask and the Face: Imagination and Social Life in Russian Chat Rooms and Beyond. *Ethnos* 74: 31–50.

Ito, M., S. Baumer, M. Bittanti, d. boyd, R. Cody, B. Herr-Stephenson, H. Horst, P. Lange, D. Mahendran, K. Martinez, C. Pascoe, D. Perkel, L. Robinson, C. Sims and L. Tripp, eds. 2010. *Hanging Out, Messing Around, Geeking Out: Living and Learning with New Media.* Cambridge, MA: MIT Press.

Ito, M., D. Okabe and M. Matsuda. 2005. *Personal, Portable, Pedestrian: The Mobile Phone in Japanese Life.* Cambridge, MA: MIT Press.

Jones, G., B. Schiefflin and R. Smith. 2011. When Friends Who Talk Together Stalk Together: Online Gossip as Metacommunication. In *Digital Discourse: Language in the New Media*, ed. C. Thurlow and K. Mroczek, 26–47. Oxford: Oxford University Press.

Jones, S., ed. 1998. *Cybersociety 2.0.* London: Sage.

Juris, J. S. 2008. *Networking Futures.* Durham, NC: Duke University Press.

Karanović, J. 2008. *Sharing Publics: Democracy, Cooperation, and Free Software Advocacy in France.* PhD diss. New York University.

Kelty, C. 2008. *Two Bits: The Cultural Significance of Free Software.* Durham, NC: Duke University Press.

Kirschenbaum, M. 2008. *Mechanisms: New Media and the Forensic Imagination.* Cambridge, MA: MIT Press.

Landzelius, K. 2006. *Native on the Net: Indigenous and Diasporic Peoples in the Virtual Age.* London: Routledge.

Lange, P. G. 2007. Publicly Private and Privately Public: Social Networking on YouTube. *Journal of Computer-Mediated Communication* 13(1): article 18. http://jcmc.indiana.edu/vol13/issue1/lange.html.

Lange, P. G. 2009. Conversational Morality and Information Circulation: How Tacit Notions About Good and Evil Influence Knowledge Exchange. *Human Organization* 68(2): 218–29.

Lewis, M. 1989. *Liar's Poker.* London: Hodder and Stoughton.

Lindholm, C. 2007. *Culture and Authenticity.* Oxford: Blackwell.

Livingstone, S. 2009. *Children and the Internet.* Cambridge: Polity Press.

MacKenzie, D. 2009. *Material Markets: How Economic Agents Are Constructed.* Oxford: Oxford University Press.

Madianou, M., and D. Miller. 2011. *Migration and New Media: Transnational Families and Polymedia.* London: Routledge.

Malaby, T. 2009. *Making Virtual Worlds: Linden Lab and Second Life.* Ithaca, NY: Cornell University Press.

Manuel, P. 1993. *Cassette Culture.* Chicago: University of Chicago Press.

Maurer, W. Forthcoming. Mobile Money: Private Sector and Philanthropic Interests in the Payments Space. *Journal of Development Studies.*

Meyer, B. 2008. Religion Sensations: Why Media, Aesthetics and Power Matter in the Study of Contemporary Religion. In *Religion: Beyond a Concept*, ed. H. de Vries, 704–23. New York: Fordham University Press.

Meyer, B. 2011. Mediation and Immediacy: Sensational Forms, Semiotic Ideologies and the Question of the Medium. *Social Anthropology* 19: 23–39.

Miller, D. 1987. *Material Culture and Mass Consumption*. Oxford: Blackwell.

Miller, D. 1995. Introduction. In *Worlds Apart*, ed. D. Miller, 1–22. London: Routledge.

Miller, D. 2000. The Fame of Trinis: Websites as Traps. *Journal of Material Culture* 5: 5–24.

Miller, D. 2007. What Is a Relationship. *Ethnos* 72(4): 535–54.

Miller, D. 2008. *The Comfort of Things*. Cambridge: Polity Press.

Miller, D. 2011. *Tales from Facebook*. Cambridge: Polity Press.

Miller, D., and D. Slater. 2000. *The Internet: An Ethnographic Approach*. Oxford: Berg.

Morawczynski, O. 2007. Surviving in the 'Dual System': How MPESA Is Fostering Urban-to-Rural Remittances in a Kenyan Slum. Mss. Department of Anthropology, University of Edinburgh.

Morozov, E. 2011. *The Net Delusion*. London: Allen Lane.

Munn, N. 1973. *Walbiri Iconography*. Ithaca, NY: Cornell University Press.

Myers, F. 1986. *Pintupi Country, Pintupi Self*. Washington, DC: Smithsonian Institution Press.

Nafus, D., J. Leach, and B. Krieger. 2006. Gender: Integrated Report of Findings. Free/Libre and Open Source Software: Policy Support (FLOSSPOLS), no. D16. http://www.flosspols.org/deliverables.php.

Nardi, B., and Y. M. Kow. 2010. Digital Imaginaries: How We Know What We (Think We) Know about Chinese Gold Farming. *First Monday* 15(6–7).

Negroponte, N. 1995. *Being Digital*. New York: Knopf.

Panagakos, A., and H. Horst, eds. 2006. Return to Cyberia: Technology and the Social Worlds of Transnational Migrants. Special issue. *Global Networks* 6.

Park, L., and D. Pellow. 2002. *Silicon Valley of Dreams: Immigrant Labor, Environmental Injustice, and the High Tech Global Economy*. New York: New York University Press.

Parks, M. 2011. Social Network Sites as Virtual Communities. In *A Networked Self*, ed. Z. Papacharissi, 105–23. London: Routledge.

Parrenas, R. 2005. *Children of Global Migration: Transnational Families and Gendered Woes*. Stanford, CA: Stanford University Press.

Pertierra, R., E. Ugarte, A. Pingol, J. Hernandez and N. Dacanay. 2002. *TXT-ING Selves: Cellphones and Philippine Modernity*. Manila: De La Salle University Press.

Postill, J. 2008. Localizing the Internet Beyond Communities and Networks. *New Media Society* 10: 413.

Rowland, M. 2005. A Materialist Approach to Materiality. In *Materiality*, ed. D. Miller, 72–87. Durham, NC: Duke University Press.

Schmidt, C. 2006. Unfair Trade e-Waste in Africa. *Environmental Health Perspectives* 114(4): A232–35.

Schull, N. 2005. Digital Gambling: The Coincidence of Desire and Design. *Annals of the American Academy of Political and Social Science* 597: 65–81.

Silverstone, R., E. Hirsch and D. Morley. 1992. Information and Communication Technologies and the Moral Economy of the Household. In *Consuming Technologies*, ed. R. Silverstone and E. Hirsch, 15–31. London: Routledge.

Simmel, G. 1978. *The Philosophy of Money.* London: Routledge.

Spiegel, L. 1992. *Make Room for TV: Television and the Family Ideal in Postwar America.* Chicago: University of Chicago Press.

Suchman, L. 2007. *Human–Machine Reconfigurations.* Cambridge: University of Cambridge Press.

Taylor, E. B., E. Baptiste and H. A. Horst. 2011. *Mobile Banking in Haiti: Possibilities and Challenges.* Institute for Money, Technology and Financial Inclusion, University of California Irvine. http://www.imtfi.uci.edu/files/imtfi/images/2011/haiti/taylor_baptiste_horst_haiti_mobile_money_042011.pdf.

Thorner, S. 2010. Imagining an Indigital Inteface: Ara Iritija Indigenizes the Technologies of Knowledge Management. *Collections: A Journal for Museums and Archives Professionals* 6: 125–47.

Thrift, N. 2005. *Knowing Capitalism.* London: Sage.

Turkle, S. 1984. *The Second Self: Computers and the Human Spirit.* New York: Simon & Schuster.

Turkle, S. 2011. *Alone Together.* New York: Basic Books.

Turner, F. 2006. *From Counterculture to Cyberculture: Stewart Brand, the Whole Earth Network and the Rise of Digital Utopianism.* Chicago: University of Chicago Press.

Turner, T. 1992. Defiant Images: The Kayapo Appropriation of Video. *Anthropology Today* 8(6): 5–16.

Van Dijck, J. 2007. *Mediated Memories in the Digital Age.* Stanford, CA: Stanford University Press.

Vertovec, S. 2004. Cheap Calls: The Social Glue of Migrant Transnationalism. *Global Networks* 4: 219–24.

Wallerstein, I. 1980. *The Modern World System.* New York: Academic Press.

Wallis, C. 2008. Techno-mobility and Translocal Migration: Mobile Phone Use Among Female Migrant Workers in Beijing. In *Gender Digital Divide*, ed. M. I. Srinivasan and V. V. Ramani, 196–216. Hyderabad, India: Icfai University Press.

Wesch, M. 2008. The Anthropology of YouTube. Lecture, 23 June, Library of Congress, Washington, D.C. http://hdl.handle.net/2097/6520.

Wiener, N. 1948. *Cybernetics.* Cambridge, MA: MIT Press.

Woolgar, S., ed. 2002. *Virtual Society?* Oxford: Oxford University Press.

Xiang, B. 2007. *Global Body Shopping: An Indian Labour System in the Information World Technology Industry.* Princeton, NJ: Princeton University Press.

Zelizer, V. 1994. *The Social Meaning of Money.* Princeton, NJ: Princeton University Press.

Part II
Positioning Digital Anthropology

–2–

Rethinking Digital Anthropology

Tom Boellstorff

If there is to be such a thing as digital anthropology, we must carefully consider both component terms constituting that promising phrase. In this chapter I respond to a staggering analytical imbalance: while anthropology has long been subjected to forms of critique—postcolonial, reflexive and poststructuralist, among others—to date the notion of the digital has been met by a profound theoretical silence. For the most part, as I have noted elsewhere, it 'does little more than stand in for "computational" or "electronic"' (Boellstorff 2011: 514). However, if digital is but a placeholder, simply marking interest in that which you plug in to run or recharge, the enterprise of digital anthropology is doomed to adjectival irrelevance from the outset. Technology is now ubiquitous worldwide, and few, if any, future fieldwork projects could ever constitute 'ethnography unplugged'. If digital is nothing more than a synonym for Internet-mediated, then all anthropology is now digital anthropology in some way, shape or form. Should we allow to take root a conception of digital anthropology founded in an uninformed notion of the digital, we thus short-circuit our ability to craft research agendas and theoretical paradigms capable of grappling effectively with emerging articulations of technology and culture.

This highly consequential project of rethinking the digital with regard to digital anthropology is my analytical goal in this chapter. In Part 1, I begin by addressing an issue with foundational implications for what we take digital anthropology to mean: the relationship between the virtual (the online) and the actual (the physical or offline).[1] This relation has pivotal ontological, epistemological and political consequences: it determines what we take the virtual to be, what we take knowledge about the virtual to entail and what we understand as the stakes of the virtual for social justice. I focus on the greatest negative ramification of an undertheorized notion of the digital: the mistaken belief that the virtual and the actual are fusing into a single domain. In Part 2, I engage in the classic anthropological practice of close ethnographic analysis, through case studies drawn from two early days of my research in the virtual world Second Life. In Part 3, I link the theoretical discussion of Part 1 with the ethnographic discussion of Part 2—another classical anthropological practice, that of 'tack[ing] between the most local of local detail and the most global of global structure in such a way as to bring them into simultaneous view' (Geertz 1983: 68).

The linchpin of my analysis will be an argument for treating the digital not as an object of study, but as a methodological approach, *founded in participant observation*, for investigating the virtual and its relationship to the actual. I thereby suggest that digital anthropology is not analogous to, say, medical anthropology or legal anthropology. The parallel to these would be virtual anthropology (Boellstorff 2008: 65). Digital anthropology is a technique, and thus a domain of study only indirectly. It is an approach to researching the virtual that permits addressing that object of study in its own terms (in other words, not as merely derivative of the offline), while keeping in focus how those terms always involve the direct and indirect ways online sociality points at the physical world and vice versa. Crucially, it is predicated on participant observation. An alarming number of researchers of the online claim to do ethnography when their methods involve interviewing in isolation or in conjunction with other elicitation methods, such as a survey. But while such elicitation methods can produce valuable data, a research project using *only* such elicitation methods is not ethnographic (though it may be qualitative). Just saying something is ethnographic does not make it so.

In short, while some will likely equate digital anthropology with virtual anthropology, I here wish to consider a more focused conception, one inspired by originary meanings of the digital and that offers specific methodological benefits for studying online culture. To foreshadow the crux of my argument, I develop a notion of the digital that hearkens back to its original meaning of digits on a hand.[2] Rather than a diffuse notion of the digital as that which is merely electronic or online, this opens the door to a radically more robust conceptual framework that contains two key elements. The first is a foundational appreciation for the constitutive role of the gap between the virtual and actual (like the gaps between 'digits' on a hand). This resonates with the dialectical understanding of the digital developed by Miller and Horst in their introduction to this volume. The second element of this digital framework, drawing from the etymology of *index* as 'forefinger', is a whole set of theoretical resources for understanding the *indexical* relationships that constantly co-constitute both the virtual and actual. I thus push toward an indexical theory for understanding how the virtual and the actual 'point' at each other in social practice.

Part 1: Challenging the Notion of Blurring

Before turning to this theory of digital anthropology and the ethnographic encounters that inspired it, it is imperative to first identify the core problem to which a more carefully articulated notion of digital anthropology can respond. This is the idea that we can no longer treat the virtual and the physical as distinct or separate. It lies beyond the scope of this chapter to catalogue examples of scholars framing the study of the online in this manner, as this is not a review essay or even a critique as such.[3] In her insightful overview of the ethnography of digital media, E. Gabriella Coleman nicely summed up this perspective when noting that, with regard to research on virtual worlds, 'the bulk of this work, however, continues to confound sharp boundaries between off-line and online contexts' (Coleman 2010: 492). Coleman's phrasing captured the sense that 'sharp boundaries' are to be avoided—that they are scholarly conceits that falsely separate online and offline contexts rather than ontologically consequential gaps that constitute the online and offline. In fact, these sharp boundaries are real, and therefore vital topics for anthropological inquiry.

While less evident in this particular quotation, the sense that one can no longer see the online and offline as separate—despite the obvious fact that they are, depending on how you define 'separate'—encodes a historical narrative that moves from separation to blurring or fusion. Such presumptions of an impending convergence between the virtual and actual mischaracterize the careful work of earlier ethnographers of the online.[4] For instance, Vili Lehdonvirta has claimed that much virtual-world scholarship is 'based on a dichotomous "real-virtual" perspective' (Lehdonvirta 2010: 2).[5] He could sustain this view that scholars have detached virtual worlds from 'the rest of society' (2) only through a sociology of the obvious—noting, for instance, that players of an online game like World of Warcraft often seek to play with persons 'based on the continent and time zone in which they reside' (2), as if World of Warcraft researchers were not aware of this fact. Lehdonvirta correctly concluded that 'scholars should place [virtual worlds] side-by-side with spheres of activity such as family, work or golf, approaching them using the same conceptual tools' (2) and that 'the point is not to give up on boundaries altogether and let research lose its focus, but to avoid drawing artificial boundaries based on technological distinctions' (9). What needs questioning is Lehdonvirta's assumption that virtual worlds are artificial boundaries, while spheres of activity such as family, work or golf are somehow not artificial.[6] At issue is that technological distinctions are central to the human condition: artifice, the act of crafting, is a quintessentially human endeavour. To presume otherwise sets the stage for the 'principle of false authenticity', which, as Miller and Horst note, occludes the fact that 'people are not one iota more mediated by the rise of digital technologies' (this volume: 11–12).

Thus, the most significant danger lies not in scholarly misrepresentation but in the three-part narrative of movement embedded in these concerns over authenticity, dichotomies and blurring: an originary separation, a coming together and a reunification. This narrative is a teleology insofar as there is a defining endpoint: the impending nonseparation of the virtual and the actual, often presented in the apocalyptic language of 'the end of the virtual/real divide' (Rogers 2009: 29). Indeed, such contentions of an end times represent not just a teleology but a theology—because they so often appear as articles of faith with no supporting evidence, and because they resemble nothing so much as the Christian metaphysics of incarnation, of an original separation of God from Man in Eden resolved in the Word made flesh (Bedos-Rezak 2011).[7] This speaks to pervasive Judeo-Christian assumptions of 'the antagonistic dualism of flesh and spirit' that have strongly shaped dominant forms of social inquiry (Sahlins 1996: 400).

Without cataloguing further examples of these narratives that the online and offline are becoming blurred, it is important to note their persistence despite the fact that this transcendental understanding of the virtual is clearly wrong: the virtual is as profane as the physical, as both are constituted 'digitally' in their mutual relationship. This language of fusion undermines the project of digital anthropology; it is an eschatological narrative, invoking an end times when the virtual will cease to be. This recalls how some scholars of the online seem unable to stop referring to the physical as the 'real', even though such inaccurate phrasing implies that the online is unreal—delegitimizing their field of study and ignoring how the virtual is immanent to the human. The persistence of such misrepresentations underscores the urgent need for rethinking digital anthropology.

Some readers may have recognized the homage at play in my phrase 'rethinking digital anthropology'.[8] In 1961, the eminent British anthropologist Edmund Leach published the essay 'Rethinking Anthropology'. In it, he chose a fascinating analogy to justify anthropological generalizations:

> Our task is to understand and explain what goes on in society, how societies work. If an engineer tries to explain to you how a digital computer works he doesn't spend his time classifying different kinds of nuts and bolts. He concerns himself with principles, not with things. He writes out his argument as a mathematical equation of the utmost simplicity, somewhat on the lines of: 0+1 = 1; 1+1 = 10...[the principle is that] computers embody their information in a code which is transmitted in positive and negative impulses denoted by the digital symbols 0 and 1. (Leach 1961: 6–7)

Leach could have not have predicted the technological transformations that now make digital anthropology possible. Nonetheless, we can draw two prescient insights from his analysis. First, 39 years after Bronislaw Malinowski established in *Argonauts of the Western Pacific* that 'the essential core of social anthropology is fieldwork' (Leach 1961: 1; see Malinowski 1922), Leach emphasized that anthropologists must attend to the 'principles' shaping everyday life. Second, to illustrate these principles, Leach noted the centrality of gaps to the digital: even a computer of nuts and bolts depends on the distinction between 0 and 1.

Leach's observations anticipate my own argument. The persistence of narratives bemoaning the distinction between the physical and the online miss the point—literally 'miss the point', as my discussion of indexicality in Part 3 will demonstrate. The idea that the online and offline could fuse makes as much sense as a semiotics whose followers would anticipate the collapsing of the gap between sign and referent, imagining a day when words would be the same thing as that which they denote.[9]

Clearly, we need a range of conceptual resources to theorize traffic across constitutive gaps; allow me to provide an example from my research on sexuality. In my studies of men who use the Indonesian term *gay* to describe their sexualities, I sought a framework that would not lead me to presume these men were becoming the same as Western gay men. I found such a resource from the kind of unexpected quarter one often discovers via an ethnographic approach. I learned that the Indonesian state had tried to ban the dubbing of foreign television shows and movies into the Indonesian language with the justification that to see 'Sharon Stone speak Indonesian' would cause Indonesians to lose the ability to tell where their culture ended and Western culture began (Oetomo 1997; see Boellstorff 2005).

What is interesting about dubbing is its explicit predication on meaning-making across a gap. In a dubbed movie—say, an Italian movie dubbed into Japanese—the moving lips of the Italian actors will never exactly match the Japanese voices. Yet no members of an audience will leave the theatre because of this mismatch: it is expected, not a failure so long as the lips and voices are close enough in synch so that understanding can take place.[10] Inspired by these antiteleological implications, I developed a notion of 'dubbing culture' to avoid a narrative in which Western gay identity represented the assumed endpoint for homosexualities worldwide. Indonesian gay men dub Western gay sexualities. They are perfectly aware that the Indonesian term *gay* is shaped by the English term *gay*, yet they are also perfectly aware that their subjectivities are not merely derivative of the West.

The notion of dubbing culture helped me avoid assuming that Indonesian and Western sexualities were converging or blurring and underscored how all semiosis involves movement across gaps. Similarly, extending the notion of the digital can help avoid any assumption that the virtual and actual are converging or blurring.[11] In Part 3, I discuss what such a rethought notion of the digital might entail and how, for such a rethinking to apply to digital *anthropology*, questions of theory cannot be divorced from questions of method. In Part 2, I turn to two case studies: I want the trajectory of this argument to reflect how my thinking has emerged through ethnographic engagement. This is not a detour, digression or mere illustration; a hallmark of anthropological inquiry is taking ethnographic work as a means to develop theory, not just data in service of preconceived paradigms.

Part 2: Two Days in My Early Second Life

Given the scope of this chapter, I cannot devote much space to background on Second Life.[12] Briefly, Second Life is a virtual world—a place of human culture realized by a computer programme through the Internet. In a virtual world, you typically have an avatar body and can interact with other persons around the globe who are logged in at the same time; the virtual world remains even as individuals shut their computers off, because it is housed in the 'cloud', on remote servers.

When I first joined Second Life on 3 June 2004, residents paid a monthly fee and were provided a small plot of virtual land. In February 2005, I sold the land I had been initially allocated and moved to another area. However, at the time I write this chapter in 2011, to get myself into an ethnographic frame of mind, in another

Figure 2.1. The land where my first home in Second Life once stood.

window on my computer I have gone into Second Life and teleported back to the exact plot of virtual land where my original home once stood in 2004. At this moment—late morning according to my California time—there are no avatars nearby. The large house that once stood here, my first experiment at building in Second Life, disappeared long ago, and nary a virtual nail remains of my prior labour. But looking at my old land's little patch of coastline, I think I can still make out the remnants of my terraforming, my work to get the beach to slope into the water just so, in order to line up with the view of the distant shore to the east. Even in virtual worlds, traces of history endure (Figure 2.1).

The current owners of my onetime virtual homestead have not built a new house to replace the one I once crafted; instead, they have made the area into a wooded parkland. To one side, swings rock to and fro with automated animations, as if bearing unseen children. On the other side, at the water's edge, a dock invites repose. In the centre, near where the living room of my old home was located, there now stands a great tree, unlike any I have ever seen in Second Life. Its long branches slope gracefully up toward the bright blue virtual sky. One branch, however, snakes out horizontally for some distance; it contains an animation allowing one's avatar to stretch out, arms folded behind one's head and feet swinging in the digital breeze. So here on this branch, where my first Second Life home once stood, my virtual self will sit as I reflect on those first days of virtual fieldwork (Figure 2.2).

In what follows, I recount hitherto unpublished fieldwork excerpts from two concurrent days early in my research. (Second Life at this time had only text communication, which I have edited for concision. As is usual in ethnographic writing, to protect

Figure 2.2. At rest in the virtual tree.

confidentiality all names are pseudonyms.) None of these interactions were noteworthy; it is unlikely anyone else bothered to record them. Yet in each case I encountered traces of broader meaning that point toward rethinking digital anthropology.

Day 1: A Slow Dance for Science

At 12:28 p.m. on 30 June 2004, I walked into my home office in Long Beach, California, and turned on my computer. I 'rezzed' (that is, my avatar appeared) in Second Life in my recently constructed house, right where my avatar will sit in a tree seven years later as I write this narrative. But on this day, only a month into fieldwork, I left my virtual home and teleported to a dance club at the suggestion of Susan, who was already at the club with her friends Sam, Richard and Becca. At this point Second Life was quite small and there were only a few clubs. At this club the featured attraction was ice skating; the club had been decked out with a rink, and ice skates were available on the walls to attach to your avatar. In fact you bought the skates and they appeared in a box; if you did not know how to do things correctly, you would end up wearing the box on your head, not the skates on your feet. Most residents were new to the virtual world's workings; Susan was having a hard time getting her skates to work, and Sam and Richard were helping as best they could:

Sam: Susan, take them off your head lol [laugh out loud]
Sam: put them onto the ground

Susan:	thanks
Susan:	hehe, I'm new to this game
Susan:	have I got them on?
Richard:	click on the box on your head and choose edit
Richard:	then click the 'more' button
Richard:	then 'content' and you'll see them
Susan:	I have the skateson... I think I do anyway
Richard:	she has the box on her head

Susan (and others) continued to have trouble using the skates. In the meantime, I had managed to figure it out and was soon skating near Becca, who saw from my profile that I was an ethnographer:

Becca:	Tom would you like to slow dance?
Richard:	they [the skates] are still in the box I believe
Susan:	But I can't see it [the box] on my head
Becca:	for science
Tom:	how do you do it?
Becca:	lol
Susan:	hehe
Becca:	um... not sure
Sam:	I don't see a box on her head.
Becca:	hehe
Richard:	I do
Susan:	So is it on my head then or not?
Sam:	So Susan... you get a set of skates in a box?
Susan:	hehe, I think that might work
Becca:	oh there we go
Becca:	lol
Susan:	Yeah, I got them from the box, moved them into my inventory and then put them on
IM [instant message]:	Becca: just don't put your hand up my skirt... hehe

Despite the fact that I have edited this conversation for the sake of brevity, the ethnographic detail in this excerpt alone could take many pages to properly analyse, and it illustrates the kinds of data obtainable from participant observation that could not be acquired via interviews or other elicitation methods. I will note just six insights we can glean from this fieldwork encounter.

First, residents worked together to educate each other rather than relying on the company that owns Second Life or some kind of instruction manual.

Second, gender seems to be shaping the interaction: it is largely men advising women. Since everyone knows that physical-world gender might not be aligning with virtual-world gender, this has implications for social constructions of gender.

Third, during this period when Second Life had only text chat (and even after the introduction of voice in 2007, chat remained common), residents had learned to parse conversations in which there were multiple threads of overlapping talk. For instance, Sam asked Susan, 'you get a set of skates in a box?' and Susan answered three lines later, after first answering, 'I think that might work', in reference to a different thread of conversation.

Fourth, when Becca made a slightly risqué comment to me ('just don't put your hand up my skirt'), she switched to an instant message, meaning that this text was visible to no one besides myself. This apparently trivial practice helped me realize early in my research that I should attend not just to the content of statements but to their modality of articulation—'chat', 'shout' (text that, like chat, is publicly visible but to avatars at a greater distance) and instant messages sent both to individuals and groups of residents. These various modalities of articulation link to long-standing linguistic interest in codeswitching but can also take forms of 'channelswitching' between different technological modalities of communication (Gershon 2010a).

Fifth, these insights (and many more) had precedents and contemporary parallels. Peer education, the impact of gender norms even when physical-world gender cannot be ascertained and the existence of multiply threaded and multimodal conversations were not unique to this interaction, to Second Life or even to virtual worlds. Thus, an awareness of relevant literatures proved helpful in analysing these phenomena.

Sixth, this encounter underscored how the ethnographer is not a contaminant. The fact that I was participating in Second Life culture without deception was not an impediment; rather, it made the research more scientific. My 'slow dance for science' illustrated the practice of participant observation, online and offline.

Day 2: Here and There

On 1 July 2004, one day after my slow dance for science, I logged into Second Life again to conduct fieldwork, appearing as usual in my house. Rather than teleporting instantaneously to another part of the virtual world, I walked down a nearby paved path. In the distance I saw three avatars, Robert, Karen and Timothy:

Robert: Why, hello!
Karen: Hi Tom
Timothy: Hi tom
Tom: Hello! I'm your neighbor down the road
Karen: Ahh cool
Karen: Sorry for all the mayhem here, I have crazy friends
Robert: Hope the hoopla hasn't been a problem
Tom: What hoopla are you talking about?
Robert: Hee hee
Karen: rofl [rolling on the floor laughing] whew
Robert: just asking for it!

Timothy:	whew
Karen:	Oh the avie [avatar] launch game we had . . . the explosions, lap dances
Tom:	Whatever it is, is hasn't bothered me!
Karen:	Very good
Karen:	So which way down the road are you?
Tom:	To my right
Karen:	Ah very good
Karen:	Got a house, or doing something else there?
Tom:	Just got a place for now
Karen:	cool
Karen:	Gonna turn this into a small boutique
Tom:	cool!

Already from the discussion, I had noted how copresence in a virtual neighbourhood could help shape online community: place matters online. Karen then changed the subject:

Karen:	wow Tom, reading your profile here.
Karen:	very interesting
Karen:	um . . . Indonesia, really?
Tom:	Yep! Cool place. Not cool really, hot and humid, but fun.
Karen:	lol how'd you end up over there?
Tom:	Random life events, backpacking there after college & meeting people
Karen:	that's gotta be quite interesting I imagine
Tom:	very!
Tom:	is that your glowing dance floor over there to my left?
Karen:	nope, no clue who it's for
Karen:	a little bright
Tom:	there's a lot of building right now in this area! It's cool—every day the landscape is transformed
Karen:	yes, a lot of this land was just released
Timothy:	happens in new areas
Timothy:	finally got a house on one side of mine
Timothy:	mini tower going in behind
Tom:	laugh
Karen:	lol
Timothy:	as long as they don't cut off my view
Karen:	they screwed up my view in Shoki [region]
Robert:	Yeah, its just sad.
Karen:	even though he said he wouldn't
Timothy:	think I am safe there

After a brief discussion of my positionality as a researcher, the conversation turned once again to virtual place. In my fieldnotes I noted the importance of one's view across a virtual landscape. Encounters like this led me to realize the importance of place to virtual worlds (see Boellstorff 2008: chap. 4). The topic then turned to multiple avatars, and I asked about The Sims Online, another virtual world I had briefly explored:

Tom:	do you play more than one avie at the same time? I know people who did that in The Sims Online but it seems that would be hard to do here.
Karen:	no, not here, in TSO [The Sims Online] I did
Robert:	Never saw the Sims, did I miss much?
Timothy:	I never tried TSO
Karen:	Didn't miss shit
Karen:	so you missed There altogether?
Tom:	Yes, I missed There completely. What was it like?
Timothy:	I remember that
Tom:	Was it more like Second Life than TSO?
Karen:	Very much like this, but more cartoonish and everything had to be pg13
Robert:	Stepford Disney World
Tom:	Is it still around?
Timothy:	and not quite as open
Karen:	yes, Stepford Disney lol
Karen:	but there's still a lot of charm to There
Timothy:	but it has its nice parts
Robert:	Better chat, great vehicles
Timothy:	Meeting Karen being one of em
Robert:	Card games!
Karen:	yes, I met both you guys in There
Karen:	the horizon is clear, not foggy like here

This section of the discussion reveals how understandings of Second Life were shaped by previous and sometimes ongoing interaction in other virtual worlds. This influenced not only how the users experienced Second Life, but their social networks (for instance, Karen first met Robert and Timothy in There.com). Yet to learn about how other virtual worlds shaped Second Life sociality, it was not necessary for me to conduct fieldwork in these other virtual worlds. Multisited ethnographic research is certainly useful given the appropriate research question—for instance studying a virtual diaspora that moves across several virtual worlds (Pearce and Artemesia 2009). However, it was clearly possible to explore how other places shape a fieldsite without visiting them personally. Indeed, in his well-known discussion of multisited ethnography, George Marcus was careful to note the value of 'the strategically situated (single-site) ethnography' (Marcus 1995: 110). This was an unexpected methodological resonance between my research in Second Life and Indonesia: to learn about gay identity in Indonesia, it was unnecessary to visit Amsterdam, London or other places that *gay* Indonesians saw as influencing their understanding of homosexual desire.

Once again, virtually embodied presence was critical to my ethnographic method. In this one encounter, I gained a new appreciation for virtual place, the importance of vision and 'a good view', and the impact of other virtual worlds. I mentioned none of these three topics in my original research proposal, even though they all turned out to be central to my conclusions. The insights were emergent, reflecting how 'the anthropologist embarks on a participatory exercise which yields materials for which analytical protocols are often devised after the fact' (Strathern 2004: 5–6).

Part 3: Digital Anthropology, Indexicality and Participant Observation

These ethnographic materials highlight how the gap between online and offline is culturally constitutive, not a suspect intellectual artefact to be blurred or erased. This distinction is not limited to virtual worlds. For instance, Daniel Miller has noted that for persons in Trinidad who have difficulty with physical-world relationships, 'Facebook provides an additional space for personal expression' (Miller 2011: 169). That is, forms of expression and relationship can take place on Facebook, but the space of Facebook and the space of Trinidad do not thereby collapse into each other. You can be on Facebook without being in Trinidad, and you can be in Trinidad without being on Facebook. Another example: in her study of breakups online, Ilana Gershon noted that such disconnections 'are emphatically not the disconnections between supposedly real interactions and virtual interactions. Rather, they are disconnections between people—the endings of friendships and romances' (Gershon 2010b: 14). These endings are both online and offline in character. To rethink digital anthropology, we must build upon such insights to identify a common set of issues that make digital anthropology cohere, and we can then explore in particular fieldsites. This is why I now scope out from the specificities of Second Life, and even virtual worlds, toward a theoretical and methodological framework for digital anthropology.

Indexicality as a Core Theory for Digital Anthropology

In the introduction, I suggested that an indexical theory for understanding the relationship between virtual and actual could help in rethinking digital anthropology. Scholars of language have long noted the existence of words that lie outside traditional notions of reference, because their meaning depends on the context of social interaction. For instance, the truth of the sentence:

> Letizia de Ramolino was the mother of Napoleon
>
> [I]n no way depends on who says it, but simply on the facts of history. But now suppose we try to analyze:
>
> I am the mother of Napoleon
>
> We cannot assess the truth of this sentence without taking into account who the speaker is…we need to know, in addition to the facts of history, certain details about the context in which it was uttered (here, the identity of the speaker). (Levinson 1983: 55–6)

The philosopher Charles Sanders Peirce termed words like these 'indexical signs' (Levinson 1983: 57) and emphasized their causal rather than symbolic relationship to referents. To use two examples familiar to linguists, smoke is an index of fire, and a hole in a piece of metal is an index of the bullet that passed through the metal. In each case, a causal relationship 'points back' from the index to the referent. A hole in a piece of metal does not conventionally symbolize a bullet in the same way that a drawing of a bullet shape or the word *bullet* can stand for an actual bullet. Instead, the hole in the piece of metal refers to the bullet causally—the bullet made the hole. Similarly, 'the smoke does not "stand for" the fire the way in which the word *fire* might be used in telling a story about a past event. The actual smoke is connected, spatio-temporally and physically, to another, related, phenomenon and acquires "meaning" from that spatio-temporal, physical connection' (Duranti 1997: 17).

While these examples indicate that indexical signs do not have to be words, a whole range of words are indeed indexicals (indexical denotationals, to be precise), including 'the demonstrative pronouns *this, that, those,* personal pronouns like *I* and *you,* temporal expressions like *now, then, yesterday,* and spatial expressions like *up, down, below, above*' (Duranti 1997: 17). For instance *this* is an indexical because its meaning shifts based on the cultural context of the utterance. To say 'the sun is round' or 'the sun is square' can be assigned a truth value regardless of my position in time and place. However, I cannot assign a truth value to the utterance 'this table is round' unless I know the context to which the word *this* can be said to point. Indexicals can be found in all human languages, and interesting variations exist. For instance in French and German, formal versus informal second-person pronouns (*tu/vous* and *du/Sie*, respectively, which in English would all be translated *you*) mark obligatory forms of social indexicality.[13]

As noted by Duranti, indexicals are 'grounded' in spatially and temporally specific social realities: 'A basic property of the indexical context of interaction is that it is dynamic. As interactants move through space, shift topics, exchange information, coordinate their respective orientations, and establish common grounds as well as non-commonalities, the indexical framework of reference changes' (Hanks 1992: 53). This 'interactive emergence of the indexical ground' (Hanks 1992: 66) provides the point of entrée for rethinking digital anthropology in terms of indexicality. The spatially and temporally specific social realities are no longer limited to the physical world; the processes of moving though space and establishing common grounds can now take place online as well as offline. Confronted with multiple embodiments, and thus with indexical *fields of reference* that are multiple in a new way, we thereby face the virtual as an emergent set of social realities that cannot be straightforwardly extrapolated from the physical world. For instance the social intentions, emotions, decisions and activities that take place on Facebook cannot be reduced to the physical-world activities and identities of those who participate in it, even though these can have physical-world consequences ranging from a romance's dissolution to a political revolution. It is possible, for example, to become a closer friend with someone on Facebook without meeting that person in the physical world along the way.

The reason why it is possible to rehabilitate the digital so as to transcend its common conflation with 'online' is that the concept is fundamentally linked to indexicality. The etymology of *index* (Latin, forefinger) and *digit* (Latin, finger) both refer to the embodied act of pointing—and this has momentous implications when you can have multiple bodies and multiple fields of reference (even when there is not a clear avatar body involved). Building upon this characteristic of the digital through the framework of indexicality results in a far more precise notion of digital; it compels attention to the indexical ground of virtual culture.[14]

The greatest strength of an indexical perspective is that it avoids the conceptual danger discussed in Part 1: the idea that the gap between the virtual and actual is headed down a teleological path to a blurring that we might celebrate or rue. It would be nonsensical to contend that the distinction between smoke and fire might someday vanish, that the gap between the word *sun* and the massive orb of gas at the centre of our solar system might blur or that the difference between 1 and 0 might converge into a fog of 0.5s. Yet just such an absurdity is entailed by the idea that the online and offline can no longer be separated. At issue are myriad forms of social practice, including meaning-making, that move within virtual contexts but also across the gap between virtual and actual—from skates on an avatar's feet to embodied views across a virtual landscape, from a friendship in the actual world altered though a text message to a friendship on Facebook between two people who never physically meet.

At a broader level, the virtual and actual stand in an 'inter-indexical relationship' (Inoue 2003: 327); it is through the general gap between them that the emerging socialities so in need of anthropological investigation are taking form. As online socialities grow in number, size and genre, the density and rapidity of these digital transactions across the inter-indexical gap between virtual and actual increase exponentially. Like standing back from a pointillist painting, it appears that the dots have blurred into brush strokes. But no matter how high the resolution, when one looks carefully, one sees the discreteness of the dots as well as the gaps of white space that allow them to convey meaning. This recalls how no matter how fast a computer becomes, no matter how quickly millions of 0s and 1s stream by, millions of gaps will stream by as well, for the computer's functioning depends on the gaps themselves.

In setting out this idea of an anthropology that is digital by virtue of its attunement to the indexical relationships constituting the virtual and the actual, I do not mean to imply that virtual meaning-making is exclusively indexical in character. I am not saying that digital anthropologists need to become semioticians or that digital anthropology projects need to prioritize indexicality. At issue is that indexicality provides an empirically accurate and conceptually rich perspective from which to rethink digital anthropology and virtual culture. This is because indexicality entails strong linkages to context (Keane 2003), and we now grapple with a human reality in which there are multiple contexts, multiple worlds, multiple bodies—all with historical precedent but no true historical parallel.

While a detailed examination of semiotic theory lies beyond the scope of this chapter, we can note in passing that symbols and icons, the other two types of sign in Peirce's analysis, are ubiquitous in online contexts (consider the icons that are so central to computing cultures). Nor do we need to limit ourselves to a Peirceian approach to language and meaning. But while not all dimensions of culture are like language, this particular aspect of language—the centrality of indexicality to meaning-making—is more indicative of virtual sociality than the structural-grammatical dimensions of language that 'cannot really serve as a model for other aspects of culture' (Silverstein 1976: 12). What I am suggesting is, first, that for digital anthropology to make sense, it must mean more than just the study of things you plug in or even the study of Internet-mediated sociality and, second, that one promising avenue in this regard involves drawing from the digital's indexical entailments of pointing and constitutive gaps. These entailments have theoretical consequences that suggest research questions and lines of inquiry. They also have important consequences for method, the topic to which I now turn.

Participant Observation as the Core Method for Digital Anthropology

Digital anthropology typically implies 'doing ethnography'.[15] But ethnography is not a method; it is the written product of a set of methods, as the suffix *-graphy* (to write) indicates. Rethinking digital anthropology must therefore address not just (1) the theoretical frameworks we employ and (2) the socialities we study, but (3) how we engage in the research itself.

Ethnographers of virtual socialities work in a dizzying range of fieldsites (and are not always anthropologists, since ethnographic methods have a long history in sociology and other disciplines). One of the greatest virtues of ethnographic methods is that researchers can adapt them to the contexts of particular fieldsites at particular periods in time. Ethnographic research online does not differ in this regard. However, this flexibility is not boundless. A serious threat to the rigor and legitimacy of digital anthropology is when online researchers claim to have 'done an ethnography' when they conducted interviews in isolation, paired at most with the analysis of blogs and other texts. Characterizing such research as ethnographic is misleading because participant observation is the core method of any ethnographic research project. The reason for this is that methods such as interviews are *elicitation* methods. They allow interlocutors to speak retrospectively about their practices and beliefs as well as speculate about the future. But ethnographers combine elicitation methods (like interviews and focus groups) with participant observation, which, as a method not predicated on elicitation, allows us to study the differences between what people say they do and what they do.

The problem with elicitation methods in isolation is that this methodological choice surreptitiously encodes a theoretical presumption that culture is present to consciousness. It is predicated on the belief that culture is something in people's heads: a set of viewpoints that an interviewee can tell the researcher, to appear later as an authoritative block quotation in the published account. Of course, persons can often be eloquent interpreters of their cultures; as a result, interviews should be part of any ethnographic project. But what interviews and other elicitation methods can never reveal are the things we cannot articulate, even to ourselves. Obvious cases of this include things that are repressed or unconscious, an insight dating back to Freud. Language is another example. Consider a basic phonological rule like assimilation, where for instance the *n* in *inconceivable* becomes *m* in *impossible* because *p* is a bilabial plosive (made with the lips), and the nasal *n* assimilates to this place of articulation. Almost no English speakers could describe this rule in an interview, even though they use the rule hundreds of times a day in the flow of everyday speech.

Such aspects of culture are by no means limited to language and the psyche. In particular, theorists of practice have worked to show how much of everyday social action involves tacit knowledge. Pierre Bourdieu emphasized this point when critiquing anthropologists who speak of 'mapping' a culture: 'it is the analogy which occurs to an outsider who has to find his way around in a foreign landscape' (Bourdieu 1977: 3). Take any route you traverse as part of your daily routine. If there is a staircase in your home or office, do you know how many stairs are there? The peril is to seek a representation of such tacit knowledge via an interview, where the informant's discourse is shaped by the framework of elicitation 'inevitably induced by any learned questioning' (Bourdieu 1977: 18). As a result,

> the anthropologist is condemned to adopt unwittingly for his own use the representation of action which is forced on agents or groups when they lack practical mastery of a highly valued competence and have to provide themselves with an explicit and at least semi-formalized substitute for it in the form of a repertoire of rules. (Bourdieu 1977: 2)

Elicitation not interwoven with participant observation can lead researchers to confuse representation with reality, and thereby mistakenly equate culture with rules, scripts or norms rather than embodied practices.

If there is one thing that ethnographers have shown over the years, it is that 'what is essential *goes without saying because it comes without saying*: the tradition is silent, not least about itself as a tradition' (Bourdieu 1977: 167, emphasis in original). When ethnographers ask interview questions, they obtain representations of social practice. Representations are certainly social facts (Rabinow 1986) and have cultural effects. But they cannot be conflated with culture as a whole. If you ask someone 'what does friendship mean to you?' you will get a representation of what that person takes friendship to be. That representation is socially consequential; it is embedded in (and influences) a cultural context. However, that elicited representation is not identical to friendship in practice.

The methodological contribution of participant observation is that it provides ethnographers insight into practices and meanings as they unfold. It also allows for obtaining nonelicited data—conversations as they occur, but also activities, embodiments, movements though space, and built environments. For instance in Part 2, I observed Second Life residents teaching each other how to skate on a virtual ice rink, in part by learning how to skate myself. Had I just walked up to an avatar and asked out of the blue, 'how do you learn in Second Life?' I would have likely received a formal response emphasizing things traditionally seen as learning-related; rich detail about a group of avatars learning to skate would not have been in the offing. Participant observation allows researchers to identify cultural practices and beliefs of which they were unaware during the process of research design.

Some persons terming themselves ethnographers may not wish to hear this. On more than one occasion I have counselled scholars who claim to be 'doing ethnography' but use interviews in isolation—in one case, because a colleague told the scholar that participant observation would take too long. Participant observation is never rapid: 'not unlike learning another language, such inquiry requires time and patience. There are no shortcuts' (Rosaldo 1989: 25). You cannot become fluent in a new language overnight, or even in a month or two. Similarly, someone claiming to have conducted ethnographic research in a week or even a month is mischaracterizing his or her work unless it is part of a more long-term engagement. There is no way the researcher could have *become known to a community* and participated in its everyday practices in such a compressed time frame.

Conclusion: Time and Imagination

When I think about the exciting possibilities that inhere in rethinking digital anthropology, I find my mind wandering back to an image. A webpage, to be precise, that has haunted me for years despite its apparent triviality. I think—of all things!—about the original McDonald's home page from 1996, from the early days of the Internet's ascendance.[16] Despite its simplicity from a contemporary perspective (basically, the Golden Arches logo on a red background), the webpage represented the best that a major corporation could offer in terms of web presence; it likely involved considerable expense to design and implement.

When I think about what this website represents, I compare it to some contemporary phenomenon like Facebook or Twitter. For instance, the well-known microblogging site Twitter was founded in 2006 and allows users to post text messages up to 140 characters in length. Such sites are simple; broadband Internet connections and blazing graphics cards are unnecessary for their operation. One could effectively access Twitter with a slow dial-up connection, using a 1990s-era computer with what would now be minuscule processing power. In fact, there is no technological reason why Twitter could not have existed in 1996, alongside that original McDonald's home page.

Why did Twitter not exist in 1996, coming into being only ten years later? It was not a limit of technology; it was a limit of imagination. In the early years of widespread web connectivity, we did not yet realize the affordances of the technology in question.

Virtual worlds, online games, social networking sites and even instant messaging and smartphones in the 2010s are analogous to that McDonald's webpage from 1996. Current uses of these technologies push against the horizon of the familiar, and it could not be otherwise. Transformative potential uses of these technologies certainly exist, but at present they are no more conceivable than the idea of a Twitter feed would have been to a user of the McDonald's website in 1996, despite its feasibility from a technical standpoint. It is a matter of time and imagination.

Leach concluded 'Rethinking Anthropology' by emphasizing: 'I believe that we social anthropologists are like the mediaeval Ptolemaic astronomers; we spend our time trying to fit the facts of the objective world into the framework of a set of concepts which have been developed a priori instead of from observation' (Leach 1961: 26). Leach was frustrated that social researchers often fail to *listen* to the empirical realities they ostensibly study. Despite our best intentions, we often fall back on folk theories and preconceived notions from our own cultural backgrounds. This is particularly the case when speaking about the future. The problem with the future is that there is no way to research it. It is the domain of the science fiction author and the entrepreneur on the make. Social scientists study the past, and many of them, including ethnographers, study the present; in this chapter I have worked to demonstrate how digital anthropology might contribute to studying this emergent present. But if we see that contribution as showing that the virtual and actual are no longer separate, we will have substituted a mistaken teleology for empirical reality: we will remain in a Ptolemaic frame of mind.

The virtual and the actual are not blurring, nor are they pulling apart from one another. Such spatial metaphors of proximity and movement radically mischaracterize the semiotic and material interchanges that forge both the virtual and the actual. Digital anthropology as a framework can provide tools to avoid this conceptual cul-de-sac—via a theoretical attention to the indexical relationships that link the online and offline *through similitude and difference* and by a methodological focus on participant observation.

Social researchers are constantly asked to engage in the work of forecasting or 'trending' to predict what will happen with regard to new technologies. But lacking access to a time machine and confronted by the failure of the most savvy futurists to predict even the rise of blogging, our only real explanatory power lies in investigating the past and present. Digital anthropology can play an important role in this regard, but for this to happen it must stand for more than ethnography online. Time is a necessity for digital anthropology—you cannot do ethnographic research over a weekend. But *imagination* is also needed. Rethinking digital anthropology will fall short if it does not include imagining what, 'digital' might mean and what its consequences might be for social inquiry.

Notes

I thank Daniel Miller and Heather Horst for their encouragement to write this chapter and Paul Manning for his helpful comments.

1. In this chapter I treat *actual*, *physical* and *offline* and *virtual* and *online* as synonyms. It is possible to craft frameworks in which these terms differ, but it is a flawed folk theory of language that the mere existence of multiple lexemes entails multiple corresponding entities in the world.
2. I have briefly discussed these meanings of the digital elsewhere with regard to embodiment (Boellstorff 2011: 514–15).
3. For reviews of the history of digital anthropological work, see, inter alia, Boellstorff (2008: chap. 2); Boellstorff, Nardi, Pearce and Taylor (2012: chap. 2) and Coleman (2010).
4. For example Curtis ([1992] 1997), Kendall (2002) and Morningstar and Farmer (1991). Such uses of convergence diverge from Henry Jenkins's (2008) notion of convergence culture, which references differing media.
5. Lehdonvirta used the unwieldy phrase 'massively-multiplayer online games and virtual environments (MMO[s])'; I will simply use 'virtual worlds' here.
6. This is true as well with regard to Huizinga's much-maligned and poorly understood notion of the 'magic circle' (Huizinga [1938] 1950: 57; see Boellstorff 2008: 23).
7. Of course, many religious traditions have influenced understandings of the virtual (as exemplified by the notion of avatars, drawn from Hinduism). However, the Christian tradition has dominated, given its hegemony in the Western contexts, where the Internet revolution began. See Boellstorff (2008: 205–11).
8. In their introduction to this volume, Miller and Horst also speak of the need to rethink basic anthropological ideas in light of the impact of the digital.

9. Even the varied post-Saussurean approaches to language provide for the constitutive role of gaps (and movement across those gaps). This includes notions of iteration which 'contains *in itself* the discrepancy of a difference that constitutes it as iteration' (Derrida 1988: 53, emphasis in original).
10. These debates, and my engagement with them, preceded and took place separately from debates over dubbing versus subbing that appear in some contemporary debates over Internet-mediated fan production.
11. The ethnographic contexts of Indonesia and Second Life are of course very different; the common need to challenge teleological narratives says as much about scholarly assumptions as the contexts themselves.
12. For a detailed theoretical and methodological discussion of this research, see Boellstorff (2008) and Boellstorff et al. (2012).
13. In English and many other languages (for example Indonesian), speakers use lexical items like *sir* or *madam* to optionally index intimacy. For a discussion of social indexicality and social deixis more generally, see Manning (2001).
14. What was likely the first contemporary virtual world originated in two hands pointing at each other while superimposed on a computer screen (Krueger 1983; see Boellstorff 2008: 42–7).
15. Phrases such as 'digital archaeology' usually connote a historical approach rather than a true engagement with archaeological approaches and paradigms (for one notable exception, see Jones 1997).
16. You can see this webpage at http://web.archive.org/web/19961221230104/http:/www.mcdonalds.com/.

References

Bedos-Rezak, B. 2000. Medieval Identity: A Sign and a Concept. *American Historical Review* 105(5). http://www.historycooperative.org/journals/ahr/105.5/ah001489.html.

Boellstorff, T. 2005. *The Gay Archipelago: Sexuality and Nation in Indonesia.* Princeton, NJ: Princeton University Press.

Boellstorff, T. 2008. *Coming of Age in Second Life: An Anthropologist Explores the Virtually Human.* Princeton, NJ: Princeton University Press.

Boellstorff, T. 2011. Placing the Virtual Body: Avatar, Chora, Cypherg. In *A Companion to the Anthropology of the Body and Embodiment*, ed. F. E. Mascia-Lees, 504–20. New York: Wiley-Blackwell.

Boellstorff, T., B. A. Nardi, C. Pearce and T. L. Taylor. 2012. *Ethnography and Virtual Worlds: A Handbook of Method.* Princeton, NJ: Princeton University Press.

Bourdieu, P. 1977. *Outline of a Theory of Practice.* Cambridge: Cambridge University Press.

Coleman, E. G. 2010. Ethnographic Approaches to Digital Media. *Annual Review of Anthropology* 39: 487–505.

Curtis, P. [1992] 1997. Mudding: Social Phenomena in Text-Based Virtual Realities. In *Culture of the Internet*, ed. S. Kiesler, 121–42. Mahwah, NJ: Lawrence Erlbaum.

Derrida, J. 1988. Signature Event Context. In *Limited Inc.*, 1–24. Evanston, IL: Northwestern University Press.

Duranti, A. 1997. *Linguistic Anthropology.* Cambridge: Cambridge University Press.

Geertz, C. 1983. 'From the Native's Point of View': On the Nature of Anthropological Understanding. In *Local Knowledge: Further Essays in Interpretive Anthropology*, 55–72. New York: Basic Books.

Gershon, I. 2010a. Breaking Up Is Hard To Do: Media Switching and Media Ideologies. *Journal of Linguistic Anthropology* 20(2): 389–405.

Gershon, I. 2010b. *The Breakup 2.0: Disconnecting over New Media.* Ithaca, NY: Cornell University Press.

Hanks, W. F. 1992. The Indexical Ground of Deictic Reference. In *Rethinking Context: Language as an Interactive Phenomenon*, ed. C. Goodwin and A. Duranti, 43–76. Cambridge: Cambridge University Press.

Huizinga, J. [1938] 1950. *Homo Ludens: A Study of the Play-Element in Culture.* Boston: Beacon Press.

Inoue, M. 2003. Speech without a Speaking Body: 'Japanese Women's Language' in Translation. *Language and Communication* 23(3/4): 315–30.

Jenkins, H. 2008. *Convergence Culture: Where Old and New Media Collide.* New York: New York University Press.

Jones, Q. 1997. Virtual-Communities, Virtual Settlements, and Cyber-Archae-ology: A Theoretical Outline. *Journal of Computer-Mediated Communication* 3(3). http://onlinelibrary.wiley.com/doi/10.1111/j.1083-6101.1997.tb00075.x/full (accessed April 12, 2012).

Keane, W. 2003. Semiotics and the Social Analysis of Material Things. *Language and Communication* 23(3/4): 409–25.

Kendall, L. 2002. *Hanging Out in the Virtual Pub: Masculinities and Relationships Online.* Berkeley: University of California Press.

Krueger, M. W. 1983. *Artificial Reality.* Reading, MA: Addison-Wesley.

Leach, E. R. 1961. Rethinking Anthropology. In *Rethinking Anthropology*, 1–27. London: Robert Cunningham and Sons.

Lehdonvirta, V. 2010. Virtual Worlds Don't Exist: Questioning the Dichotomous Approach in MMO Studies. *International Journal of Computer Game Research* 10(1): 1–16.

Levinson, S C. 1983. *Pragmatics.* Cambridge: Cambridge University Press.

Malinowski, B. 1922. *Argonauts of the Western Pacific.* New York: E. P. Dutton.

Manning, H. P. 2001. On Social Deixis. *Anthropological Linguistics* 43: 54–100.

Marcus, G. 1995. Ethnography in/of the World System: The Emergence of Multi-Sited Ethnography. *Annual Review of Anthropology* 24: 95–117.

Miller, D. 2011. *Tales from Facebook.* Cambridge: Polity Press.

Morningstar, C., and F. R. Farmer. 1991. The Lessons of Lucasfilm's Habitat. In *Cyberspace: First Steps*, ed. M. Benedikt, 273–301. Cambridge, MA: MIT Press.

Oetomo, D. 1997. Ketika Sharon Stone Berbahasa Indonesia [When Sharon Stone speaks Indonesian]. In *Bercinta Dengan Televisi: Ilusi, Impresi, dan Imaji Sebuah Kotak Ajaib* [In love with television: Illusions, impressions, and images from a magical box], ed. D. Mulyana and I. Subandy Ibrahim, 333–7. Bandung, Indonesia: PT Remaja Rosdakarya.

Pearce, C., and Artemesia. 2009. *Communities of Play: Emergent Cultures in Multiplayer Games and Virtual Worlds.* Cambridge, MA: MIT Press.

Rabinow, P. 1986. Representations Are Social Facts: Modernity and Post-Modernity in Anthropology. In *Writing Culture: the Poetics and Politics of Ethnography*, ed. J. Clifford and G. E. Marcus, 234–61. Berkeley: University of California Press.

Rogers, R. 2009. *The End of the Virtual: Digital Methods.* Amsterdam: Vossiuspers UvA.

Rosaldo, R. 1989. *Culture and Truth: The Remaking of Social Analysis.* Boston: Beacon Press.

Sahlins, M. 1996. The Sadness of Sweetness: The Native Anthropology of Western Cosmology. *Current Anthropology* 37(3): 395–428.

Silverstein, M. 1976. Shifters, Linguistic Categories, and Cultural Description. In *Meaning in Anthropology*, ed. K. H. Basso and H. A. Selby, 11–55. Albuquerque: University of New Mexico Press.

Strathern, M. 2004. *Commons and Borderlands: Working Papers on Interdisciplinarity, Accountability, and the Flow of Knowledge.* Wantage: Sean Kingston.

–3–

New Media Technologies in Everyday Life

Heather A. Horst

Domestic life constitutes one of the primary concerns of the discipline of anthropology. Beginning with Lewis Henry Morgan's classic study *Houses and House Life of the American Aborigines* (Morgan 1966), Lévi-Strauss's (1983, 1987) notion of house societies and Bourdieu's structuralist approach to understanding the symbolism of the Kabyle house, understanding domestic life emerged a way through which anthropologists began to formulate theories around kinship, lineage, social organization and reproduction (Bloch 1998; Carsten and Hugh-Jones 1995). As anthropology has broadened its inquiry from small-scale societies and the focus upon traditional or non-Western lives to the urban, Western and the middle class, anthropological attention also shifted from outlining social structure to the interpretation of and processes underpinning social change. Indeed, Bourdieu's formulation of the habitus and social practice in shaping taste and aesthetics in French homes (Bourdieu 1972, 1984) and Moore's (1986) analysis of the ways in which gender is structured and restructured in domestic space through practice represent seminal work on the ways which gender and other forms of difference become inscribed and reinscribed in domestic space.

Patterns stemming from processes such as modernization, urbanization and globalization have recently reinvigorated our understanding of the relationship between domestic spaces, particularly with respect to social change. This work has chronicled alternative political visions such as the construction and negotiation of socialist cities and dwellings (Holston 1989; Buchli 1999); the development of gated communities and neoliberal governance (Low 2003); historicized accounts of the ways in which notions of gender are renegotiated through the introduction of time-saving kitchen devices, Tupperware and related projects such as domestic science programs (Clarke 1999; Hancock 2001; Pink 2004; Shove 2003) and the relationship between consumption and the microdynamics of decorating, redecorating and moving furniture (Cieraad 2006; Miller 2001). In addition, research has examined the role that home plays in the project of the self in late modernity (see Giddens 1991; Clarke 2001; Garvey 2001, 2010; Low and Lawrence-Zuñiga 2003; Marcoux 2001; Miller 2001). This chapter will focus upon one of these new arenas—new media technologies in the home—and the implications of the rapidly changing media ecology for social life.

New Media Technologies in the Home

As previous research on radio and television revealed (Tacchi 2002; Wilk 2002), new media technologies altered the infrastructure and rhythms of everyday life. For example, Lynn Spigel's (1992, 2010) work on television reveals how, in conjunction with the process of suburbanization, the television in 1950s America became part of the everyday fabric of the home, structuring the ways families came together to watch news and broadcast programming. As Bakardjieva (2005), Dourish and Bell (2007), Livingstone (2002) and others have observed, kitchens, dens, basements, bedrooms and other domestic spaces such as cars have also changed with the introduction of computers, mobile phones, gaming devices, MP3 players and a range of other digital and networked media (Baym 2000; Bull 2008; Horst 2010; Horst and Miller 2006; Ito, Okabe and Matsuda 2010; Lally 2002; Ling 2004; Stevens, Satwicz and McCarthy 2008).

One of the important distinctions between new media technologies and technologies such as dishwashers and Tupperware involves the concept of double articulation; new media technologies are not only objects, but they also link the private sphere with the public sphere and, in turn, facilitate the negotiation of meaning both within and through their use (Silverstone, Hirsch and Morley 1992). Silverstone, Hirsch and Morley (1992) argue that the capacity for double articulation also has implications for the processes through which new media technologies are incorporated into everyday life. As they describe,

> Objects and meanings, technologies and media, which cross the diffuse and shifting boundary between the public sphere where they are produced and distributed, and the private sphere where they are appropriated into a personal economy of meaning (Miller 1987), mark the site of the crucial work of social reproduction which takes place within the household's moral economy…objects and meanings, in their objectification and incorporation within the spaces and practices of domestic life, define a particular semantic universe for the household in relation to that offered in the public world of commodities and ephemeral and instrumental relationships. (18–19)

The 'moral economy of the household' is expressed through the process of objectification, incorporation and conversion, wherein new media technologies become a normal and accepted part of everyday life; they become domesticated.

Building upon the work on domestication, Elaine Lally (2002) studied the introduction of the home computer and the processes underpinning the appropriation and ownership of computers and other related assemblages in the home. Her work critiques Silverstone, Hirsch and Morley's notion that new media technologies are the only domestic objects that exhibit double articulation. Lally contends that other objects such as the refrigerator door and filing cabinets also play a dual role in the household. Moreover, Lally emphasizes the importance of understanding the dynamism of objects by illustrating how the biography of the home computer has changed over time. These changes bring about alterations in notions of ownership and the role that new media technologies continue to play in the constitution or project of the self—a core characteristic of personhood in many Western contexts. Lally further argues that computers and other objects become extensions of the self through acts such as personalization, self-transformation and 'material projection(s) of an imagined possible self' (Lally 2002: 214; see also Miller and Slater 2000 and their discussion of expansive realisation). Through such processes, objects can become de-alienated; however, this may change over time as the relationship to a particular new media technology changes and one seeks to alienate or divest oneself from the object. For Lally, possession, ownership and the process of domestication are both mutable and relational.

This chapter builds upon this literature on domestication, the moral economy of the household, possession and imagined futures as they are expressed through the integration of new media technologies in everyday life. Highlighting the three key issues that emerge in the previous literature—the management of space and time, the microdynamics of the household and the boundaries between private and public—I describe three case studies from recent research on new media and the family to examine how new media technologies (especially networked media) extend and challenge earlier conceptions of technology appropriation. The cases take place in Silicon Valley, the centre of the technology industry where residents are envisioned as tech savvy 'digital natives' (Gasser and Palfrey 2008; Prensky 2001).

The first case study examines how families place new media in their home. Illustrating the emergence of bedroom culture, gaming and entertainment rooms and office/homework spaces for adults and youth, I focus upon the increasing specialization of domestic space and the importance of activities in shaping the spatial, social and temporal boundaries of these spaces. The second case study explores the relationship between place, notions of the self and coming of age in social network sites such as Facebook and MySpace. The third case study examines the relationship between different practices and spaces inhabited by young people who are also playing a role in the creation and dissemination of content historically in the domain of broadcasters and producers. I use Christine Nippert-Eng's (1996) work on the relationship between home and work (see also Broadbent, this volume), particularly notions of segmentation and integration, to analyse the ordinary ways in which relationships with media figure into the lives of the families and young people in the study. The three case studies capture the tension between the material and symbolic (Livingstone 2007) exhibited in new media technologies as well as the multiple spaces and negotiations of home by exploring the relationship between home and work, the representations and expressions of the self across domestic space and profile pages and the relationship between hobbies, school and leisure spaces.

Case Study One: From Kitchen Society to Desktop Society

In contrast to the industrial workplace, where the factory gate establishes a clear boundary between work and domestic life, workers in the knowledge economy maintain fluid boundaries between home and work (Gregg 2011; Nippert-Eng 1996). Joining a conference call during dinner, sorting e-mail while watching a movie with the kids and logging in to work for a few hours after putting the kids to bed characterize just a few of the routine ways that work permeates the domestic sphere in Silicon Valley, California (Darrah, Freeman and English-Lueck 2007; English-Lueck 2002; see also Broadbent, this volume). For youth and children growing up in Silicon Valley, innovation, self-regulation, competition and other values associated with work in the technology industry are as much a part of everyday life as the company logos emblazoned on shirts, hats and bags hanging in their closets. The dot.com bust of 2000 further reconfigured this relationship between home and work as companies have downsized and made redundant many of their employees. In response, parents in the families I've been researching over the past five years established new careers as independent contractors and consultants. In most instances, the shift towards consulting and independence increased the permeability of the boundary between home and work for parents and other family members (Broadbent, this volume).

The material assemblages associated with adult labour clearly influence the infrastructure of home. Yet they also shape what is seen as the labour of childhood among middle-class families: school and homework. One of the most interesting aspects of Silicon Valley professional households involves the shift from the 'kitchen table society'—a term coined by Marianne Gullestad (1984) to signal the centrality of the kitchen table for sociality among Norwegian women—to what I call the 'desktop society'. For example, Jeff, a fourteen-year-old middle school student, lives with his parents and his elder brother in one of the wealthiest areas of Silicon Valley. Both of Jeff's parents are professionals, but his mother recently decided to become a consultant so she could devote more time to the boys' school and extracurricular activities. Within this remit is the remodelling of their five-bedroom house. Although there are two offices (one for each parent) and the two brothers have desk space in their bedrooms, Jeff's mother decided to remove the kitchen table to construct a large desk space where Jeff and his brother could do their homework each evening. Out of concern for their media usage, she then decided to make an addition to the home to separate the 'work' computer from the 'play' computer. Reflecting on her sons' use of technology and media, she notes,

> We do restrict the use of the computer games and media during homework. And—so and I think one of the things that we just had a discussion on is the distractibility of IM [instant messaging] and that's something that my husband and I have really talked to Jeff about…And the concern is the IM and the music and homework. So those three media is [*sic*] happening. So we're concerned about his ability to stay focused on task

> when all that's happening. And I think he's been working on that, disciplining himself, right J?

As becomes evident in Jeff's mother's discussion, it is by no accident that kids' workspaces are constructed in the traditional site of household and familial reproduction: the kitchen and dining room. The creation of a workplace in a shared domestic space creates the sense that what kids are doing on the computer and online is public and thus keeps them disciplined and on task (see also Lally 2002). A few parents have explicitly stated that the transformed office space is conveniently proximate to where they are cooking, and thus parents can keep a watchful eye on computer monitors while children do their schoolwork. In addition, the decision to install a desktop computer rather than a more portable laptop computer solidifies this particular area as a homework space, akin to their parent's home offices.

But parents are not the only ones structuring homework spaces in and through technology. Evalyn, a thirteen-year-old middle school student, lives in a four-bedroom house in a suburban neighbourhood with her parents and two siblings. Evalyn and her older brother attend private school, and her older sister recently started high school at a respected public school in the area. Evalyn's parents are both professionals who have worked for a few of the region's large technology firms, but, in the wake of the dot.com bust, they have become independent contractors and thus work primarily at home. Now that Evalyn has started middle school and is 'not really a kid anymore', she has been spending more time with her older sister. One weekend they were talking and listening to music together, and they came up with an idea—it might be fun to share a bedroom and convert the extra bedroom into their own home office. They moved 'work stuff' and desk stuff into Evalyn's room and moved clothing, jewellery and beds to the other room. The work stuff Evalyn refers to consists of desktop computers, a printer, paper, schoolbooks and media devices, including a shared iPod and digital camera. As a place designated for doing their homework, the kids' office is also a space set apart from the shared family computers and printers that their brother and parents use. For teenagers, Evalyn and her sister are unusual in opting out of their own, private bedrooms—an act that seems to run contrary to almost all of the values of individualism and privacy associated with U.S. middle-class life. But as a semiprivate space for Evalyn and her sister, there is a curious symmetry between the integration of work spaces in the home through the office and the resegmentation of the spaces through the designation of one space as an office and another as a bedroom. While this practice is not as prevalent as the transformation of the kitchen table space into an office space for homework, there are a variety of forms of this consolidation and sharing of office resources among siblings in other families as they gradually learn to integrate work in their own lives.

As Mary Douglas (1991) has argued, the creation of home is ultimately tied to controlling time and space to create an infrastructure to frame the household as a community. In Jeff's home and others like it, where the home office is constructed in the kitchen and dining room, parents (Jeff's mother in particular) play a key role in structuring the public space in the home and attempting to discipline time. Young peoples' strategies—looking like they're doing homework or hiding their use of certain programs—in using these media and technologies may belie their structure. However hidden or revealed, they nonetheless continue to discern the relationship between home and work, where it is already quite clear to them that within the home there should be spaces for work. The youth-driven creation of a home office suggests an even deeper incorporation of work into home spaces and poses provocative questions about the changing experience of childhood in late capitalism.

Case Study Two: Coming of Age in Social Network Sites

A common transformation in household structure over the past few decades is the presence of media in the bedroom.[1] Historically, bedrooms emerged as a key space in the home because they represented a space of containment, a place where middle-class parents could keep their children, and particularly their daughters, protected from the outside world (Calvert 1992; Gutzman and de Connick Smith 2008). As a location that tends to be private (or at least is ideally associated with privacy), the bedroom represents an important space for exploration, experimentation and play (Bloustein 2003; Bovill and Livingstone 2001). While some parents prefer to place media in the public spaces of the home, young people often articulate the need for privacy and their own media to be placed in private spaces such as their bedroom. As McRobbie and Garber ([1978] 2000) note in relation to girls, bedrooms are important spaces where young people feel relatively free to develop or express their sense of self or identity, particularly through decoration and organization (Amit-Talal and Wulff 1995; Bovill and Livingstone 2001; Clarke 2001; Kearney 2006; Mazzarella 2005). Many parents in Silicon Valley feel that when bedrooms become the focal point of their children's activities at home, they lose the ability to monitor and guide their children's activities. Yet, where parents discursively distinguish between public and private spaces in the home and attempt to organize their children's activities in relation to that principle, most young people contested the notion of the bedroom as a definitely private space, even when they are conferred ownership. In practice, young people note that their parents can hear through bedroom walls and possess the ability to move through spaces. Sharing a room (as well as media and technology) with a sibling has an impact on the sense of privacy teens feel and, in some instances, renders privacy almost impossible. Erecting barriers to separate the parts of the room and creating passwords are a few of the strategies young people use to carve out their own space. Many young people turn to sites like Facebook because they feel that what they can do and express in these spaces are more private than their physical homes (see also Miller, this volume).

For young adults such as eighteen-year-old Ann, who lives on the outskirts of Silicon Valley, the entrée into networked public culture came through MySpace (Varnelis 2008). During her junior and senior years of high school, Ann was an active MySpace user who uploaded pictures and commented on friends' comments on a daily basis. Ann also participated in what she and her friends called 'MySpace parties', or sleepovers that involved dressing up and taking photographs to post on their respective MySpace pages. Ann and her friends enjoyed trying on sexy clothing such as short skirts, bra tops and fishnet stockings. They also began to make videos of themselves doing 'funny stuff', such as dancing or imitating celebrities. While the pictures, songs, personality quizzes and other content on her MySpace page changed on an intermittent basis, Ann's favourite part of her page, and the most consistent feature of her MySpace page and profile, involved the incorporation of Ann's signature colours, brown and pink. Describing her MySpace page, Ann notes, 'It's actually the colors of my room so it's like brown and pink. And then I don't know. I had... a default pink so it's like what everyone sees when they see a comment.' As Ann suggests, her personal page mirrors the private space of her bedroom at home. The walls of her room are painted a matte brown, and the main features of her room—such as her twin-sized comforter, a large desk and a large French bulletin board—are pink. Other pink and brown accents—such as throw pillows on the bed, the ribbon on her bulletin board, the cushion on her desk chair and picture frames—have been carefully selected and arranged throughout her bedroom. For Ann, brown and pink constitute the backdrop to her daily life in both online and offline spaces.

After accepting an offer to attend a small liberal arts college in Washington State, Ann received an invitation from her future dorm's resident assistant (RA) to participate in Facebook, a social network site that (at the time) primarily catered to the college community. Ann's RA sent her an invitation to be a member of the 'Crystal Mountain' wing, part of a wider network of ninety dorm residents attending her new college. Ann began spending hours at a time perusing different people's sites, looking for familiar names and faces and checking out friends of friends. As the summer progressed, Ann increasingly felt that she was becoming 'addicted' to Facebook, checking it whenever she had a free moment for status updates (e.g. a change to someone's profile). She checked in about four or five times per day, and a typical session lasted about ten minutes. Through this brief, repetitive engagement, Ann started to meet the other students slated to live in her dorm, the most important and exciting of these new connections being her future roommate, Sarah. Describing her fascination with her own Facebook page, Ann explained:

> And you can see everyone else's dorm room and I have groups. Like everyone in my dorm room is in this group. And you can see all the others... and so I can see who my RA is going to be and stuff and so it's really cool. And then I have... I can show you my

> roommate. It's really exciting. So I can see her. And so it... I don't know, I can just see a picture of her instead of having to wait and stuff.

Over the summer, Ann and Sarah 'poked' each other and sent each other short messages and comments. Some of these messages were pragmatic, such as when they planned to move into their dorm room, what furnishings they would be bringing or which classes they planned to take. In addition to using Facebook to communicate, Ann delved into the details of Sarah's Facebook page for insight into what she imagined would be shared interests. Decisions around what to bring to college were aligned with a desire to construct an aesthetic balance. She viewed buying new, trendy iPod speakers as a complement to the 'really nice TV' Sarah would be contributing to their room. Ann also hoped that the speakers might create an acoustic space wherein Ann and Sarah could hang out and listen to music together. Ann and Sarah decided to upload a few pictures of their bedrooms at home onto their Facebook pages to get a sense of each other's style and tastes. Ann was excited when she looked at the photographs and saw Sarah's signature colours: 'I'm brown and pink stuff and she's brown and blue stuff!' Ann surmised that this aesthetic harmony would also signify a harmonious relationship (Clarke 2001; Young 2005).

For Ann, and many individuals like her, social network sites such as MySpace and Facebook play or have played an important role in structuring and sustaining social worlds, including Ann's ability to imagine her future college life in the dorm and establish relationships with new individuals and communities. Social network sites also provided Ann with opportunities to understand and assert her own sense of who she is and who she would become in the transition from high school to college. Much like homecoming, prom and graduation, Facebook, MySpace and other spaces of networked public culture (boyd 2008; boyd and Ellison 2007; Goffman 1959; Miller 1995; Robinson 2007; Strathern 2004; Varnelis 2008) have become part and parcel of the coming-of-age process for teenagers in the United States.

Case Study Three: Locating Connection and Disconnection

Fangrrl and her parents lived in a humble, two-bedroom home characteristic of Silicon Valley's early history as ranch land. Like the outside of the home, the interior had been only moderately updated and retrofitted to accommodate new media technologies. The back porch was modified into a small office where the family shared a PC with a dial-up connection to the Internet, established in the late 1990s; Fangrrl's home was the only one in my study of families in Silicon Valley that still had dial-up Internet access. The family also had an older-model television, a VCR, a gaming system and desktop PC computers. Despite the lack of cutting-edge technology in her home, Fangrrl's online practices and *use* of new media technologies represented a model of the digital native that is glorified in the media and academic press. At the age of sixteen, Fangrrl was an award-winning fan fiction writer with followers throughout the world and a presence on a number of fan fiction community sites. Like other youth who are interest-driven (Ito, Okabe and Matsuda 2010), Fangrrl began her fan fiction career rather early, at the age of twelve, when she started reading the *Harry Potter* book series. After enjoying the books, she heard about a website, fanfiction.net, where stories were created by amateur writers using characters from the *Harry Potter* series. Similar to the alternative and subaltern readings of soap operas and television shows highlighted by Abu-Lughod (2004), Mankekar (1999) and others (Askew and Wilk 2002; Ginsburg, Abu-Lughod and Larkin 2002), writers of fan fiction develop new relationships between characters and develop alternative interpretations and storylines in conversation with the series producers and other readers and writers.[2] After a year or so of avidly reading and, eventually, drafting a few of her own stories, Fangrrl began to concentrate on writing fan fiction for the *Buffy the Vampire Slayer* television series which aired between 1997 and 2003 and has a steady following through reruns, DVRs and rentals. Fangrrl typically wrote a story or two each month during the school year and wrote at least one story per week during the summer.[3]

Like other amateur cultural activities (Jenkins 2006; Lange and Ito 2010), being a fan fiction writer in an era of what Jenkins (2007) terms 'participatory culture' takes a great deal of effort. Rather than spending endless hours online like some of her peers who have unlimited broadband access, Fangrrl used her limited time online very strategically. She logged into her e-mail account for updates and went to sites that she enjoyed and valued to download and save others' stories, which she read later. After reading other people's work, she provided feedback in a Microsoft Word document to be copied and pasted into the comments section online. Just as Lave and Wenger's (1991) extensive work on communities of practice highlights, Fangrrl took on roles in the community, eventually engaging in what Ito et al. (2010) define as 'geeking out', a genre of participation that reflects deep commitment and engagement in a particular site, community or practice which often involves feedback, commenting and other forms of interactions in (this case) networked spaces (see also Horst et al. 2010; Livingstone 2008).[4] As Fangrrl describes her own participation,

> I'm good at commenting on other people's [stories], just do a lot of comments. But it bothers me when I like have lot of hits but no comments. So I try to comment if I can. Like I generally have more time to read than I have to write because I can read in a minutes. Often I'll kinda check various long, ongoing ones to see if they've updated, and if they have, I'll try to write a quick comment. Sometimes I'll write longer comments if I have more time. Sometimes I don't have time at all.

In addition to being a reader and commentator, part of honing her craft (and maintaining her credibility) involved routinely watching *Buffy the Vampire Slayer*. Fangrrl made a fan out of her younger sister, who loved to watch hours of *Buffy* with her; one weekend the sisters spent ten hours watching the series. Fangrrl's sister also likes to suggest new ideas for storylines and new couple configurations between the characters. However, Fangrrl's most valued feedback came from one of her 'beta readers', who she met through their participation in a fan fiction community. Fangrrl also started to take a more active role in other aspects of production, such as creating the art for her stories. As she described,

> I will sometimes, instead of doing homework, fool around with Photoshop and the digital pictures... Before, we had one [digital camera], it was a lot harder to, you know, use pictures. I had to like lift stuff off the internet like a picture of Angelina Jolie... I mean now it's a lot more fun because I can actually, like you know decide what images I want and then make them.... But, like, I would also do the Buffy stuff or whenever I take pictures that are screen captures, I edit them or mix two together or something and kinda make a picture for the title page of the story or something I've written.

Fangrrl's enthusiasm for her fan fiction writing reflects the increasing engagement of audiences and alternative communities in the production of media. As notions of production and consumption have become more complex and, in some ways, more flexible, frameworks such as 'participation' and 'participatory culture' have been introduced. Participation and participatory culture define the new relationships between the medium of digital media and engagement, particularly the ability to create and produce, interact and receive feedback on productions and distribute them to broader publics. Proponents of the shift to participatory culture and participation argue that a focus on participation acknowledges a broader cultural shift in the access to basic tools of production via laptops, smart phones, editing software and so on that often come prepackaged with computers, smartphones and handheld gaming devices (among other objects). It also acknowledges a shift from what is largely viewed as passive consumption to active participation that is multiple and varied.

While a textual analysis of Fangrrl's writings might yield interesting insights about the nature of growing up in the contemporary media ecology, it was clear that the frame for her participation was as much about her activities in a variety of fan fiction sites and communities, and the structures and opportunities for expression they provided, as it was about the navigation of these worlds in her everyday life. Indeed, what always remained fascinating about Fangrrl was the relationship between her participation in fan fiction communities and her place-based communities (e.g. friends, family, school and other organizations and institutions). Despite her online reputation as a fan fiction writer, reader and commentator, she noted that only two of her friends at school knew about her writing and achievements. At school, she had friends, played sports and was considered to be one of the smart kids (and, crucially, was well regarded by her teachers, who, in turn, allowed her extra access to computers during lunch, breaks and after school). Despite her teachers' assistance providing access to the Internet and her recognized proficiency as a writer, Fangrrl did not tell her teachers about her writing. When she started applying to colleges, she decided it would be best to leave out her fan fiction awards and achievements in her applications. She thought the writing would help her in her personal statement and writing samples (what educators describe as transfer) but that outlining her accomplishments might hinder her in a more academic domain. In Fangrrl's case, participation in fan fiction communities became an outlet for expression and participation, but she did not see these communities or places as any more (or less) legitimate for her sense of self. She relished the challenge of improvement and tended to find writing fan fiction more interesting than her homework, but, unlike claims about 'girl geeks' being socially inept or disconnected from so-called real life, Fangrrl felt no antagonism or unease in place-based communities.

In her book *Home and Work*, Christine Nippert-Eng (1996) describes the relationship between home and work in terms of two frameworks: segmentation and integration. Segmentation is found in the industrial workplace, where all connectedness with home is suspended when one walks through the factory gate. Most of the Silicon Valley families in my study can be characterized as integrated, meaning that they maintain fluid boundaries between home and work. Describing the distinctions between working-class attitudes towards the boundary between home and work, Nippert-Eng notes:

> We show our larger mutually exclusive realm territories by separating out a larger amount of artifacts, activities, and associates into their 'proper' realms. There is a distinct time and a distinct place for everything, as people, objects, thoughts, actions, and behaviors are assigned to either the 'home' or 'work' territories. As we integrate more, possessing smaller mutually exclusive home and work territories, we display less of these visible, segmenting strategies. Compared to our more segmenting counterparts, we are ready for most of these artifacts and endeavors, any time, any place, paying very little attention to their classification and containment. (Nippert-Eng 1996: 581)

Fangrrl's ability to segment her various worlds was, in part, by her own family's experience and position in Silicon Valley. At one level, this was basic economics. While centrally located in one of the hub towns in Silicon Valley, the public schools in the area were not as highly ranked and tended to offer 'normal' courses and stressed 'competition', as Fangrrl characterized her parent's decisions. To send their daughters to private schools (US$10,000 per child annually), the family had to weigh a number of priorities. Their decisions were also driven by values around expression, experience and equity rather than what Bourdieu and others would identify as 'conspicuous consumption' practised by others in the region (Shankar 2008). Trained as artists and educators with roots in some of the more liberal arenas of the San Francisco Bay area, Fangrrl's parents valued experience and worked quite arduously to support their two daughters' interests in and out of school.

This process of segmentation also resonates with the strategies parents and youth exhibited in the two previous case studies. What is particularly interesting about Silicon Valley families and their framing and use of media and space to structure these activities is that there are, at times, at least two moral economies of the household: one for the parents and one for children. The construction of the kids' home office, the customization of different media spaces like bedrooms and profile pages and the other rather explicit strategies to segment and specialize media use represent a return to the work culture of childhood that characterized industrial pre–World War II culture. As work on the construction of childhood demonstrates (Bucholz 2002; Buckingham 2000; James, Jenks and Prout 1998; Zelizer 1994), the separation of children from the world of work is a relatively recent construction. While young people in Silicon Valley families are not expected to bring income into the household, the youth-driven creation of a home office suggests an incorporation of work into home spaces and, in turn, a transformation in the experience of childhood in late capitalism. Play and leisure give way to work, focus and specialization, and the expressions of these emerge in the separation and segmentation of physical spaces. Parents in Silicon Valley teach their children strategies to segment as a response to the rapid changes not only resulting from the convergence of new media platforms and the media ecology but also to the life stages and changes associated with the constitution of and power dynamics within the household. Rather than media objects moving towards a stable state of domestication, there is a much more dynamic and mutable relationship between new media technologies and families.

Towards a Digital Anthropology of Everyday Life

This chapter has focused on the ways in which the creation and engagement with media is embedded in the everyday lives of youth and family and becomes part and parcel of coming of age and the attendant project of the self in Western contexts such as Silicon Valley. As I suggested previously, the focus on new media technologies signals a return to the focus on the home and domestic space. As social and cultural life is enacted in and through various screens that are situated inside homes and domestic settings such as cars, the locations and contexts of these activities often matter a great deal, even if the meaning-making may be located in networked and distributed communities (Karanovic, this volume). And while many new methods and forms of research material explore the digitalization of everyday life through the media and the Internet, many of these forms gain analytic power when they are accompanied by a commitment to a number of core values associated with classic anthropological ways of knowing: the attention to change over time, relationships and relationality and a broad sense of commitment to a site, place, people or practice.

In a recent tribute to Roger Silverstone, media studies scholar Sonia Livingstone (2007) considered the theoretical and methodological challenges of carrying out research that reflects symbolic and material dimensions of new media technologies (Silverstone, Hirsch and Morley 1992). While studying patterns and practices in online domains has value, from an ethnographic perspective, the challenge has been to take seriously the relationships between the worlds created in these online spaces and places. Doing so does not necessarily mean privileging one space over the other as more or less authentic but rather understanding how these practices come together and diverge at different points in time. Indeed, and depending upon the research question at hand, Boellstorff (2008) and others compellingly argue for understanding these practices within the integrity of the worlds themselves. One of the key challenges of a digital anthropology is to discover new ways to understand the relationship between media practices and the constitution of media worlds in an individual's, community's or group's life and the different spaces, media and modes through which such endeavours take place. Here, notions of the networked self—where strong and weak ties dominate the interpretations and meaning of the network—tend to collapse these relationships as well as their dynamism over time.

As noted in the introduction to this volume, one of the characteristics of work on the digital is the penchant or quest for the new. Indeed, in one sense this chapter may be viewed as acquiescing to this drive for the new and esoteric with its focus on a high-profile region like Silicon Valley as well as youth; one might expect that the tech-savvy youth who constituted the core of my study would yield quite extraordinary practices. Yet the day-to-day practices of youth and their families in Silicon Valley—selecting profile pictures, situating media in the home or navigating infrastructures—tend to look rather normative and routine. In part, the mundane nature of these practices reflects the research focus upon the domestic and family life. However, it also reflects attention to moving beyond snapshots to understanding how these media practices emerge and change over time. Ann's moves from MySpace to Facebook, from high school to college and from the family home to the dorm room, while occurring in a relatively short time span, involve shifts in the relationships between these spaces as well as in the other key relationships in her life. For Fangrrl, the ambivalence that she felt in her late high school years about integrating her participation in fan communities with her academic achievements changed over time as she went to college and discerned that she could integrate some of these interests into her coursework and major. This ethos of time and attention is not necessarily a core value in other disciplines or with other methodologies; I am often approached for tips on speeding up the process of doing ethnography or for designing diary studies and other tools that enable researchers to see change over time through analyses of back-end data. Anthropological approaches to research do, indeed, leave plenty of room for these innovative tools (Broadbent, this volume; Drazin, this volume), but they cannot be used to sidestep long-term relationship building, trust and rapport. Moreover, anthropological and ethnographic approaches cannot be reduced to participant observation and the ethnographic present. To contrast what people say and do and to understand what practices mean over time takes more than one way of knowing. Anthropology has always been well positioned to understand and analyse changes over time; this will become even more important for a digital anthropology to distinguish itself and its analytical perspective in the drive to understand contemporary practices in their proper context.

Connected to the value of time, the third commitment revolves around the humanity of our work and the people we study. While certainly we have moved beyond naïve notions of giving voice to the people we work with (see Tacchi, this volume, for a critical reflection on voice), anthropology continues to value the emic perspective. One of the hallmarks of anthropology and an anthropological approach is a broad commitment not only to participant observation and thick description but also to particular sites, places, peoples and practices. While we perhaps no longer identify with or value identities as Africanists, Melanesianists and so on with the same vigour as anthropologists did in the past (although see Thomas and Slocom 2003 on the salience of area studies), anthropologists continue to value particularity and believe that an understanding of humanity as a whole can be gleaned through the same ethnographic approaches to analysing small-scale societies that have been the hallmark of the discipline for some time. While the research questions may change and we integrate new forms of material and analyses—from visualizations, use of profiles and other possibilities that come with the digital—the focus upon the everyday lived experience and the ways in which it is intricately connected to the big picture continues to be anthropology's particular perspective on and contribution to our understanding of humanity.

Notes

1. A lengthier version of this section was published in the chapter titled 'Aesthetics of the Self: Digital Mediations', in Daniel Miller, ed., *Anthropology and Individuals* (Oxford: Berg, 2009).
2. From studies of television and celebrity to work on fans' readings of popular culture such as *Star Trek*, *Buffy the Vampire Slayer* and other popular shows, there continues to be a growing recognition that audiences are not passive consumers of media and, in fact, often write and produce their own amateur interpretations. These interpretations often circulated underground through zines and other subcultural forms of dissemination and, increasingly, have found voice in online venues such as fanfictionalley.com and other specialist sites (Baym 2000; Jenkins 2006).
3. Because Fangrrl still actively writes fan fiction and the stories are searchable online, I have not included excerpts of the writing discussed here.

4. Ito, Okabe and Matsuda (2010) utilize the notion of 'genres of participation' to capture the focused attention to a particular activity as well as the interpretations of those activities in socially meaningful and contextual ways.

References

Abu-Lughod, L. 2004. *Dramas of Nationhood: The Politics of Television in Egypt.* Chicago: University of Chicago Press.

Amit-Talal, V., and H. Wulff, eds. 1995. *Youth Cultures: A Cross-Cultural Comparison.* London: Routledge.

Askew, K., and R. R. Wilk, eds. 2002. *The Anthropology of Media Reader.* Malden, MA: Blackwell.

Bakardjieva, M. 2005. *Internet Society: The Internet in Everyday Life.* London: Sage.

Baym, N. 2000. *Tune In, Log On: Soaps, Fandom, and Online Community.* Thousand Oaks, CA: Sage.

Bloch, M. 1998. *How We Think They Think: Anthropological Studies in Cognition, Memory and Literacy.* Boulder, CO: Westview Press.

Bloustein, G. 2003. *Girl Making: A Cross-Cultural Ethnography on the Processes of Growing Up Female.* New York: Berghahn Books.

Boellstorff, T. 2008. *Coming of Age in Second Life.* Princeton, NJ: Princeton University Press.

Bourdieu, P. 1972. *Outline of a Theory of Practice.* Ed. J. Goody, trans. R. Nice. New York: Cambridge University Press.

Bourdieu, P. 1984. *Distinction: A Social Critique of the Judgment of Taste.* Cambridge, MA: Harvard University Press.

Bovill, M., and S. M. Livingstone. 2001. Bedroom Culture and the Privatization of Media Use. In *Children and Their Changing Media Environment: A European Comparative Study*, ed. M. Bovill and S. M. Livingstone, 179–200. Mahwah, NJ: Lawrence Erlbaum Associates.

boyd, d. 2008. Why Youth (Heart) Social Network Sites: The Role of Networked Publics in Teenage Social Life. In *Youth, Identity, and Digital Media*, ed. D. Buckingham, 119–42. John D. and Catherine T. MacArthur Foundation Series on Digital Media and Learning. Cambridge, MA: MIT Press.

boyd, d. m., and N. B. Ellison. (2007). Social Network Sites: Definition, History, and Scholarship. *Journal of Computer-Mediated Communication* 13(1): article 11. http://jcmc.indiana.edu/vol13/issue1/boyd.ellison.html.

Buchli, V. 1999. *An Archaeology of Socialism: The Narkomfin Communal House, Moscow.* Oxford: Berg.

Bucholz, M. 2002. Youth and Cultural Practice. *Annual Review of Anthropology* 31(1): 525–52.

Buckingham, D. 2000. *After the Death of Childhood: Growing Up in the Age of Electronic Media.* Cambridge: Polity.

Bull, M. 2008. *Sound Moves: iPod Culture and Urban Experience.* London: Routledge.

Calvert, K. 1992. *Children in the House: The Material Culture of Early Childhood, 1600–1900.* Boston: Northeastern University Press.

Carsten, J., and S. Hugh-Jones, eds. 1995. *About the House.* Cambridge: Cambridge University Press.

Cieraad, I., ed. 2006. *At Home: Anthropology of Domestic Space.* Syracuse, NY: Syracuse University Press.

Clarke, A. J. 1999. *Tupperware.* Washington, DC: Smithsonian Institution Press.

Clarke, A. J. 2001. Setting Up Home in North London: Ambition and Actuality. In *Home Possessions: Material Possessions Behind Closed Doors*, ed. D. Miller, 23–46. Oxford: Berg.

Darrah, C. N., J. M. Freeman and J. A. English-Lueck. 2007. *Busier Than Ever! Why American Families Can't Slow Down.* Palo Alto, CA: Stanford University Press.

Douglas, M. 1991. The Idea of a Home: A Kind of Space. *Social Research* 58(1): 288–307.

Dourish, P., and G. Bell. 2007. The Infrastructure of Experience and the Experience of Infrastructure: Meaning and Structure in Everyday Encounters with Space. *Environment and Planning B: Planning and Design* 34(3): 414–30.

English-Lueck, J. 2002. *SiliconValley@Cultures.* Stanford, CA: Stanford University Press.

Garvey, P. 2001. Organized Disorder: Moving Furniture in Norwegian Homes. In *Home Possessions: Material Culture Behind Closed Doors,* ed. D. Miller, 47–68. Oxford: Berg.

Garvey, P. 2010. Consuming IKEA and Inspiration as Material Form. In *Design Anthropology*, ed. A. J. Clarke. New York: Springer-Verlag.

Gasser, U., and J. Palfrey. 2008. *Born Digital: Understanding the First Generation of Digital Natives.* New York: Basic Books.

Giddens, A. 1991. *Modernity and Self-Identity: Self and Society in the Late Modern Age.* Cambridge: Polity Press.

Ginsburg, F., L. Abu-Lughod and B. Larkin. 2002. *Media Worlds: Anthropology on New Terrain.* Berkeley: University of California Press.

Goffman, E. 1959. *The Presentation of Self in Everyday Life.* New York: Anchor Books.

Gregg, M. 2011. *Work's Intimacy.* Cambridge: Polity.

Gullestad, M. 1984. *Kitchen-Table Society: A Case Study of the Family Life and Friendships of Young Working-Class Mothers in Urban Norway.* Oslo: Universitetsforlaget

Gutzman, M., and N. de Connick Smith, eds. 2008. *Designing Modern Childhoods: History, Space and the Material Culture of Childhood.* New Brunswick, NJ: Rutgers University Press.

Hancock, M. 2001. Home Science and the Nationalization of Domesticity in Colonial India. *Modern Asian Studies* 35(4): 871–904.

Holston, J. 1989. *The Modernist City: An Anthropological Critique of Brasília.* Chicago: University of Chicago Press.

Horst, H. 2010. Families. In *Hanging Out, Messing Around and Geeking Out: Living and Learning with New Media*, ed. M. Ito et al., 149–94. Cambridge, MA: MIT Press.

Horst, H., B. Herr-Stephenson, and L. Robinson. 2010. Media Ecologies. In *Hanging Out, Messing Around and Geeking Out: Living and Learning with New Media*, ed. M. Ito et al., 29–78. Cambridge, MA: MIT Press.

Horst, H., and D. Miller. 2006. *The Cell Phone: An Anthropology of Communication.* Oxford: Berg.

Ito, M., D. Okabe and M. Matsuda, eds. 2005. *Personal, Portable, Pedestrian: The Mobile Phone in Japanese Life*. Cambridge, MA: MIT Press.

James, A., C. Jenks and A. Prout. 1998. *Theorizing Childhood.* Cambridge: Cambridge University Press.

Jenkins, H. 2006. *Fans, Bloggers, and Gamers: Media Consumers in a Digital Age.* New York: New York University Press.

Jenkins, H. 2007. *Confronting the Challenges of Participatory Culture: Media Education for the 21st Century.* Chicago: John D. and Catherine T. MacArthur Foundation.

Kearney, M. C. 2006. *Girls Make Media.* London: Routledge.

Lally, E. 2002. *At Home with Computers.* Oxford: Berg.

Lange, P., and M. Ito. 2010. Creative Production. In *Hanging Out, Messing Around and Geeking Out: Living and Learning with New Media*, ed. M. Ito et al., 243–94. Cambridge, MA: MIT Press.

Lave, J., and E. Wenger. 1991. *Situated Learning: Legitimate Peripheral Participation.* Cambridge: Cambridge University Press.

Lévi-Strauss, C. 1983. *The Way of the Masks.* London: Jonathan Cape.

Lévi-Strauss, C. 1987. *Anthropology and Myth: Lectures 1951–1982.* Oxford: Blackwell.

Ling, R. 2004. *The Mobile Connection: The Cell Phone's Impact on Society.* San Francisco: Morgan Kaufman.

Livingstone, S. 2002. *Young People and New Media.* Thousand Oaks, CA: Sage.

Livingstone, S. 2007. On the Material and the Symbolic: Silverstone's Double Articulation of Research Traditions in New Media Studies. *New Media and Society* 9(1): 16–24.

Livingstone, S. 2008. Taking Risky Opportunities in Youthful Content Creation: Teenagers' Use of Social Networking Sites for Intimacy, Privacy, and Self-Expression. *New Media and Society* 10(3): 393–411.

Low, S. 2003. *Behind the Gates: The New American Dream.* New York: Routledge.

Low, S., and D. Lawrence-Zuñiga. 2003. *The Anthropology of Space and Place: Locating Culture.* Oxford: Blackwell.

Mankekar, P. 1999. *Screening Culture, Viewing Politics: An Ethnography of Television, Womanhood, and Nation in Postcolonial India.* Chapel Hill, NC: Duke University Press.

Marcoux, J.-S. 2001. The 'Casser Maison' Ritual: Constructing the Self by Emptying the Home. *Journal of Material Culture* 6: 213–36.

Mazzarella, S. R. 2005. Claiming a Space. In *Girl Wide Web*, ed. S. R. Mazzarella, 141–60. New York: Peter Lang.

McRobbie, A., and J. Garber. [1978] 2000. Girls and Subcultures. In *Feminism and Youth Subcultures*, 2nd ed., ed. A. McRobbie, 12–25. London: Routledge.

Miller, D. 2001. *Home Possessions: Material Culture Behind Closed Doors.* Oxford: Berg.

Miller, D., and D. Slater. 2000. *The Internet: An Ethnographic Approach.* Oxford: Berg.

Miller, H. W. 1995. Goffman on the Internet: The Presentation of Self in Electronic Life. Paper presented at the Embodied Knowledge and Virtual Space Conference, Goldsmith's College, University of London, June. http://www.ntu.ac.uk/soc/psych/miller/goffman.htm.

Moore, H. 1986. *Space, Text and Gender: An Anthropological Study of the Marakwet of Kenya.* Cambridge: Cambridge University Press.

Morgan, H. L. 1966. *Houses and House Life of the American Aborigines.* Classics in Anthropology. Chicago: University of Chicago Press.

Nippert-Eng, C. 1996. *Home and Work: Negotiating Boundaries Through Everyday Life.* Chicago: University of Chicago Press.

Pink, S. 2004. *Home Truths: Gender, Domestic Objects and Everyday Lives.* Oxford: Berg.

Prensky, M. 2001. Digital Natives, Digital Immigrants. *On the Horizon* 9(5): 1–6.

Robinson, L. 2007. The Cyberself: The Self-ing Project Goes Online, Symbolic Interaction in the Digital Age. *New Media and Society* 9(1): 93–110.

Shankar, S. 2008. *Desi Land: Teen Culture, Class and Success in Silicon Valley.* Durham, NC: Duke University Press.

Shove, E. A. 2003. *Comfort, Cleanliness and Convenience: The Social Organization of Normality.* Oxford: Berg.

Silverstone, R., E. Hirsch and D. Morley. 1992. Information and Communication Technologies and the Moral Economy of the Household. In *Consuming Technologies: Media and Information in Domestic Spaces*, ed. R. Silverstone and E. Hirsch, 15–31. London: Routledge.

Spigel, L. 1992. *Make Room for TV: Television and the Family Ideal in Postwar America.* Chicago: University of Chicago Press.

Spigel, L. 2010. *Electronic Elsewheres: Media, Technology and Social Space.* Minneapolis: University of Minnesota Press.

Stevens, R., T. Satwicz and L. McCarthy. 2008. In-Game, In-Room, In-World: Reconnecting Video Game Play to the Rest of Kids' Lives. In *the Ecology of Games: Connecting Youth, Games, and Learning*, ed. K. Salen, 41–66. The John D. and

Catherine T. MacArthur Foundation Series on Digital Media and Learning. Cambridge, MA: The MIT Press.

Strathern, M. 2004. The Whole Person and Its Artifacts. *Annual Review of Anthropology* 33: 1–19.

Tacchi, J. A. 2002. *Radio Texture: Between Self and Others.* In *The Anthropology of Media: A Reader*, ed. K. Askew and R. R. Wilk, 241–57. Malden, MA: Blackwell.

Tacchi, J. A. 2009. Finding a Voice: Digital Storytelling as Participatory Development in Southeast Asia. In *Story Circle: Digital Storytelling around the World*, ed. J. Hartley and K. McWilliam, 167–75. London: Wiley-Blackwell.

Thomas, D., and K. Slocum. 2003. Rethinking Global and Area Studies: Insights from the Caribbean. *American Anthropologist* 105(3): 553–65.

Varnelis, K., ed. 2008. *Networked Publics.* Cambridge, MA: MIT Press.

Wilk, R. 2002. Television, Time, and the National Imaginary in Belize. In *Media Worlds*, ed. F. Ginsburg, L. Abu-Lughod and B. Larkin, 171–86. Berkeley: University of California Press.

Young, D. 2005. The Colours of Things. In *Handbook of Material Culture*, ed. P. Spyer, C. Tilley, S. Kuechler and W. Keane, 173–85. Thousand Oaks, CA: Sage.

Zelizer, V. A. 1994. *Pricing the Priceless Child: The Changing Social Value of Children.* Princeton, NJ: Princeton University Press.

–4–

Geomedia: The Reassertion of Space within Digital Culture

Lane DeNicola

Space, Media and Their Globalization

Anthropology has recognized for some decades that the questions of culture with which it has been engaged for so long are today ineluctably entangled with contemporary developments in technologies of mediation. Several years prior to Google's transformation from the research project of two Stanford doctoral students into an incorporated commercial firm (and more than a decade and a half before *google* would become a common verb) Gupta and Ferguson (1992) made what was then a profound claim: 'Existing symbiotically with the commodity form, profoundly influencing even the remotest people that anthropologists have made such a fetish of studying, mass media pose the clearest challenge to orthodox notions of culture' (18–19). That claim and the challenges they observed have mushroomed in the last twenty years, even if—in the context of an anthropology of digital culture—the claim's potency seems diminished in hindsight. What is perhaps more striking is that the focus of that article and related work of that era was not mass media but *space*, and especially the process of deterritorialization.

> The idea that space is made meaningful is of course a familiar one to anthropologists; indeed, there is hardly an older or better established anthropological truth. East or West, inside or outside, left or right, mound or floodplain—from at least the time of Durkheim, anthropology has known that the experience of space is always socially constructed. The more urgent task... is to politicize this uncontestable observation. With meaning-making understood as a practice, how are spatial meanings established? Who has the power to make places of spaces? Who contests this? What is at stake? (Gupta and Ferguson 1992: 11)

This line of inquiry can today be traced more deeply into digital culture, not only through the fields of social geography and media studies but via a broader spatial turn within the social sciences generally. The work I will elaborate on here attempts to perform that tracing, but with a specific class of technologies and social relations (here given the name *geomedia*) as its anthropological subject.[1] I am interested first in clarifying how this work is contiguous with earlier social inquiry into new media and knowledge production, and interested further in suggesting some related paths along which digital anthropology could most productively develop its spatial analyses. Underlying my discussion are two suspicions I can only incompletely articulate or support here. First, geomedia demands special analytic treatment, insofar as it is collapsible to neither digital medium, place-making practice nor representational technology. It comprises, in fact, an ineluctable convergence of all three. More speculatively, I perceive room for an argument that geomedia will yet again reconfigure orthodox notions of culture. Far from being a type of media that anthropologists should scrutinize in established ways, geomedia are critical to understanding the full rationale for an anthropology of the digital.

Media scholars and critical historians of communication technology have illustrated how grandiose claims about the 'death of distance' were just as central to the utopian rhetoric of 'the electronic revolution' in the nineteenth century as they were in the digital revolution of the twentieth (Carey 1989). With European cultural norms of leisure travel and technologies such as the steam locomotive, the possibility of two-way communication over long distances via radio heralded a new age in the popular imagination, the 'conquering of space' and the entrenchment of cosmopolitanism as intrinsic to the order of modernity. Arguably, few aspects of digital media, cyberspace or the network society are as commonly perceived as fundamental as its disembodying aspects, its placelessness and subordination of physical proximity to network connectivity (Castells 1996). Critical geographers, meanwhile, have led a long-term and highly reflexive engagement with the tools of their discipline, not unlike anthropology's engagement with photography. The production and circulation of maps and globes, the development of cartographic techniques and apparatuses, coordinate systems, land use classification schemes and many other spatial technologies of their trade have been scrutinized. Neither unequivocally objective nor value-neutral, they have long been employed in the construction of nationhood, colonial exploitation and the planning and administrative functions at the core of urban planning and global development (Barnes and Duncan 1992; Gregory 1994; Soja 1989). Most recently, this scrutiny has been levelled at the newer digital tools of their trade, in particular *satellite-based navigation systems* such as the geographic positioning system (GPS), *geographic information systems* (GIS) and *earth remote sensing* (Curry 1998; Harris 2003; Monmonier and Blij 1996; Pickles 1995, 2004; Porteous 1986; Sieber 2004).[2] Though these two academic traditions have developed largely in parallel and occasionally even drew from a common conceptual terrain, they remain segregated by one simple assumption: mass media are essentially *cultural phenomena*, consumer-driven and of the masses, while maps and cartographic technologies are more clearly *scientific domains* and generally within an expert purview.

Beginning at least with Latour's *We Have Never Been Modern* (1993), it was precisely this presumed schism between culture and science that brought anthropologists into proximity with the burgeoning field of science and technology studies or STS, and this interaction warrants a brief elaboration.[3] Prior to the interventions of Latour and his contemporaries (e.g. Forsythe 1994; Pfaffenberger 1992), STS was largely an interdisciplinary amalgam of the history of technology (a comparatively venerable field with strong ties to museum communities), the (also well-developed) field of the philosophy of science and certain specific schools within the sociology of knowledge. Since at least the mid-1990s, anthropology and STS have shared a predilection for empiricism at the social and experiential levels, an interest in comparative, cross-cultural analysis, an understanding of the researcher as the lens through which knowledge production happens and a subordination of the narratives of elites to those of otherwise peripheral populations. As Hess and colleagues (1998) suggested:

> Perhaps anthropology's most profound contribution to STS as a whole at this point has been the ethnographically-based analysis of the viewpoints of users, patients, consumers, employees and other publics outside the citadels of technical expertise. Anthropology has helped shift the focus of social studies of science and technology from the epistemologically and politically problematic question of the social construction of science and technology to the much more interesting—and relevant—question of the reconstruction of science and technology by new groups within science, and by the various consumers and publics of science and technology. (176)

These fields also share the perspective that material forms can erode, catalyze or entrench systems of value and specific social relations. STS also makes the (often explicitly political) move of taking two of the conceptual linchpins of the modern era (science and technology) as the most appropriate axes along which critical inquiry into contemporary global society should be developed. This certainly offers a route through which we might 'politicize the constructed experience of space', as called for by Gupta and Ferguson. In that task both STS and anthropology face striking a tricky balance between, on the one hand, critical scrutiny of dominant institutions (e.g. state-based mapping agencies) and, on the other hand, adding the voices of underrepresented groups (e.g. communities within mapped landscapes) to the pool of human knowledge. Yet for all the critical work on spatial knowledge and experience performed within this domain (Bender 2006; Hirsch and O'Hanlon 1995; Low and Lawrence-Zuaniga 2003; Tilley 1994), little, if any, of it has yet had to confront the tacit division of the spatial sciences from common experience, the analytic segregation of exotic scientific apparatus from the mediation of landscapes via consumer technology. With the emergence of geomedia, however, such a confrontation becomes unavoidable.

Two aspects of space and media are foregrounded by anthropological work on contemporary digital culture and must be taken into account in the analysis of geomedia. The first is the *mobilization of digital technology*, the untethering of online interaction via the shift away from the computer as a domestic or business appliance or scientific device (Edwards 1996) to appurtenances that are personal, portable and pedestrian (Ito, Okabe and Matsuda 2005). Mobile phones, only the most common manifestation of that shift, have seen the broadest analysis in spatial terms, with portable music players, portable game consoles and vehicular navigation units receiving considerably less critical scrutiny. Some have argued that this shift, intuitively suggestive of a newly liberated or connected subjectivity, can just as easily yield the reverse, tethering users to their workplaces or shutting out that which is physically near in order to privilege the remote (Bull 2008). In the dystopian extreme, human bodies themselves are incorporated as nodes within a network, normativizing constant surveillance. Others have observed that this mobilization has precipitated important secondary effects, such as the shift away from the business-oriented desktop to that of the map as the dominant metaphor for the ordering of information. A second observation with special import for geomedia is the *destabilization and ongoing reconfiguration of the dominant media institutions* (journalistic conventions, the publishing and film production industries, intellectual property law). In comparison with the powerfully hierarchical ordering of twentieth-century commercial media, the volatile social and political landscape of journalistic bloggers, YouTube regulars, mesh network advocates and open-source software seem complex indeed. Arguably this trend is indicative of a broadened attribution of authority, a more distributed and (in the ideal) participatory form of knowledge production. Undoubtedly, the research specialities mentioned so far can contribute some insights into that trend in the form of work on indigenous media, participatory GIS, community informatics and citizen science (Epstein 1996; Ginsburg, Abu-Lughod and Larkin 2002; Monmonier 2002; Sieber 2004).

Two examples from my own research illustrate the ramifications of these observations for geomedia. First I discuss the field of earth remote sensing (ERS), and in particular ethnographic work I conducted on the training of satellite image interpreters at a renowned institution in India. As a field site, this institution is situated within India's tightly regulated cartographic community and is an important participant in India's neoliberal information economy. As the back office to the world, India's software development and data-processing expertise has a global reputation, one that—along with the particularities of India's experience with cartography (Edney 1997)—foreground some of the most important aspects of geomedia. Next I outline research on location awareness, location-aware artefacts and the location-based services industry. In many ways the conceptual converse of eye-in-the-sky data-gathering systems, inexpensive location-tracking technology now piggybacking on cellular communications is finding its way into an expanding array of artefacts and Internet services. In so doing, location and locatability are being attributed new significance within digital culture, and while this is not without irony, it is also in congruence with an underlying supposition of this volume as a whole: that at the same time digital culture is posited as placeless and homogenizing, when it comes to actual practice, digital culture remains thoroughly socialized and materially entangled with spatial experience.

Earth Remote Sensing in India

In a special issue of *Technology and Culture* devoted to earth remote sensing, Brugioni (1989) recounted a striking personal experience in his article on the impact and social implications of that technology:

> In 1978, 34 years after World War II, my curiosity about the Nazi death camp at Auschwitz-Birkenau was rekindled when a television program on the Holocaust was aired. With Robert Poitier, a research colleague, we began to look back into old aerial photographic files. I knew that in 1944 aerial reconnaissance and bombing missions were conducted on the I. G. Farben Synthetic Fuel and Rubber Plant, only 5 miles from the Auschwitz-Birkenau Camps. Because the aerial cameras were turned on a few minutes prior to arriving over the target and left running a few minutes after the bomb strike or reconnaissance run, we found detailed aerial photos of the death camp in operation—something that had been entirely overlooked during and after the war. Analyzing the photos, we could see four large complexes of gas chambers, undressing rooms and crematoriums whose round-the-clock operation was killing about 12,000 people a day. Bodies were also being burned in large open pits or buried in trenches. On one mission, we could spot victims being marched to their death and in another a line of prisoners being processed for slave labor. Israeli experts on the Holocaust have described the aerial photos as among 'the largest caches of information ever uncovered on Auschwitz.' The photos are now on display at the Yad Vashem Holocaust Museum in Jerusalem, the Auschwitz Museum in Poland, and at the National Archives in Washington. (81)

While the remarkable serendipity of this anecdote is likely clear, its immediate relevance to digital anthropology is probably less so.[4] Images collected by aircraft (and later satellites) were recognized as having potent strategic value even before the outbreak of World War I, so it is unsurprising that the technology was (like the Internet) gestated within the military-industrial complex of dominant states. Beginning in the 1960s, the utility of such imagery for civil applications (weather forecasting, natural resource prospecting and inventory, disaster assessment) was realized, resulting in the deployment of a variety of new satellites and supporting infrastructure (initially by the Cold War superpowers but later by a diverse array of states). The first tentative foray into ERS commercialization was marked by the French SPOT system (Satellite Pour l'Observation de la Terre), the first satellite-based ERS system designed from the start to fulfil explicitly commercial purposes. In the three decades since, the number and technical capabilities of commercial ERS systems have expanded dramatically. That development has had two profound results. First, the collection of aerial images—once a logistically complex bespoke activity focused on limited geographic regions—is now routine, continuous and global in scope. ERS represents, in fact, a massive (and rapidly expanding) visual database of the terrestrial surface, one that specialists admit is outpacing our data-mining abilities (and data-handling policies). Second, though previously confined to highly specialized facilities run by state and commercial actors, the vast majority of today's Internet users have easy access to satellite imagery, in many cases imagery that is timely enough and of high enough resolution to identify small buildings and quite recent construction. Further, that imagery is increasingly woven into pedestrian experience, both online and off.

India's earth remote sensing programme is a prominent feature on this landscape. I have noted previously (DeNicola 2007) how Western discourse often depicts space research and industry at a double-remove from the so-called developing world, where high technology and nationalistic goals are overshadowed by patent human needs and a lack of basic infrastructure. Yet advocates of space industrialization allege a specific utility for ERS in socially relevant applications, and India has amassed more than five decades of experience in space, with systems and capabilities rivalled today only by those of the United States and China. My interest in ethnographic research into India's ERS programme was not to seek a resolution to debates about developmentalism and space research, but to understand the meaning-making occurring around and through what I perceived as a nascent visual medium. Clearly the meaning-making attached to such big science efforts does not occur outside the postcolonial context (Prakash 1999) nor outside the rhetorical and material advocacy of ERS in the developing world by institutions such as the World Bank and the United Nations (Morgan 1990), but I was at least as interested in the peculiarities of satellite images as a digital commodity, how they were being circulated—or blocked from circulation—in a highly competitive and volatile global data market where it is often difficult to discern commercial entities from organs of the state, military from civil applications. Further, I wanted to know about the construction of expertise and professional identity among trained satellite image interpreters in India, particularly given the rapid popularization of the visual forms that are their subject.

In a triangulation on these questions, my fieldwork and research crystallized along three analytic threads. First, I noted the conspicuous rhetorical presence of India's ERS satellites themselves, in everything from newspaper accounts to industry trade literature to the published musings of India's president:

> We seem to have a blind admiration of anything done outside our borders and very little belief in our own abilities…I have in my possession a glossy, superbly produced German calendar with maps of Europe and Africa based on remote sensing. When people are told that the satellite that took the picture was the Indian Remote Sensing Satellite, they find it hard to believe. They have to be shown the credit line under the pictures. (Kalam and Tiwari 2004: 27)

A diachronic analysis of the Indian space programme and especially its ERS satellites is illuminating. Mainstream media coverage of India's launch of CARTOSAT-1, for example, lauded the local firm responsible (Mecon) for the launchpad construction and described the launch vehicle as an 'engineering marvel—a totally indigenous affair—[that] has brought the nation [into] the select club of countries having this rare expertise'. The special relevance of the claim lies in the context that India had previously been importing the cryogenic technology crucial to heavy-lift boosters from the United States. When the Americans halted that import as part of international sanctions against India's 1992 nuclear test detonation, India successfully developed its own cryogenics capacity. The spectacular launch and deployment of ERS satellites invokes what Nye has labelled 'the technological sublime', the 'repeated experiences of awe and wonder, often tinged with an element of terror, which people have when confronted with particular natural sites, architectural forms, and technological achievements' (Nye 1994: xvi). With their remoteness from and invisibility within our everyday experience, ERS satellites operate as an allegory of statehood. If, as Abraham (1998) has suggested, nuclear test detonations have reified the Indian state in their construction of an 'enunciatory' capacity, ERS satellites have worked similarly in constructing the Indian state as a particular *observational* capacity with global purview.

A second analytic thread in this work examined the social life of Indian ERS imagery itself, as discursive artefact and global information commodity. Despite the shared genealogy of ERS and cartography (not to mention the continued application of the former to the latter), the planning and infrastructure that supports satellite image collection is quite distinct from that of ground survey and measurement. While such images often may be used to produce maps, they represent in a way quite distinct from them. ERS is clearly a genre of scientific visualization akin to the cloud chamber images of high-energy physics (Galison 1997) or the ultrasound images employed by obstetricians (Yoxen 1994). Yet its applications and popular circulation are considerably broader than most such examples. Its subjects and visual grammar are not only less alien to the layperson, they are often of direct and obvious political relevance (e.g. Amos 2003). ERS imagery is also a high-volume commodity in comparison with most scientific visual forms, with a consumer base that spans a dizzying variety of industries. Insofar as it is a strategic technology (like uranium purification and cryptographic algorithms), state governments have a vested interest in regulating access to both the technological artefacts (e.g. satellites) and data of ERS. As a technology of surveillance (like closed-circuit television and DNA analysis), ERS—even in its environmental applications—introduces many of the difficult ethical (Marx 2007) and sociolegal (Lynch 2003) issues typical of surveillance and forensics technologies, and in fact ERS has seen growing forensic and evidentiary use (Markowitz 2002). Despite the acknowledged expertise required for rigorous interpretation, ERS imagery draws technically and visually on a photographic vernacular that moderns are acculturated to, and it is increasingly recognized as an artefact with aesthetic potential (U.S. Geological Survey 2002). The dense intersection of meanings attached to ERS as a visual form suggest it may transgress the circulatory patterns of other media, challenging conventional analytic approaches.

The third and final analytic thread of this multisited ethnography followed satellite image interpreters, and more specifically their early socialization and formal education as observed at the Indian Institute of Remote Sensing (IIRS), the premier institution in India and arguably most of Asia for such training. I documented the visual and spatial practices of this interpretive community of experts while formally enrolled as a student at IIRS in the city of Dehradun. Like the first-year students of Good's (1994) ethnographic account of medical school, neophyte satellite image interpreters must go through a transformation in how they see, taking images that are often quite abstract or misleading to the layperson, parsing them into relevant features and projecting them mentally as shadows of three-dimensional landscapes. Inevitably, classificatory ambiguities arise—is this bright red patch productive, healthy forest, or is it useless scrub?—and in such cases the fledgling interpreter must rely on a quite partial and subjective set of categories (Robbins 2003), typically one inherited from the state. Also of interest here was the fact that image interpreters perceived themselves not only as key participants in India's new information economy but as ineluctably caught between analogue and digital, between old and new. In comparison with their colleagues in most other information technology subfields working in telecommunications, business or finance, students of remote sensing and geoinformatics seemed to acknowledge a greater level of intimacy with the physical world, insofar as it is, by definition, their subject. This suggested a possible tension between material and immaterial (and more broadly between different concepts of space) that have persisted throughout this vein of research.

ERS has been a comparatively easy target for critique on multiple fronts. The mutually constitutive relationship between, on the one hand, geographic knowledge (and the tools for its production) and, on the other hand, cultural concepts of society and environment has been well theorized (Aitken and Michel 1995; Harvey and Chrisman 1998; Macnaghten and Urry 1998; Pickles 1995; Sheppard 1995). Geographers in particular have noted that, as with any cartographic technology, geographic technologies present a variety of thorny issues, particularly to those interested in supporting more inclusive scientific research and more just social policy, *without* simultaneously enabling surveillance or environmental exploitation (Monmonier 2002; Sieber 2007). ERS has enjoyed substantial growth in civil application and now circulation into popular discourse, but it has also been criticized as a tool that can displace more humanistically engaged forms of knowledge (Parks 2005) or telescope historical phenomena into a distorted, 'presentist' narrative (Litfin 2001). For example, the centuries of deforestation and overdevelopment in Europe and North America that occurred prior to the advent of aerial photography could not possibly have been documented with the same comprehensiveness or level of detail that much more recent activity in the developing world has seen. While unquestionably enhancing state ability to delineate boundaries, conserve resources, improve agricultural yields and mitigate the effects of natural and artificial disasters, as a discursive subject (the critique holds), civil ERS is fundamentally based on a number of problematic assumptions 'rooted in a paradigm of rationality and control' (Litfin 1997: 26). I return to this critique at the end of this chapter, after shifting first to an entirely different case of geomedia.

Figure 4.1. IIRS students examine a satellite photo on a ground-truthing exercise. Photo by Lane DeNicola © 2005.

When Things Know Where They Are (and Remember Where They've Been)

In 2007, New York City taxi drivers staged a two-day strike when city administrators mandated that all taxicabs would be required to have onboard GPS trackers installed.[5] The location-finding devices would be accompanied by credit card processing equipment and displays that would make routes clearly visible to passengers. Officials viewed this as a mechanism for addressing a variety of transportation management and consumer protection functions, while drivers felt the measures were tantamount to a new and unnecessary surveillance regime. The cabbies' initial argument—that the monitoring of their location constituted an invasion of privacy—got little traction in the mainstream press, but when the New York City Taxi Workers Alliance filed suit in the US District Court of Manhattan, they took a different tack. The recorded paths taken by cabbies constituted their own behavioural patterns and expert knowledge, they argued, and so were a proprietary resource which they were simultaneously the producers and rightful owners of. This shift—from a framing of individual privacy and surveillance as a tool of coercion to one of information traces as property and surveillance as enabling—is indicative of yet another development in the spectrum of phenomena referred to as geomedia.

Commercially available satellite navigation (or 'satnav') receivers of the type commonly installed in vehicles are only the most overt of location-aware devices. Significantly more pervasive are the location-finding technologies (which often do not rely on satellites at all) now typically embedded within mobile phones. Ironically, the continuous personal locatability that mobile phones provide was of little general interest prior to its integration with mobiles. In the United States, when the first mobiles (cell phones) become available to the average consumer, US 911 emergency management systems were overwhelmed by calls from panicked individuals struggling to identify their whereabouts (such systems having been designed around the norm of fixed landlines). Since cellular telecommunications technically required that individual units be able to determine their location within a given 'cell' anyway, the federal government mandated that all new mobile phones would automatically provide that location information to emergency responders. It was not long before the general utility (and commercial potential) of providing location information to the user was realized, and within the last two decades the location-based services industry has shown explosive growth. Location awareness has become an expected capability of smartphones such as Apple's iPhone, and given that such mobile devices are rapidly displacing desktop computers as the dominant interface with the Internet, location awareness is arguably an understudied aspect of digital culture.

The location-based services industry emerged largely from the idea that commercial services could be targeted to consumers when they were physically proximate to them (e.g. advertising for a local restaurant sent to the mobiles of those passing nearby), but the concept has expanded beyond such straightforward applications. Consider for example the recent emergence of the check-in on social networking sites. Foursquare, for example, is a social network built entirely around physical places. Members perform a simple check-in via their mobiles upon arriving at specific locales—home, work, the shopping mall or the local pub. Other members of their Foursquare network receive a message indicating their new whereabouts, possibly precipitating an impromptu rendezvous. Members are also rewarded for checking in by accruing points attached to each locale, and acquiring sufficient points earns badges displayed prominently alongside the members' profiles. Those with the most check-ins within a given time span may be tagged as the 'mayor' of the locale in question, with many game-style scavenger hunts and other variants regularly hosted by Foursquare. Similar functions have since been employed in Google's Latitude service and Facebook Places. Just as interestingly, the dangers peculiar to routinely publishing one's physical location have been spectacularly highlighted by sites such as PleaseRobMe.com and ICanStalkU.com. The crucial anthropological insight in these examples is that, far from the erasure of space or the subordination of physical location as irrelevant to our social networks, physical places are reappropriated as indelible nodes or strata within those networks (DeNicola 2006a, 2006b).

Figure 4.2. High-precision professional-grade GPS receiver. Photo by David Monniaux, available under Creative Commons 'Share-Alike' 3.0.

It is important to take note of how these developments play out at the macro level as well as the micro. The term *GPS* has become synonymous with satellite-based navigation, but the Global Positioning System—controlled by the US Department of Defense—is actually only one of a growing number of such systems. Though it has yet to achieve its envisioned status, the Russian Glonass system began deployment in the early 1980s and has been partially operational since 1993. A global, all-weather navigation system independent of the US military was of obvious utility during the waning years of the Cold War. Galileo, on the other hand—a civilly controlled alternative to GPS—has been under development by the European Union since 1999. It promises several levels of service, including a robust 'life critical' service for specialized applications. In 2003, China began backing out of its participation in the Galileo programme and moved instead to design its own system, called BeiDou or Big Dipper. Scheduled to be operational in 2015, it is slated to serve not only

China but the sprawling pan-Asian telecommunications market generally. India has been the latest nation to chime in, announcing that the Indian Regional Navigational Satellite System is scheduled for operation by 2014.

While the observational capacities of earth remote sensing satellites have moved beyond their roles in intelligence gathering and state administration to being an apparatus of commercial enterprise, it would appear that the spatial-ordering capabilities afforded by navigational satellites are still firmly held as exclusive functions of the state. Further, we see in this prioritization that location and the locatability of things and persons has been transformed, taking on a heightened status in the millennial era in a fashion similar to that of 'attention' in the nineteenth century (Crary 1999). Following the reconfiguration of labour by industrialization and the rise of behavioural psychology, attention became the principal capacity of the 'sane' or mentally healthy subject. Today, instantaneous locatability has become the principal capacity of the 'secure' subject.

It is crucial in this context to acknowledge not only the shift from desktops to mobiles, but the equally profound shift from the computer as a dedicated appliance to computing as a generalized capacity (DeNicola 2010). Location awareness is no longer exclusive to dedicated handheld receivers nor even a capability integrated

Figure 4.3. An array of location-aware devices. Photo by Mike Roach, available under Creative Commons 'Attribution ShareAlike' 2.0 Generic.

into mobile telecommunications devices. It is a function appearing in a growing array of pedestrian artefacts not typically perceived as information technology. We can find, for example, a number of social networking sites for bicyclists or runners built around the exchange of user-generated maps and paths. The data for these paths may be collected using a smartphone, but often they are more seamlessly acquired using athletic trainers (tennis shoes) embedded with a GPS receiver. Several styles of such digitally enabled footwear have been available to consumers for a number of years, originally marketed in the United States as a means of keeping tabs on one's children or elderly relatives.

Spime is a neologism coined by science fiction author and design theorist Bruce Sterling in his brief monograph, *Shaping Things* (Sterling 2005). We can think of the term as an abstract placeholder akin to the term *widget.* While a widget is any artefact that can be mass produced, a spime is any artefact whose history and contextual details of production, consumption and exchange have been embedded within the artefact itself and rendered legible to the user. As its advocates would have it, the spime represents a revolution in the relationship between humans, artefacts and the built environment. With an amalgam of other technologies, Sterling stipulates that ubiquitous location awareness would be key in the development of spimes, and he optimistically proposes an 'Internet of Things' that could dramatically enable ethical consumption and more sustainable design. Once inscribed with their own material histories and dependencies, artefacts themselves would serve as links into the networks of individuals and communities that produce and consume them. They become animated to an extent and are accorded agency, interacting with humans and each other via a literal network. We could go so far as to describe the proliferation of spimes as the emergence of a 'Facebook of things': if part of the effect of Facebook is to put on display the various activities comprising social relations (Miller 2011), populating the world with spimes (according to advocates) would do the same for human–artefact relations, rendering them visible to the individuals and communities with which that object is entangled.[6] From the perspective of digital anthropology, the spime represents a complex of desires and anxieties that have utility in the analysis of contemporary digital culture. It is a conceptual vanishing point, ordering a growing diversity of material objects and information technologies. With theoretical work in space, experience and material culture, the spime provides a framework that could tie together both previous work and proposed research across a number of otherwise quite distinct communities. These are actors for whom physical artefacts and even human bodies are 'mashable', contiguous and combinable with the aforementioned forms of geomedia.

An Anthropology of Geomedia

In introducing their important *Anthropology of Place and Space*, Low and Lawrence-Zuaniga (2003) echo Gupta and Ferguson's concerns about the spatial turn:

> The most significant change for anthropology is found not in the attention researchers increasingly pay to the material and spatial aspects of culture, but in the acknowledgement that *space is an essential component of sociocultural theory.* That is, anthropologists are rethinking and reconceptualizing their understandings of culture in spatialized ways. (1, emphasis added)

One of my points in presenting the work above and its framing as geomedia is that critical investigators of digital culture would do well to follow suit. If indeed we accept that 'space is an essential component of sociocultural theory', the conceptualization of geomedia extends that precept into the digital domain. Spatial aspects of *digital* culture must be seen as an essential component of sociocultural theories of the digital. If (to paraphrase Lefebvre), space is produced as and through social relations (Lefebvre 1991), we do not escape spatial constraints via geomedia any more than we escape the constraints of language through communications technology. Acknowledging the continuing significance of space is one thing; however, analysing it is quite another. The physical and the virtual become intermingled with ever finer granularity; for example the anthropologist must increasingly contend with the limitations of conventional conceptualizations of media and mediation. The two broad observations discussed earlier—the mobilization of digital technology and the reconfiguration of dominant institutions—reach an apotheosis in geomedia. It is no longer sufficient to talk of landscapes being mediated; what we must recognize are those instances where *media have become 'landscaped'*, ordered in meaning according to some quite traditional spatial sensibilities. What was once unquestionably an esoteric scientific literacy, exotic technological assemblage and strategic information asset is today perceived as a routine digital fluency, everyday consumer technology and vernacular visual form. How can we address such profound changes?

A straightforward step in the right direction would be an expansion of ethnography of everyday geomedia use and associated changes to our sense of place, particularly with well-established technologies such as satnav systems and Google Earth. Further, we need to develop a repertoire of methodological techniques for the observation and analysis of geomedia as a genre of digital culture. Theodolites, physical maps and aerial photographs have been subject to analysis as material and visual culture, but equating such objects with the sociotechnical phenomenon of location awareness is like trying to understand the subjective human experience of vision solely through the study of cameras and photographs. The immaterial paths and continuously updated location streams of geomedia present quite differently from other textual and visual forms, and a holistic treatment demands a modified perceptual approach.

Finally, it is worth considering once again Gupta and Ferguson's spatial prescriptions:

> Instead of stopping with the notion of deterritorialization, the pulverization of the space of high modernity, we need to theorize how space is being *re*territorialized in the

> contemporary world. We need to account sociologically for the fact that the 'distance' between the rich in Bombay and the rich in London may be much shorter than that between different classes in 'the same' city. Physical location and physical territory, for so long the only grid on which cultural difference could be mapped, need to be replaced by multiple grids that enable us to see that connection and contiguity—more generally the representation of territory—vary considerably by factors such as class, gender, race, and sexuality, and are differentially available to those in different locations in the field of power. (Gupta and Ferguson 1992: 20)

Along with place making and identity, *resistance* was identified by Gupta and Ferguson as one of the major themes arising from their collected explorations (1997: 17). As a subject, resistance takes many forms in the context of geomedia. 'Spatial hacktivism', for example, has included the production of so-called counter-maps, the coordination of protest activities, the inventory of indigenous resources and the public disclosure of large-scale toxic releases or illegal resource extraction by state or commercial entities. In a different vein, resistance to spatial digitalization is observable in a diversity of phenomena, from blockades of Google's Streetview vehicles to location-tracking consumer watchdog groups to new markets for mobile-blocking materials, mobile phone jammers and mobile-free or WiFi-free zones. These developments might be usefully compared, for example, with examinations of 'technology rejectors' (e.g. Weaver, Zorn and Richardson 2010). In maintaining a sensitivity to questions of power, and by continuing its tradition of including voices and scenes of resistance, ethnographic work would continue to yield crucial insights into geomedia in all its manifestations.

Notes

1. The term *geospatial* (from whence geomedia derives) is distinct from *spatial* in that it concretely refers to the terrestrial globe, whether in the specific quantitative sense of an earth coordinate system or in the more abstract human sense of landscapes. Domiciles, churches and business offices have often been analysed spatially, but to analyse them geospatially pulls them out of abstraction and situates them within a particular and finite space, the terrestrial sphere.
2. *Satellite-based navigation systems* are used to ascertain precise three-dimensional locations within a global coordinate system. *Geographic information systems* are essentially databases whose principal index is a location (though they typically include specialized components for visualization, analysis and many other functions). *Earth remote sensing* entails the gathering and analysis of photographs or images of the earth's surface (typically via aircraft or satellite), a technique employed in a broad array of civil and military applications.
3. STS is also referred to variously as science, technology and society or simply science studies. For more detail on this genealogy, see Hess (1997).

4. It is interesting to note, however, that anthropology—and in particular archaeology—has a long-established relationship with ERS, principally in its application to the survey and planning of archaeological sites and digs.
5. GPS trackers consist of a GPS receiver (which provides position and velocity data) and a recorder that stores the location data at regular intervals.
6. I would be remiss were I to not mention Tales of Things (http://talesofthings.com), a project of the Centre for Advanced Spatial Analysis at University College London. The website opines:

   > Wouldn't it be great to link any object directly to a 'video memory' or an article of text describing its history or background? Tales of Things allows just that with a quick and easy way to link any media to any object via small printable tags known as QR codes. How about tagging a building, your old antique clock or perhaps that object you're about to put on eBay?

   Technologies such as QR (quick response) codes provide a different aspect of spimes—*unique identification*—than location technologies such as GPS.

References

Abraham, I. 1998. *The Making of the Indian Atomic Bomb: Science, Secrecy and the Postcolonial State.* New York: Zed Books.

Aitken, S. C., and S. M. Michel. 1995. Who Contrives the 'Real' in GIS? Geographic Information, Planning and Critical Theory. *Cartography and Geographic Information Systems* 22(1): 17–29.

Amos, J. 2003. *Environmental Aspects of Modern Onshore Oil and Gas Development.* Testimony to the Committee on Resources of the United States House of Representatives, Subcommittee on Energy and Mineral Resources (17 September session).

Barnes, T. J., and J. S. Duncan, eds. 1992. *Writing Worlds: Discourse, Text, and Metaphor in the Representation of Landscape.* New York: Routledge.

Bender, B. 2006. Place and Landscape. In *Handbook of Material Culture*, ed. C. Y. Tilley, W. Keane, S. Küchler, M. Rowlands and P. Spyer, 303–24. London: Sage.

Brugioni, D. A. 1989. Impact and Social Implications. *Technology in Society* 11: 77–87.

Bull, M. 2008. *Sound Moves: iPod Culture and Urban Experience.* London: Routledge.

Carey, J. W. 1989. *Communication as Culture: Essays on Media and Society.* Boston: Unwin Hyman.

Castells, M. 1996. *The Rise of the Network Society.* Vol. 1. Cambridge, MA: Blackwell.

Crary, J. 1999. *Suspensions of Perception: Attention, Spectacle, and Modern Culture.* Cambridge, MA: MIT Press.

Curry, M. 1998. *Digital Places?: Living with Geographic Information Technologies.* London: Routledge.

DeNicola, L. A. 2006a. GPS. In *Encyclopedia of Privacy*, ed. W. G. Staples, 256–9. Westport, CT. Greenwood Press.

DeNicola, L. A. 2006b. The Bundling of Geospatial Information with Everyday Experience. In *Surveillance and Security: Technological Politics and Power in Everyday Life*, ed. T. Monahan, 243–64. New York: Routledge.

DeNicola, L. A. 2007. Techniques of the Environmental Observer: India's Earth Remote Sensing Program in the Age of Global Information. PhD diss., Rensselaer Polytechnic Institute. Troy, New York.

DeNicola, L. A. 2010. The Digital as Para-world: Design, Anthropology and Information Technologies. In *Design Anthropology: Object Culture in the 21st Century*, ed. A. J. Clarke, 196–205. Wien, NY: Springer Vienna Architecture.

Edney, M. H. 1997. *Mapping an Empire: The Geographical Construction of British India, 1765–1843.* Chicago: University of Chicago Press.

Edwards, P. N. 1996. *The Closed World: Computers and the Politics of Discourse in Cold War America.* Cambridge, MA: MIT Press.

Epstein, S. 1996. *Impure Science: AIDS, Activism, and the Politics of Knowledge.* Vol. 7. Berkeley: University of California Press.

Forsythe, D. E. 1994. STS (Re)constructs Anthropology: A Reply to Fleck. *Social Studies of Science* 24(1): 113–23.

Galison, P. L. 1997. *Image and Logic: A Material Culture of Microphysics.* Chicago: University of Chicago Press.

Ginsburg, F. D., A.-L. Lila and B. Larkin, eds. 2002. *Media Worlds: Anthropology on New Terrain.* Berkeley: University of California Press.

Good, B. 1994. *Medicine, Rationality, and Experience: An Anthropological Perspective.* Cambridge: Cambridge University Press.

Gregory, D. 1994. *Geographical Imaginations.* Cambridge, MA: Blackwell.

Gupta, A., and J. Ferguson. 1992. Beyond 'Culture': Space, Identity, and the Politics of Difference. *Cultural Anthropology* 7(1): 6–23.

Gupta, A., and J. Ferguson. 1997. *Culture, Power, Place: Explorations in Critical Anthropology.* Durham, NC: Duke University Press.

Harris, C. 2003. Satellite Imagery and the Discourses of Transparency. PhD diss., University of California San Diego.

Harvey, F., and N. Chrisman. 1998. Boundary Objects and the Social Construction of GIS Technology. *Environment and Planning A* 30(9): 1683–94.

Hess, D. J. 1997. *Science Studies: An Advanced Introduction.* New York: New York University Press.

Hess, D., G. Downey, L. Suchman, D. Hakken and L. Star. 1998. Obituary: Diana E. Forsythe (11 November 1947–14 August 1997). *Social Studies of Science* 28(1): 175–82.

Hirsch, E., and M. O'Hanlon. 1995. *The Anthropology of Landscape: Perspectives on Place and Space.* Oxford: Oxford University Press.

Ito, M., D. Okabe and M. Matsuda, eds. 2005. *Personal, Portable, Pedestrian: The Mobile Phone in Japanese Life*. Cambridge, MA: MIT Press.

Kalam, A.P.J.A., and A. Tiwari. 2004. *Wings of Fire: An Autobiography.* Hyderabad: Universities Press (India).

Latour, B. 1993. *We Have Never Been Modern.* Cambridge, MA: Harvard University Press.

Lefebvre, H. 1991. *The Production of Space.* Oxford: Blackwell.

Litfin, K. 1997. The Gendered Eye in the Sky: A Feminist Perspective on Earth Observation Satellites. *Frontiers: A Journal of Women's Studies* 18(2): 26–37.

Litfin, K. 2001. The Globalization of Transparency: The Use of Commercial Satellite Imagery by Nongovernmental Organizations. In *Commercial Observation Satellites: At the Leading Edge of Global Transparency*, ed. J. C. Baker, K. M. O'Connell and R. A. Williamson, 463–84. Santa Monica, CA: RAND and the American Society of Photogrammetry and Remote Sensing.

Low, S. M., and D. Lawrence-Zuaniga. 2003. *The Anthropology of Space and Place: Locating Culture.* Blackwell Readers in Anthropology. Malden, MA: Blackwell Publishing Professional.

Lynch, M. 2003. God's Signature: DNA Profiling, the New Gold Standard in Forensic Science. *Endeavor* 27(2): 93–7.

Macnaghten, P., and J. Urry. 1998. *Contested Natures.* Thousand Oaks, CA: Sage.

Markowitz, K. J. 2002. Legal Challenges and Market Rewards to the Use and Acceptance of Remote Sensing and Digital Information as Evidence. *Duke Environmental Law and Policy Forum* (Spring): 219–64.

Marx, G. T. 2007. Surveillance. In *Encyclopedia of Privacy*, ed. W. G. Staples, 534–44. Westport, CT: Greenwood Press.

Miller, D. 2011. *Tales from Facebook.* Cambridge, UK: Polity Press.

Monmonier, M. S. 2002. *Spying with Maps: Surveillance Technologies and the Future of Privacy.* Chicago: University of Chicago Press.

Monmonier, M., and H. J. de Blij. 1996. *How to Lie with Maps.* 2nd ed. Chicago: University of Chicago Press.

Morgan, G. 1990. Remote Sensing Activities in the World Bank: A Review of Experiences and Current Technical Capabilities. In *Satellite Remote Sensing for Agricultural Projects*, ed. J. P. Gastellu-Etchegorry, 1–10. Washington, DC: World Bank.

Nye, D. E. 1994. *American Technological Sublime.* Cambridge, MA: MIT Press.

Parks, L. 2005. *Cultures in Orbit: Satellites and the Televisual.* Durham, NC: Duke University Press.

Pfaffenberger, B. 1992. Social Anthropology of Technology. *Annual Review of Anthropology* 21: 491–516.

Pickles, J., ed. 1995. *Ground Truth: The Social Implications of Geographic Information Systems.* New York: Guilford Press.

Pickles, J. 2004. *A History of Spaces: Cartographic Reason, Mapping, and the Geo-Coded World.* London: Routledge.

Porteous, J. D. 1986. Intimate Sensing. *Area* 18: 250–1.

Prakash, G. 1999. *Another Reason: Science and the Imagination of Modern India.* Princeton, NJ: Princeton University Press.

Robbins, P. 2003. Beyond Ground Truth: GIS and the Environmental Knowledge of Herders, Professional Foresters, and Other Traditional Communities. *Human Ecology* 31(2): 233–53.

Sheppard, E. 1995. GIS and Society: Towards a Research Agenda. *Cartography and Geographic Information Systems* 22(1): 5–16.

Sieber, R. E. 2004. Rewiring for a GIS/2. *Cartographica* 39(1): 25–39.

Sieber, R. E. 2007. Spatial Data Access by the Grassroots. *Cartography and Geographic Information Science* 34(1): 47–62.

Soja, E. W. 1989. *Postmodern Geographies: The Reassertion of Space in Critical Social Theory.* New York: Verso.

Sterling, B. 2005. *Shaping Things.* Cambridge, MA: MIT Press.

Tilley, C. 1994. *A Phenomenology of Landscape: Places, Paths, and Monuments.* Oxford: Berg.

U.S. Geological Survey. 2002. Earth as Art. Earth Resources Observation and Science Center. http://eros.usgs.gov/imagegallery/.

Weaver, C. K., T. Zorn and M. Richardson. 2010. Goods Not Wanted. *Information, Communication and Society* 13(5): 696–721.

Yoxen, E. 1994. Seeing With Sound: A Study of the Development of Medical Images. In *The Social Construction of Technological Systems: New Directions in the Sociology and History of Technology*, ed. W. E. Bijker, T. Parke Hughes and T. J. Pinch, 281–303. Cambridge, MA: MIT Press.

Part III
Socializing Digital Anthropology

–5–

Disability in the Digital Age

Faye Ginsburg

> It is only when I type something in your language that you refer to me as having communication. I smell things, I listen to things, I feel things, I taste things, I look at things. It is not enough to look and listen and taste and smell and feel, I have to do those to the right things, such as look at books, and fail to do them to the wrong things, or else people doubt that I am a thinking being, and since their definition of thought defines their definition of personhood so ridiculously much, they doubt that I am a real person as well. I would like to honestly know how many people if you met me on the street would believe I wrote this. I find it very interesting by the way that failure to learn your language is seen as a deficit but failure to learn my language is seen as so natural that people like me are officially described as mysterious and puzzling rather than anyone admitting that it is themselves who are confused, not autistic people or other cognitively disabled people who are inherently confusing. We are even viewed as non-communicative if we don't speak the standard language but other people are not considered non-communicative if they are so oblivious to our own languages as to believe they don't exist. In the end, I want you to know that this has not been intended as a voyeuristic freak show where you get to look at the bizarre workings of the autistic mind. It is meant as a strong statement on the existence and value of many different kinds of thinking and interaction in a world where how close you can appear to a specific one of them determines whether you are seen as a real person or an adult or an intelligent person.
>
> Amanda Baggs, excerpt from audio track of YouTube video, *In My Language*

In Her Language: Case Study One

On 14 January 2007, Amanda Baggs, a then twenty-six-year-old woman with autism and a neurodiversity activist, launched a video titled *In My Language* on YouTube.[1] The nine-minute work was shot in Baggs's apartment in Vermont in the do-it-yourself style typical of many user-generated video works shared on that platform.[2] For some viewers, the unusual combination of sight and sound and the sense of an alternative aesthetic suggests experimental video of the sort seen in museum galleries and art venues.[3] *In My Language* offers a riveting glimpse into Baggs's life, immersing the audience into how she experiences the world differently from 'neurotypicals'. Explaining the video in a way that clearly anticipates and invites nonautistic viewers, Baggs writes: 'The first part is in my "native language," and then the second part provides a translation, or at least an explanation. This is not a look-at-the-autie gawking freak show as much as it is a statement about what gets considered thought, intelligence, personhood, language, and communication, and what does not.' The first part of the video shows Baggs engaged in a variety of repetitive gestures around her apartment—playing with a necklace, typing at her keyboard, sitting on her couch, moving her hand back and forth in front of a window—to the sound of a wordless tune she hums off camera, creating a meditative, almost mesmerizing effect. Baggs, who stopped speaking verbally in her early twenties, provides the translated portion of the piece from which the chapter opening quote is taken about four minutes into the video. Her spoken voice is rendered via an augmentative communication device, a DynaVox VMax computer. When she is feeling well, she can type on the device at a rate of 120 words per minute. Her typed words emerge into spoken speech—as well as in yellow subtitles—via a synthetic female voice that, as one interviewer remarked, 'sounds like a deadpan British schoolteacher' (Wolman 2008).

I begin my contribution to a book on digital anthropology with this particular case, because *In My Language* makes stunningly clear how interactive digital technologies can provide unanticipated and powerful platforms that allow those with disabilities to communicate to a broad range of publics.[4] These media enable people with disabilities to engage in a first-person discussion of their world and experiences—often asserting an alternative sense of personhood, as does Baggs—without requiring others to interpret for them. Moreover, the accessibility of media forms such as YouTube have dramatically enhanced the possibilities of forming community for those who have difficulty speaking or sustaining face-to-face conversation. As Baggs explained on National Public Radio in 2006:

> Many of us have a lot of trouble with face to face interaction and are also extremely isolated. Like a lot of autistic people, I rarely even leave the house. A lot of us have trouble with spoken language, and so a lot of us find it easier to write on the Internet than to talk in person. There's a lot of us where we might not be able to meet anywhere else but online, and so that's been a lot of where we've organized. (Shapiro 2006)

In a future video project (Wolman 2008), Baggs hopes to further explore her understandings of communication, empathy and self-reflection—core elements of the human experience that have at times been used to define personhood, thus illuminating how the digital might help us rethink the cultural parameters of humanity and deeper social discriminations along the lines of ability.

This chapter contains several cases that illustrate how, in the twenty-first century, people with disabilities and their supporters—such as Amanda Baggs, those who support her and people who respond to her videos and blogs—are developing emergent forms of digital media practices that enable their self-representation in ways that expand our collective sense of personhood and publics.[5] The cases I discuss here use social media platforms—YouTube, the immersive virtual world of Second Life[6] and web-based outreach attached to documentary projects—and are only a small part of the remarkable embrace of digital media by many of the estimated 15 per cent of the American population who live with some kind of disability.[7] The cases are exemplary of the enhanced capacity of these media to provide counterdiscursive sites of representation for cultural actors who rarely have had opportunities to enter the public (or counterpublic) sphere. Of course, people with disabilities might choose to present themselves in ways that do not require the disclosure of identity, given the now well-documented flexibility for self-presentation enabled by virtual environments, a circumstance discussed later in this chapter. In either case, inequalities in *access* to digital technologies raise questions regarding how the very design of digital interactivity can 'disable' potential users who may have any of a range of impairments from vision or hearing loss to difficulty with fine motor coordination to many other atypical circumstances of mind or body. While the question of accessible design is less frequently discussed than are issues of representation on the screen, work on accessibility in terms of the design of digital media demonstrates how the very materiality of digital media builds in assumptions about embodiment, personhood and even citizenship. In their groundbreaking 2003 work, *Digital Disability: The Social Construction of Disability in New Media*, Gerald Goggin and Christopher Newell rightly remind us that questions of access and new media are cause to 'curb our digital enthusiasm'. They write:

> In this book, we have sought to show how society, consciously and unconsciously, has built in disability into digital technologies. Time and time again in the field of new media and communications technologies, our needs as people with disabilities are not met by a preexisting product or service. (147)

> As we interrogate our technologies, and see them as reflecting the values and lived social policy, we propose that society dare to ask: whom do I count as a member of my moral community, and whom do I exclude in the everyday taken-for-granted technology and its uses? Whom do we disable in the scramble to the networked digital society? Or, more hopefully, how can we bring about a future in which disability in its digital incarnations may unfold in new, unexpected, and fairer ways to the genuine benefit, and with the assured, ubiquitous participation every day, individually and collectively, we engage with a pressing reality: disabling new media. (154)

Whether people with disabilities can access digital technologies or whether poor design continues to exclude certain users of these technologies—despite the remarkable efforts of people like Amanda Baggs—the battles that were fought for ramps, elevators, Braille signage and visual signals for the hearing impaired, to name a few of the more well-known efforts of disability activists to make public space available and accessible to all citizens, are now being extended to the digital media world. New media enthusiasts such as Clay Shirky—whose popular 2008 book title, *Here Comes Everybody*, made clear his position on the world of digital possibility—might not always be mindful of the concerns raised by people with disabilities, whose movement long ago adopted the slogan, 'nothing about us without us'.[8] The essential question Goggin and Newell raise in the previous quote when discussing the consequences of inaccessible digital technology—whom do I count as a member of my moral community?—reminds us that issues of digital design concern more than political economy or tweaking technology; they reflect the politics of recognition and the need to extend the 'everybody' of Shirky's title to include the full range of people who constitute the body politic (Ellis and Kent 2010; Goggin and Newell 2003).

Screening Disabilities

My interest in this question of the impact of digital media on the experiences and categorical understandings of disability grows from several sources. First is my several decades of interest in transformations in media worlds (Ginsburg, Lughod and Larkin 2002) as a form of cultural activism, a central focus in my long-standing work on the development of indigenous media worldwide (Ginsburg 2011). Second is the twenty-two-plus years that I have spent raising a child with a rare and debilitating genetic disorder, familial dysautonomia.[9] This circumstance has, since 1989, profoundly changed my understanding of disability and its consequences and turned me into an advocate, activist and daily observer of the difference that media forms and representations make in the lives of those who routinely face the challenges of communication, mobility, chronic illness and discrimination. I watched as my daughter, Sam, grew increasingly frustrated at the stunning lack of kids with disabilities on any of her favourite forms of popular media. She eventually told her own story on television at age ten and started a blog at age eleven. Her encounters with this form of prejudice—the sense that one's experience and body are virtually invisible—and the growing range of media during the decade or so since then that address the lack of representation for disabled people have taught me where, when and how to pay attention. Throughout the past two decades, I have watched the uneven expansion of what I call the 'disability media world' through participating in, inventing and running disability film festivals and screenings as well as getting involved in online communities on a variety of platforms.

The impact of disability on digital media is increasingly evident in the growth of digital photographic and video work and, of course, Web 2.0 social media, including interactive websites, Facebook groups, virtual worlds, blogging and YouTube, all of which have dramatically expanded the range of locations for the mediation of disability to a variety of publics. New scholarship in disability studies, visual culture and media has opened lively discussions on how such media are deeply implicated in the creation of a more inclusive sense of citizenship for nonnormative social actors (Coleman 2010). In their recent book, *Disability and New Media* (2010), Kate Ellis and Mike Kent point out that

> Technological advancement does not occur as something separate from ideology and stigma, and web 2.0 has been developed in and by the same social world that routinely disables people with disability [*sic*]. However, a resistance has emerged in an attempt to reverse this trend in the form of critical disability studies, a discipline that seeks to reveal the workings of a disabling social world. (3)

Rosemarie Garland-Thomson's 2009 book *Staring* provides a valuable discussion of 'visual activism', a term she deploys to describe how people with disabilities are increasingly putting themselves in the public eye, saying 'look at me' instead of 'don't stare'. The public presence of people with disabilities as powerful social actors, she argues, 'stretches our shared understanding of the human variations we value and appreciate and invites us [instead] to accommodate them' (195). The radical nature of this insight, and the fact that most of the work she discusses is so recent—only two decades or so at most—is compelling testimony to how rapidly these changes are occurring (and to their profound nature as well).

Disability scholars and filmmakers Sharon L. Snyder and David T. Mitchell (2008) interpret the potential for transformation that occurs via encounters with self-determined disability films (most of them produced digitally). Snyder and Mitchell suggest that exposure to a broad range of disabilities, which can occur in utopian spaces such as disability film festivals, can produce what they call 'aesthetic reprogramming' for audiences who watch an array of works that reframe the everyday experience of visual *doxa*—the taken-for-granted aspects of the social world (Bourdieu [1972] 1977)—inviting all to 'stare' in Rosemarie Garland-Thomson's sense. This experience, they argue, allows audiences to vicariously experience the remarkable variety of lives with a difference through documentaries as well as fictional accounts that include protagonists with disabilities ranging from autism, Down syndrome, attention deficit disorder, cerebral palsy, blindness, deafness, brain injury and depression to wounded warriors and stutterers. Snyder and Mitchell reframe the insights of theorists such as B. Ruby Rich (1999), who have argued that film festivals organized by and for queer counterpublics are dynamic sites where distinctive features of that world emerge.

> As one of the few public spaces within which to actively fashion alternative disability identities, film festivals challenge internal and external orthodoxies that tend to quickly sediment within politicized identity gatherings. They not only serve the important function of historical recovery; they also seek out a variety of perspectives on the meaning of disability from older and younger generations of disabled people and non-disabled allies.

> Disability film festivals actively disrupt static boundaries of disability identity—even with respect to disabled people's concepts of their own collective makeup. (Snyder and Mitchell 2008: 14)

Such exposure, Snyder and Mitchell maintain, can lead to an embrace of disability in all its diversity. However, while newly evolving concepts of being disabled emerge in such settings, they also resist articulating a shared identity based on collective coherence of experience, affect or diagnosis.

As an example, New York City's Reelabilities Film Festival (for which I serve as a founding advisor) draws a larger audience every year; attendance tripled between its inaugural year in 2008 and 2011.[10] The festival has shown outstanding films—almost all of them made on digital media—from all over the world dealing with topics such as brain injury, autism, mental illness and Down syndrome. These are not what Snyder and Mitchell call (with some disdain) 'awareness' films (2008: 13), but rather show people with disabilities as agents of their own creative interventions, resisting the conventions of exclusion. Audiences are extremely diverse and include the able-bodied and people with a remarkable range of disabilities. The kind of 'aesthetic reprogramming' that Snyder and Mitchell discuss occurs not only because of what is on the screen but also through the experience of being in a truly inclusive screening space. The closing-night film, *Wretches and Jabberers: Stories from the Road* (Wurzburg 2010), was sitting and standing room only, with the requisite adaptations for the viewing space: audio description for those with visual impairments, signing for deaf audience members, seating that allowed for at least ten power chairs in the room, a few guide dogs, a high tolerance for audience unruliness and many people with autism using assistive communication devices. The documentary, made by Gerardine Wurzberg, features Tracy Thresher and Larry Bissonnette, two men with autism who have limited oral speech. As young people, both faced lives of isolation. It was not until adulthood, when each learned to communicate by typing with digital assistive technology, that their lives changed dramatically, finally providing them with a way to express their thoughts, needs and feelings. After more than ten years of advocating for people with autism, Thresher and Bissonnette felt it was time to take their message global—to help people with autism around the world break through the isolation they both knew so well. Through an outreach campaign conducted via a website, Facebook, YouTube and e-mail, the film spread virally across the globe through the densely connected autism network.

Finally, this chapter is shaped by my current research on disability, carried out with my colleague, the anthropologist Rayna Rapp, who is also the parent of a child with a disability. Since 2007 we have been studying the emergence and social consequences of the category of learning disabilities in New York City. Because we are both so deeply implicated in this work as parents, activists and researchers, we sometimes refer to our method as 'adventures on the Möbius strip', suggesting the impossibility—on occasion—of knowing whether we are on the inside or outside of many of the situations we are studying. In our ethnographic fieldwork with families, schools, media makers and scientists we are learning how kinship, caretaking and the life course are reconfigured when a child is diagnosed with a cognitive disability. As families begin to recognize their commonalities and needs with others who share their difference—a social process that we argue is exponentially enabled by digital media—we find that a new imaginary kinship emerges, which is expressed through a variety of idioms. In the United States, as recently as the 1970s, social mores dictated that family members with disabilities be hidden from view and stories about them be silenced. Throughout the past few decades, the available cultural scripts regarding the public face of family life have been revised across a range of media practices, popular culture, parenting manuals, legal discourses and scientific narratives about human difference. A sea change has occurred from the intimacy of the household to the public worlds of educational policy, scientific research and, most relevant to this chapter, in documentary and narrative film and digital media—a process that is happening around the world. As Rapp and I have argued elsewhere,

> Anthropology is well-known for its capacious and ever-expanding framework for understanding 'human nature.' Given the centrality of diversity to our epistemology, it is puzzling that the subject of disability has not been a central topic for our discipline. Surely, this form of difference and the social hierarchies that often stigmatize it are a universal aspect of human life. Unlike the categories of race and gender, from which one can only enter or exit very rarely and with enormous and conscious effort—'passing' or 'transgendering,' for example—disability has a distinctive quality: it is a category anyone might enter unexpectedly, challenging lifelong presumptions of stable identities and normativity...As a circumstance that requires attention to subjectivity and personhood, cultural meaning and mediation, social relations and kinship, and the limits of the biological, disability seems a 'natural' topic for anthropological study. (Rapp and Ginsburg 2010: 517)

Dan Habib is one of many disability activist parents and filmmakers with whom Rapp and I have been working. His son Samuel was born with cerebral palsy and—in Samuel's parents' words—'brought the disability rights movement into our home'. As 'accidental activists', Samuel's parents soon found themselves acting on behalf of their son—particularly in regard to his education in their New Hampshire town, as they sought inclusive settings for him that combined children with and without disabilities in the same classroom. Dan began photographing their journey, and soon a documentary film was in production: *Including Samuel* (Habib 2008). Dan extended the questions he had about his son's unpredictable future to four other students with disabilities at different life stages to ask about the possibilities and limits of inclusive education from kindergarten through college. Since its completion in 2008, *Including Samuel* has screened across the country and has been widely publicized, both for its compelling story and for its visionary as well as practical advocacy carried out on- and offline. The digital video documentary, which, from the beginning, was an extension of the Habibs' commitment to social change, is now used by thousands of schools, parent organizations, nonprofit groups, universities and state agencies around the United States and internationally. The Habibs' website, the Including Samuel Project, extends the film's reach through social media applications; the site invites others to upload their stories of disability, exclusion and success, thus creating an alternative virtual community focused on issues of educational inclusion. Habib calls all of this activity emerging from the film the 'Including Samuel Effect'.[11]

This story exemplifies a recurring phenomenon that we see in our research. Like many parents of cognitively atypical children, the Habibs are not only rethinking the intimate world of kinship from the point of view of their experiences raising a child with a disability; they are also taking their insights beyond their home, into their community and, thanks to digital media, across the globe. The wide and interconnected reach of media is the key factor in the creation of such projects, producing what we call *mediated kinship.* Emerging as a neighbouring—and sometimes overlapping—field to the formal, institutionalized discourse of disability rights, mediated kinship offers a critique of normative American family life that is embedded within everyday cultural practice. Across many genres—documentaries, talk shows, online disability support groups, websites, Second Life communities and so on—a common theme is the rejection of the pressure to produce perfect families, objectified through the incorporation of difference under the sign of love and intimacy in the domain of kinship relations.

We suggest that these mediated spaces of public intimacy are crucial for building a social fund of knowledge more inclusive of the fact of disability. Such media practices—which are increasingly digital—provide a counterdiscourse to the stratification of families that for so long has marginalized those with disabilities. It is not only the acceptance of difference within families but also the embrace of relatedness that such models of inclusion present to the body politic. As groups of people with similar diagnoses—such as autism, Down syndrome, attention deficit disorder—begin to recognize each other through these practices, their emergent sense of kinship and identity makes these spaces potentially radical in their implications for an expanded understanding of personhood. As sites of information and free play of imagination, these cultural forms create a more inclusive social landscape (Rapp and Ginsburg 2001: 550). Such forms of relatedness are not necessarily genealogical or familial; they may be based on relationships created among avatars (and their humans) on Second Life, whose experiences are enriched by the virtual possibilities for social connection denied to the disabled in real life (RL). In any polysemic tradition, there are many ways to materialize a sense of relatedness; a variety of media practices, from analogue photographs to websites, can increasingly be understood as forms beyond 'blood' and other bodily substances that can produce a sense of relatedness among those with disabilities and their supporters (Bouquet 2001). The fact that these media practices have been embraced in the context of the late-twentieth-century global disability rights movements has provided a robust social environment that shapes and is shaped by these media practices.

Found in Digital Translation

In My Language is exemplary of the productivity of digital media for people with disabilities. Baggs uploaded the video approximately two years into the existence of YouTube, the digital social media platform for uploading and sharing video of all kind. Perhaps because YouTube was a relatively young medium in 2007 or possibly because of the video's novelty as an intervention into the presumptions of typicality exhibited by most other videos on the site—and certainly due to the rising interest in the nature and diagnosis of autism spectrum disorders in the early twenty-first century (Grinker 2007)—*In My Language* provoked considerable response and some controversy, with more than 300,000 views in the first three weeks of its posting (Gupta 2007).

Within a month of its launch, CNN ran a story on Amanda Baggs and the video; two days later, she guest-blogged with CNN television journalist Anderson Cooper (2007). A year later, she was the subject of an article by David Wolman in *Wired* magazine titled 'The Truth About Autism: Scientists Reconsider What They Think They Know' (Wolman 2008).[12] In the article Wolman wrote,

> I tell her [Amanda Baggs] that I asked one of the world's leading authorities on autism to check out the video. The expert's opinion: Baggs must have had outside help creating it, perhaps from one of her caregivers. Her inability to talk, coupled with repetitive behaviors, lack of eye contact, and the need for assistance with everyday tasks are telltale signs of severe autism. Among all autistics, 75 percent are expected to score in the mentally retarded range on standard intelligence tests—that's an IQ of 70 or less... After I explain the scientist's doubts, Baggs grunts, and her mouth forms just a hint of a smirk as she lets loose a salvo on the keyboard. No one helped her shoot the video, edit it, and upload it to YouTube. She used a Sony Cybershot DSC-T1, a digital camera that can record up to 90 seconds of video (she has since upgraded). She then patched the footage together using the editing programs RAD Video Tools, VirtualDub, and DivXLand Media Subtitler. 'My care provider wouldn't even know how to work the software,' she says. (Wolman 2008: 4)

In April 2008, CNN's celebrity medical expert and neurosurgeon, Sanjay Gupta, interviewed Baggs at her Vermont home. Chronicling the transformation in his own understanding of the personhood of Baggs (and people like her), whose humanity he had not previously recognized, Gupta explained that when he 'first came across Amanda on YouTube, her appearance there was so startling, I wanted to meet her. I had so many questions'. After Gupta met her and saw the remarkable access that was opened to her by media platforms such as YouTube or blogging,[13] he quipped: 'The Internet is like a "get out of jail for free" card for a new world of autistics. On the Internet, Amanda can get beyond names and expectations. She can move at her own pace, live life on her own terms' (Gupta 2008).

Baggs's use of digital platforms illustrates the striking potential benefit that this kind of technology holds for certain groups of people with disabilities—especially those with autism and related communicative disorders. Digital platforms reach beyond the local and constitute networks organized along other modes of recognition rendered intimate or at least available because of the rapid and democratizing (if unequal) spread of social media. In his book *Tales from Facebook,* Danny Miller's case of 'Dr. Karamath'—who is able to create a network of like-minded people despite the fact that a disability renders him homebound—makes this poignantly clear (Miller 2011: 28–39). A number of researchers have pointed out that the Internet has features that make it especially appropriate for those who can be easily overwhelmed by the many simultaneous channels of communication that govern face-to-face interaction, such as body language and facial expressions.[14] Another autistic activist, Canadian researcher Michelle Dawson, finds face-to-face interaction an ordeal. She is an avid blogger, especially with 'scientists, parents' groups, medical institutions, the courts, journalists, and anyone else who'll listen to their stories of how autistics are mistreated' (Wolman 2008: 10).

Not Being Able to Talk Doesn't Mean You Don't Have Anything to Say

People like Amanda Baggs sometimes seem to neurotypicals as if they have no language because they do not speak. But, of course, Baggs and others with communicative disorders *can* communicate—and at times they are strikingly articulate—by using a keyboard and augmented communication technologies and interactive tablet technologies such as the iPad (Fox 2011). As Baggs has remarked regarding her own situation: 'Not being able to talk doesn't mean you don't have anything to say.'

The thirty or more videos she has posted on YouTube of her everyday activities are testimony to that; they range from angry manifestos against the inhumanity shown to those with disabilities or other forms of 'unacceptable' difference, such as *Being an Unperson*, to the wry yet revelatory *How to Boil Water the Easy Way.*[15] In the latter piece, the viewer sees Baggs first sitting on her couch figuring out how to get to her kitchen, then standing in her kitchen opening cupboards, the microwave and refrigerator, coping with the range of cues presented by the materiality of her kitchen, until she figures out which ones will help her to actually accomplish the task of heating water. The piece is introduced with a series of title cards that guide the viewer:

> This is meant to explain why it takes me five hours or longer to boil water sometimes. This is a shortened version of what goes on. Feel free to laugh as long as it's not to make yourself feel superior or something. But even though it can be funny, be aware this is a serious and real situation for a lot of autistic people among others.

A quick, unscientific read of many of the 30,000 responses to this particular video in the uploaded comments section (where there are only twenty 'dislikes') gives a sense of how this digital self-presentation strikes viewers. The comments of Suzanne expressed the sentiments of many:

> You are amazing:) Brilliant video! I am thankful for the videos you produce. Sincerely, Suzanne, mother of an autistic 3 (almost 4) yr old. p.s. and I'd like to give you a cyber (((hug))) =). maybe I can meet up with you some day in Second Life and give you a hug there. Hehe.[16]

Suzanne is clearly aware that, in addition to the use of video platforms such as YouTube and blogging, Amanda Baggs is an avid participant in the virtual immersive community of Second Life, where Baggs has created an avatar who looks and acts like her—typing and rocking back and forth—but who can fly to different destinations and attend autism meetings with far less anxiety than in real life.

In real life, according to David Wolman's interview with Baggs from *Wired* magazine,

> Baggs lives in a public housing project for the elderly and handicapped near downtown Burlington, Vermont. She has short black hair, a pointy nose, and round glasses. She usually wears a T-shirt and baggy pants, and she spends a scary amount of time—day and night—on the Internet: blogging, hanging out in Second Life, and corresponding with her autie and aspie friends. (For the uninitiated, that's *autistic* and *Asperger's*.) On a blustery afternoon, Baggs reclines on a red futon in the apartment of her neighbor (and best friend). She has a gray travel pillow wrapped around her neck, a keyboard resting on her lap, and a DynaVox VMax computer propped against her legs. Autistics like Baggs are now leading a nascent civil rights movement. 'I remember in '99,' she says, 'seeing a number of gay pride Web sites. I envied how many there were and wished there was something like that for autism. Now there is.' The message: We're here. We're weird. Get used to it. (Wolman 2008: 4–5)

While her 'celebrity crip' status is unique, Amanda Baggs's experiences with such technologies offer unprecedented pathways for expressing a sense of personhood and dignity that are appreciated by many who have autism and their supporters. Baggs's creative and interventionist uses of YouTube, blogging and Second Life are, I suggest, metonymic of a broader change in the zeitgeist, at least in the First World for those who have access to computers, and arguably in many other locations (e.g. Miller 2011; Sreberny and Khiabany 2010). The rise of the global movement for disability rights since the 1980s (Charlton 1998) and the simultaneous emergence of enabling digital technologies for people with disabilities have created a modest but nonetheless transformative effect. The phenomenon can be seen as a kind of digital 'structure of conjuncture' (Sahlins 1985)—that is a historical moment when various interests within a field converge in ways that lead to paradigmatic change.

If one of the central goals of the contemporary disability rights movement worldwide is self-determination, then there is no question that being able to represent oneself in digital public (or counterpublic) spheres on one's own terms is consistent with that project. As Amanda Baggs's case illustrates, self-determination might include:

1. passing as typical (as with 'Dr. Karamath', one of the profiles in Miller (2011)) or coming out as a person with disabilities;
2. having control over channels of communication in ways that are suitable for particular issues faced by those who are not neurotypicals; and
3. locating and developing relationships with others with similar circumstances as well as supportive fellow travellers in the broad, nonlocal world of the Internet.

The emerging literature on the impact of digital media for people with disabilities suggests that these new forms of digital access provide distinctive possibilities for virtual sociality and self-determined recognition, a fundamental aspect of personhood. This is not a universal social fact, and problems of discrimination and abuse persist, as do unintended consequences of digital innovation (Ellis and Kent 2010: 7). Indeed, the case of Baggs—and the kind of wonder, attention and scepticism that her digital media projects have attracted—is a reminder of how new this kind of digital media practice is for people with disabilities. Thirty or forty years ago, life would have been different and much harder for Amanda, says Morton Ann Gernsbacher, a cognitive psychologist who specializes in autism at the University of Wisconsin–Madison. 'The Internet is providing for individuals with autism, what sign language did for the deaf', she says. 'It allows them to interact with the world and other like-minded individuals on their own terms' (quoted in Gajilan 2007). In the United States, it was only four decades ago that the so-called ugly laws were abolished; for over a century, this legislation had made it illegal for persons with 'unsightly or disgusting disabilities' to appear in public in most US cities. As disability scholar Susan Schweik (2009) explained in her important book on this subject, the laws laid the groundwork for the widespread acceptance of eugenics and institutionalization in the nineteenth and twentieth centuries.

In addition to the alternative but clearly indexical representation of her life offered by Amanda Baggs, another corner of the digital media world—the virtual world of Second Life—has become home to a small but growing presence of participants with disabilities. A remarkable number of avatars created by people with disabilities live fully social lives in ways not otherwise available to them in real life. Taking a different approach, a number of disability activists joined together to create Virtual Ability in 2008. The website provides support for those with disabilities both in Second Life—including how to gain access if one has difficulty using standard software and hardware—and in real life, with counselling and support provided in ways that demonstrate the difficulty of rendering online and offline worlds fully separable.

Getting a (Second) Life: Case Study Two

At a Friday afternoon workshop about Jewish religious practice in the online world at New York University's Center for Religion and Media,[17] a virtual lighting of the Shabbat candles was about to take place in the Jewish section of the online world of Second Life.[18] The assembled group waited eagerly, watching a projection of a computer screen while a group of online avatars (or 'javatars' as some call those virtual representatives of the self created by those who identify as Jewish) gathered for the first set of candles to be lit (virtually) based on Israeli time, seven hours ahead of New York City. As the avatar named Namav Abramovitch carried out the ritual, scholar Chava Weissler (who was conducting the workshop as part of a demonstration of her research) asked Abramovitch if he would be leaving soon to light candles in real life. To the group's astonishment, he wrote back, 'No, I can't light candles in RL because I am disabled. Second Life is the only space where I can be a practicing Jew.' Abramovitch is Nick Dupree, a Medicaid reform activist with muscular dystrophy who uses a ventilator to breathe. He had been active on Second Life for only a few months prior to the encounter just described; he joined this media world after reading an article in the *Washington Post* about how people with disabilities creatively use Second Life and other social media (Stein 2007). Dupree can not use a keyboard or lift his hands; he types with one thumb on a trackball mouse, creating text by hitting letters using on-screen keyboard software. As he explains, 'I had run a support group online in the past, and am interested in using virtual community to support people with disabilities…and now have founded Open Gates, a project to provide 24/7 peer support in Second Life.'

Dupree is not alone. In an issue of the online magazine *2Life*, an article described how a woman used the virtual world to be more active in a religious community in ways not available to her offline: 'On [the Jewish holidays of] Rosh HaShana and Yom Kippur, Serafina, who is homebound in RL, had an open house in the synagogue, welcoming everyone who had no other possibility to attend services, to join her in the virtual world.'[19] These stories of Dupree and Serafina—and many others—offer a parable of digital possibility for those who find real life less than accommodating of their impairments.[20] Much as YouTube has offered an important platform for Amanda Baggs and others, the experiences of disabled participants on Second Life suggest that participation in this virtual world offers a chance to engage in social practices that previously might not have been available to them. Research on the impact of this virtual activity on offline lives suggests that these opportunities to be part of a virtual community are 'existentially therapeutic'. Rob Stein, in his influential 2007 *Washington Post* article, 'Real Hope in a Virtual World', described a number of such cases.[21] One woman had a devastating stroke in 2003 that left her in a wheelchair with little hope of walking again; she has since regained the use of her legs and 'has begun to reclaim her life, thanks in part to encouragement she says she gets from an online "virtual world" where she can walk, run and even dance'. Another person who had severe agoraphobia gained the confidence to venture outdoors after exploring the world of Second Life. One of Stein's (2007) interviewees makes a compelling case for her experiences in virtual reality.

> 'It's kind of like getting your life back again, but even better in some ways', said Kathie Olson, 53, who uses a wheelchair, lives alone and rarely leaves her home near Salt Lake City. In Second Life, she roams about as Kat Klata, a curvy young brunette who runs the Dragon Inn nightclub. 'I've met so many people. I can walk. I can dance. I can even fly. Without this I'd just be staring at four walls. Mentally it's helped me so much.

Stein (2007) suggests that the uplift and even jouissance people feel by participating in second life are so powerful in part because 'the full-color, multifaceted nature of the experience offers so much more "emotional bandwidth"'. In his ethnography of Second Life, based on fieldwork that took place from 3 June 2004 to 30 January 2007, anthropologist Tom Boellstorff (2008) talks about the consequences that actual-world embodiment has for virtual participation on this online world. The Second Life residents he encountered who have physical disabilities were able to expand their social networks and gain an enhanced sense of agency. These people included a deaf participant who liked the fact that text chat equalized his capacity to talk with everyone, because in real life, many people are not familiar with sign language. Another Second Life resident who was recovering from a stroke explained that 'you lose your role and sense of control in real life; in Second Life you can take the bits of you that work and forge a new one' (Boellstorff 2008: 137).

Clinical research confirms these reports on the practical and existential effects of participating in virtual worlds for people with disabilities.[22] These effects include disabled users gaining a sense of control over their environment and their interactions with others (Alm et al. 1998; Stevens 2004; Williams and Nicholas 2005); developing an enhanced spatial awareness, eye–hand coordination and fine motor skills and finding sources of social support and medical information (Hill and Weinert 2004; Kalichman et al. 2003); and achieving greater independence, communication and learning for those with mobility impairments (Anderberg and Jönsson 2005) and traumatic brain injury (Thornton et al. 2005). Participation in virtual reality has been shown to help those with cognitive impairments focus attention and learn life skills such as shopping and food preparation (Alm et al. 1998; Christiansen et al. 1998; Standen and Cromby 1995). People with autism spectrum disorders often find virtual reality communication more comfortable than communication in real life (Biever 2007; Parsons and Mitchell 2002).

Boellstorff (2008) draws attention to the ways that the design of digital media can be 'disabling'. However liberating life as an avatar might be, creating that version of the self requires that 'one saw or heard with actual eyes and ears, typed on a keyboard and moved a mouse with actual hands and fingers' (2008: 134–5).[23]

Boellstorff notes the frequency of comments he heard during his two years of fieldwork in Second Life regarding the lack of consideration for universal design that might accommodate users with a variety of disabilities. Complaints included the difficulty of reading small fonts for those with visual impairments, the impact of seizure-inducing flash effects for those with epilepsy, difficulties managing avatars with a track ball and problems with abstract reasoning required for scripting. Boellstorff also found that many people who self-disclosed created avatars that did not reflect their impairments—an online practice of passing noted since the days of text-only chat rooms (Damer 1998; Van Gelder [1985] 1991: 366). As one resident in Boellstorff's study explained, having virtual capacities in Second Life that otherwise are not available 'allows you to be free to explore yourself' (2008: 137). Others, like Amanda Baggs, have created embodied representations that reflected their actual-life disabilities (Boellstorff 2008: 136).

The case of Second Life residents with what Boellstorff calls psychological disabilities (or what others might call cognitive differences) opens discussion of what he calls virtual agency, the presumption of 'a self who can discover interests and desires and respond to them through acts of creativity' (Boellstorff 2008: 147). As discussed in the case of Amanda Baggs, Boellstorff astutely observes that:

> Second Life's reliance on textual chat instead of voice during the period of [his] fieldwork, the limited capacity for avatar facial expression, and a general tolerance for delayed or unexpected responses (for instance, because persons were often afk [away from the keyboard]) made it possible for many residents with autism to be competent social actors to a significantly greater degree than in the actual world. (147)

Similarly, those with attention deficit disorder found that 'they were perceived like any other resident, analogous to the manner in which a person who could not walk in the actual world could walk like anyone else' in Second Life (Boellstorff 2008: 147). One woman, Suzee, whose brother, Joseph, had severe schizophrenia, found her relationship with her brother catalyzed in Second Life. While in real life, Joseph lives with his mother (despite the fact that he is in his thirties), in Second Life, he built and decorated a cabin for himself and spends hours with Suzee talking and creating things with her. Citing these and other cases, Boellstorff observes, 'This theme of Second Life permitting access to an interior self that in the actual world is masked by an unchosen embodiment and social obligations was common…Avatars were not just placeholders for selfhood but sites of self-making in their own right' (2008: 148–9).

Importantly (and not surprisingly), discrimination was still a challenge for Second Life residents with disabilities, despite their having crafted avatars that enabled them to pass as people without disabilities. One person notes that virtual friends sometimes 'run away, and I think it bothers me more in here. It's like they are looking for the perfect person. It happens here just as easy as in the real world, so many here don't tell they have a disability' (Boellstorff 2008: 138). At the same time,

Boellstorff notes the capacity of virtual worlds to generate compassionate identification, as was seen in some of the comments generated in response to YouTube videos by Amanda Baggs. 'Virtual worlds can be sites of griefing [bullying/harassing] and inequality, but they can also produce new ways of living, including a kind of empathy that recalls the ethnographic project itself' (Boellstorff 2008: 249).

Some of the benefits of having an extension into virtual reality are practical, especially for the 38 per cent of Americans with disabilities who are unemployed due to discrimination and less-than-accommodating workplaces.[24] Seshat Czeret has a painful disability that makes it difficult for her to leave her home or participate in community life in the physical world. She is unable to work away from home, leave the house for social visits and participate in her local community. In Second Life, she runs a successful clothing and furniture business and is an avid role-player. She describes her use of Second Life not as escape into fantasy but as 'escape from persecution'.[25]

Boellstorff's fieldwork ended in January 2007, six months before the emergence of a remarkable community of support for people with disabilities on Second Life, largely due to the efforts of disability activist Alice Krueger.[26] According to the Virtual Ability website, prior to becoming involved with Second Life, Krueger

> worked part time from home as a technical writer and editor for an education research firm for five years using adaptive office equipment. As a woman with Multiple Sclerosis, she found it increasingly difficult to participate in her real life community. No longer able to leave home to work, volunteer, or socialize with friends, she turned to virtual worlds to fulfill these basic human needs. Ms. Krueger is the mother of three young adults with disabilities and has been a special education teacher. Ms. Krueger's avatar in Second Life® is Gentle Heron. Gentle can stand and walk without crutches.[27]

The community that Krueger founded with two other disabled friends began in June 2007, when they

> began thinking about how important the concept of community was for those who faced barriers to participation in the physical community in which they lived. They began asking other disabled people what their idea of 'community' was and what they expected from being a member of a community. From this research, the friends determined that people with disabilities want the same things everyone else does. They want companionship and friendship especially with people who understand the limitations placed on them by their disabling conditions. They need to learn more about their own conditions, about health and wellbeing, and about resources available to make their lives better. They want a chance to be employed or to do volunteer work since both give back to our community. And, they want to have fun. This was really no surprise, nor was it a surprise that these things were difficult to achieve in the world outside their homes. People who are disabled are often socially isolated, even physically isolated, within their geographic communities. So the three friends…decided to explore virtual reality as a setting within which to build a supportive community…and chose Second Life as the one to colonize

first, since it seemed to be the richest cultural environment and the most fully developed. (Whiteberry 2008)

Originally, the three friends called the online community they had created the Heron Sanctuary, but the site was frequently mistaken as 'an organization that provided a safe place for large, blue-feathered wading birds'. While doing research, they came across the Accessibility Center on Second Life's HealthInfo Island, where they met Lorelei Junot, a librarian responsible for setting up the Information Island archipelago within Second Life. Junot allowed them to use a plot of land on EduIsland 4, and the project began. Within its first eight months, the community grew to 150 subjects and quickly earned a reputation as the primary group on Second Life supporting people with real-world disabilities. After discussion, in January 2008 this group formed Virtual Ability, Inc., a nonprofit corporation based in Colorado, where Krueger lives. Virtual Ability has six Second Life properties that reflect the concerns first articulated by the founders. These are: (1) Virtual Ability Island (VAI), which provides new resident orientation and training for people with disabilities or chronic illnesses on how to navigate Second Life; (2) HealthInfo Island, which is attached by a drawbridge to VAI and offers information on physical, emotional and mental health through interactive displays, links to outside resources, events and personalized assistance as well as an Accessibility Center with floors that focus on different aspects of accessibility: vision, hearing, mobility and dexterity and learning impairments; (3) Cape Able, which is for those who are deaf or have hearing impairments; (4) Cape Serenity, which is a haven featuring a library with books written by people with disabilities as well as a patio for storytelling and poetry readings; (5) Wolpertinger property, which offers twenty-three inexpensive apartments and (6) AVESS (Amputee Virtual Environment Support Space), which was built to establish best practices and protocols for the provision of online peer-to-peer support services for military amputees and their families.[28] From 2006 to 2010, Wellness Island, founded by SL counsellor Avalon Birke, provided one of the first support centres on Second Life to offer mental health resources, counselling and education. It closed after three and a half years due to constraints of time and money.[29]

Unlike most other participants with avatars in Second Life and other virtual communities, those involved in Virtual Ability do not regard their participation on Second Life as a game. Their goal—to provide a support community for people with disabilities and their friends and families—is a serious project that does not regard the boundary between virtual and real life as significant. Consistent with their interest in disability rights both online and offline, their most recent project was the organizing and hosting of a virtual world conference about real-world rights.[30] That supportive environment includes making Second Life more accessible to people with different kinds of disabilities. As explained on the Virtual Ability website:

You probably have friends with disabilities. You know that people with disabilities face many barriers in living in the 'real' world. There are also barriers to entering into a

> virtual world. Some people have only one hand or even one finger they can control to type. Some use a stylus, or type with their toes. Some can't type at all, and use voice recognition software to control their computer. Virtual Ability, Inc. helps people with these kind of challenges get into and become successful in virtual worlds like Second Life® During our unique intake process, we conduct an individualized skills assessment, refer clients for help with assistive hardware and software as appropriate, and provide customized training and orientation.[31]

Making the technology available to people with disabilities is central to the Virtual Ability project. The website discusses how attention to this form of accessibility is indeed part of the making of the kind of 'moral community' that Goggin and Newell recognize can only happen when access to a medium is taken into account.

The language the site uses to describe the activities available once people gain access to Virtual Ability is very much in that spirit. Virtual Ability helps members

> integrate into the virtual society, and provides an ongoing community of support. The community offers members information, encouragement, training, companionship, referrals to other online resources and groups, ways to contribute back to the community, and ways to have fun. We take virtual field trips as part of our curriculum with our new intakes. We also have volunteers who love to go shopping, and enjoy helping folks with virtual makeovers. While almost anyone new to a virtual online world would enjoy a little early guidance, we are finding that this individualized attention is often critical for the success of those who have disabilities. We also do a lot of dancing. We have taken folks to walk in the virtual woods, climb mountains, go virtual skydiving—all kinds of things that are profound and a pleasure to someone with physical or mental limitations. It's an amazing experience helping someone who will never walk again in real life to jump on a virtual trampoline.[32]

Conclusion

Virtual Ability's mindful approach to digital design—that meeting the requirements of people with disabilities for access to digital media is a fundamental statement about who counts as part of the moral community—suggests that the hopes expressed by Goggin and Newell in 2003 are no longer entirely about the future. Their words could easily describe the philosophy and practice of Virtual Ability.

> From this knowledge—provided directly from people with disabilities as experts about their lives and opportunities—a different understanding of people with disabilities and the new media can be fashioned. This requires us to recognize and affirm in practice different ways of knowing the world and to map the diversity of abilities people have in our societies. (Goggin and Newell 2003: xix)

There is still considerable ground to cover before we truly achieve digital *doxa*, in which 'disability in its digital incarnations may unfold in new, unexpected, and fairer ways to the genuine benefit...of people with disabilities' (Goggin and Newell 2003: 154). My daughter, at age 22, still finds it hard to find characters with disabilities on television or at the movies. And those who occupy positions as public pundits on things digital rarely call attention to the inequalities of access to this media world for those with disabilities—or, for that matter, other marginalized groups (Ginsburg 2008), with the occasional exceptions to the rule, such as Amanda Baggs.

Nonetheless, the cases discussed here suggest a sea change is occurring, from the expanded sense of experience and personhood that Amanda Baggs created for audiences across the globe through her YouTube videos and blog entries to the visionary expansion of Second Life's accessibility by Alice Krueger/Gentle Heron in her quest to use digital media to create an alternative world full of possibility and support for those with disabilities, to the mobilizing capacity of social networks on- and offline for disability activist filmmakers such as Dan Habib. These cases help us see how the capacities of digital media enable significant interventions in our everyday understandings of what it means to be human for the estimated 15 to 20 per cent of the world's population that lives with disabilities, a category that any one of us might join in a heartbeat.

It seems only fitting in a chapter that emphasizes the significance of self-determination for those with disabilities to let Amanda Baggs have the last word. In *In My Language*, she makes clear the existential motivation of her presence in social media and its liberatory potential:

> There are people being tortured, people dying, because they are considered non-persons because their kind of thought is considered so unusual as to be not be considered thought at all. Only when the many types of personhood are recognized will justice and human rights be possible.

Acknowledgements

I am grateful to Danny Miller and Heather Horst for inviting me to be part of this volume. They encouraged me to explore a new angle in a longer research project that I have been working on for several years with Rayna Rapp, which is supported by the Spencer Foundation and New York University's Institute for Human Development and Social Change. I also want to thank Gabriella Coleman, Emily Martin, John Michalczyk and Rayna Rapp for their thoughtful readings of earlier drafts of this chapter.

Notes

1. There has been some controversy regarding whether Amanda Baggs is 'truly' autistic. These kinds of authenticity arguments are precisely the kind of policing of identity she objects to, and not relevant to the argument of this chapter.

YouTube is a video-sharing website where users can upload, share and display a wide variety of user-generated video content, including movie and TV clips, music videos and amateur content such as short original videos.

2. *Do it yourself*, or DIY, is a broad term that refers to independent music, art and film that cultivates a homemade, low-tech sensibility.
3. Interestingly, when I have shown a clip of *In My Language* during public talks, people involved in experimental film find this work a riveting example of the experimental film genre, although that is not Baggs's intention.
4. I am honoured to contribute to a collection that seeks to extend the ideas and methods of anthropology as a way to understand the profound changes in cultural worlds that are catalyzed by digital technologies. However, I find the term *digital anthropology* to be rather awkward; did we ever think of our work as *analogue anthropology*? When writing about the complexities of the transformations produced by the presence (or absence) of digital media, I prefer to use terms such *the digital age*—which clearly means different things to New Yorkers than it does to indigenous people in Australia—a point I underscore in my article, 'Rethinking the Digital Age' (2008), which cautions against the ethnocentric enthusiasms produced by the illusion that digital technologies have indeed created a global village.

   To reinforce that point, according to Internet World Stats, an excellent resource on global Internet usage, as of March 2011, only 30 per cent of the world population has access to the Internet (http://www.internetworldstats.com/stats.htm). Discovering what that uneven distribution of the Internet means in terms of people's everyday experience of communication, identity, community and so forth in the digital age—despite the popular illusion that the whole world is wired—is exactly the work of books such as this collection.
5. What counts as digital is a vast array of technologies; by necessity, this chapter will be limited to only a few of these forms. As Goggin and Newell point out in their 2003 book, *Digital Disability: The Social Construction of Disability in New Media*,

   > New digital communications technologies, or new media, include the Internet and broadband networks (fast, high-capacity data services), advanced telecommunications networks (offering services such as caller ID, digital mobile phones, third generation mobile telecommunications, video telephones), and digital broadcasting (with digital television). There is a bewildering proliferation of communications and media technologies that are promised to revolutionize our lives. (xiii)

6. Second Life (SL or 2Life) is an immersive virtual world launched in 2003 and is accessible via the Internet. A free client program called the *Second Life Viewer* enables users, called residents, to interact with each other through avatars. Built into the software is a three-dimensional modelling tool based on simple

geometric shapes that allows residents to build virtual objects. Residents can explore, meet other residents, socialize, participate in individual and group activities, create and trade virtual property and services and travel throughout the world, which residents refer to as the grid.

7. According to the U.S. Census Bureau, 15.1 per cent of the population has some kind of disability (http://factfinder.census.gov/servlet/STTable?_bm=y&-geo_id=01000US&-qr_name=ACS_2007_3YR_G00_S1801&-ds_name=ACS_2007_3YR_G00_). Estimates in some other parts of the world are much higher.
8. The slogan 'nothing about us without us' became the title of James Charlton's 1998 book chronicling the disability rights movement. Charlton first heard the term in talks by South African disability activists Michael Masutha and William Rowland, who had in turn heard the phrase used by an East European activist at an international disability rights conference (Charlton 1998).
9. Familial dysautonomia is an Ashkenazi Jewish genetic disease causing dysfunction of the autonomic and sensory nervous systems. See Dysautonomia Foundation, Inc., 2008, *What Is Familial Dysautonomia?*: http://www.familialdysautonomia.org/whatisfd.htm.
10. For further information, see http://www.reelabilities.org/.
11. The Including Samuel website, created by filmmaker Dan Habib, is a remarkable intereactive resource offering readers not only information about the documentary *Including Smauel* but also the opportunity to be in dialogue with others and to find resource listings for people with disabilities and the educational system. See http://www.includingsamuel.com/home.aspx.
12. *Wired* magazine reports on how new and developing technologies—especially digital technologies—affect culture, the economy, the body and politics.
13. Baggs is also a prolific blogger. I recommend spending some time on her blog, Ballastexistenx, in which she elaborates on her philosophy and experiences. See http://ballastexistenz.wordpress.com/gossip-free-zone/.
14. For a review of this research, see the section entitled 'Medical Benefits' on the Virtual Ability Island website: http://www.virtualability.org/va_medical_benefits.aspx.
15. Amanda Baggs, *Being an Unperson*, uploaded to YouTube on 3 November 2006 (http://www.youtube.com/watch?v=4c5_3wqZ3Lk); Amanda Baggs, *How to Boil Water the Easy Way*, uploaded to YouTube on 17 June 2007 (http://www youtube.com/watch?v=4c5_3wqZ3Lk).
16. This comment on Baggs' YouTube can be found at: http://www.youtube.com/watch?v=9fUi1EYq6Rs.
17. I am a founding co-director of the Center for Religion and Media (at New York University), which began in 2003. The workshop described here was organized by the ongoing working group 'Jews, Media, Religion' organized by Barbara

Kirshenblatt-Gimblett and Jeffrey Shandler. For more information on the centre, see http://crm.as.nyu.edu/page/home; on the activities of the working group, see the MODIYA Project: http://modiya.nyu.edu/.

18. Virtual Ability, Inc., is a website that collects a range of resources for people with disabilities. It is a nonprofit corporation based in Colorado. As the website explains, 'Our mission is to enable people with a wide range of disabilities by providing a supporting environment for them to enter and thrive in online virtual worlds like Second Life.' See http://virtualability.org/vanamav.aspx.
19. See the magazine *2Life* at http://www.2lifemagazine.com/.
20. Parables are stories that ask us to examine our everyday assumptions about the usual order of things, 'a traditional technique for coping with problematic social situations' providing 'a microcosm of the life situation and a projected resolution' (Kirshenblatt-Gimblett 1975: 107, 123). The term 'parable of possibility' has been used by economist Russell Roberts (2008) in his novella about the virtues of the free market and the creativity of the American economy and by literary scholar Terence Martin's (1995) study of the American literary fixation with 'beginnings'.
21. Stein (2007) offers a quote indicating how preliminary our knowledge of digital life is, from the National Science Foundation social scientist William Sims Bainbridge: 'Researchers say they are only starting to appreciate the impact of this phenomenon. "We're at a major technical and social transition with this technology. It has very recently started to become a very big deal, and we haven't by any means digested what the implications are."'
22. For more information see http://virtualability.org/va_medical_benefits.aspx.
23. Citing Mauss ([1935] 1979) on body techniques and Ellul (1964) on the age of *techne* and drawing on the experiences of Second Life residents with disabilities, Boellstorff argues that all forms of embodiment—both virtual and actual—are informed by *techne*, 'which is one reason why the notion of the posthuman inadequately characterizes virtual selfhood. Yet this very continuity also allows virtual embodiment to destabilize the human' (2008: 135).
24. According to the US Census Bureau, among the 15.1 per cent of the total US population classified as disabled, only 36.7 per cent of those between the ages of sixteen and sixty-four are employed (as opposed to approximately 90 per cent or higher among the general population in the same age group). The American Factfinder is an online resource created by the US Census Bureau. The numbers cited here are based on their 2010 census reports. See http://factfinder.census.gov/servlet/STTable?_bm=y&-geo_id=01000US&-qr_name=ACS_2007_3YR_G00_S1801&-ds_name=ACS_2007_3YR_G00_.
25. A blog created to teach people how to make avatars, clothing, skins, textures and animations in Second Life can be found at http://seshat-czeret.blogspot.com/.

26. Thanks to John Michalczyk for a very helpful conversation on this.
27. For more information see http://www.virtualability.org/aboutus.aspx.
28. For more information see http://www.virtualability.org/aboutus.aspx.
29. Second Life Healthy consolidates information on all SL activity related to health care taking place in this virtual world. See *Wellness Island*, http://slhealthy.wetpaint.com/page/Wellness+Island.
30. The International Disability Rights Affirmation Conference took place on 23–4 July 2011 at Sojourner Auditorium on Virtual Ability Island; see http://etechlib.wordpress.com/2011/07/26/second-life-international-disability-rights-affirma tion-conference-overview/.
31. For more information see http://virtualability.org/aboutus.aspx.
32. For more information see http://virtualability.org/aboutus.aspx.

References

Alm, N., J. L. Arnott, I. R. Murray and I. Buchanan. 1998. Virtual Reality for Putting People with Disabilities in Control. *Systems, Man, and Cybernetics* 2: 1174–9.

Anderberg, P., and B. Jönsson. 2005. Being There. *Disability and Society* 20(7): 719–33.

Baggs, A. 2007. *In My Language*. YouTube, 14 January. http://www.youtube.com/watch?v=JnylM1hI2jc.

Biever, C. 2007. Let's Meet Tomorrow in Second Life. *New Scientist* 2610 (June): 26–7.

Boellstorff, T. 2008. *Coming of Age in Second Life: An Anthropologist Explores the Virtually Human.* Princeton, NJ: Princeton University Press.

Bouquet, M. 2001. Making Kinship with an Old Reproductive Technology. In *Relative Values: Reconfiguring Kinship Studies*, ed. S. Franklin and S. McKinnon, 85–115. Durham, NC: Duke University Press.

Bourdieu, P. [1972] 1977. *Outline of a Theory of Practice.* Vol. 16, trans. R. Nice. Cambridge: Cambridge University Press

Charlton, J. 1998. *Nothing About Us Without Us: Disability Oppression and Empowerment.* Berkeley: University of California Press.

Christiansen, C., B. Abreu, K. Ottenbacher, K. Huffman, B. Masel and R. Culpepper. 1998. Task Performance in Virtual Environments Used for Cognitive Rehabilitation after Traumatic Brain Injury. *Archives of Physical Medicine and Rehabilitation* 79(8): 888–92.

Coleman, G. 2010. Ethnographic Approaches to Digital Media. *Annual Review of Anthropology* 39: 487–505.

Cooper, A. 2007. Why We Should Listen to 'Unusual' Voices. 21 February. http://www.cnn.com/CNN/Programs/anderson.cooper.360/blog/2007/02/why-we-should-listen-to-unusual-voices.html.

Damer, B. 1998. *Avatars! Exploring and Building Virtual Worlds on the Internet.* Berkeley, CA: Peachpit Press.

Ellis, K., and M. Kent. 2010. *Disability and New Media.* New York: Routledge.

Ellul, J. [1954] 1964. *The Technological Society.* Trans. J. Wilkinson, intro. R. K. Merton. New York: Alfred A. Knopf.

Fox, Z. 2011. *Four Ways iPads Are Changing the Lives of People with Disabilities.* http://mashable.com/2011/07/25/ipads-disabilities/. Accessed 18 August 2011.

Gajilan, C. 2007. Living with Autism in a World Made for Others. CNN.com. 22 February. http://edition.cnn.com/2007/HEALTH/02/21/autism.amanda/index.html. Accessed 18 August 2011.

Garland-Thomson, R. 2009. *Staring: How We Look.* New York: Oxford University Press.

Ginsburg, F. 2008. Rethinking the Digital Age. In *The Media and Social Theory*, ed. D. Hesmondhalgh and J. Toynbee, 129–44. New York: Routledge.

Ginsburg, F. 2011. Native Intelligence: A Short History of Debates on Indigenous Media and Ethnographic Film. In *Made to Be Seen: Perspectives on the History of Visual Anthropology*, ed. M. Banks and J. Ruby, 234–55. Chicago: University of Chicago Press.

Ginsburg, F., L. A. Lughod and B. Larkin. 2002. *Media Worlds: Anthropology on New Terrain.* Berkeley: University of California Press.

Goggin, G., and C. Newell. 2003. *Digital Disability: The Social Construction of Disability in New Media.* New York: Rowman & Littlefield.

Grinker, R. R. 2007. *Unstrange Minds: Remapping the World of Autism.* New York: Basic Books.

Gupta, S. 2007. Behind the Veil of Autism. 20 February. http://www.cnn.com/HEALTH/blogs/paging.dr.gupta/2007/02/behind-veil-of-autism.html.

Gupta, S. 2008. Finding Amanda. 2 April. http://thechart.blogs.cnn.com/2008/04/02/.

Habib, D. 2008. *Including Samuel.* Film. Durham, NH: Institute on Disability. www.includingsamuel.com/.

Hill, W. G., and C. Weinert. 2004. An Evaluation of an Online Intervention to Provide Social Support and Health Education. *Computers, Informatics, Nursing* 22(5): 282–8.

Kalichman, S. C., E. G. Benotsch, L. Weinhardt, J. Austin, W. Luke and C. Cherry. 2003. Health-Related Internet Use, Coping, Social Support, and Health Indicators in People Living with HIV/AIDS: Preliminary Results from a Community Survey. *Health Psychology* 22(1): 111–16.

Kirshenblatt-Gimblett, B. 1975. A Parable in Context: A Social Interactional Analysis of Storytelling Performance. In *Folklore: Performance and Communication*, ed. D. Ben-Amos and K. S. Goldstein, 107–23. The Hague: Mouton.

Martin, T. 1995. *Parables of Possibility: The American Need for Beginnings.* New York: Columbia University Press.

Mauss, M. [1935] 1979. Body Techniques. In *Sociology and Psychology: Essays by Marcel Mauss*, trans. B. Brewster, 95–123. London: Routledge and Kegan Paul.

Miller, D. 2011. *Tales from Facebook.* Cambridge: Polity Press.

Parsons, S., and P. Mitchell. 2002. The Potential of Virtual Reality in Social Skills Training for People with Autistic Spectrum Disorders. *Journal of Intellectual Disability Research* 46(5): 430–43.

Rapp, R., and F. Ginsburg. 2001. Enabling Disability, Rewriting Kinship, Reimagining Citizenship. *Public Culture* 13(3): 533–56.

Rapp, R., and F. Ginsburg. 2010. The Human Nature of Disability. Vital Topics Column. *American Anthropologist* 112(4): 517.

Rich, B. R. 1999. Collision, Catastrophe, Celebration: The Relationship Between Gay and Lesbian Film Festivals and Their Publics. *GLQ: A Journal of Lesbian and Gay Studies* 5(1): 79–84.

Roberts, R. 2008. *The Price of Everything: A Parable of Possibility and Prosperity.* Princeton, NJ: Princeton University Press.

Sahlins, M. 1985. *Islands of History.* Chicago: University of Chicago Press.

Schweik, S. M. 2009. *The Ugly Laws: Disability in Public.* New York: New York University Press.

Shapiro, J. 2006. Autism Movement Seeks Acceptance, Not Cures. *All Things Considered*, National Public Radio. 26 June. http://www.npr.org/templates/story/story.php?storyId=5488463.

Shirky, C. 2008. *Here Comes Everybody: The Power of Organizing Without Organizations.* New York: Penguin.

Snyder, S. L., and D. T. Mitchell. 2008. 'How Do We Get All These Disabilities in Here?': Disability Film Festivals and the Politics of Atypicality. *Canadian Journal of Film Studies* 17(1): 11–29.

Sreberny, A., and G. Khiabany. 2010. *Blogistan: The Internet and Politics in Iran.* London: I. B. Tauris.

Stein, R. 2007. Real Hope in a Virtual World. *Washington Post*, 6 October. http://www.washingtonpost.com/wp-dyn/content/article/2007/10/05/AR2007100502391.html.

Stevens, L. 2004. Online Patient Support: Mostly a Boon, but Challenges Remain. *Medicine on the Net* 10(3): 1–6.

Thornton, M., S. Marshall, J. McComas, H. Finestone, A. McCormick and H. Sveistrup. 2005. Benefits of Activity and Virtual Reality Based Balance Exercise Programmes for Adults with Traumatic Brain Injury: Perceptions of Participants and Their Caregivers. *Brain Injuries* 19(12): 989–1000.

Van Gelder, L. [1985] 1991. The Strange Case of the Electronic Lover. In *Computerization and Controversy: Value Choices and Social Conflicts*, ed. C. Dunlop and R. Kling, 364–75. Boston: Academic Press.

Whiteberry, W. 2008. The Story of the Heron Sanctuary. *Imagination Age*, 24 January. http://www.theimaginationage.net/2008/01/story-of-heron-sanctuary.html.

Williams, P., and D. Nicholas. 2005. Creating Online Resources for the Vulnerable. *Library and Information Update* 4(4): 30–1.

Wolman, D. 2008. The Truth About Autism: Scientists Reconsider What They Think They Know. *Wired* 16(3). http://www.wired.com/medtech/health/magazine/16-03/ff_autism?currentPage=all. Accessed June 6 2012.

Wurzburg, G. 2010. *Wretches and Jabberers: Stories from the Road.* Film. Area 23A.

–6–

Approaches to Personal Communication

Stefana Broadbent

This chapter is concerned with a particular field within digital anthropology—that of personal communication. It will show that the advent of digital technologies has had particularly personal consequences, because communication itself is so central to the way relationships are constituted and negotiated. The intention of the chapter is to move beyond speculative suggestions as to the consequences of the proliferation of new communication media and to concentrate instead upon the findings that are now available through detailed ethnographic research.

The core of the chapter consists of two case studies. The first is concerned with an extraordinary transformation in the relationship between work and nonwork situations, such that boundaries that had been developed for over a century and assumed to be essential for the effective carrying out of work in the modern world have almost entirely been breached by new technologies. The second case study considers the sheer number of new channels and devices available and shows that these have become more than the sum of their individual forms—that together they effectively resocialize the relationship between people and technology. Before presenting the case studies, the first part of the chapter focuses upon some general findings from recent research and describes the ongoing debate regarding the effect of mediated communication on sociality.

The context for this discussion is the rise of several new communication technologies. In the last twenty years, we have seen the widespread adoption of a variety of new communication channels: e-mail, which for many years constituted the main driver for users to go online; instant messaging in various formats; usenet groups; online forums; mobile voice calls; texting; voice-over-Internet protocol (VoIP); and an array of social networking sites. Interestingly, the adoption of these channels did not follow a linear sequence, and in different countries the discovery and uptake of the various channels followed different routes. Some countries led the way in mobile telephony usage, with very intense early use of short message service (SMS, or texting) (as discussed by Igarishi, Takai and Yoshida 2005 in Japan; Kasesniemi 2003 in Finland; Paragas 2005 in the Philippines). Others anticipated the wider adoption of instant messaging, as did the United States with AIM (AOL instant messaging), China with QQ and South Korea with Cyworld social networking. The reasons for such diversity had more to do with national policies leading to differences in the availability of broadband connections or mobile services than with cultural specificities. Currently in most affluent countries, infrastructural development and a greater harmonization of policies mean that there is a greater uniformity of access and pricing across markets, and users are exposed daily to the whole palette of communication possibilities, accessing all the channels mentioned above from different devices and often within single services.

Turning to social dimensions, the advent of digital communication technologies has generally been presented as an expansion of our social environments. We talk of the death of distance and imagine that this is an expansive world that brings us out of the claustrophobia of constrained personal relationships and leads us to wide landscapes of networking and extension. In this perspective, place-based ties are shattered in favour of interest-based connections created remotely, independent of physical proximity. This idea has permeated the culture of software development in the last fifteen years and has given rise to innumerable platforms for online communities to flourish. Online, interest-based communities also became the object of scrutiny by the social sciences as soon as such communities started attracting the early adopters of the Internet. In the 1990s, new fields of research emerged from the interaction between the social and computing sciences, such as computer-mediated communication, whose main object of analysis were the first online collaborative environments: usenet newsgroups, chat rooms and multi-user dungeons (MUDs). These groups, which only involved a fraction of Internet users at the time, were extensively researched because of their novelty and because they embodied the features of what seemed to be the major social transformation the Internet was introducing. Newsgroups aggregated people who wanted to discuss and collaborate on specific issues of interest, and MUDs were the first multiplayer role-playing games in which users created fictional characters for themselves and played with other gamers online. In her analysis of MUDs, Sherry Turkle (1995) described the first cases of multiple virtual identities, an experience that has now become far more widespread. The idea that people could entertain intense, fruitful and emotionally rich relationships in virtual spaces that were created to bring together similar-minded people with common interests regardless of their geographical situation and their social and cultural belonging elicited an initial intellectual euphoria. Manuel Castells, in *The Rise of the Network Society* ([1996] 2000), argued for the transformative nature of information networks on social, political and economic relations; Howard Rheingold (2002) was a vocal advocate of the role of communication technology in amplifying the human capacity for cooperation. In the related fields of computer-supported collaboration and computer-supported collaborative work, Dourish and Belloti (1992) and Nardi, Whittaker and Bradner (2000) also pointed out the role of technology in transforming cooperation in social groups. Researchers in computer-supported learning found potential avenues for online 'communities of practice'—a term used by Lave and Wenger (1991) that was highly influential in the analysis of online communities (Sproull and Kiesler 1991; Suchman 1987).

The advent and even more staggering speed of adoption of mobile phones introduced a completely different angle to our understanding of remote personal communication. Much more personal devices than computers, mobile phones sustained one-to-one conversations rather than group exchanges. Designed for voice calls, which are principally person-to-person, and then extended to support texting, which again is primarily a dyadic form of exchange, mobile phones surpassed PCs in number of users, in intensity of exchanges and in the significance users attributed to them as social tools.

Between 2000 and 2006, a series of seminal works on mobile phone usage by Katz and Aakhus (2002); Ito and Okabe (2005); Ito, Okabe and Matsuda (2005); Ling (2004); Fortunati (2003); de Gournay and Smoreda (2003) and Licoppe and Smoreda (2005) identified what have proven to be enduring features of mobile communication. Mobile phones are allowing people to maintain perpetual contact with an intimate sphere of relationships. Ito and Okabe (2005) described the sense of permanent mutual awareness that Japanese teenagers were experiencing while texting. The tightening of connections has also been found in Africa (De Bruijn, Nyamnjoh and Nyamnjoh 2009), Asia Pacific (Hjorth 2008), China (Wallis 2008) and India (Lee 2009; Priyanka 2010). Jonathan Donner (2006) reported the intense social and personal use of mobile phones by microentrepreneurs in Rwanda, where he found that more than two-thirds of calls and texts were directed to family and friends. Horst and Miller (2006) argue that Jamaicans cultivate extensive personal networks to subvert the limits of their local community or familial networks, and they also use the mobile phone to intensify existing relationships. Surveys such as those of the Australian Research Council (Bittman, Brown and Wajcman 2009) or by Hampton, Sessions and Her (2011) in the United States later confirmed on large samples of users that the vast majority of calls and texts are exchanged between close family members and friends, highlighting what Ling (2008) has called the 'bounded solidarities'.[1]

Paradoxically, these studies swung the debate on digital communication in a different direction from the initial euphoria about the renewal of communities and new forms of extensive sociality. Other social scientists critically examined the opposite hypothesis: that mediated communication triggers a process of individualization (Boase and Wellman 2006; Kraut et al. 1996, 1998; Ling and Campbell 2009). This debate was rooted in a well-established sociological discussion on the historical evolution of sociality towards a reduction of social cohesion and public engagement (Fisher 1982; Granovetter 1973; Putnam 2000; Sennett 1998). A number of common practices among mobile phone users (such as making private calls in public spaces) were taken as signs of disengagement from the public sphere and a clear concentration on close personal ties (Harper 2010; Ling 2008). People were seen as detaching themselves from their surroundings to focus on more distant but also often more intimate and established relationships through their mobile phones. The attention of callers was directed to their remote interlocutors, excluding the people they were in the presence of. Similar patterns of isolation were described by Bull (2000) in his analysis of the use of personal music devices such as MP3 players to create boundaries for the self. This set of behaviours were interpreted as a tendency to privilege the private ties at the detriment of the public ones (Campbell 2007). The interactional violations that occur when a person is negotiating both private/remote conversations and public/co-present exchanges have been analysed within the frame of reference of Goffman's (1959) theory of front and backstage. These findings suggested that the accepted understandings of what represents the private sphere and the public sphere were undergoing fundamental and rapid change which was best appreciated through an ethnographic encounter with the minutiae of everyday communication.

Once the personal nature of mobile communication was identified, other digital channels were also found to be dedicated primarily to a small number of contacts: instant messaging users, for instance, regardless of long 'buddy' lists, interacted primarily with a few family members and close friends (Kim et al. 2007). Nardi, Whittaker and Schwarz (2002) found that IM users 'chatted' regularly with only four or five of their IM buddies, which is the same number Schiano and colleagues (2002) found for teenagers. A report from the Pew Internet and American Life Project (2000) on e-mail practices also found that in private usage, the main recipients of messages were family connections.

More recently, data on users' practices in social networking sites—a platform that, by definition, was designed to support extensive social group interaction—have revealed that intense communication is concentrated among a few regular contacts. Researchers distinguish between reciprocal active exchanges and maintaining a sense of background awareness of others through public status updates (Facebook Data Team 2009; Kim and Yun 2007; Park, Heo and Lee 2008). One-to-one reciprocal conversations on social networking sites are still dedicated to a small group of interlocutors (fewer than ten, according to the Facebook Data Team) who tend to be people who communicate via other media. Baym (2010) also points out that very strong bonds can emerge based on intense online exchanges around a common interest (such as music or the need for mutual support or companionship) but that these often move on to other communication channels as well or evolve into face-to-face encounters. Haythornthwaite (2005) had already shown that the closer a relationship is, the greater the number of channels that are used to keep in touch. On the contrary, distant, weak ties are usually contacted with only one medium, and any breakdown in that medium can unintentionally sever the relationships. danah boyd (2007) and Nancy Baym evoked this point in their personal blogs in May 2010 (zephoria.org and onlinefandom.com), where they debated why people cannot give up Facebook even in light of the company's breaches of privacy. Shutting down Facebook would, in many cases, permanently sever the ties with many contacts that are maintained only through this channel.

Most observations concur that the main consequences of the proliferation of new media channels for people's everyday lives is not necessarily the extension of new social connections on a global scale or the cultivation of social capital, but rather the intensification of a small group of highly intimate relationships that have now managed to match the richness of their social connectedness with a richness of multiple communication channels. The transformative nature of digital communication channels as a means of shattering the limitations of the local is therefore not perceived as a means of transcending existing ties, but as a way of achieving something else: the possibility to expand the co-present into the remote and thus maintain relationships that are emotionally close but geographically distant and the invasion of private personal exchanges in spaces that banned them for different normative reasons.

Regarding the first point, a growing body of research examines the use of different channels in transnational relationships, and in migration in particular (Ros and De la Fuente 2011). These studies show the extent of migrants' implication in video calls, photo sharing, online chatting and all other means of maintaining contact. These studies are delving into issues of remote parenting, distant romance and social remittance (Levitt 1998). On the second aspect, the expansion of the private, I have mentioned the research on public spaces such as transport and restaurants. In my own research I have started looking at spaces that are not only public but also institutional—workplaces, schools, hospitals; places where the social structures are explicitly manifested in institutionalized norms of behaviour. In particular, I have analysed the effect of private communication on organizations in which the personal sphere had been explicitly banned for many years (Broadbent 2011).

Case Study One: Communication at Work

Workplaces have historically erected a strict barrier between the realms of work and nonwork, as though workers would be incapable of fulfilling their commitments to labour if they were to have the distraction of potential communication with the wider world. It is these spheres which at the moment are most subject to change. Even though there has been a rise of other, more flexible forms of work, the conception which equates work to a paid job obtained through universalistic criteria and carried out away from home in a dedicated organization is still dominant and is possibly expanding geographically (Edgell 2006). The separation between workplace and home, derived from the generalization of the organizational models of industrial capitalisms, continues to imply a strong correlation between attention, time and productivity. The control of attention, in particular, as a source of effective labour has become an integral part of the management of human resources. Within this context, the wide adoption of private mobile phones and private digital communication in the workplace not only challenges the social boundaries erected around the workplace, but also reestablishes a certain autonomy in the management of individual attention

(Madden and Jones 2008). Restrictions of access to certain websites and to mobile phones and other communication channels are therefore to be understood as attempts to preserve the boundaries between social spheres and as forms of organizational control on attention. But the widespread use of computers with Internet connections in the workplace represented a fundamental challenge to the maintenance of this strict duality between work and leisure.

Starting in 2004, the Observatory of Usage within the telecoms operator Swisscom ran a variety of studies on digital life in Switzerland (Broadbent and Bauwens 2008). The studies combined traditional network data analysis with ethnographic projects on various aspects of communication, employing a number of anthropologists in this task. Our approach was both longitudinal and systematic, as we wished to repeat our research over a period of years. Every year, for instance, we collected communication diaries from hundreds of respondents. For four days, each informant filled in a paper diary indicating the following details for each mediated exchange: the interlocutor, the channel used, the content, the time and the place where it took place. Once completed and analysed, the diary, in an exercise of autoconfrontation (Mollo and Falzon 2004), became the basis of discussion with the informants on their communication practices and relationships. The data were also collated to identify patterns of usage. For instance we scrutinized correlations between communication partners and locations of contact. These studies were not specifically intended to uncover communication behaviours at work or in school, but they did provide a first reliable insight on how much private communication was happening outside the house.

Between 2009 and 2011, I carried out a series of studies on private communication in the workplace in Italy, France and the United Kingdom. I observed that, while personal communication from the workplace has become the norm, there is a persistent social tension surrounding this practice. The availability of multiple channels has become a vehicle for circumventing institutional regulations and for enabling communication between people in different institutional settings (Broadbent 2011). Employees are simply choosing the channels that are most compatible with the restrictions present in their work environment and with the limitations of the situational context of their interlocutors. Employers vary in their level of acceptance of these practices. While some employers are tolerant of private e-mails, they may be less so of personal calls. Other organizations may block access to all but internal e-mail and may tolerate mobile phones. We observed that in workplaces where there were no rules and an easy and personal access to the Internet, employees simply used all the channels at their disposal, from e-mail to social networks to instant messaging. Institutions that were controlling and that banned mobile phones or limited Internet access to certain websites simply encouraged individuals to find a solution—such as hiding or accessing a remote server—to use at least one channel to stay in touch. Once the walls of the workplace have been breached, and employees become used to the idea that being at work should not be at the expense of key forms of connectivity, such as with their close family, they will devise a solution to ensure the communication.

Regardless of the degree of digital freedom, we found that textual channels (e-mail, texting, instant messaging) were preferred to voice, for their unobtrusive nature and for their asynchronocity, which allows both speakers to manage their attention. The use of texting and other text-based channels is spread evenly throughout the day (Office of Communication 2010); voice calls are clustered in the evening. The timing of the exchanges during the day do not occur at random moments, though; rather, they follow some generalized patterns. For instance, at Swisscom, when we analysed the diaries of communication concentrating on the time of exchanges relative to the recipient, we found that the closest ties were most likely to be contacted between 11:00 a.m. and 6:00 p.m., with peaks at 3:00 p.m. and 5:00 p.m.; weaker ties were contacted after 6:00 p.m. This is not surprising and confirms what we know about the different forms of communication people use according to how distant they are both geographically and emotionally (Calabrese et al. 2007). Weaker or distant ties need longer exchanges, because more mutual ground has to be constructed during the conversation.

Calls from Work to Support Boundary Transitions

Other temporal patterns emerged within the working schedule indicating routines that intersected with the different phases of the working day: travelling to work, entering the workplace, the various phases of activity, breaks and leaving the workplace. Exchanges with friends and family seem to match the transitional phases of the day and in particular to support the moments in which people change their roles and their focus of attention. Peak moments of communication are when leaving work or when finishing a set of activities.

The journey to work is not only a physical transportation, but also a psychological transformation from the home persona to the work persona. In her book *Home and Work* (1996), Christena Nippert-Eng described how people go through a set of rituals to move from their home mentality to their work mentality. The separation between home and workplace is not just a spatial one; the two environments correspond to two social identities. Nippert-Eng's respondents had elaborate techniques and habits to shed their home mentality in the morning and get into the work mentality, and then leave the professional mode behind them in the evening to resume their private persona at home. These practices could be as simple as putting on specific clothes for each environment, reading the newspaper, drinking coffee or having a beer at the end of the day.

Three phenomena seem to be happening in the morning: people put on a face or persona compatible with their professional role, they build up their concentration for the execution of their job and, in order to achieve this, they actively remove personal issues from their attention span. This last point is accomplished by activities such as tidying up before leaving the house and performing separation rituals with family members. In our observations in Switzerland, respondents listened to different types of music and radio channels on the way to work than they did on the way back home, and they read different newspapers and drank different drinks. Everything on the way to work was oriented towards building up focus, attention and concentration. On the way back home, it was all about winding down and reentering the private space.

So when we think in terms of new communication technologies disrupting the prior boundaries between work and nonwork, this is not a simple or absolute change. Rather, we see a process of gradual adoption and adaptation which has, in effect, humanized the conventional distinctions and allowed a more gradual transition and more liberal interpretation of difference. Data from mobile operators shows a peak of calls in the early evening (5:00 p.m. to 7:00 p.m., depending on the habitual working schedule of a country). This time usually corresponds to the moment when most people leave their workplace. In the diaries that we collected, calls and messages were done on a routine basis, all around the same time. These were not simply coordination/functional calls. They were daily conversations that marked the transition from the professional world to the private world. What these calls do is help people shed the professional stance and regain their private persona. In a certain sense, the calls redefine the person, who can quickly reenter the private or intimate role that was left at the door of the office in the morning. People have told us that, when they text to say 'I'm out', they are making manifest that they have crossed a threshold; they feel they can fully reconnect with personal objects of attention which they have largely set aside during their work time. What this means is that communication technologies are used not to abolish the distinction of work and home but to help people manage and take control over that transition.

Contact during Work Activity

Our data showed that when people are at work, they only contact their closest ties—family and close friends. More distant friends and relations are instead contacted from home. The private calls, e-mails and messages that are sent during work hours fit a pattern that can also be defined as transitional. In the diaries we studied, we realized that calls and texts during working hours had a routine quality, just as did calls at the end of the day: they were repeated at more or less the same time every day and often matched transitions in the interlocutor's day.

People who work night shifts or early morning shifts, for instance, always find a moment to wish their partners good morning or goodnight. In general, people who have nonstandard working hours suffer from the fact they cannot be at home for some ritual activities such as breakfast or preparing for sleep. Along with the disruption of their sleeping cycles, this missing out on rituals at home has always been the main complaint of shift workers. Their calls from work, at exactly the times that correspond to the rituals they are missing, are therefore highly routinized and are seen as attempts to compensate for what is felt to be a major sacrifice imposed by their position. A classic example of what Ling (2008) refers to as ritual interactions, the calls actually become part of the household's ritual, contributing to reinforce the family cohesion.

Even couples that are on similar schedules exchange some messages during the day—often little more than a 'how are you doing?' or 'how did it go?'. In many cases, the exchanges follow the closure of a certain phase of activity—the conclusion of a task, the end of a meeting or the end of a period of some sort. What is important is not the content of the exchange but the contact, the extraction from the physical context of the workplace to a space of intimacy. Changing the focus of attention and the social sphere seems to be an effective way of marking a pause and signalling a break in the flow of activity. By calling, texting or posting or updating a status, the worker indicates that this time is not professional time; it is a time of personal agency and control of attention.

When we examine digital media usage in institutional settings, we do not see a process of disengagement from the public sphere, a focalization on small personal cohesive groups, but rather the coexistence in the same place of multiple registers of social affiliation. These multiple affiliations coexist in people's social networks, as well illustrated by Spencer and Pahl (2006) in their book on friendship. Mediated communication allows these connections to be accessible concurrently. People who call their mothers from work are demonstrating the capacity to entertain multiple roles and relationships, even within constrained and highly regulated settings. The techniques of closing into the phone, creating a sort of enclosed, private space of conversation that excludes all other co-present individuals—which Gergen (2008) describes as absent presence—are in my view simply techniques to allow the physical and spatial coexistence of the different social engagements. These behaviours are enacted to preserve the interactional patterns proper to the public stance, not to destroy them.

Case Study Two: Multiple Channels

The second case study concerns the consequences of the current availability of multiple communication channels that lead people to make informed decisions about the medium they use for each exchange and that add a new level of communicational power to digital media. The choice of a text or a call to contact someone on a specific topic is not seen as neutral, neither by the recipient nor the emitter; on the contrary, it is highly meaningful information. The book by Ilana Gershon, *The*

Breakup 2.0 (2010), offers the best example of the interconnection between channel choice and relationship. Gershon analyses media ideologies through students' narrations of their breakups. By dissecting with them the texts, posts and e-mails that have accompanied the process of breaking up with a partner, Gershon analyses the subtle differences between communication channels and between people's beliefs about technologies. Not only do breakups happen on multiple media, with people moving their conversations from media to media, but the choice of medium is a second-order information that, according to Gershon's informants, provides crucial emotional cues on the nature of their relationships and their partners.

Generalizing from such cases, Madianou and Miller (2011) have proposed the word 'polymedia' for this new condition of multiplicity of channels. On the basis of their study of Filipina mothers in London and the mothers' relationships to their children left behind in the Philippines, Madianou and Miller argue that there are two key conditions for polymedia. First, the availability of several alternative channels must exist—from text and voice phone to webcam, e-mail, social networking and others. But, equally important, once a computer with an Internet connection is purchased and a phone contract is secured, the cost of communication is embedded in this infrastructure, so any individual act of communication is no longer seen in relation to its cost. Under such conditions, Madianou and Miller find that the mothers can no longer explain their choice of this or that media in terms of either access or cost. The situation (as with that of Gershon) implies that an individual is now held morally responsible for which particular channel he or she employs. People recognize that one type of medium is good for avoiding arguments, another for keeping track of commitments; one gives power to the young, who understand its complexities, while another favours older people because it depends on costly infrastructure.

This means that, instead of thinking about any individual communicative medium, we have to consider each medium not only in terms of its specific affordances (see Baym 2010), but also in terms of the wider media ecology (see Horst, Herr-Stephenson and Robinson 2010), where it is defined relative to all the others that might have been chosen instead. Indeed most relationships now depend on using several channels for different aspects of the same relationship. This also means that communication channels now speak more directly to issues such as the control over emotions, differences in power and the moral responsibility of media choice. In Gershon's study, people may be as incensed by the selection of an inappropriate medium for dumping a boyfriend or girlfriend as the fact that they have been dumped. For Madianou and Miller, this means that the subtlest of media differences can start to come much closer to the complexities of relationships, such as that between a mother and her left-behind children.

In our own research, when we stopped tracking the adoption of a single channel at a time[2] and started looking at how people were using the whole palette of digital media, our object of research shifted from the domestication (Haddon 2004, 2006) of technology to communication itself and the relationships being entertained. From our initial interest in how people were integrating communications technologies in their daily life and how the process of domestication was impacting their household practices, we found ourselves focusing more and more on how different channels were weaving into relationships such as friendship, parenting or collaboration.

One of our most ambitious studies in the Observatory of Usage within Swisscom was a longitudinal study that ran between 2005 and 2010. Over a period of four years, my colleagues (Petra Hutter, Carolyne Hirt, Daniel Boos, Veronica Pagnamenta, Susanne Jost, Cora Pauli and Jeanne Caruzo) and I followed the evolution of the digital life of sixty households (which included 140 people). Households were located in the three linguistic regions of Switzerland, in urban and rural areas, and included families with children, single parents, retired couples, young singles and couples. Participants also had a range of professional activities and levels of employment. The households were visited twice a year, and all household members were asked to fill in communication diaries, draw maps of their homes, create a social map of their contacts and draw up a time line of two workdays and a day in the weekend. We sat with our informants in front of their computers and observed them navigate the Internet. We asked them to show us the websites they preferred and the online activities they usually pursued. When possible we looked at the content they were storing on their PCs, such as pictures, music files, texts or videos. We discussed TV and video consumption and musical preferences and habits. We distinguished between individual and collective activities. Over time we came to know them well and observed the changes in their lives as much as in their digital habits. Year after year, we returned to households where children were born, couples formed and dissolved, jobs changed or were lost and homes were sold or rented. By systematically observing these transformations over time, we were attempting to identify the triggers for change in digital behaviours. We obviously observed a number of adjustments in the use of the Internet as people discovered new websites and services and they adopted new devices for media consumption and communication. Changes, however, were far slower than we had anticipated; new practices emerged very gradually, with most people tentatively trying out new activities without giving up prior habits. For instance taking pictures with mobile phones started slowly, coexisting with digital cameras and analogue cameras for different occasions. Social networking sites started off on very specific services with specialized interests fully integrated in existing offline social activities—such as tillate.com, a website supported by discos and clubs to share pictures and comments of parties members had attended, and Xing.com, which aimed at sustaining professional connections. Only later did our informants adopt more personal forms of social networking services such as MySpace, which included a much wider and personal variety of friends.

Two among the myriad results we collected are particularly relevant for this discussion. First, nearly all the transformations in digital practices we observed were triggered by life events such as a job change, a move of house or the departure of a family member. This was particularly true of communication. In a number of households, for instance, parents adopted e-mail or Skype when a child moved abroad, left for military service or started working in another city. Teenagers stopped using instant messaging when they started apprenticeships and shifted most of their exchanges to texting. This effect of life phases on communication had been described by Manceron, Lelong and Smoreda (2002) in an article regarding the changes in communication behaviours following the birth of the first child and by Mercier, de Gournay and Smoreda (2002) on the new patterns of calls after a move of residence.

Second, we never observed any communication channel being abandoned. When a new service or channel was adopted, it was simply added to the others and it reorganized the way in which previous services were used (e.g. instant messaging did not supplant e-mail or texting but just redefined their scope, and social networking sites did not replace phone calls or instant messaging). This process is compatible with what Jay Bolter and Richard Grusin (2000) called remediation, the process by which new media refashion older media. In some cases, the adoption of new channels led to increased usage of an older one, as is happening with texting, which is constantly growing despite the adoption and intense use of social networking sites. This confirms what Haythornthwaite (2005) found regarding the increase of communication exchanges among heavy users of e-mail and the Internet. We also found that there is a snowball effect and that the greater the intensity of exchanges, the more likely people will be to use multiple channels.

What emerged from the longitudinal study and from the diary studies mentioned in the previous section was that the reorganization of channels and the allocation of new functions followed very determined patterns. Not just any channel can replace another for certain exchanges, because each channel is perceived as significantly different and there are sophisticated strategies for selecting one or another for a particular exchange. Long, periodic calls with a distant relative could not be transformed into occasional texting, but would more easily be replaced by a regular Skype call. Similarly, e-mails to distant friends could be replaced by status updates on social networking sites but not by mobile calls. One of our more stable results, when we compared the usage of different channels by individuals over the years, was that channel switch was always among written or among oral channels, but never between modalities; for example, texting would give way to e-mail and voice calls to VoIP calls. The reasons for this rigidity are to be found in the social expectations that underlie synchronous remote communication.

Synchronicity/asynchronicity is without doubt the factor that has the strongest effect on communication practices, because it carries such strong implications for social interaction. Synchronous mediated communication has a very strong prerequisite: that both interlocutors be available at the same time for the conversation—available, willing and ready to dedicate the necessary amount of attention required for the conversation. When two people are face-to-face, it is easy for both interlocutors to see and understand if the other person is available for a conversation. When they are distant, this readiness for conversation must be inferred or negotiated. Many sophisticated social techniques have been developed to ensure readiness, such as sending a text or an e-mail first to ask if a call can be made or prearranging an appointment for a call. Most people are well aware of the demand for attention that a call implies, and this type of request is not done lightly or unconsciously of the social implications. Respondents in the Swisscom studies mentioned that they always thought twice before calling someone they did not know well on their mobile. They would, in any case, not choose a synchronous channel to communicate with a person in a very different hierarchical position, such as a superior or a teacher.[3]

Giving and asking for attention in communication is far from a neutral social behaviour; it requires a sophisticated understanding of social norms and practices. The social practices regarding who we should give attention to first, for how long, how much attention we should request and so forth are highly complex, and there are clear links between attention and power, attention and gender and attention and education. Charles Derber (2000), for instance, argues that status relations, in general, are fundamentally about the distribution of attention-getting and attention-giving across the social hierarchy. Those of lower status are expected to give attention to others. Those of higher status are expected to demand and receive the attention of others. Thus, when either lower-status individuals give attention or upper-status individuals get attention, they confirm their status.

Among our Swiss respondents, we observed that women and men tended to appreciate text messaging for the exact opposite reason. Women liked the fact that they could communicate without disturbing or grabbing attention, and men liked it because they didn't need to get involved in a conversation. Conversely, the people we encountered who didn't like texting were mostly men who claimed that they couldn't stand waiting for an answer and wanted immediate feedback. In other words, men's and women's attitudes to synchronous or asynchronous channel selection are good indicators of their attitudes regarding attention request in their relationships. Similar gendered attitudes to texting and calling were found by my students at the École Nationale Supérieure des Arts Décoratifs (ENSAD) in Paris among young women from North Africa who were studying in France. The young women always sent texts to their brothers also living in France and waited for the brothers to choose the moment to call them. Sending a text rather than calling was done not to save money, but because they felt that it was up to their brothers to decide when they were available for a voice conversation.

To conclude, again and again we see that the choice of a channel has little to do with accessibility and price, but rather reflects people's beliefs about the appropriate communication modality for a certain relationship and a certain context. Attention and power are two of the many factors that are taken into account in this process of selection. There are now several approaches that are engaging with this new complexity, including work on media ecologies by Horst et al. (2010) and the analysis of affordances by Baym (2010). One of the key points made by Madianou and Miller (2011) that is central to a digital anthropology is that polymedia is a resocializing of the media. In my studies, the implications of media difference are now much more closely related to the specifics of the social situation people find themselves in and the nature of their relationships. Moving from availability towards moral responsibility for media choice and a sense of what each media is good or bad for in terms of a given relationship leads us from media studies to more evidently anthropological studies.

Conclusions and Future Directions

The multiplication and diversification of channels is an ongoing process, and we can expect a wide adoption of new media in the next few years. Most of the media that have emerged recently are explicitly aimed at communicating with a larger sphere of ties than the intimate set of contacts that has been addressed with e-mail, cell phones, and voice channels. Although we have argued that, even with social networking sites, most people are still communicating primarily with a close sphere of contacts, there are clear indications that more and more people are also addressing themselves, albeit less frequently, to a wider audience and to weaker connections. This raises a variety of questions on how weaker relationships are maintained and how different social groups present themselves and engage with much less familiar relations. This in turn shifts our investigations of the communicational modalities that people choose from when addressing themselves to a less known social sphere: Which channel will be deemed most appropriate for self-presentation in different contexts and cultures? Which modality is required for different contents and interlocutors and how to speak of others?

Just as in the case of intimate and personal communication, anthropology has much to offer to explain the interaction between digital media and the social norms, agency and practices that emerge in their usage. All of this amounts to an argument for the advancement of digital anthropology itself. An emphasis upon the social context of media use—and communication more generally—is best understood in the light of long-term ethnographic observations on the changing patterns of usage in the context of good knowledge about the social relationships that these media are increasingly integral to.

We are witnessing an exponential increase of available data on users' interactions with digital media with analytics tools that allow us to capture and record the interaction events and the details of individuals' exchanges. This mass of data is, however, often underspecified, lacking the meaning that these interactions actually have for the individuals who engage in them. This is where an anthropological approach brings a unique value; it can transform the interactions into relationships. From a methodological point of view, therefore, the challenge for digital anthropology is to be able to push the limits of traditional ethnographic investigation to incorporate the quantitative data produced by the web analytics, telecom log data and traffic data (which tend to flatten out differences and highlight the generic) and enrich and augment it with the minutiae of the particular. By understanding the where, when, who and what of each communicational event, we can understand how digital media become an integral part of the social experience. By following the evolution of practices over time in a longitudinal approach, we can, as digital anthropologists, contribute to the understanding of the real social implications of digital media.

Notes

1. The Australian study of more than 2,000 people revealed, for instance, that nearly two-thirds of all communications were to family and friends; only 12 per cent of the 13,978 calls made were work-related.
2. We tracked the onset of Internet adoption in France and Italy in a series of studies with novices (Broadbent and Cara 2003; Broadbent and Carles 2001).
3. This difficulty of negotiating attention may explain why voice calls do not seem to increase over the years while the number of text messages continues to increase exponentially. Trade data from CTIA 2010 show that the average length of mobile calls has diminished over time, from just over two minutes to just below two minutes. The International Telecommunication Union (World Telecommunication 2011) estimated that there were 6.1 trillion messages sent in 2010, compared to 1.8 trillion in 2007.

References

Baym, N. 2010. *Personal Connections in the Digital Age.* Cambridge: Polity Press.

Bittman, M., J. E. Brown and J. Wajcman. 2009. The Cell Phone, Constant Connection and Time Scarcity in Australia. *Social Indicators Research* 93(1): 229–33.

Boase, J., and B. Wellman. 2006. Personal Relationships: On and Off the Internet. In *Cambridge Handbook of Personal Relationships*, ed. Anita Vangelisti and Daniel Perlman, 1–19. Cambridge: Cambridge University Press.

Bolter, G., and R. Grusin. 2000 *Remediation: Understanding New Media.* Cambridge, MA: MIT Press.

boyd, d. 2007. Why Youth (Heart) Social Network Sites: The Role of Networked Publics in Teenage Social Life. In *Youth, Identity, and Digital Media Volume*, ed. David Buckingham, 119–42. MacArthur Foundation Series on Digital Learning. Cambridge, MA: MIT Press.

Broadbent, S. 2011. *L'Intimité au Travail.* Paris: FYP Editions.

Broadbent, S., and V. Bauwens. 2008. Understanding Convergence. *Interactions* 15(1): 29–37.

Broadbent, S., and F. Cara. 2003. The New Architectures of Information. In *Texte-e: Le texte à l'heure d'Internet*, ed. G. Origgi and N. Arikha, 197–215. Paris: BPI.

Broadbent, S., and L. Carles. 2001. Evolution des usages de l'Internet. In *Comprendre les usages de l'Internet*, ed. E. Guichard, 156–65. Paris: Presses de l'Ecole Normale Supérieure.

Bull, M. 2000. *Sounding Out the City: Personal Stereos and the Management of Everyday Life.* London: Berg.

Calabrese, F., Z. Smoreda, V. D. Blondel and C. Ratt. 2011. Interplay between Telecommunications and Face-to-Face Interactions: A Study Using Mobile Phone Data. *PLoS ONE* 6(7): e20814. doi:10.1371/journal.pone.0020814.

Campbell, S. W. 2007. Perceptions of Mobile Phone Use in Public Settings: A Cross-Cultural Comparison. *International Journal of Communication* 1: 738–57.

Castells, M. [1996] 2000. *The Rise of the Network Society.* The Information Age: Economy, Society and Culture Vol. I. 2nd ed. Cambridge, MA: Blackwell.

De Bruijn, M., F. Nyamnjoh and I. Brinkman, eds. 2009. *Mobile Phones: The New Talking Drums of Everyday Africa.* Bamenda, Cameroon: Langaa; Leiden: African Studies Centre.

de Gournay, C., and Z. Smoreda. 2003. Communication Technology and Sociability: Between Local Ties and 'Global Ghetto'. In *Machines That Become Us: The Social Context of Personal Communication Technology*, ed. J. E. Katz, 57–70. New Brunswick, NJ: Transaction Publishers.

Derber, C. 2000. *The Pursuit of Attention: Power and Ego in Everyday Life.* New York: Oxford University Press.

Donner, J. 2006. The Use of Mobile Phones by Microentrepreneurs in Kigali, Rwanda: Changes to Social and Business Networks. *Information Technologies and International Development* 3(2): 3–19.

Dourish, P., and V. Bellotti. 1992. Awareness and Coordination in Shared Workspaces. In *Proceedings of the 1992 ACM Conference on Computer-supported Cooperative Work*, 107–14. New York: ACM Press.

Edgell, S. 2006. *The Sociology of Work.* London: Sage.

Facebook Data Team. 2009. Maintained Relationships on Facebook. *The Facebook Data Team Blog.* http://www.facebook.com/note.php?note_id=55257228858.

Fisher, C. 1982. *To Dwell Among Friends: Personal Networks in Town and City.* Chicago: University of Chicago Press.

Fortunati, L. 2003. The Mobile Phone and Democracy: An Ambivalent Relationship. In *Mobile Democracy: Essays on Society, Self and Politics*, ed. Kristóf Nyíri, 239–58. Vienna: Passagen Verlag.

Gergen, J. K. 2008. Mobile Communication and the Transformation of the Democratic Process. In *Handbook of Mobile Communication Studies*, ed. J. E. Katz, 297–310. Cambridge, MA: MIT Press.

Gershon, I. 2010. *The Breakup 2.0.* Ithaca, NY: Cornell University Press.

Goffman, E. 1959. *The Presentation of Self in Everyday Life.* Garden City, NY: Doubleday.

Granovetter, M. 1973. The Strength of Weak Ties. *American Journal of Sociology* 78(6): 1360–80.

Haddon, L. 2004. *Information and Communication Technologies in Everyday Life: A Concise Introduction and Research Guide.* Oxford: Berg.

Haddon, L. 2006. The Contribution of Domestication Research to In-Home Computing and Media Consumption. *The Information Society: An International Journal* 22(4): 195–203.

Hampton, K. N., L. F. Sessions and E. Her. 2011. Core Networks, Social Isolation and New Media. *Information, Communication and Society* 14(1): 130–55.

Harper, R. 2010. *Texture: Human Expression in the Age of Communications Overload.* Boston: MIT Press.

Haythornthwaite, C. 2005. Social Networks and Internet Connectivity Effects. *Information, Communication and Society* 8(2): 125–47.

Hjorth, L. 2008. *Mobile Phone Culture in the Asia Pacific: The Art of Being Mobile.* London: Routledge.

Horst, H., B. Herr-Stephenson and L. Robinson. 2010. Media Ecologies. In *Hanging Out, Messing About and Geeking Out*, ed. M. Ito et al., 29–78. Cambridge, MA: MIT Press.

Horst, H., and D. Miller. 2006. *The Cell Phone: An Anthropology of Communication.* London: Berg.

Igarashi, T., J. Takai and T. Yoshida. 2005. Gender Differences in Social Network Development via Mobile Phone Text Messages: A Longitudinal Study. *Journal of Social and Personal Relationships* 22(5): 619–713.

Ito, M., and D. Okabe. 2005. Contextualizing Japanese Youth and Mobile Messaging. In *Inside the Text: Social Perspectives on SMS in the Mobile Age*, ed. R. Harper, L. Palen and A. Taylor, 1–17. London: Springer Verlag.

Ito, M., D. Okabe, and M. Matsuda, eds. 2005. *Personal, Portable, Pedestrian: The Mobile Phone in Japanese Life.* Cambridge, MA: MIT Press.

Kasesniemi, E. L. 2003. *Mobile Messages: Young People and a New Communication Culture.* Tampere: Tampere University Press.

Katz, J., and M. Aakhus, eds. 2002. *Perpetual Contact: Mobile Communication, Private Talk, Public Performance.* Cambridge: Cambridge University Press.

Kim, H., G. J. Kim, H. W. Park and R. E. Rice. 2007. Configurations of Relationships in Different Media. *Journal of Computer-Mediated Communication* 12(4): article 3.

Kim, K.-H., and H. Yun. 2007. Cying for Me, Cying for Us: Relational Dialectics in a Korean Social Network Site. *Journal of Computer-Mediated Communication* 13(1): article 15.

Kraut, R. E., M. Patterson, V. Lundmark, S. Kiesler, T. Mukhopadhyay and W. Scherlis. 1998. Internet Paradox: A Social Technology That Reduces Social Involvement and Psychological Well-being? *American Psychologist* 53(9): 1017–32.

Kraut, R., W. Scherlis, T. Mukhopadhyay, J. Manning and S. Kiesler. 1996. The HomeNet Field Trial of Residential Internet Services. *Communications of the ACM* 39: 55–63.

Lave, J., and E. Wenger. 1991. *Situated Learning: Legitimate Peripheral Participation.* Cambridge: Cambridge University Press.

Lee, D. 2009. The Impact of Mobile Phones on the Status of Women in India. PhD diss., Stanford University. http://www.mobileactive.org/files/file_uploads/MobilePhonesAndWomenInIndia.pdf.

Levitt, P. 1998. Social Remittances: Migration Driven Local-Level Forms of Cultural Diffusion. *International Migration Review* 32(4): 926–48.

Licoppe, C., and Z. Smoreda. 2005. Rhythms and Ties: Towards a Pragmatics of Technologically-mediated Sociability. In *Domesticating Information Technologies*, ed. R. Kraut, M. Brynin and S. Kiesler, 911–61. Oxford: Oxford University Press.

Ling, R. 2004. *The Mobile Connection.* San Francisco: Morgan Kaufman.

Ling, R. 2008. *New Tech New Ties.* Cambridge, MA: MIT Press.

Ling, R., and S. W. Campbell, eds. 2009. *The Reconstruction of Space and Time: Mobile Communication Practices.* New Brunswick, NJ: Transaction Publishers.

Madden, M., and S. Jones. 2008. *Networked Workers.* The Pew Internet and American Life Project, September. www.pewinternet.org.

Madianou, M., and D. Miller. 2011. *Migration and New Media: Transnational Families and Polymedia.* London: Routledge.

Manceron, V., B. Lelong and Z. Smoreda. 2002. La naissance du premier enfant. *Réseaux* 20(115): 91–121.

Mercier, P., C. Gournay and Z. Smoreda. 2002. Si loin, si proches. Liens et communications à l'épreuve du déménagement. *Réseaux* 20(115): 121–50.

Mollo, V., and P. Falzon. 2004. Auto- and Allo-confrontation as Tools for Reflective Activities. *Applied Ergonomics* 35(6): 531–40.

Nardi, B. A., S. Whittaker and E. Bradner. 2000. Interaction and Outeraction: Instant Messaging in Action. In *Proceedings of the 2000 ACM Conference on Computer Supported Cooperative Work*, 79–88. New York: ACM Press.

Nardi, B., S. Whittaker and H. Schwarz. 2002. NetWORKers and Their Activity in Intentional Networks. *Journal of Computer-supported Cooperative Work* 11(1–2): 205–42.

Nippert-Eng, C. 1996. *Home and Work.* Chicago: University of Chicago Press.

Office of Communication (OFCOM). 2010. *Communications Market Report.* 19 August. London. http://www.ofcom.org.uk/.

Paragas, F. 2005. Migrant Mobiles: Cellular Telephony, Transnational Spaces and the Filipino Diaspora. In *A Sense of Place: The Global and the Local in Mobile Communication*, ed. K. Nyíri, 241–50. Vienna: Passagen Verlag.

Park, Y., G. M. Heo and R. Lee. 2008. Cyworld Is My World: Korean Adult Experiences in an Online Community for Learning. *International Journal of Web Based Communities* 4(1): 33.

The Pew Internet and American Life Project. 2000. *Tracking Online Life: How Women Use the Internet to Cultivate Relationships with Family and Friends.* http://pewinternet.org/Reports/2000/Tracking-Online-Life/Main-Report/Part-1.aspx.

Priyanka, M. 2010. Mobile Phone Usage by Young Adults in India: A Case Study. PhD diss., University of Maryland.

Putnam, R. D. 2000. *Bowling Alone: The Collapse and Revival of American Community.* New York: Simon & Schuster.

Rheingold, H. 2002. *Smart Mobs: The Next Social Revolution.* New York: Basic Books.

Ros, A., and G. De La Fuente Vilar. 2011. Through the Webcam: Bolivian Immigrant Women in Barcelona Communicating with Their Families Back Home. In *Conference Proceedings Digital Diasporas Cambridge 2011.* http://www.crassh.cam.ac.uk/events/1328/77.

Schiano, D., C. Chen, J. Ginsberg, U. Gretarsdottir, M. Huddleston and E. Isaacs. 2002. Teen Use of Messaging Media. In *Extended Abstracts of ACM CHI 2002 Conference on Human Factors in Computing Systems*, 594–5. New York: ACM.

Sennett, R. 1998. *The Corrosion of Character: The Personal Consequences of Work in the New Capitalism.* New York: W. W. Norton.

Spencer, E., and R. Pahl. 2006. *Rethinking Friendship: Hidden Solidarities Today.* Princeton, NJ: Princeton University Press.

Sproull, L., and S. Kiesler. 1991. *Connections: New Ways of Working in the Networked Organization.* Cambridge, MA: MIT Press.

Suchman, L. 1987. *Plans and Situated Actions: The Problem of Human–Machine Communication.* New York: Cambridge University Press.

Turkle, S. 1995. *Life on the Screen: Identity in the Age of the Internet.* New York: Simon & Schuster.

Wallis, C. 2008. Technomobility in the Margins: Mobile Phones and Young Migrant Women in Beijing. Dissertation Abstracts International. A, The Humanities and Social Sciences. ProQuest Information & Learning.

World Telecommunication. 2011. *ICT Indicators Database 2011.* 15th ed. http://www.itu.int/ITU-D/ict/publications/world/world.html.

–7–

Social Networking Sites

Daniel Miller

The Particular Significance of Social Networking Sites for Anthropology

The study of digital anthropology juxtaposes two terms. *Anthropology* is traditionally associated with the study of custom and tradition in small-scale societies rather than with the cutting edge of modernity. Then there is the *digital*, which, by contrast, seems to ratchet up the speed of social change and represents the epitome of rapid transformation. It is no surprise that social networking sites (SNS), the very latest of the major digital media, seem also to have been the fastest in terms of their ability to become a global infrastructure. The first mass usage of SNS was probably that of Cyworld in Korea in 2005, but the best known is the rise of Facebook from an instrument for connecting students at Harvard University to become, within six years, a site used by half a billion people. Facebook has seen recent growth areas in countries such as Indonesia and Turkey and is heading towards older rather than younger persons.

If the rapidity of the development of SNS seems antithetical to anthropology, then their substance seems to suggest close affinity. After all, the very term *social networking* could have been a definition of an anthropological perspective as against, for example, that of psychology. Anthropologists refused to study persons as mere individuals, but, as in the study of kinship, an individual was regarded as a node in a set of relationships, a brother's son or sister's husband, where kinship is understood to be a social network. In contrast to anthropology, sociology was principally concerned with the consequences of an assumed decline from this condition as a result of industrialization, capitalism and urbanism. Still, many of today's most influential books in sociology—such as Putnam's (2001) *Bowling Alone*, Sennett's (1977) *Fall of Public Man* and works by Giddens, Beck and Bauman—remain clearly within this dominant trajectory. In all such work, there is an assumption that older forms of tight social networking colloquially characterized by words such as *community* or *neighbourhood* are increasingly replaced by individualism.

Furthermore within sociology there has been an increasing interest in the idea that these individuals are best understood as networked. So the idea of social networking matched the developments in theory associated with Castells, Granovetter and Wellman (though probably not Latour, who uses the idea of a network for the rather different purpose of incorporating nonhuman agency). Castells made dramatic claims about the rise of the Internet and how 'Our societies are increasingly structured around a bipolar opposition between the Net and the Self' (1996: 3). Over three volumes, Castells (2000) presented what he termed the 'network society', though the main focus was on presumed linkages between new information technologies and new forms of political economy, governance, power and globalization. Coming after the fashion for postmodernism in academic theory, these developments in networking were seen as further extensions of an assumed individualism and fragmentation in modern life.

The theorist who has done the most to keep open the dialogue between online and offline forms of sociality has been Barry Wellman (Boase and Wellman 2006). In his case, it is location-based networking such as neighbourhoods and community that have been, in some measure, replaced by Internet-based networking. Research suggested that online networking may foster a renewal of some degree of offline sociality in new residential settlements (Hampton and Wellman 2003). A further influence was the work of Granovetter (1973), who suggested that sometimes people's weaker and more distant ties could be highly significant—not just their immediate, strong ties. This seemed important for Internet communities which were often partial and transitory.

Postill (2008) provides an anthropological critique of this work (see also Woolgar 2002), urging caution in using the older terminology of community and neighbourhood, but also noting the increasing fetishism of the term *network* arising from this new sociological subdiscipline of social network analysis. Instead (as in this volume), he favoured a more nuanced and contextualized ethnography of the many different social fields in which people engage on—for example short-term activist-related political collectives that emerged from his fieldwork in a Malaysian suburb. This view was supported by Miller and Slater (2000), who had criticized Castells but also argued that Internet-based networks were too dispersed and partial to equate with these older forms of sociality.

The premise of this chapter, however, is that SNS correspond neither to the sociological work of Castells and Wellman on networks nor to the critiques of Postill, Miller and Slater. Rather, SNS have turned out to be something much closer to older traditions of anthropological study of social relations such as kinship studies. The critical points made by Postill, Miller and Slater followed evidence that Internet networks tended to be specialist and partial, associated with specific interests. By contrast, SNS are, in several important respects, quite the opposite of the earlier Internet. On Facebook, peer-to-peer friendships were joined by family and kin-based networks and, in some cases, also saw the dissolution of the distinctions between home and work (Broadbent 2011), thereby bringing together in one place what had been separate networks. As such, SNS challenge the fundamental premise that separates sociology from anthropology: that the overlapping social relationships that were foundational to anthropological study inevitably decline towards the more separated-out networks that are central to sociology.

A similar problem arises with the idea of networked individualism as fostered by Castells and Wellman. To preempt my second case study on usage by migrants, a recent article by McKay (2011) demonstrates the flaws in such arguments. McKay has been working for many years with people from the northern Philippines and with their dispersed migrant families. She notes how those who remain in the Philippines often juxtapose their presentation of themselves on SNS with old black-and-white historical photographs of kin. In addition, they use photographs of old buildings from the local town or iconic photographs from collections made about the Philippines in older times. They recognize that when a family member in the diaspora comes to their site, they have to represent not just an autonomous individual, but a node within an extended and ancestral family and site. McKay theorizes that these extensions, using the work of Strathern (1996) and Melanesian concepts of personhood, are premised on entirely different concepts of the person from the individualism presumed by Wellman.

From this evidence we may construct a larger argument. Instead of focusing on SNS as the vanguard of the new, and the rapidity of its global reach, it may well be that SNS are so quickly accepted in places as such as Indonesia and Turkey because their main impact is to redress some of the isolating and individualizing impacts of other new technologies and allow people to return to certain kinds of intense and interwoven forms of social relationship that they otherwise feared were being lost. SNS have, then, an extraordinary ability to return the world to the kinds of sociality that were the topic of traditional anthropological concern and, as such, are hugely important to contemporary anthropology and the future of the discipline. As suggested in the introduction to this volume, we have most to learn from the normativity quickly imposed upon these technologies.

Studies of SNS

The first attempt to create a more systematic engagement with SNS was probably that of danah boyd building on her initial thesis work on platforms such as Friendster. Her review (boyd and Ellison 2007) of the history and range of SNS has become even more important now that journalistic treatments (and the influential film *The Social Network*) seem to be simplifying that history as though there was some inevitable trajectory that led towards the current dominance of Facebook, based on the particular personality and vision of Mark Zuckerberg. By contrast, boyd shows that Facebook arose alongside a whole slew of SNS and that much of what subsequently developed was more happenstance than intention. SNS could migrate quickly from their intended base and their intended function. So a US site such as Orkut could end up as the main SNS of Brazil, and a dating site such as Friendster could evolve into a very different genre that dominated SNS usage in South East Asia. At least initially, movement was rapid between SNS, most conspicuously in the rise and decline of MySpace, whose impact was less on sociality per se than on new ways of disseminating music to mass audiences. Cyworld was already almost ubiquitous amongst South Korean youth by 2005 and remains dominant there. So the triumph of Facebook may not reflect any particular superior functionality, but merely the overwhelming desire of everyone to be on the same site combined with a unique ability to spread through emulation. Just as US colleges took to Facebook in emulation of its origins at Harvard, so I could observe, over the course of 2009 to 2010, how Facebook took over from Friendster in the Philippines, principally based on the prestige of early adoption in key Manila universities.

Recent anthropological work, including that of boyd, Heather Horst and Mimi Ito (Ito et al. 2010), looks at more general use within friendship circles of teenagers in the United States, while Gershon (2010) has documented the importance of Facebook in relationship breakup amongst US students. All such work contributes to what has probably become the single most sustained discussion of the implications of SNS, which was predicted in the title of boyd's (2008) article, 'Facebook's Privacy Trainwreck'. The argument was that the ideology behind Facebook, where the default was complete openness, had led users into a level of public exposure that was both unintended and could have quite problematic consequences (especially for children; see Livingstone 2008, 2009). Questions arose as to whether individuals' relationships could be threatened by the evidence of who else they spent time with, or whether having fun misbehaving at a party could result in being refused a job, as employers inspected applicants' Facebook pages. The ultimate threat was the exposure of children to sexual predation. As anthropologists have noted, SNS simply do not correspond to more traditional oppositions between a public sphere and the private (boyd 2007; Gershon 2010). Rather, SNS such as Facebook tend to reflect an aggregate of an individual's private spheres, the previously dyadic contact with each friend or relative co-present in the same space. This is not at all the same as broadcasting to a more general public, though the latter may be fostered in the more journalistic style of Twitter.

There is a singularly important trajectory from the work of anthropologists who are focused on issues of privacy and exposure in private and intimate life to the increasing concern with the same conundrum about exposure and privacy in respect to politics. The point is evident in the contrast between two recent high-profile books about SNS. *The Facebook Effect* (Kirkpatrick 2010) starts with a story about how a Facebook site became the catalyst for a popular movement in Colombia, mobilizing ten million people in street demonstrations, which curbed the violence and kidnapping by the Fuerzas Armadas Revolucionarias de Colombia (or Revolutionary Armed Forces of Colombia) guerrilla movement. By contrast, Morozov (2011), in *The Net Delusion* suggests that the claims made for Twitter and Facebook in facilitating the

Green protests in Iran were wildly exaggerated. He suggests that there is rather more evidence that these media represent documentation that can be used by repressive regimes for locating and suppressing dissent (see Postill, this volume). Similar issues arise on the development side of anthropological work, where SNS have been instrumental in relief efforts ranging from typhoons in the Philippines to earthquakes in Haiti—but, again, we lack the ethnographic evidence to properly assess such claims.

Case One: The Comparative Anthropology of SNS

One would expect that a major part of any anthropological contribution to the study of SNS would be that of cultural relativism, based on the assumption that different regions gradually appropriate SNS through processes of localization to emerge as specific to the cultural concerns of that region. A classic argument of that kind, though not strictly related to SNS, was Humphrey's (2009) study of Russian chat rooms. She notes how many users view their avatars and other aspects of their online presence in a singularly Russian manner. As one of her informants puts it, 'The *avatar* is not designed to demonstrate the person's face. It should convey the inner state of the person, his soul, one might say, or the condition of his soul' (40–1). The analogy, familiar from Russian literature, is that ordinary life is a suppression of the true inner being of the person, which lies deep in the soul and which is both profound and expressive. Viewing these avatars as somehow closer to that inner being and capable of the more direct expression of powerful emotions suggests that online activity accords with what has been taken as quintessentially Russian (compare Miller 2011: 40–52, on the idea of Facebook as the book of truth).

As already noted, notwithstanding all the current attention to Facebook, the first significant establishment of SNS was Cyworld which was ubiquitous amongst South Korea youth by 2005. Studies by Hjorth (2009, 2010) and others (e.g. Qiu 2009) suggest that many features of this and other East Asian SNS closely reflect the underlying cultural priorities of those regions. For example, in Cyworld, one's friends and contacts are subject to a series of circles from the closest to the most distant. This seems to be modelled on the same idea of concentric circles as defined within Korean kinship. East Asian sites also tend to use a genre of the 'cute', which is seen as a kind of warm domestication of what otherwise might be experienced as the colder edge of new technologies. SNS such as QQ in China show more concern with the development of an avatar than the mere representation of the user and have tighter integration of gaming. Far more money tends to be spent on the 'interior decoration' of such sites, all of which suggests that there are elements which may be distinctly regional.

After using anthropological relativism to establish regional difference, we are then in a position to engage in the comparative analysis of SNS. The potential is evident in the work of Stefana Broadbent (2011, also this volume), who has developed the concept of attention. Synchronous communication such as instant messaging or phone calls demand immediate attention from one's correspondent, and this claim to attention raises various issues of power and control. By contrast, Facebook is one of the least engaging and demanding channels. Being a semipublic act, a posting is not to anyone in particular and so doesn't require or demand the attention of any other particular correspondent. The significance of Broadbent's point becomes much clearer through her comparison of Facebook and Cyworld. If in Cyworld you agree to be a Cy-ilchon—a very close relation—then you are socially bound by expectations of immediate reciprocity to comment on each other. Most people have fewer than twenty Cy-ilchons. So Cyworld comes with the demands for attention and the burdens of intense sociality that are what make media such as e-mail and instant messaging feel a bit like work, even when they are used for leisure communication. This is in clear contrast to Facebook.

This stage of comparative studies is based on noting the differences between regions with respect to their particular dominant SNS. But the possibility of making such comparisons might seem negated by the rise of Facebook at the expense of all other alternative SNS. Once Facebook becomes globally ubiquitous, then the only way we can retain the insights of comparison is by focusing instead upon the regional differences of the use of Facebook. So, for example, we can still address Broadbent's issue of attention by noting that, in the Philippines, there seems to be much more pressure to respond to postings by friends than there is in the United Kingdom.

At the same time, there are dangers in any claim to localized difference. For example several commentators have suggested that Facebook is some kind of emanation or reflection of the neoliberalism of the contemporary US political economy, and that Happy Farm, the most popular SNS-related game in China, differs from the Facebook equivalent, Farmville, because stealing crops is an integral element in the former but not the latter. The presence of stealing is claimed to show the ambivalence felt in China towards capitalism as represented in the game. But it would be just as easy to argue that China today is far less ambivalent about capitalism than most other regions. Arguments about comparison and regional localism need to be based on more sustained analysis of wider contexts of usage rather than glib assertions that SNS must embody the entire political economy of their context.

In our earlier study of the Internet in Trinidad (Miller and Slater 2000), we argued for a larger dialectical analysis. Most studies at that time understood their brief as documenting processes of globalization and localization. So they might have written an account of what happens to the Internet when it becomes appropriated by Trinidadians. But we argued that there simply was no such thing as *the Internet* per se. Rather, the Internet was that which people engaged in online in some particular place. We should not privilege US or UK usage as *the Internet*, which could be equally exemplified by each and every place. With respect to any given region, we could only document what the Internet is through its use by Trinidadians, or what Trinidadians had become thanks to the Internet. A similar argument is implied by the very way Trinidadians talk about Facebook. Quite often the site is referred to as either *Fasbook* or *Macobook.* In Trinidadian dialect, to be *fas* is to try and get to know another person rather too quickly, as compared to the accepted etiquette. To be *maco* is to be nosy, constantly prying into other people's private business. Since both of these terms are seen as particularly characteristic of Trinidadian behaviour, there seems to be a natural affinity between the propensity within the infrastructure of Facebook itself and the cultural inclination of Trinidadians. A leading historian of Trinidad told me a story about how, when the Caribbean islands were considering coming together in a united political entity in the late 1950s, they decided against making the Trinidadian capital of Port of Spain the base for the new federation for fear of the disruptive effect of the Trinidadian love of rumour and gossip. So this idea that Trinidadians are naturally *fas* and *maco* is nothing new.

In a previous work (Miller 1992), I argued that the word *bacchanal* is perhaps the most common expression of what people feel it means to be distinctly Trinidadian and that this had been previously expressed through an attachment to an imported US soap opera, *The Young and the Restless.* Bacchanal in turn relies upon the central role of sex in Trinidad as an expression of the truth about what humans in the end really are, and what they will inevitably end up doing despite themselves. Gender itself is constituted by a basic exchange relationship between sex and labour. Women, for example, are sceptical of formal marriage since their husbands may then take sex for granted, rather than it being dependent on men continuing to work on behalf of the wider family (Miller 1994: 168–201). All these concepts gain their most explicit expression in the annual festival of Carnival, which celebrates the values of bacchanal.

In these studies I was attempting to map out the core values of Trinidadian life, often in contrast with other values such as respectability and religious ideals promulgated within Pentecostalism. In *Tales from Facebook* (Miller 2011), I examine in detail the degree to which Facebook is now viewed as expressive of these core Trini values. There are many examples within that book which demonstrate why it feels as though Facebook was predestined for Trinidad, notwithstanding its origins at Harvard University. For example the way Facebook's technology of tagging photographs of people seen in public leads to the exposure of individuals in the company of the wrong people is one of the main sources for the eruption of bacchanal in contemporary Trinidad.

The first of the portraits in *Tales from Facebook* is of a marriage breaking down because of Facebook. This occurs not because of what the husband thinks people in general do with Facebook, but because of what his wife can't help but do: as a typical *macotious* Trini, she constantly looks into the private world of every woman her husband has any contact with on Facebook. It is less clear whether the fact that the verb 'to friend' already existed in Trinidad and traditionally meant 'to have sex with' has a bearing on such cases. When a person I call Vishala says that the truth of another person is more likely to be found in his or her Facebook profile than through meeting the person face-to-face, this again implies a very Trinidadian concept of truth and authenticity as found in appearance as opposed to the deception which is found deep within a person. Similarly, when the businessman Burton argues that, to understand Facebook, you need first to appreciate how people are themselves social networking sites, he frames this by what he regards as the particular way Trinis engage in business as opposed to business practices he witnessed working abroad. Even the particular Trinidadian version of Pentecostal and Apostolic churches manages to find ways to express their specific values and ideals through Facebook. Indeed, the whole experience of using Facebook may be described using the term *liming*, which is how Trinidadians understand their particular mode of socializing. Originally associated with street-corner life and hanging out with others, liming has gradually broadened in connotation to a more general hanging out. But its significance here is that it is used to render Facebook once more as a specifically Trinidadian practice rather than as an imported infrastructure.

These arguments are crucial to contemporary anthropology. If the globalization of drinks such as Coca-Cola, or of digital instruments such as Facebook, indicate only global homogenization, then this implies a decline in cultural diversity and specificity—the core concerns of anthropological investigation. However, if these imported products become subject to processes that make their regional appropriation distinctive, then they can become the source of new forms of cultural diversity. If, as I have argued above, they only ever exist in respect to the specific cultural practices of some particular population, then there is really no difference from traditional anthropological apprehensions of cultural diversity. So anthropology is showing some self-interest here. It becomes a more relevant and necessary discipline to the degree that Facebook is transformed into *Fasbook.* Though to take this one stage further, the point is not that Facebook is localized so much as that *Fasbook* is invented by Trinidadians at the same time as Trinidadians are dialectically changed through their use of *Fasbook.* For the anthropologist, there is no such thing as Facebook; there is only the aggregate of its particular usages by specific populations. The relativism of anthropology pertains, then, not just to the differences between Orkut, Twitter, QQ, Facebook and Cyworld; it is also the heterogeneity of each SNS as made evident from what we may hope will soon be multiple ethnographic encounters.

Case Two: The Use of SNS by Migrants

The importance of the Internet for migrant populations who are separated from their families has been clear for some time (e.g. Horst and Panagakos 2006). It is not surprising that this importance has extended to SNS for their ability to unite diaspora populations and facilitate their connections with their homeland. An example is provided by Oosterbaan (2010a, 2010b), who studied the way in which Orkut has quickly established itself as a major point of reference and organization for the diaspora Brazilian populations of Europe, often based around virtual groups associated with particular cities such as Barcelona and Amsterdam. Similarly in Shenzhen, perhaps the world's fastest-growing modern city, QQ is being used by migrant taxi drivers to bring together the new local social networks based around work with their originally kin-based networks. QQ is seen as more personal and less instrumental than telephone calls back to one's place of origin (Wei and Qian 2009: 819). Other studies in China note how internal migrants also chat to strangers as another pool of sociality (Qiu 2009: 99), with mobile QQ often dominating for reasons of cost (Cheng 2011). In most regions, SNS are generally used by migrants as part of a constellation of media. For example the Polish migrants in Ireland studied by Komito and Bates (2009) mainly use the Polish-based SNS Nasza-Klasa in a relatively passive manner simply to keep up to date with other Poles and use other media for more active social engagement.

Between 2008 and 2010, I carried out a research project with Mirca Madianou on Filipina migrant mothers and their left-behind children (Madianou and Miller 2011). Much of our research was conducted in the United Kingdom, but we also travelled to the Philippines to meet the children of the women we had worked with. At that time, the most common social networking sites we encountered in the Philippines were Friendster, Facebook and Multiply. SNS are used alongside other media in retaining connections—for example when someone finds that many of his or her school friends have now emigrated for work. Sometimes one SNS is used for maintaining formal family connections (including posting photographs of family events such as births and weddings), while another SNS is used for informal postings. Many of the older women in the United Kingdom learned to use such sites mainly for communicating with kin.

In the Philippines, as elsewhere, a pivotal moment in the transformation of SNS was when individuals started to receive friends requests from their mothers. This signalled a movement from college or peer linkages to the incorporation of core kinship networks. Some of these linkages were experienced as highly positive encounters—such as when children felt that this combination of distance and intimacy allowed them to achieve a more adult relationship with their parents. Their physical separation combined with easy communication had provided just the right degree of autonomy to facilitate this change in their relationship. In another case, however, a left-behind child found his idealized imagination of his mother shattered when he gained access to her Friendster account and saw the kinds of party pictures that women commonly post on SNS. SNS can also lead to closer surveillance—for example over the use of remittances, meeting children's boyfriends and girlfriends and compensating for absence by imposing high degrees of control on left-behind children.

The importance of this research is that it challenges the simple idea that migration leads to a loss of communication in relationships that is then repaired by the advent of new media. What we encountered was more complex and ambivalent, with at least some of the children claiming that the ease of communication with their mothers that came from new media made their lives worse rather than better. Some of these children felt an overuse of such sites for surveillance. And some children felt that the increased media contact exposed the inability of absent parents to relate to them as they grew and changed—evident, for example, in the way that parents still sent them presents more suited to younger children. In the Philippines, SNS are also the main places for blogging, and issues arose when children blogged their private anxieties and resentments with regard to their absent parents (see also Rettberg 2008: 77–80). In some cases, the highly public nature of posting led the entire diasporic extended family to acknowledge disputes that otherwise would have been managed more privately. We also found that, while the etiquette was to accept all friend requests in the Philippines, usage in the United Kingdom sometimes reflected growing class divisions, for example between nurses and domestic workers (compare Hargittai 2007).

McKay's (2011) work on the use of Facebook amongst Filipino migrants in London reinforces this view of the ambiguous and sometimes negative consequences of SNS for migrants. She also brings us back to issues of politics and privacy and the way these connect the intimate with wider politics. These migrants mainly use Facebook so that they can follow each other's social lives in detail—where someone has visited, what they wore, who they were with and so forth. Mostly they belong to the same church network, which itself runs a Facebook group, and they enthusiastically examine photos from church events. Most of the photographs posted are typically domestic and quotidian. This is a population whose origin is in a northern rural area where close kinship, ritual and trust are retained as aspects of community, and these features of social life are exported to the new London environment.

But as I have argued with respect to the Trinidadian study (Miller 2011), real communities have always been subject to contradictory forces, including petty jealousies, long-term quarrels and exclusions. Most of these migrants are illegal, and at the extreme there is a constant fear that internal quarrels might lead to one person reporting another to the police, with subsequent deportation. The problem is that they find it impossible to limit this Facebook openness, for reasons that McKay (following Strathern 1996) argues are intrinsic to the way kinship and reciprocity tends to work within bilateral systems of kinship.

So Facebook can exacerbate quarrels and tensions, leading to people being cropped out of photographs or accused of witchcraft, all of which activity is as much followed by those who remain in the villages in the Philippines as those who are based now in London. In short, Facebook tends to up the ante on the critical tension between trust and risk that is bound to arise for a migrant community in a situation of semilegal status in a foreign land. So instead of distancing them from traditional contradictions of community, it makes these community-like aspects of social life even more intense.

The initial literature on migration naturally focuses upon the use of SNS to recover and maintain links with the homeland. But it is also possible to take a more radical view of where SNS might lead in the future. Instead of regarding SNS as simply a means to communication between two given localities, it is also possible to start thinking about SNS as places in which people in some sense actually live. A Filipina worker in London whom I know well makes no use any of the local facilities, never going out to pubs or to watch films. Apart from working, sleeping and eating in London, she spends her time on SNS in the company of friends and kin. In *Tales from Facebook* (Miller 2011), we find the story of Dr. Karamath, who is disabled and so never steps out of his house in Trinidad. He lives as much as possible within Facebook, where he 'works' aggregating activist information on human rights and 'socializes' with a group of friends from the South Asian diaspora. It makes more sense to see such individuals as living inside the SNS rather than in the physical location in which they sleep and eat.

Viewing Facebook more as a kind of home than as a type of communication between homes helps make sense of one of the key ways in which people use SNS: as a site for 'interior decoration'. It helps explain how people tidy, decorate and adorn their sites. As Horst has shown, it may be quite hard to distinguish between a US teenager decorating her bedroom and decorating her MySpace site. The teen may even deliberately choose a common colour scheme for both (Horst 2009). In Trinidad, much of the time spent on Facebook is in uploading photographs or links that effectively create a personal aesthetic. Indeed, the term *interior decoration* makes for a convenient pun, since it is even more evident on Facebook than in room decoration that what is emerging in the public space is a sense of the interior—that is the private space of the individual externalized onto this digital domain. This seems still more appropriate when we see that many of the exchanges taking place are trivial, inconsequential items about the day's events that are more like the communication between people who are co-present in the same home. So one ironic effect of the increasing transnationalism and cosmopolitanism of migration is that SNS are also in the vanguard of creating a new form of domesticity, where such sites are emerging as places within which migrants could be said to live rather than being merely technologies of communication. This linkage with the domestic is the subject of Horst's chapter within this volume.

Future Studies

This chapter has focused narrowly on SNS, but in the future it is likely that studies of specific digital media will have to consider the wider context of polymedia. *Polymedia* is a term developed by Madianou and myself to reflect a critical transformation in digital communicative media more generally (see also Baym 2010). Polymedia follows where a population has paid for computer usage or a smartphone. This means that they have access to up to a dozen different ways of communicating and that the cost of an individual act of communication lies in the background expense of the infrastructure rather than the actual act of communication. Under such circumstances, it is harder to assert that the reason for picking this or that media was one of either cost or access. Rather, a person is held responsible for which media he or she chooses to use. Gershon (2010) shows that when boyfriends and girlfriends are dumped, the key question may be why they chose to do this by phone or text or e-mail or Facebook and what that says about the person. Madianou and Miller (2011) argue that this attribution of moral responsibility in effect resocializes media use in general, as we move from technological considerations to the new normativities that exist in any given society around the meaning of any particular media.

At the same time that we may contextualize SNS as one of many alternative media that are being used, we also see that SNS have themselves been transformed into instruments of polymedia, as they allow people to use instant messaging or other forms of messaging within the SNS site. Similarly, SNS are currently migrating from computer to smartphone, increasing the sense that SNS are always-on media which can be checked incessantly. In conclusion, one future direction of study is likely to be the subsuming of SNS within researching polymedia more generally.

A similar issue to that of polymedia is an increasing appreciation of how SNS expand in their connectivity with many other topics within this volume. For example, to take Malaby's contribution, SNS may become linked to games such as World of Warcraft (e.g. Golub 2010). More than that, they may represent a fundamental change in gaming culture itself. Today the most important online games in global terms may have become those that are actually embedded within SNS such as Facebook and QQ. Hjorth (2010) points out that Happy Farm and Farmville look nothing like the teenage world of traditional hardcore gaming such as Halo and World of Warcraft. Happy Farm and Farmville are more likely to be dominated by an entirely different demographic, such as older women. Other growing links are with YouTube, where the following of sites can lead to the development of particular networks (Lange 2007) and the entire spectrum of digital media discussed in this volume.

Although some SNS such as Facebook are increasingly seen as global in scope, there has also been a proliferation of more specialist and targeted SNS that pertain to more particular anthropological studies, such as the elderly or various subcultures of sexual orientation or music (Baym 2007; Madden 2010). For example gay men in the Philippines tend to retain links to SNS specifically associated with that subculture while maintaining other links to family and others in Friendster and Facebook. Detailed study of such usage helps depose common stereotypes. In Australia, not only do the elderly use the Internet, but a seventy-year-old may be quicker at turning such contacts into direct sexual activity than the young (Malta and Farquharson 2010). So the study of dominant and global SNS needs to be complemented by the continued importance of more specialist SNS. We are also likely to see more specialist anthropological analysis, for example exploiting the evidence of such textual material for work in anthropological linguistics (e.g. Jones and Schiefflin 2009; Jones, Schiefllin and Smith 2011).

Anthropology is a discipline that balances its concern for the particular with more universal ambitions. In the last sections of *Tales from Facebook* (Miller 2011), I indicated the potential for a much wider anthropological engagement with SNS, exploring issues of cosmology and theory. In studying Facebook, it is soon apparent that the site exhibits a surplus communicative economy in that people seem to do all sorts of things with it that are hard to reduce to some simply communicative need or any other form of instrumentalism. At one stage, I turn the usual logic around and ask whether, instead of seeing Facebook as a means to facilitate friendships between people, many of us use friendships between people to facilitate a relationship to Facebook itself. SNS could be then seen as a meta–best friend who we could turn to when no one else wanted to be socially engaged with us, such as in the early morning when we feel lonely and are unable to sleep.

This accounts for some but not all of the observable surplus communicative economy. It still doesn't explain the large number of SNS friends who are not part of any active SNS interaction or the more recent trend—at least in Trinidad—to post quite revealing material that may not place the user in the most flattering light. Social networks also seem to generate their own compulsion to visibility. Just as people don't feel they are actually on holiday unless they see photographs of themselves enjoying that holiday, so today some people don't seem to feel they have had an experience of an event unless they have broadcast it through Facebook or Twitter. In *Tales from Facebook*, I speculate about a cosmological aspect to SNS in which it acts as a point of 'witnessing' which allows us to view ourselves as moral beings whose actions are always subject to adjudication—something that traditionally we might have ascribed to the gaze of the divine but here is rendered as a generic *other* consisting of that wide canopy of SNS friends beyond those we actually communicate with. In short it suggests that SNS are also a form of moral encompassment that gives them a cosmological significance.

The implication of such arguments is to bring SNS back to the terrain of anthropological theory and the wider ambitions of anthropology as a discipline for understanding the fundamental nature of society and culture. This is also the reason why *Tales from Facebook* ends with a detailed analogy drawn between the study of the Kula ring and that of SNS. The argument is that, at least for Munn (1986) in her book *The Fame of Gawa*, Kula served as emblematic of culture, because it was an instrument for what she calls 'intersubjective spacetime': the scale of the world within which people can live and gain fame. There are positive transformations that expand this spacetime and negative transformations that shrink it. My proposition is that Facebook acts to replace the immediate consumption of conversation, just as Gawa forbids the immediate consumption of produce. These conversations must first be sent out into wider spheres, where they create an expansion of spacetime, with a much greater range of people involved in that communication. But the same instruments that assist in this expansion of spacetime also retain the potential for destroying and diminishing spacetime, such as bachannal in Trinidad or witchcraft in Gawa. These also operate as an important sanction which secures normative and moral usage of Facebook or Kula. So culture itself can grow or it can shrink, and Facebook is analogous to Kula as an instrument for this growth and contraction. At this level, SNS can contribute to the further development of core theory in anthropology.

The sheer ubiquity of SNS means that they are likely to become an aspect of almost any area of anthropological study in the future—from economic life and religion to development studies and medical anthropology. But the reason for focusing so tightly upon SNS within the more general realm of digital anthropology is that SNS possess qualities that seem to have a particular affinity with the discipline of anthropology itself. If my argument is correct, then the importance of SNS is not the unprecedented brave new world they open up, but their inherent conservatism, which helps to bring back the intense social relationships and the interconnectedness between what had become separated-out fields of sociality. Throughout this chapter I have argued that it is not just that anthropologists can study SNS, it is that SNS may be bringing the world back closer to the premises of anthropological research.

References

Baym, N. 2007. The New Shape of Online Community: The Example of Swedish Independent Music Fandom. *First Monday* 12(8) (6 August). http://firstmonday.org/htbin/cgiwrap/bin/ojs/index.php/fm/rt/printerFriendly/1978/1853.

Baym, N. 2010. *Personal Connections in the Digital Age.* Cambridge: Polity Press.

Boase, J., and B. Wellman. 2006. Personal Relationships: On and Off the Internet. In *Handbook of Personal Relations*, ed. D. Perlman and A. Vangelisti, 709–26. Cambridge: Cambridge University Press.

boyd, d. 2007. Why Youth (Heart) Social Network Sites: The Role of Networked Publics in Teenage Social Life. In *Youth, Identity, and Digital Media*, ed. D. Buckingham, 119–42. Cambridge, MA: MIT Press.

boyd, d. 2008. Facebook's Privacy Trainwreck: Exposure, Invasion, and Social Convergence. *Convergence* 14(1): 13–20.

boyd, d., and N. B. Ellison. 2007. Social Network Sites: Definition, History and Scholarship. *Journal of Computer-Mediated Communication* 13(1): article 11.

Broadbent, S. 2011. *L'Intimité au Travail.* Paris: Fyp Editions.

Castells, M. 1996. *The Rise of the Network Society, The Information Age: Economy, Society and Culture.* Vol. 1. Cambridge, MA: Blackwell.

Castells, M. 2000. *The Information Age: Economy, Society and Culture.* Updated ed., 3 vols. Oxford: Blackwell.

Cheng, C.-T. 2011. Migration, Diaspora and Information Technology in Global Societies. In *Routledge Research in Migration, Diaspora and Information Technology in Global Societies*, ed. L. Fortunati, R. Pertierra, and J. Vincent, 218–29. London: Routledge.

Gershon, I. 2010. *Breakup 2.0: Disconnecting over New Media.* Ithaca, NY: Cornell University Press.

Golub, A. 2010. Being in the World (of Warcraft): Raiding, Realism, and Knowledge Production in a Massively Multiplayer Online Game. *Anthropological Quarterly* 83(1): 17–45.

Granovetter, M. 1973. The Strength of Weak Ties. *American Journal of Sociology* 78(6): 1360–80.

Hampton, K., and B. Wellman. 2003. Neighboring in Netville. *City and Community* 2(4): 277–311.

Hargittai, E. 2007. Whose Space? Differences among Users and Non-users of Social Network Sites. *Journal of Computer-Mediated Communication* 13(1): article 14. http://jcmc.indiana.edu/vol13/issue1/hargittai.html.

Hjorth, L. 2009. Gifts of Presence: A Case Study of a South Korean Virtual Community, Cyworld's Mini-Hompy. In *Internationalising the Internet Anthology*, ed. G. Goggin and M. McLelland, 237–51. London: Routledge.

Hjorth, L. 2010. The Game of Being Social: Web 2.0, Social Media, and Online Games. *Iowa Journal of Communication* 42(1): 73–92.

Horst, H. 2009. Aesthetics of the Self: Digital Mediations. In *Anthropology and the Individual*, ed. D. Miller, 99–114. Oxford: Berg.

Horst, H., and A. Panagakos. 2006. Return to Cyberia: Technology and the Social Worlds of Transnational Migrants. *Global Networks* 6(2): 109–24.

Humphrey, C. 2009. The Mask and the Face: Imagination and Social Life in Russian Chat Rooms and Beyond. *Ethnos* 74(1): 31–50.

Ito, M., S. Baumer, M. Bittanti, d. boyd, R. Cody, B. Herr-Stephenson, H. Horst, P. Lange, D. Mahendran, K. Martinez, C. Pascoe, D. Perkel, L. Robinson, C. Sims and L. Tripp. 2010. *Hanging Out, Messing Around, Geeking Out: Living and Learning with New Media*. Cambridge, MA: MIT Press.

Jones, G., and B. Schiefflin. 2009. Talking Text and Talking Back: 'My BFF Jill' from Boob Tube to YouTube. *Journal of Computer-Mediated Communication* 14: 1050–79.

Jones, G., B. Schiefllin and R. Smith. 2011. When Friends Who Talk Together Stalk Together: Online Gossip as Metacommunication. In *Digital Discourse: Language in the New Media*, ed. C. Thurlow and K. Mroczek, 26–47. Oxford: Oxford University Press.

Kirkpatrick, D. 2010. *The Facebook Effect.* London: Virgin Books.

Komito, L., and J. Bates. 2009. Virtually Local: Social Media and Community among Polish Nationals in Dublin. *ASLIB Proceedings: New Information Perspectives* 61(3): 232–44.

Lange, P. G. 2007. Publicly Private and Privately Public: Social Networking on YouTube. *Journal of Computer-Mediated Communication* 13(1): article 18. http://jcmc.indiana.edu/vol13/issue1/lange.html.

Livingstone, S. 2008. Taking Risky Opportunities in Youthful Content Creation: Teenagers' Use of Social Networking Sites for Intimacy, Privacy and Self-expression. *New Media and Society* 10: 393–411.

Livingstone, S. 2010. *Children and the Internet.* Cambridge: Polity Press.

Madden, M. 2010. *Older Adults and the Social Media.* Report from the Pew Internet and American Life Project. http://pewinternet.org/Reports/2010/Older-Adults-and-Social-Media/Report.aspx.

Madianou, M., and D. Miller. 2011. *Technologies of Love: Migration and the Polymedia Revolution.* London: Routledge

Malta, S., and K. Farquharson. 2010. Old Dogs, New Tricks? Online Dating and Older Adults. In *Proceedings of the Emerging Researchers in Ageing (ERA) Conference*, Newcastle, Australia, 21–2 October, 115–19.

McKay, D. 2011. On the Face of Facebook: Historical Images and Personhood in Filipino Social Networking. *History and Anthropology* 21(4): 483–502.

Miller, D. 1992. The Young and the Restless in Trinidad: A Case of the Local and the Global in Mass Consumption. In *Consuming Technologies*, ed. R. Silverstone and E. Hirsch, 163–82. London: Routledge.

Miller, D. 1994. *Modernity: An Ethnographic Approach.* Oxford: Berg.

Miller, D. 2011. *Tales from Facebook.* Cambridge: Polity Press.

Miller, D., and D. Slater. 2000. *The Internet: An Ethnographic Approach.* Oxford: Berg.

Morozov, E. 2011. *The Net Delusion.* London: Allen Lane.

Munn, N. 1986. *The Fame of Gawa.* Cambridge: Cambridge University Press.

Oosterbaan, M. 2010a. Virtual Migration: Brazilian Diasporic Media and the Reconfigurations of Place and Space. *Revue Européenne des Migrations Internationales* 26(1): 81–102.

Oosterbaan, M. 2010b. Virtual Re-evangelization: Brazilian Churches, Media and the Postsecular City. In *Exploring the Postsecular: The Religious, the Political, the Urban*, ed. J. Beaumont, A. Molendijk and C. Jedan, 281–308. Leiden: Brill.

Postill, J. 2008. Localizing the Internet beyond Communities and Networks. *New Media Society* 10: 413.

Putnam, R. 2001. *Bowling Alone.* New York: Simon & Schuster.

Qiu, J. 2009. *Working-Class Network Society: Communication Technology and the Information Have-Less in Urban China.* Cambridge, MA: MIT Press.

Rettberg, J. 2008. *Blogging.* Cambridge: Polity Press.

Sennett, R. 1977. *The Fall of Public Man.* New York: Knopf.

Strathern, M. 1996. Cutting the Network. *Journal of the Royal Anthropological Institute* 2: 517–35.

Wei, D., and T. Qian. 2009. The Mobile Hearth: A Case Study on New Media Usage and Migrant Workers' Social Relationship. Paper presented at the ANZCA Conference, June. http://www.anzca.net/conferences/anzca09proceedings.html.

Woolgar, S., ed. 2002. *Virtual Society?* Oxford: Oxford University Press.

Part IV
Politicizing Digital Anthropology

–8–

Digital Politics and Political Engagement

John Postill

The growing use of digital media by political actors of all kinds (including politicians, journalists, activists and religious leaders) has given rise to a thriving literature, albeit one that is divided along disciplinary and technological lines. It is only very recently that the term *digital politics* has begun to acquire currency. This appears to signal the birth of an interdisciplinary field that studies both the digitization of traditional politics as well as the rise of new forms of political life originating in the digital world, such as WikiLeaks or the Anonymous movement. Whilst there is as yet no digital politics textbook, three useful entry points into the subfield of Internet politics are Chadwick and Howard's (2008) *Routledge Handbook of Internet Politics*; Oates, Owen and Gibson's (2006) *The Internet and Politics*; and Chadwick's (2006) *Internet Politics.* This chapter starts with four review sections that cover similar ground to the material discussed in these works, although I broaden the inquiry to include mobile media. For example the next section is titled 'digital government' rather than 'e-government'—the latter a term usually associated with the Internet but not with mobile technologies. The subsequent sections exemplify the application of an anthropological approach to the study of digital politics. Drawing from my own fieldwork in Malaysia and Spain, I argue that anthropology brings to this nascent field a rich political lexicon, processual analyses, ground-up comparisons and participatory research. I conclude with a brief discussion of the potential for future anthropological studies in this area.

Digital Government (Executives and Bureaucracies)[1]

One of the more influential introductions to the study of digital government is Fountain's (2001) *Building the Virtual State*, which explores the relationship between new Internet technologies and institutional change within government agencies in the United States. Fountain argues that the US bureaucracy must modernize and move towards a more decentralized system, yet one that can still guarantee citizens' right to privacy. The system's 'structural obsolescence' presents, however, a formidable obstacle. Researchers working in Europe and Asia have similarly reported a wide chasm between the visions and realities of digital government. Thus, in the early 2000s, Malaysia's e-government flagship sought to 'improve the convenience, accessibility and quality of interactions with citizens and businesses' (Yong 2003: 189). The vision was, and remains, 'for government, businesses and citizens to work together for the benefit of the country and all its citizens' (Yong 2003: 190). In practice, however, officials report poor digital practices and a resistance to information and communication technology (ICT) integration throughout the Malaysian public sector (Karim and Khalid 2003: 81–7)—a finding familiar to researchers studying e-government projects in Europe (see Kubicek, Millard and Westholm 2003).

As new digital technologies and practices have spread, digital government advocates have sought to recruit them to the elusive task of improving the functioning of government agencies. For instance, Noveck (2008) favours the adoption of open-source practices to democratize government decision making (with Wikipedia as the template) and sees great potential in the collaborative use of simple digital tools by citizens to assist 'isolated bureaucrats'. Other scholars place their hopes in the transition from e-government to m-government, based on mobile platforms, particularly in the global South, where 'last mile connection' infrastructure is often lacking (Kuschchu and Kuscu 2003; Narayan 2007). They see m-government as a way of bridging the digital divide, especially in rural areas of Africa and South Asia, creating a world in which citizens will have 'anytime, anywhere access' to public services (Alrazooqi and De Silva 2010).

Digital government scholarship is hampered by its commitment to what Green, Harvey and Knox (2005) have called 'the imperative to connect'—an urge that they encountered during anthropological research into publicly funded digital projects in Manchester, UK. The overriding ambition on the part of ICT managers and staff was to link European projects across divides of geography, language, culture and organization. The aim was not to create virtual spaces but rather 'new networks of located connection' (2005: 817), a vision animated by a 'fantasy of…"flattened" connection' (2005: 817) that overlooked the constraints, tangles and disconnects that invariably accompany such endeavours (see Strathern 1996).

Digital Democracy (Community, Deliberation, Participation)

If the key digital government metaphor is connectivity, the field of digital democracy has at its core the concept of 'public sphere', associated with the social philosopher Jürgen Habermas. A public sphere is 'an arena, independent of government [and market]…which is dedicated to rational debate and which is both accessible to entry and open to inspection by the citizenry. It is here…that public opinion is formed' (Holub, quoted in Webster 1995: 101–2). Despite Habermas's insistence that his concept of public sphere referred to a particular phase in European history, for many authors the public sphere has become a normative ideal (Benson 2007; Chadwick 2006). Thus,

Dahlberg (2001) has evaluated the citizen-led initiative Minnesota e-Democracy, built around an e-mail list forum, against five predefined public sphere criteria: autonomy from state and market, reciprocal critique, reflexivity, sincerity, and discursive inclusion. Like the term *community* (see below) or indeed *connectivity*, public sphere is used both as a 'rhetorical token' (Benson 2007: 3) and as a normative notion that guides research away from what is and towards what *ought to be*. Instead of this romantic ideal, Chadwick (2008: 10) argues for a new approach to democracy where 'a plurality of different sociotechnical values and mechanisms' can find their place, taking advantage of the low entry threshold and ease of use of Web 2.0 tools.

More recently, Carty (2010) has explored the potential of digital media in the development of new ways of mobilization, participatory democracy and civic engagement. This requires leaving behind earlier models of mobilization based on face-to-face communication, taking the logic of digital technologies on its own terms. Roberts (2009) urges a more cautious and critical stance towards the democratic possibilities of Web 2.0 tools. More pessimistically, Hindman (2009) concludes that the corporate media have maintained their audience share of web content, and ordinary citizens are not 'empowered' by the new digital tools.

Digital Campaigning (Parties, Candidates, Elections)

The scholarly literature on digital political campaigning has been dominated by the wide use of Internet and mobile technologies in US presidential campaigns since 2000 (Hara 2008). On the whole, this literature is descriptive, quantitative and under-theorized, though it provides a rich seam of empirical evidence. For example, Bimber and Davis (2003) focus on candidate websites during the elections of 2000 and the impact they had on voters' behaviour. Four years later, Cornfield (2005) found that the Internet made a substantial difference to both candidates and voters, with very large numbers of adults using the Internet. Most candidates had to embark on a steep learning curve to maximize the campaigning potential of the by-now-familiar Internet. Hara (2008) followed the online activist group MoveOn.org to document participants' 'voices', noting a discrepancy between this group's nonhierarchical and decentralized image and the traditional nature of its actual practices. Howard (2005) found that the Internet disseminated valuable data about policies, programmes, candidates and other political actors ('deep democracy'). But he also encountered a prevalence of expressive, overengaged politics ('thin citizenship') as well as privacy concerns raised by the extensive use of data mining by political parties. This intensified with the popularization of social networking sites, a trend documented for the 2008 campaign (Pew Research Centre for the People and the Press 2008). By the 2008 campaign, nearly half of all Americans used the Internet to keep informed (a finding confirmed by Smith and Rainie 2008), with younger voters and Obama supporters more likely to use these technologies.

Other researchers have investigated political blogging. In Canada, Elmer et al. (2009) have mapped the relationship between blogs and party loyalty through hyperlink analyses, discovering that Conservative Party bloggers are particularly loyal to their party in their blog recommendations.

Digital Mobilization (Interest Groups and Social Movements)

A useful entry point into this research area is Melucci's (1996) *Challenging Codes*. Critical of resource mobilization theory, Melucci stresses the cultural dimensions of social movements and regards collective action as being invariably tethered to relational structures (or social fields) that constrain action, although 'breakthrough social agency is always possible' (Venkatesh 2003: 344–5). Castells (2001) argues that cultural movements are built around communication, especially via the mass media and the Internet. He famously posits networks as the defining social formations of our era, highlighting the importance of networked social movements such as the Zapatista uprising in Chiapas, Mexico, or the anticorporate globalization movement in Seattle (see also Castells 2009).

Juris (2008) extends these ideas through anthropological fieldwork among antiglobalization activists in Barcelona, Spain. Following Massey, he argues that transnational networks are invariably entangled with 'a complex nexus of translocal ties and articulations' (Juris 2008: 63). Thus the field of Catalonian activism is a product of this region's strong anti-Francoist, nationalist and anarchist traditions (63). With Zapatista ideals and web technologies added to the mix in the 1990s, the result was 'a unique form of activism guided by emerging networking logics and practices' (70).

Another strand of research explores the use of mobile technologies for activism, social protest and mobilization. Rheingold (2002) writes about the growing importance of 'mobile ad hoc social networks' (or 'smart mobs') to collective action. Early examples of these 'spontaneous social experiments' include the massive use of text messages to mobilize against President Estrada in the Philippines in 2001 (although this has been subsequently questioned, see Rafael 2003) or against Spain's ruling Popular Party following terrorist attacks in 2004.

The debate was reignited in 2009 with the publication of Shirky's *Here Comes Everybody*, a much-commented-on account about how new digital tools foster collective action by greatly lowering the financial and time costs incurred. One of the many examples cited by Shirky was how Chinese parents used Twitter and other Web 2.0 media to swiftly form protest groups against the local authorities following an earthquake in May 2008 in which nearly 7,000 schools collapsed, killing thousands of children. Shirky's most vocal critic has been Morozov (2011), who challenges the idea that the Internet serves to advance freedom and democracy. If anything, he suggests, the Internet tightens the grip of repressive regimes like China or Iran. Taking a middle path, Hands (2010) seeks to avoid false dichotomies (e.g. virtual versus real life) and media polemics of the 'Twitter revolution' variety. Hands sees digital technologies as being integral to political struggles, not as alien artefacts impacting upon an otherwise apathetic civil society.

In a recent review of the digital ethnography literature, Coleman (2010) points out that ethnographers have documented a range of digital activism forms, including Juris's just mentioned antiglobalization study, 'banal activism' in suburban Malaysia (Postill 2008), diaspora mobilization and social media (Costanza-Chock 2008), political blogging in Iran (Doostdar 2004; Sreberny and Khiabany 2010) and non-governmental organization technological activism (McInerney 2009)—a list to which we could add ethnographies of Internet-mediated war (Bräuchler 2005), mobile phones and village politics (Tenhunen 2008) and local e-governance (Hinkelbein 2008; Strauss 2007).

The next section draws from my work on digital politics in Malaysia to exemplify three key anthropological strengths. First, anthropology brings to the table a rich political lexicon developed over decades of cross-cultural research and theorization around the globe. Second, political anthropology has a long tradition of 'following the conflict' (Marcus 1995) that is highly pertinent to today's digitally mediated struggles. Third, ethnographic research lends itself to post hoc comparisons of political phenomena encountered in the field. For instance, what I have termed 'banal activism' is a species of digital activism that I did not set out to study in Malaysia but rather encountered in the course of fieldwork.[2]

Case Study One: Suburban Malaysia

A Rich Political Lexicon

Subang Jaya and its sister township, USJ, make up a largely middle-class, ethnic Chinese suburb of Kuala Lumpur. Most residents arrived in this award-winning suburb in the 1990s hoping to find a green and safe environment in which to raise their young families. Their plans were soon complicated, however, by a series of regional, national and local crises. In 1997 the collapse of South East Asia's financial markets caused a sharp economic downturn in Malaysia after many years of robust growth. A deep political crisis ensued when the then deputy prime minister, Anwar Ibrahim, was imprisoned without trial. This led to an explosion of pro-Anwar websites that Prime Minister Mahathir's government was unable to defuse, having guaranteed foreign ICT investors that the Internet would remain free from governmental meddling.

It was precisely in 1997 that Subang Jaya's municipal council was established. Two years later, in 1999, the new council faced the first of many challenges from residents' groups when it raised local taxes by 240 per cent. This episode gave rise to a type of 'banal activism' that has predominated in Subang Jaya ever since—an activism led by technology-savvy residents who use the rhetoric of community to campaign on issues such as taxation, traffic congestion, waste disposal, school provision and local crime. These issues would seem mundane to the urban intelligentsia in Kuala Lumpur or to the young antiglobalization activists in Barcelona studied by Juris (2008), but they are crucial to suburban parents embarked on family-building projects.

From 2003 to 2004, I conducted fieldwork in Subang Jaya, followed by intermittent online research from Britain until 2009 and a brief visit in 2010. I found a plethora of digital projects during my stay, ranging from a multimedia library and a 'cybermosque' to several web forums and a townshipwide 'smart community' initiative. On returning home, my initial attempt at placing these various initiatives along a community–network continuum (with community-like initiatives at one end and network-like initiatives at the other) soon foundered. Eventually I realized that I had fallen into the community/network trap that lies at the heart of Internet studies (Postill 2008). The trap consists of reducing the plurality and flux of social and political formations that one invariably finds in contemporary localities (e.g. peer groups, cohorts, associations, gangs, clans, sects, mosques, factions, families, action committees, mailing lists, Facebook groups, Twitter trends) to a crude community-versus-network dichotomy. This originates in the misguided idea that our local communities are being impacted upon by a global network society and by that network of networks known as the Internet.

In search of a way out of this impasse, I revisited the early work of Gluckman, Turner, Epstein and other members of the Manchester School of Anthropology. I also found unexpected links between this ancestral literature and more recent anthropological explorations (e.g. Amit and Rapport 2002; Gledhill 2000) as well as signs of a renewed interest in their pioneering studies (Evens and Handelman 2006). The Manchester scholars conducted fieldwork in a very different part of the world (British Central Africa) and under radically different historical conditions: the end of empire. Yet the conceptual issues they confronted were strikingly similar to those I was struggling with after returning from postcolonial Malaysia. The problem boils down to how to study a locality under conditions of rapid social and political change when tribal, regional, linguistic and other groupings appear to be in flux and new kinds of affiliations and social formations are being constantly made and remade. Faced with such fluid actualities on the ground, the Manchester scholars moved away from the then-predominant structural-functionalist paradigm and towards historical-processual accounts informed by new concepts such as 'field', 'ego-centred network', 'social drama' and 'arena'.

In my book *Localizing the Internet* (Postill 2011), I synthesize this approach with the equally historical and processual field-theoretical model developed by Bourdieu, best demonstrated in his *The Rules of Art* (1996). Rather than positing the existence of a local community being impacted upon by global networks, I discuss how variously positioned field agents and agencies in Subang Jaya (residents, politicians, committees, councillors, journalists and others) compete and cooperate over matters concerning the local residents, often via the Internet. I call this dynamic set of projects, practices, technologies and relations 'the field of residential affairs'. This can be described as a digital field in that the set of social relations and practices that sustain it are inextricably entangled with digital technologies such as e-mail, mailing lists, web portals, online forums, blogs and mobile phones.

Like Epstein (1958) in his late 1940s fieldwork in northern Rhodesia's mining areas, I found that processes of change were unevenly spread across Subang Jaya's field of residential affairs, with some regions of the field changing more rapidly than others. For example, the fight against crime is an ecumenical issue that has brought together people and agencies from across the governmental divide in the township. Crime prevention initiatives led by residents have received governmental support and mass media coverage and have undergone considerable technological development, including new mobile applications. By contrast, a nationwide campaign to reinstate local elections made no lasting impact.

Besides having two or more main sectors, typically a field of residential affairs will exhibit both 'stations' and 'arenas' (the latter are described later). Adapting Giddens's (1984: 119) notion of stations, I define field stations as those stopping places in which field agents interact with other agents, ideas and technologies on a regular basis, an interaction that in turn (re)produces the station. Examples include a leading resident's daily tweets on local issues, a politician's weekly surgery or the regular public meetings of a parish council. For a local leader, a regular presence in such settings is an essential part of maintaining good working relations with allies and supporters. By the same token, a prolonged absence from such stations is likely to undermine a leader's position within the field of residential affairs, a domain suffused with metaphors of copresence, collaboration and rootedness.

So far the picture of the field I have painted is one of Giddensian routinization—the predictable cycles of political agents as they go about coordinating their activities and (re)producing their practices in clock-and-calendar time (Postill 2002). But to complete the picture we must also consider those irregular, often unpredictable patterns of collective action that disrupt the regular schedules of a field of practice. In other words, we need to follow the conflict.

Following the Conflict

Today we associate field theory with Bourdieu, whose analytical preference is for the slow-moving, cumulative changes that take place within a field (Couldry 2003; Swartz 1997: 129), not for potentially volatile processes such as court trials or popular uprisings that often migrate *across* fields. The Parisian salons, brasseries and courthouses of Bourdieu's *The Rules of Art* provided him with a fixed spatial matrix of objective relations—the sociophysical backdrop to a slowly changing field of practice (Bourdieu 1996: 40–3).

Political processes were, in fact, central to the collaborative work of the Manchester School, whose field theories predate Bourdieu's by many years. By political process they meant that kind of social process that is 'involved in determining and implementing public goals [as well as] in the differential achievement and use of power by the members of the group concerned with those goals' (Swartz, Turner and Tuden 1966: 7). One key Manchester School concept is 'social drama'. Coined by Victor Turner, a social drama is a political process that originates within a social group but can spread across a wider intergroup field unless appropriate 'redressive action' is taken (Turner 1974: 128–32). Social dramas undergo four stages: (1) breach, (2) crisis, (3) redressive action and (4) either reintegration or schism.

The Subang Jaya digital drama I wish to recount revolved around a seemingly banal issue: the building of a food court. As the theory predicts, the conflict was triggered by a perceived breach of the regular norms governing relations between two local parties—in this case, the residents versus the municipal council.

Breach The drama began when a local activist named Raymond Tan announced online that construction of a food court had begun on land earmarked for the building of a police station in the crime-ridden suburb. He urged local residents to cast their vote on an online poll that was created to solicit their reactions. The following day another leading activist, Jeff Ooi, replied suggesting that there may be somebody in the council promoting food courts. The fact that the land was reserved for a police station made the issue 'even fishier'.

Crisis Within a few days, the discussion had spread to a number of local electronic mailing lists. Raymond encouraged residents to feed the politicians' responses to their texting campaign back to the mailing list or, alternatively, to either of two local portals. The next day, Jeff Ooi sent subscribers of all five mailing lists a citizen journalism item he had recently posted on the portal's news section. The piece chided the members of parliament and assemblymen for their inaction. It then noted the absence of the mandatory project notice board at the building site. This remark resonates with reports of local activism from elsewhere. Faced with powerful interests, people around the world 'have quickly invented resourceful means of resistance' (Abram 1998: 13).

Later that day, Raymond used both the web forum and five mailing lists to announce the recent formation of an action committee. He listed the names and affiliations of the pro tem committee members, with himself at the helm and a close associate as his right hand. The other eleven members were recruited from across the field of residential affairs. The campaign was spearheaded not by an imaginary community but rather by a subset of Raymond's local contacts in the shape of a small action committee. This improvised committee is best described as an action set—a group of individuals mobilized to attain a specified goal who will disperse when that goal is either reached or abandoned (Mayer 1966; Turner 1974).

Within twenty-four hours, Raymond's deputy informed forum subscribers that the campaign to lobby local politicians via text messages had 'resulted in jolting each and every one of them into action'. He appended a list of politicians and their reactions to the text messages, which ranged from 'full support' to a promise to 'look into the matter'. Here we can see clearly Turner's (1974) notion of arena at work through a new technological articulation—that between Internet and mobile media. In an arena, nothing must be left unsaid; all actors drawn into the drama ('jolted into action') must state publicly where they stand on the dispute at hand.

The following day, Raymond contributed a post in which he identified a number of procedural lapses in the food court project. This suggested there may be a 'higher power at play'. Soon the drama's central arena shifted offline when some two hundred residents demonstrated at the building site 'under full media coverage', as Raymond put it.

Redressive Action The climax of the drama came when the deputy home minister paid a visit to Subang Jaya and promised to resolve the dispute. This redressive move by the authorities was promptly reciprocated by the local activists, who were only too eager, as one of them put it, to 'complete the cycle' of the campaign. To this end, the action committee deputy leader circulated a message asking residents to show their elected representatives their gratitude via SMS.

Reintegration Only two months after these auspicious events, fresh rumours began to circulate online that the operator was planning to resume construction of the food court. Soon thereafter, the local council approved the project, and physical work resumed at the site. Raymond's reaction was unequivocal: 'Friends and neighbours, are we going to allow these clowns [to] push the FOOD court down our throats?' Space limitations here preclude a discussion of the subsequent unfolding of events, which included a highly unusual offline arena—namely a public hearing. The police station was eventually completed after a five-year struggle.

This digital drama demonstrates the limitations of the community/network paradigm for the study of Internet localization (Postill 2008). By broadening the analysis from the neighbourhood domain to the wider field of residential affairs, we gained an understanding of local leaders' individual and collective agency, relations with other local agents and their multiple uses of digital media at a critical point in the suburb's history.

Raymond emerged from the drama as a formidable field broker. Like Internet activists in other parts of the world, Raymond possesses 'an unusual combination of technical, political and cultural skills' (Coleman 2005: 39). Throughout the digital drama, he connected and coordinated the disparate parties involved using a range of technologies as well as face-to-face encounters. At least five mailing lists, two web forums, personal e-mail and mobile telephony were recruited to the intensive campaigning. Two key 'Internet affordances' (Wellman et al. 2003) were exploited to the full: hypertextuality and interactivity. Whilst the widely circulated hyperlinks ensured a high degree of message redundancy, the interactive web forum and e-mail threads aided the active participation of residents in the fast-moving drama. The effect was magnified by the grassroots journalism of Jeff Ooi and ample mass media coverage.

The crisis spread virally, spilling over into the powerful fields of federal government and the mass media through the deft use of a range of digital media by an unprecedented alliance of residents' groups. The ensuing drama reveals the field's dynamics of factionalism, alliance building and technological mediation as well as its entanglements with powerful neighbouring fields at a given point in time.

Ground-up Comparisons

Anthropology is a comparative endeavour. However, because ethnographic fieldwork is a participant-driven, open-ended process, this can lead into new research directions, complicating any prior comparative framework. Rather than seeing this as a problem, though, I regard it as an opportunity to carry out what we might call 'ground-up comparisons'—that is, post hoc comparisons arising from the researcher's experiences on the ground. On returning from Malaysia, I discovered intriguing parallels in the digital media literature between my own findings and those from other middle-class suburbs in places that were geographically and culturally remote from Subang Jaya, including Tel Aviv, Toronto, Melbourne and Plano, Texas (see Arnold, Shepherd and Gibbs 2008; Durington 2007; Hampton 2003; Hampton and Wellman 2003; Mesch and Levanon 2003). With the benefit of hindsight, I now regard my study as paving the way for future comparisons with analogous 'natural experiments' (Diamond and Robinson 2010) in digital localization in neighbourhoods worldwide.

To illustrate this comparative potential, consider a recent study of media and activism in an upmarket housing estate near Melbourne, Australia, named 'Kookaburra Hollow' (a pseudonym, see Arnold et al. 2008). Like their Subang Jaya counterparts, Kookaburra Hollow incomers arrived in pursuit of the dream of a green, safe and high-tech suburbia away from the chaos and pollution of urban life. They too, however, soon found that all was not well in their leafy neighbourhood. As part of an attractive package, the developers had offered prospective buyers high-speed broadband connections in every household. Alas, this failed to materialize in many homes, triggering the onset of Kookaburra Hollow's own brand of banal activism aimed at securing this technology. (Other complaints centred on allegations of poorly built houses and a scarcity of public amenities.) Residents turned to the local intranet facility—originally envisaged by the developers as a site for convivial community building—to plan and carry out their campaign along with face-to-face meetings and homemade banners. The fledgling intranet station morphed into a field arena where the two camps clashed as a local social drama unfolded. Representing the developers was Bill Flanders (jocosely known as 'Big Brother'), who was the intranet forum moderator. Opposing him stood the controversial figure of Anthony Briggs, a vocal resident regarded by some neighbours as being too confrontational.[3] The drama escaped the control of local actors when a popular current-affairs programme on television covered the conflict at the request of leading residents. Following the airing of this show, a 'growing chorus' of residents expressed their concern that the media coverage might undermine local property values (Arnold et al. 2008).

As this synopsis shows, Kookaburra Hollow's field of residential affairs is divided into two main subfields or sectors: a private sector (the developers) and a residents' sector. The authors describe the arrangement as one of 'privatised governance', in which most of the functions that one would normally associate with a local council are devolved to a private firm (see Low 2003). As in Subang Jaya, there is a strong rhetoric of community, solidarity and rootedness at work across this divide. What I have termed for Subang Jaya 'an interest in disinterestedness' (Bourdieu 1996), Arnold and his coauthors label 'interested solidarity' (2008: 10). Residents constantly remind one another that it is in their self-interest to throw in their lot with the rest of the community. Yet just as in the early days of banal activism in Subang Jaya, Kookaburra Hollow residents soon learned that involving the mass media in a local dispute can sometimes do more harm than good.

Case Study Two: Urban Spain

Participatory Research

Today we live in a very different world from that which framed my Malaysian fieldwork in 2003–04. Whilst the United States, Britain, Japan and other developed nations have been mired in a deep economic crisis since 2008, emerging economies such as China, India and Russia continue to experience strong growth. At the same time, increasingly affordable participatory media such as blogs, microblogs, wikis, social network sites, video sharing sites and smartphones are now in the hands of millions of ordinary citizens. In countries as disparate as Iceland, Tunisia, Egypt, Spain, Britain, Israel, Malaysia and India, the convergence of these two global trends—geopolitical and economic turbulence on the one hand and widely available digital media on the other—have fuelled new forms of civil unrest and technopolitical activism that the ruling elites are finding very difficult to counter.

Given the centrality of participant observation to the ethnographic approach, anthropologists are well placed to study the use of participatory media in these complex processes. This section describes some of the potential uses of participatory research with reference to my recent fieldwork into social media and activism in Barcelona, Spain.

The aim of this 2010–11 project was to determine whether social media such as Facebook, YouTube and Twitter are making any significant difference to the work of activists, as is often claimed in the news media and in some of the literature reviewed earlier. Abiding by the political anthropology imperative to follow the conflict, my research focus shifted as did conditions on the ground, from an early focus on nationalist activism through a middle period studying Internet freedom, ending with the dramatic events of 15 May 2011, when hundreds of thousands of Spaniards mobilized to demand 'real democracy'. These protests were followed by encampments in central squares of Madrid, Barcelona and many other cities, marking the birth of the mass movement known today as 15-M or the indignados movement.

One striking feature of this movement is the pervasive, decentralized use of social media by hackers, prodemocracy activists and countless ordinary citizens to form a common front. Although a few fundamentalist hackers refused to use corporate platforms such as Facebook or Twitter, most campaigners I encountered justified their use of corporate social media on pragmatic grounds. For example, when the Barcelona hub of the umbrella organization Real Democracy Now! (Democracia Real Ya!, DRY) was created in March 2011, participants were encouraged to use both Facebook and a nonproprietary web forum to coordinate their activities. When it became apparent that Facebook was the preferred platform, the group's informal leaders readily went along with the majority.

Throughout my research into the 15-M movement, I took part in a range of collaborative activities across various online platforms. Three examples will illustrate this participatory approach to the study of digital politics and political engagement. All three entail the use of digital media to copy, paste, share and modify knowledge with like-minded citizens, representing but a small subset of practices within a rapidly expanding participatory ecology. The first example concerns the use of Facebook to coauthor political texts. As a native English and Spanish speaker, part of my modest contribution to the 15-M movement has been to act as an occasional translator and proofreader. Thus, on one occasion I shared via Facebook what I regarded as an improved version of a passage taken from the English translation of the DRY manifesto. In a matter of minutes, another user replied with a better translation, which I duly forwarded to the manifesto team. This example may seem pedestrian, but it captures neatly the sorts of micropolitical collaborations amongst strangers—including scholars—that social media enable on a much vaster scale than was possible even a few years ago, before the explosive uptake of Facebook, Twitter and other major platforms.

It is important, however, not to draw too sharp a distinction between corporate and free platforms. After all, skills and habits acquired on the former can migrate to open-source platforms—and vice versa. My second example demonstrates this transfer and its implications for research into emerging forms of digitally mediated politics. As we were nearing the 15 May deadline, a local DRY campaigner told me about a new platform set up to share information about like-minded groups in Barcelona. Having painstakingly created a directory of local groups on my research blog over a period of months, I was happy to contribute to the collective effort whilst learning to use a new technopolitical tool. Soon I was interacting with eight to ten other people—all but one of them strangers—by means of an open-source platform developed by Sweden's Pirate Party, which advocates greater Internet and democratic freedoms. The platform is aptly named PiratePad and consists of a main wiki area where users can easily coauthor public texts and a right-hand column with a chat facility. On entering the pad, each user must choose a colour through which their particular contributions can be identified. The chat area allows for real-time discussion and modification of the materials as they are being shared. Having spent months slowly building up a directory on my blog, I marvelled at the extraordinary speed, smoothness and efficiency of this colorful exercise. By pooling our individual knowledge, in less than two hours we had produced a comprehensive list with immediate practical applications.

This and similar sessions were also instructive about the mechanics of informal leadership in Web 2.0 settings. Although 15-M supporters have always insisted that the movement is horizontal and leaderless, some individuals are, of course, more influential than others. They must, however, exercise their power subtly, leading by example, not command. Like longhouse headmen among the egalitarian Iban of Sarawak with whom I lived in the late 1990s (Postill 2006), 15-M leaders govern through 'a subtle mixture of persuasion and admonition' (Freeman 1970: 113). Thus, when I copied and pasted a link to Catalonia's Pirate Party from my blog onto the pad, I was promptly challenged by an informal leader through the open chat channel. She cordially pointed out that, in keeping with the grassroots nature of the 15-M movement, we should not include political parties or trade unions in the directory, only citizens' groups. I agreed and quickly deleted the offending entry (but not without privately registering the irony of using software developed by the Swedish Pirate Party to exclude their Catalan comrades from the directory).

My third and final example involves once again my research blog, but this time paired with a very different platform: the micro-blogging site Twitter. On 20 July 2011, I launched a 15-M glossary on my blog. After a brief Google search, I found three existing glossaries which I aggregated by the simple procedure of copying and pasting their entries in alphabetical order onto my blog.

Within minutes of announcing the launch of the glossary to my Twitter followers, I received both public and private feedback. One activist suggested a minor correction. Another recommended a source that I had in fact already included in the glossary. A third activist promised to help with future drafts and asked about my preferred language. A fourth activist retweeted my message to her followers. Finally, a fifth Twitter user found that the glossary was too 'centralist' and that people outside Madrid would not be pleased with this bias. I rapidly replied that this was merely the first version of the glossary and that future versions would incorporate terms and experiences from other parts of Spain. I also used the opportunity to ask all readers for assistance identifying other materials. As I write these lines a month later, the glossary continues to grow and even enjoyed the proverbial fifteen seconds of

Twitter fame (cf. Nahon et al. 2011) when it was recommended by DRY to its over 90,000 followers.

This final instance is further proof of the participatory potential of both digital activism and digital ethnography in the current era of lowered entry access to the means of content creation—a historical phase in which coproducing and sharing contents has become a taken-for-granted daily practice for millions of people (Chadwick 2008; Shirky 2009). I do not suggest that participation is a panacea that will resolve the deep political and economic malaise that afflicts countries such as Spain, Greece or Britain. Rather, I draw attention to the strong fit between anthropological practice and popular forms of digital participation that only a few years ago were the virtual preserve of a technorati elite.[4]

Conclusion

In *Personal Connections in the Digital Age*, communication scholar Nancy Baym (2010) lists seven digital media variables: interactivity, temporal structure, social cues, storage, replicability, reach and mobility. She then differentiates two main types of online collectivity: communities and networks. This stark contrast between a rich set of technological concepts and a meagre pair of sociological concepts signals the need for anthropological studies of digital politics that borrow some of their technical terminology from media and communication studies whilst bringing to the field a strong track record of mapping the shifting terrain on which technopolitical struggles take place. Baym's positing of communities and networks as the paradigmatic social formations of the digital era is, as I argued earlier, a central feature of digital media studies (Postill 2008). Yet relying on this odd couple for our social and political mapping is unwise. For one thing, both notions have had chequered careers as social scientific concepts. More importantly, the vast diversity of social and political formations found among humans—ranging from predigital nuclear families, associations and organizations at one end of the spectrum to digital-era formations such as Facebook groups, Twitter hashtags and mobile phone contacts at the other—can hardly be captured with two terms. This is akin to expecting that a team of biologists embarking on a survey of Amazonian biodiversity make do with the terms *plant* and *animal.*

In this chapter I have argued for an integrated approach to the study of digital politics that overcomes the tacit digital divide separating Internet and mobile phone studies whilst expanding the field's conceptual and theoretical horizons. Future anthropological studies of digital politics should avoid sterile debates about technological determinism and virtual versus real-life politics and concentrate instead on the careful analysis of political processes and their digital dimensions. The devil is in the technopolitical details.

One neglected area of great potential for future anthropological research is the study of political virals—digital contents of a political nature that spread epidemically across online platforms, mobile devices and face-to-face settings. The study of virals has been so far left largely to marketing practitioners and new media gurus, and yet virals are a mainstay of contemporary media environments (Postill 2005; Wasik 2009). In the Barcelona research just described, I encountered both campaign virals and what we might call viral campaigns. Examples of campaign virals include tweets with catchy slogans, YouTube videos and digital photographs that are widely shared. But campaigns themselves can go viral. For instance, in late December 2010, tens of thousands of Spaniards mobilized overnight against the country's political elite for attempting to pass an antidigital piracy law known as Ley Sinde. The trigger was the voluntary shutdown of Spain's main link-sharing sites in protest at the imminent passing of the bill, which led to an outcry from millions of Spaniards suddenly deprived of their favourite free films and television series. Three key arenas in which the drama was played out were Twitter's 'trending topics' (the most popular topics at any given time), the Spanish Parliament in Madrid and the mainstream media.

Although our understanding of viral campaigns is still poor, their main features appear to include an explosive growth, social drama liminality, real-time participation, multiple online and face-to-face arenas and intense but ephemeral news media coverage. These campaigns raise intriguing questions about the methodological challenges of studying the technopolitical contexts that foster and inhibit the spread of virals and about the extent to which virals strengthen or undermine public discourse. One question for future research is whether we are witnessing the coming of an era in which political reality is framed by virally shared digital contents—an age of viral reality.[5]

Acknowledgements

The Malaysian and Spanish research reported here was funded by the Volkswagen Foundation through Bremen University and by the Open University of Catalonia Foundation through the Internet Interdisciplinary Institute (IN3), respectively. I am very grateful to these organizations for their support. I also wish to thank the book editors for their helpful feedback on early drafts of this chapter. The Malaysian materials are adapted from my book *Localizing the Internet: An Anthropological Account* (Berghahn Books, 2011).

Notes

1. In this and subsequent subheadings I have retained Chadwick's (2006) helpful explanatory keywords in parentheses.
2. It is telling of the ethnographic method that the political anthropologist Alexander T. Smith (personal communication, 22 May 2006) and I independently coined the term 'banal activism' within a few months of each other—in Smith's case whilst conducting fieldwork among Conservative Party supporters in Scotland.

3. Bill Flanders and Anthony Briggs are also pseudonyms (see Arnold et al. 2008).
4. For an extended discussion of how to map participation in online contexts, see Fish et al. (2011).
5. On the diffusion of viral information through the political blogosphere, see Nahon et al. (2011).

References

Abram, S. 1998. Introduction. In *Anthropological Perspectives on Local Development*, ed. S. Abram and J. Waldren, 1–17. London: Routledge.

Alrazooqi, M., and R. De Silva. 2010. Mobile and Wireless Services and Technologies for m-government. *WSEAS Transactions on Information Science and Applications*. http://www.wseas.us/e-library/transactions/information/2010/88–120.pdf.

Amit, V., and N. Rapport. 2002. *The Trouble with Community*. London: Pluto.

Arnold, M., C. Shepherd and M. Gibbs. 2008. Trouble at Kookaburra Hollow: How Media Mediate. *Journal of Community Informatics* 3: 4. http://www.ci-journal.net/index.php/ciej/article/view/329/380.

Baym, N. 2010. *Personal Connections in the Digital Age*. Cambridge: Polity Press.

Benson, R. 2007. After Habermas: The Revival of a Macro-sociology of Media. Paper presented at the American Sociological Association Annual Conference, New York, 11 August. http://steinhardt.nyu.edu/scmsAdmin/uploads/000/671/Benson_ASA.pdf.

Bimber, B., and R. Davis. 2003. *Campaigning Online. The Internet in U.S. Elections*. Oxford: Oxford University Press.

Bourdieu, P. 1996. *The Rules of Art: Genesis and Structure of the Literary Field*. Cambridge: Polity Press.

Bräuchler, B. 2005. *Cyberidentities at War: Der Molukkenkonflikt im Internet*. Bielefeld: transcript.

Carty, V. 2010. *Wired and Mobilizing: Social Movements, New Technology, and Electoral Politics*. London: Routledge.

Castells, M. 2001. *The Internet Galaxy*. Oxford: Oxford University Press.

Castells, M. 2009. *Communication Power*. Oxford: Oxford University Press.

Chadwick, A. 2006. *Internet Politics: States, Citizens and New Communications Technologies*. New York: Oxford University Press.

Chadwick, A. 2008. Web 2.0: New Challenges for the Study of E-Democracy in Era of Informational Exuberance. *I/S: A Journal of Law and Policy for the Information Society* 5: 9.

Chadwick, A., and P. N. Howard. 2008. *Routledge Handbook of Internet Politics*. New York: Routledge.

Coleman, G. 2010. Ethnographic Approaches to Digital Media. *Annual Review of Anthropology* 39: 487–505.

Coleman, S. 2005. *From the Ground Up: An Evaluation of Community-focused Approaches to e-democracy.* London: Office of the Deputy Prime Minister. http://www.bristol.gov.uk/ccm/cms-service/download/asset/?asset_id = 27704058.

Cornfield, M. 2005. *The Internet and Campaign 2004: A Look Back at the Campaigners.* Washington, DC: Pew Internet and American Life Project. http://www.pewinternet.org/pdfs/Cornfield_commentary.pdf.

Costanza-Chock, S. 2008. The Immigrant Rights Movement on the Net: Between 'Web 2.0' and Comunicacion Popular. *American Quarterly* 60(3): 851–64.

Couldry, N. 2003. Media Meta-capital: Extending the Range of Bourdieu's Field Theory. *Theory and Society* 32(5–6): 653–77.

Dahlberg, L. 2001. Extending the Public Sphere through Cyberspace: The Case of Minnesota E-Democracy. *First Monday* 6(3). http://www.firstmonday.dk/issues/issue6_3/dahlberg/.

Diamond, J., and J. A. Robinson, eds. 2010. *Natural Experiments of History.* Cambridge, MA: Harvard University Press.

Doostdar, A. 2004. The Vulgar Spirit of Blogging: On Language, Culture, and Power in Persian Weblogestan. *American Anthropologist* 106(4): 651–2.

Durington, M. 2007. Moral Panics in Suburban Texas. Paper presented to the EASA Media Anthropology Network e-Seminar, 27 February–6 March. http://www.media-anthropology.net/durington_panics.pdf.

Elmer, G., G. Langlois, Z. Devereaux, P. M. Ryan, F. McKelvey, J. Redden and A. B. Curlew. 2009. 'Blogs I Read': Partisanship and Party Loyalty in the Canadian Political Blogosphere. *Journal of Information Technology and Politics* 6(2): 156–65.

Epstein, A. L. 1958. *Politics in an Urban African Community.* Manchester: Manchester University Press.

Evens, T.M.S., and D. Handelman, eds. 2006. *The Manchester School: Practice and Ethnographic Praxis in Anthropology.* Oxford: Berghahn Books.

Fish, A., L.F.R. Murillo, L. Nguyen, A. Panofsky and C. M. Kelty. 2011. Birds of the Internet. *Journal of Cultural Economy* 4(2): 157–87.

Fountain, J. E. 2001. *Building the Virtual State: Information Technology and Institutional Change.* Washington, DC: Brookings Institution Press.

Freeman, J. D. 1970. *Report on the Iban of Sarawak,* Kuching: Government Printing Office. Reprinted as *Report on the Iban.* London: Athlone Press.

Giddens, A. 1984. *The Constitution of Society.* Cambridge: Polity Press.

Gledhill, J. 2000. *Power and Its Disguises: Anthropological Perspectives on Politics.* London: Pluto Press.

Green, S., P. Harvey and H. Knox. 2005. Scales of Place and Networks: An Ethnography of the Imperative to Connect through Information and Communications Technologies. *Current Anthropology* 46(5): 805–26.

Hampton, K. N. 2003. Grieving for a Lost Network: Collective Action in a Wired Suburb. *Information Society* 19: 417–28.

Hampton, K. N., and B. Wellman. 2003. Neighboring in Netville: How the Internet Supports Community and Social Capital in a Wired Suburb. *City and Community* 2(3): 277–311.

Hands, J. 2010. *@ Is for Activism.* London: Pluto.

Hara, N. (2008). Internet Use for Political Mobilization: Voices of the Participants. *First Monday* 13(7). http://www.uic.edu/htbin/cgiwrap/bin/ojs/index.php/fm/article/viewArticle/2123/1976.

Hindman, M. 2009. *The Myth of Digital Democracy.* Princeton, NJ: Princeton University Press.

Hinkelbein, O. 2008. Strategien zur Digitalen Integration von Migranten: Ethnographische Fallstudien in Esslingen und Hannover. Unpublished PhD thesis, University of Bremen.

Howard, P. N. 2005. Deep Democracy, Thin Citizenship: The Impact of Digital Media in Political Campaing Strategy. *Annals of the American Academy of Political and Social Science* 597(1): 153–70.

Juris, J. S. 2008. *Networking Futures:* The Movements against Corporate Globalization. Durham, NC: Duke University Press.

Karim, M.R.A., and N. M. Khalid. 2003. *E-Government in Malaysia.* Subang Jaya: Pelanduk.

Kubicek, H., J. Millard and H. Westholm. 2003. The Long and Winding Road to One-stop Government. Paper presented at the Oxford Internet Institute and Information, Communication, and Society Conference, Oxford, 18 September.

Kushchu, I., and M. H. Kuscu. 2003. From e-Government to m-Government: Facing the Inevitable. In *Proceedings of the Third European Conference on e-Government (ECEG 2003)*, 253–60. Trinity College, Dublin. http://topics.developmentgateway.org/egovernment/rc/filedownload.do~itemId=396584.

Low, S. 2003. *Behind the Gates: Life, Security, and the Pursuit of Happiness in Fortress America.* New York: Routledge.

Marcus, G. 1995. Ethnography In/Of the World System: The Emergence of Multi-Sited Ethnography. *Annual Review of Anthropology* 24: 95–117.

Mayer, A. 1966. The Significance of Quasi-Groups in the Study of Complex Societies. In *The Social Anthropology of Complex Societies*, ASA Monographs, No. 4, ed. Michael Banton, 97–122. London: Tavistock.

McInerney, P. B. 2009. Technology Movements and the Politics of Free/Open Source Software. *Science, Technology, and Human Values* 34(2): 206–33.

Melucci, A. 1996. *Challenging Codes: Collective Action in the Information Age.* Cambridge: Cambridge University Press.

Mesch, G. S., and Y. Levanon. 2003. Community Networking and Locally Based Social Ties in Two Suburban Locations. *City and Community* 2: 335–52.

Morozov, E. 2011. *The Net Delusion: The Dark Side of Internet Freedom.* New York: Public Affairs.

Nahon, K., J. Hemsley, S. Walker and M. Hussain. 2011. Fifteen Minutes of Fame: The Power of Blogs in the Lifecycle of Viral Political Information. *Policy and*

Internet 3(1): article 2. http://www.psocommons.org/policyandinternet/vol3/iss1/art2.

Narayan, G. 2007. Addressing the Digital Divide: E-governance and m-governance in a Hub and Spoke Model. *Electronic Journal on Information Systems in Developing Countries* 31(1): 1–14.

Noveck, B. S. 2008. Wiki-Government. *Democracy* 7 (Winter). http://www.democracyjournal.org/7/6570.php.

Oates, S., D. Owen and R. K. Gibson, eds. 2006. *The Internet and Politics: Citizens, Voters and Activists.* New York: Routledge.

Pew Research Center for the People and the Press. 2008. *Social Networking and Online Videos Take Off: Internet's Broader Role in Campaign 2008.* Washington, DC: Pew Research Center for the People and the Press. http://people-press.org/reports/display.php3?ReportID = 384_.

Postill, J. 2002. Clock and Calendar Time: A Missing Anthropological Problem. *Time and Society* 11: 251–70.

Postill, J. 2005. Internet y epidemiología cultural en Malaisia: reflexiones desde la antropología cognitiva. In *Antropología de los Media*, ed. E. Ardevol and J. Grau. Seville: AA.EE.

Postill, J. 2006. *Media and Nation Building: How the Iban Became Malaysian.* Oxford: Berghahn Books.

Postill, J. 2008 Localising the Internet beyond Communities and Networks. *New Media and Society* 10(3): 413–31.

Postill, J. 2011. *Localizing the Internet: An Anthropological Account.* Oxford: Berghahn Books.

Rafael, V. 2003. The Cell Phone and the Crowd: Messianic Politics in the Contemporary Philippines. *Public Culture* 15(3): 399–425.

Rheingold, H. 2002. *Smart Mobs: The Next Social Revolution.* Cambridge, MA: Perseus.

Roberts, B. 2009. Beyond the 'Networked Public Sphere': Politics, Participation and Technics in Web 2.0. *Fibreculture Journal* 14. http://journal.fibreculture.org/issue14/issue14_abstracts.html.

Shirky, C. 2009. *Here Comes Everybody: The Power of Organizing Without Organizations.* New York: Penguin Books.

Smith, A., and L. Rainie. 2008. *The Internet and the 2008 Election.* Washington, DC: Pew Internet and American Life Project. http://www.pewinternet.org/pdfs/PIP_2008_election.pdf.

Sreberny, A., and G. Khiabany. 2010. *Blogistan: The Internet and Politics in Iran.* London: Tauris.

Strathern, M. 1996. Cutting the Network. *Journal of the Royal Anthropological Institute* 2: 517–35.

Strauss, P. 2007. Fibre Optics and Community in East London: Political Technologies on a 'Wired-Up' Newham Housing Estate. Unpublished PhD thesis, Manchester University.

Swartz, D. 1997. *Culture and Power: The Sociology of Pierre Bourdieu.* Chicago: University of Chicago Press.

Swartz, D., V. Turner and A. Tuden, eds. 1966. *Political Anthropology.* Chicago: Aldine.

Tenhunen, S. 2008. Mobile Technology in the Village: ICTs, Culture, and Social Logistics in India. *Journal of the Royal Anthropological Institute (New Series)* 14: 515–34.

Turner, V. W. 1974. *Dramas, Fields and Metaphors: Symbolic Action in Human Society.* Ithaca, NY: Cornell University Press.

Venkatesh, M. 2003. The Community Network Lifecycle: A Framework for Research and Action. *Information Society* 19: 339–47.

Wasik, B. 2009. *And Then There's This: How Stories Live and Die in Viral Culture.* New York: Viking Press.

Webster, F. 1995. *Theories of the Information Society.* London: Routledge.

Wellman, B., et al. 2003. The Social Affordances of the Internet for Networked Individualism. *Journal of Computer-Mediated Communication* 8(3). http://jcmc.indiana.edu/vol8/issue3/wellman.html.

Yong, J.S.L. 2003. Malaysia: Advancing Public Administration into the Information Age. In *E-Government in Asia: Enabling Public Service Innovation in the 21st Century*, ed. J.S.L. Yong, 175–203. Singapore: Times.

–9–

Free Software and the Politics of Sharing

Jelena Karanović

The study of software extends a long-standing anthropological interest in 'the imponderabilia of actual life' (Malinowski 1922: 20). From cell phones to social networking platforms, software is the mundane infrastructure of the daily lives of people worldwide. In the shape of search engines, mapping tools and databases, it is central to the reorganizing of media experiences (Bowker and Star 1999; Miller et al. 2005; Scholz 2008; Stalder and Mayer 2009). Court cases, pedagogical guidelines and polemics about sharing films, music and texts online suggest that much remains open-ended with respect to acceptable uses of digital media. Yet the politics of digital infrastructure is often elided by the assumption—or promise—of access on market terms (Ginsburg 2008).

Free software (FS) offers a cogent entry into struggles over meanings of sharing that, in turn, are key to contentions about the appropriate legal, economic and technical frameworks for digital media. From the web browser Mozilla Firefox to the blogging platform WordPress, free software contradicts the assumption that property rights are necessary as a motivation for making sophisticated and innovative digital media. Each FS project encompasses software code as well as a licence that ensures that all users have the right to study, modify, copy and redistribute the software. These rights make FS distinct from *proprietary software*, whose modification and distribution are restricted by copyright. FS enthusiasts are sensitive about seemingly arcane technical matters such as the choice of software platforms, legal licences, data formats and technological standards. In this chapter, I argue that, by studying how these putatively specialized issues matter in daily contexts, anthropologists can address questions about (political, legal, technological and societal) choices that are routinely muted in discussions of digital media.

I proceed by surveying how anthropologists have contributed to understanding the utopian premises of free software. I then rely on the lens of ethnography to make two related points: First, I explore accounts of FS developers to scrutinize the notion of 'hacker ethic' that has animated many studies of free and open-source software. Ethnographic accounts suggest that it is not only hackers' passion for writing and sharing code but also pedagogical and legal apprenticeship that are key to making high-quality software through (almost entirely) unpaid voluntary work. On the one hand, hackers may reshape media circulation; on the other hand, media change, and especially legal claims and technical contexts of software may create pressures for new forms of hacker engagement. Second, I argue that analyses of FS have so far highlighted a few strategic campaigns while obscuring the daily practices that sustain FS projects around the world. I expand the horizon of actors and practices that count in analyses of FS to address some dilemmas of participation in FS as a movement. Drawing on my ethnographic work in France in 2004–5, I focus on one group of girlfriends and wives of French FS activists who have employed their software and web-publishing skills to create an homage to the daily travails of free software development and advocacy. The final section of this chapter presents some preliminary thoughts of how struggles over software may matter to anthropologists interested in understanding the changing practices of media production, consumption and distribution.

The Utopian Challenges of Free Software

Since the late 1990s, the conceptual and legal frameworks of FS have served as a prime example for debates about the growth in commodification and regulation of the Internet. Critical legal scholars have posited FS as a challenge to corporate efforts to radically privatize the Internet and enforce a scarcity-based market in information through software protocols (Boyle 1996; Lessig 1999; Zittrain 2008). These critical accounts rest on conceptual dichotomies of free software to give salience to the wider legal and societal stakes in technological choices. Anthropologists have joined this debate by highlighting the hybrid nature of FS projects which often blur conceptual dichotomies (Kelty 2008): FS licences are often interpreted as a subversion of copyright and the ideology of romantic authorship, yet they rely on copyright to guarantee users' rights (Boyle 1996). Much of the rhetoric surrounding FS and 'the commons' shares with corporate capitalism and neoliberalism the notions of property, creativity and freedom (Coombe and Herman 2004).[1] While FS licences foster nonproprietary distribution of software, they do not prohibit commerce, and many FS contributors encourage and rely on the support of businesses, blurring the contrast between FS and market-oriented proprietary software production (Benkler 2006; Lessig 1999). Tracing some of these derivations, Kelty (2008) has argued that FS developers aim to reform, rather than overthrow, the contemporary constellation of markets, law and technical infrastructure that shape the meanings of software.

Large-scale FS projects, such as Debian, involve thousands of contributors who volunteer their time and skills. Economists and organizational theorists spearheaded research into the motivations of FS developers who put their time and energy into making software that then is given away (Ghosh 1998; Tirole and Lerner 2002; Von Hippel 2005). Early analyses suggested that developers are driven by a competition for prestige (Ghosh 1998; Raymond 2001) or career concerns (Tirole and Lerner

2002). In an influential contribution to this debate, political scientist Steven Weber argued that software is a 'network good'—that is its value increases as more people use it, as it is implemented on diverse platforms and as it becomes accepted as a standard (Weber 2004: 154). Online distribution of code enables many diverse actors to contribute to FS; even though only a small fraction of FS users contribute to software code, the gigantic user base encompasses many interested and skilled developers. Taking into account a range of motivations among FS developers, Kelty (2008) has nevertheless singled out developers' concern with access and modifiability of software. This concern makes it possible to understand software development as a form of collective engagement with existing technical, legal and market configurations. Kelty denotes this multiprong form of public engagement by the term *recursive public*: 'a public that is vitally concerned with the material and practical maintenance and modification of the technical, legal, practical, and conceptual means of its own existence as a public' (Kelty 2008: 3). By delineating the construct of a recursive public in FS and affiliated fields, Kelty's work seeks to expand assumptions about public speech and political engagement: he analyses practices of software development alongside more conventional activities of discussion, advocacy and voting.

FS has also catalyzed debates about the possibilities that the Internet offers for efficient and costless coordination. In particular, the development of the Linux kernel in the 1990s inspired research into how FS volunteers coordinate online to produce objects that, in many aspects, rival or even surpass industrially made professional software.[2] Here there are two main directions of research: The first one grounds FS in an ethics of access to information, freedom of expression and passionate pursuit of projects valued by peers, all emergent in the transnational communities of hackers and their daily practices (Himanen 2001; Jordan and Taylor 2004; Juris 2005). Hackers are here understood as tinkerers whose association is driven by digital networks. The second body of research epitomizes FS developers' practices as a model of decentralized, nonproprietary peer production made possible through digital networks (cf. Benkler 2006). While both of these approaches suggest that distributed invention rests on flexible networks, abundance of resources and individuals' freely choosing the projects in which they invest their time, their understandings of the agency afforded by the network may be overly limited. Distributed invention is not a novel phenomenon, nor is it unique to computing, nor is it dependent on the Internet (Ghosh 2005; Noyes 2009). As Noyes (2009) has argued, vernacular invention also depends on a network of people and things, yet is shaped by scarcity of resources, inflexibility of social ties and enforced inactivity that is often accompanied by boredom or frustration. Furthermore, some of these vernacular dimensions of the network are arguably at work among FS developers. For example, Born (1996) has found that computer researchers at IRCAM shared utopian ideals of collaborative authorship that subverted commodification, conventional copyright and the institutional power of IRCAM over their software. In practice, this sometimes entailed keeping the software on a computer disconnected from IRCAM's network, obfuscating the software code by neglecting to write comments or documentation and in general 'preferring to accrue research capital by circulating [software] via the international network to other selected computer music and research centres' (Born 1996: 113). In this case, the ethic of distributed authorship went hand-in-hand with patronage.

Joining the discussion about the novelty of FS, anthropologists have foregrounded continuities in the free software ideals of freedom and individual power, which build upon long-standing liberal debates about selfhood, property, creativity, governance and the place of the market in social life (cf. Coleman 2010a; Coleman and Golub 2008; Kelty 2008; Leach, Nafus and Krieger 2009). As Miller and Horst point out in the introduction to this book, the analytic use of the term *liberalism* encompasses clashing interpretations of the term. While in the United States, invocations of liberalism often refer to left-wing social agendas, in Europe the term is more troubled and denotes laissez-faire economic policies and US right-wing social agendas. FS activists are aware of such clashing interpretations and skilfully use them to clarify their own objectives. One especially vibrant interpretation by a French activist argued that free software could 'tame the devouring and devastating flames of freedom in order to conserve their warmth. To counter liberal fanaticism with love of a calorific form [that] takes care of its embers and knows how to grapple with what it consumes' (Moreau 2005: 15, my translation). The metaphor of tempering the flames of freedom was here in explicit opposition to US president George W. Bush's celebrations of unfettered freedom.

Anthropological attention to continuities of liberal ideals in FS helps counter claims—common in the broader literature on free software—about epochal effects on human creativity and governance of specific technologies (i.e. the spread of the Internet) or laws (e.g. Digital Millennium Copyright Act). Yet, as Coleman points out, 'continuity of liberal traditions does not mean sameness' (Coleman 2004: 511). It may be helpful to remember that debates about the Internet in the 1990s questioned whether online connections were real and whether it was possible to commercialize online transactions (cf. Marcus 1996). So a reinvention of liberal tenets—in practices and languages of programming—may be a more apt term than continuity.

As explained in more detail below, FS developers are arguably the most invested among hackers in reformulating 'liberal social institutions, legal formulations and ethical precepts' (Coleman and Golub 2008: 267). Yet the possibilities for uniting technological practices and political objectives vary in time and place. Whereas in the United States, the priority may lay in claiming that software is a form of speech, in the European Union, the priority may be in finding national political allies to contest the common-sense link between software and technology. For another example, being an FS developer in France in the early 2000s meant having to read English on a daily basis. Insufficient knowledge of English prevented people from finding help in installing and using FS. For this reason, translating documentation was as important as coding or helping other people install FS on their computers. Furthermore, translation encompassed not only technical documentation but also various practical manuals, opinions and answers on online forums. So being involved in global FS debates and projects also meant being thoroughly and constantly oriented towards French interlocutors (whether political parties, user associations or media) (Karanović 2008). Thus, the specifics of time and place are especially important for understanding how activists can rely on technical language and practices to pursue diverse political attachments. At the same time, many FS developers in France and elsewhere feel ambivalent about foregrounding the national contexts of their activities (cf. Takhteyev 2009). Regional and national inflections of FS then renew the currency of anthropological remark that activism around a global medium can simultaneously accomplish a variety of projects (cf. Ginsburg, Abu-Lughod and Larkin 2002).

FS ideals of free access and modifiability have been extended into other fields, notably in the free online encyclopaedia Wikipedia, open access journals such as Public Library of Science, music labels such as Magnatune and Jamendo and even social networking sites (Diaspora). Chris Kelty has been a particularly relentless interlocutor on the ways in which FS could serve as an inspiration for transforming anthropological publishing and teaching.[3] Since 2005, the expansion of FS principles into other fields has been eclipsed by a trove of businesses that combine social networking features with possibilities for users to upload, share and comment on the networked content. Typically these platforms allow users to access the content free of charge, but media makers have no access to anything comparable to source code in software. For this reason, reuse and reworking of content on these platforms (sometimes known as Web 2.0) resemble FS only in a generic sense of sharing and deserve analysis in their own right. For example, video bloggers and other subgroups use YouTube to build social connections by exchanging videos and commenting on each other's work (Burgess 2008; cf. Jenkins 2006; Juhasz 2011; Lange 2008). At the same time, users' videos are also commodities that YouTube uses to serve marketers (Burgess and Green 2009; Gillespie 2010). Millions of Internet users around the world have become adept at downloading and uploading files on peer-to-peer networks, and some artists are embracing online circulation of their recordings free of charge (Future of Music Coalition 2007; Rodman and Vanderdonckt 2006). Yet the insistence on users' rights to legally modify and redistribute, key to FS, seems to be an increasingly minor concern in the effusive growth of sharing and repurposing cultural forms online.

Rethinking the Hacker Ethic

The term *hackers* first came into wide circulation in the early 1980s, denoting tinkerers who were enthusiastic about computers (Levy 1984; Turkle 1984). One of the most influential accounts was by journalist Steven Levy, who portrayed three cohorts of hackers from the late 1950s to 1980s and argued that they shared a set of practices that he named the 'hacker ethic' (Levy 1984). The principles of the hacker ethic included sharing code, promoting decentralization, having access to computers and code in order to improve the code and using computers to improve the world. Levy's account suggests that free software is a faithful incarnation of the hacker ethic. He describes the founder of free software, Richard Stallman, as 'the last of the true hackers' due to Stallman's commitment to preserve the hacker ethic in computing despite the growing clout of business that restricted the sharing of software and disinterest among his peers who moved on to other ventures.

By the mid-1980s, the treatment of hackers in the media already had a negative valence and was associated with potentially criminal exploits. Levy's account forged a distinct identity that countered these negative stereotypes, although the term hacking is still used to denounce a wide variety of acts from whistleblowing to corporate crime. Otherwise, his exploration of differences was subdued, even though he noted that hackers did not necessarily agree on what makes one a hacker and whether hacking encompassed practices such as transgression and breaking into computer systems, which were overblown in the media. Moreover, although the hacker ethic postulated that giving away code was key to being a hacker, hackers held divergent stances on the free distribution of information. Historian Fred Turner writes that participants at the first Hackers' Conference, shortly after Levy's book was published, 'by and large…agreed that the free dissemination of information was a worthy ideal, but in some cases, it was clearly only an ideal' (Turner 2006: 263). Along with a small group of countercultural entrepreneurs and journalists, by the mid-1990s, hackers symbolized 'the liberated information worker', who mixed cutting-edge technology skills, creativity and entrepreneurship (Turner 2006: 259). Making free software was, increasingly, only one option among diverse business models that hackers pursued.

The successful commercialization of free software services in the late 1990s inspired numerous intellectuals to rethink the contrasts, well established in FS as well as in the hacker ethic, between proprietary and shared information. An influential elaboration of the hacker ethic from the dot-com era argued that the main 'ethical dilemma facing businesses in the new information economy' is that proprietary information (key to money-making) is dependent on publicly available information (gained through research) (Himanen 2001: 59). FS hackers and their norms of distributing—rather than owning—information, Himanen argued, led the way in realizing 'a free market economy in which competition would not be based on controlling information but on other factors' (60). Himanen's analysis relies upon a few well-known free software/open-source hackers and affiliated groups: Linus Torvalds, Eric Raymond, Richard Stallman, the Electronic Frontier Foundation and the Internet Society. What makes FS (rebranded 'open source' by a vocal set of activists and business owners) hackers distinctive in his view is that they find passionate interest and joy in their work and prioritize the 'recognition within a community that shares their passion' before the pursuit of money as an end in itself (Himanen 2001: 51).

Anthropologists have been much more inclined to explore the heterogeneity of hacker practices (Coleman 2012; Coleman and Golub 2008; Lin 2007). One strategy has been to pursue a more comprehensive categorization of hackers. Coleman and Golub (2008) have identified two ethical codes that hackers in the United States acknowledge in addition to free software: proponents of 'cryptofreedom' are concerned with preserving users' privacy by putting encryption tools within the reach of the public, while 'the hacker underground' has adopted transgression as a form of political critique. The concern with preserving the rights of users to legally copy, edit and distribute files—which is central to free software but muted in cryptofreedom and the hacker underground—has led some FS hackers to feel ambivalent or outright opposed to networks that offer downloading of the latest commercial music and films, making users clearly vulnerable to prosecution. The (sometimes uneasy) coexistence of three ethical codes is key to understanding heterogeneous progeny of hacking that ranges from free software to online subcultures of trolling (Coleman 2012).

Another approach revisited the history of FS hacking and longer-term developments that, by the early 1980s, came to be recognized as the hacker ethic. Kelty (2008) has traced five distinct genealogies that converged in the late 1990s around FS: the practices of sharing source code, writing software licences that subvert copyright, coordinating numerous contributors, aligning diverse actors around competing concepts of openness and discussing the principles of free software. Kelty has also reinterpreted the origin story of FS by arguing that the creation of the best known FS licence, GNU GPL, had less to do with the hacker ethic and more to do with historically specific concerns such as the genealogy of technical contributions to the text editor EMACS and the uncertain legal status of software in the early 1980s. Along similar lines, Kelty has argued that the practices of sharing source code in FS were not developed in opposition to dominant business habits but were rooted in a series of hybrid relationships ('quasi-commercial, quasi-academic, networked, and planetwide') that computer researchers have grown accustomed to in the proliferation of UNIX distributions (Kelty 2008: 141).

Hackers, a priori invested in exploring the possibilities of digital media, may be especially predisposed to experiment with the blurring of technological practices and political speech. Usually the relationship between hacking and novel forms of public engagement is broached in one direction only. For example theorists of networked peer production tend to focus on the question of how networks of peers, usually seen as animated by principles of the hacker ethic, may reshape media-making and circulation (cf. Benkler 2006). But the ethnographic work discussed in this section raises a possibility that has so far received less attention: that changes in technological contexts (e.g. the selling of a social networking platform) and legal claims may create pressures for new forms of hacker engagement. This issue was most directly addressed by Coleman (2009) as she juxtaposed an account of high-profile legal battles (and hackers' understandings of them) with hackers' everyday means of tinkering with technology, interpreting law and developing ethical precepts.

Ethnographic accounts have also suggested several means by which FS hackers learn and reclaim links between technology, law and ethics. Some FS projects, such as Debian, have explicit ethical guidelines and social contracts that developers discuss in the process of joining the project (Coleman and Hill 2004). Coleman and Hill have argued that as Debian developers become proficient in developing code and in discussing the implications of Debian software licence and policies, they also develop a commitment to information freedom. The implication is that pedagogical and legal apprenticeship is key to both distributed authorship and shared ethical precepts. Voting systems, such as in the Apache project, are also key to distributed authorship. Even the Linux project, Kelty has argued, owes its success to 'Linus Torvalds's pedagogical embedding in the world of UNIX, Minix, the Free Software Foundation, and the Usenet' (Kelty 2008: 215). Furthermore, although scholars and hackers themselves consider online/mediated interactions to constitute the key sites for work and socializing, the growth of conferences and yearly meetings gives hackers another important venue for developing and intensifying vibrant commitments and a sense of community (Coleman 2010b). Coleman writes, 'the advent of networked hacking should not be thought of as a displacement or replacement of physical interaction. These two modes silently but powerfully reinforce each other' (Coleman 2010b: 49). Coleman focuses on large-scale yearly conventions, but the same argument could include workshops, install parties, talks and informal gatherings.

The Expansive Sociality of Free Software

So far, I have sketched how ethnographies of FS hackers and geeks have qualified or challenged some generalizations about FS. However, their limited horizon—focusing solely on FS developers—raises questions about the meanings of FS among other groups, in other times and places. It invites an exploration of the global variation in 'recursive publics' (Kelty 2008) or 'network good' (Weber 2004). In my ethnographic study of FS advocacy in France, I found that FS advocacy is affected by national labour laws and nongovernmental organizations, linguistic differences, the availability of high-speed Internet access and contingent phenomena such as European Union integration or national revision of authorship law (cf. Karanović 2008). Ethnographies here can contribute an understanding of the daily activities that constitute engagement with software beyond a small number of very well known and studied projects. In the campaign against software patents in the European Union, FS activists wrote software but also planned protest actions, organized talks and conferences, talked to members of the European Parliament (MEPs), streamed and transcribed debates at the European Commission and published activist documents about US software patents, the European Patent Office and even the voting habits of MEPs (Karanović 2010).

The close attention to actors and contexts matters in understanding why FS developers embrace specific practices and representations. For example in response to two high-profile arrests of hackers in 1999 and 2003 for publishing allegedly illegal software, US-based free software programmers asserted that software was a form of public speech. Furthermore, they crafted the link between software and speech by writing code in the form of haiku and emphasizing its expressive possibilities (Coleman 2009). Around the same time, some of the participants on the German-language mailing list Oekonux, committed to discussing social implications of free software, found the concepts of cooperation and exchange to be overly simplistic when denoting their practices in free software and similar projects (Lovink 2003).

Ethnographic accounts of the expansive sociality of FS also suggest another way of thinking about the (utopian) universality of free software: anyone is invited to contribute. If taken seriously, this widens the scope of research beyond geeks and hackers. Kelty writes that the circle of FS users and potential contributors before 1998 was limited to people in high-technology hubs who 'got it'; this 'made it possible for [the ethnographer] to travel from Boston to Berlin to Bangalore and pick up an ongoing conversation with different people, in very different places, without missing a beat' (Kelty 2008: 20). New participants have always been welcome to FS, but in the early 2000s they came from a wider geographical and social range. This has inflected the scope, practice and ideals associated with FS. For example Peruvian FS activists were willing to engage formal political representatives and link notions of citizens' political rights to the adoption of FS in their national administration. As a result, public debates about FS in Peru were less influenced by considerations of technical strength or economic advantages than 'the recodability of political and civic bodies' (Chan 2004: 535). At the same time, the high-profile adoption of FS in the Brazilian public sector was led by experts who endeavoured to challenge neoliberal assumptions about technology- and intellectual property–driven economic growth (Shaw 2011). European FS advocates involved in the campaign against software patents decried the common-sense association of software with technology. As they became familiar with EU policymaking around software patents, many acquired a critical awareness of their European citizenship. For this reason, debates about software patents shed light not only on FS in the European Union but also on competing visions of the European Union (Karanović 2010).

Furthermore, an ethnographic purview may shed light on some dilemmas of gendered participation in the FS movement. FS advocates worldwide have for several years been concerned about the low participation of women and the absence of women's voices in FS projects (Ghosh et al. 2002; Lin 2005). The existence of several projects, such as Debian Women and LinuxChix, that explicitly aim to increase the participation of women developers qualifies the assertion that an egalitarian and meritocratic imagination precludes thinking about gender imparity among developers (Leach et al. 2009). I proceed to describe how a small group of women catalyzed debates about gender and participation in FS projects, although not entirely on terms of their own choosing. My account here is based on website analysis, interviews and twenty-month participant observation, in 2004 and 2005, among voluntary associations promoting FS in France.

The term *geek* (pronounced gik or zhik) comes from English and was popularized among French FS advocates via copinedegeek.com (which translates as 'geekgirlfriend.com'), a website created and maintained by romantic partners of several French software advocates between 2002 and 2005. Two of the website founders worked in a Parisian web-hosting company with gendered divisions of labour and technological platforms. The two women, Annabelle and Elsa, were the only women employees in the company, and both worked in marketing. Their male colleagues all worked on technical support and used free software. The two women first heard of free software during lunch conversations with coworkers and then read free software magazines, looked at websites of free software associations and visited the booths at the main free software convention in Paris. A few months later, both women found themselves dating free software developers, and they noticed that conversations with their dates resembled their lunchtime conversations with coworkers. This inspired them to create a website that would draw out these similarities in a humorous way. Annabelle bought a domain name (copinedegeek.com), and a team of six women launched the site in May 2002.

The mission statement positioned the website as 'foremost a result of years of experience of living with a free software geek'. Texts and images on the site presented, and made fun of, various stereotypes associated with free software developers, under the umbrella term of geeks. For example the photo-stories featured corporate computer industry bosses, ambitious corporate employees and girlfriends alongside free software developers. Humorous firsthand testimonials discussed geek diet, sense of time, dress style, importance of machines, vocabulary and holidays, all presented from the perspective of a girlfriend talking to another woman. The 'Geek Fair' section resembled a dating website; it had personal profiles as well as sorting, searching and messaging features. Some profiles read like personal ads, and several couples met through these personals. But more often, people made new friends; for example men who were habitually very shy used this platform to find partners for in-line skating rounds in Paris.[4]

In my interview with Annabelle, she explained that she had conceived of copinedegeek.com as a website made by women for women, intending to make them and their partners laugh. Yet the site rapidly took off in a direction that eclipsed her intentions. The majority of visitors were men who were trying to understand, in Annabelle's words, 'the way in which women saw geeks'.[5] These men visitors found humorous caricatures to be an adequate framework for thinking about gender and technology. Geeks were, on this website, assumed to be heterosexual men, although

Annabelle did receive one e-mail from a gay man who offered to contribute articles for the website. He often found himself adopting the strategies presented on copinedegeek.com in dealing with his geek partner.

There was no article devoted to defining a geek girlfriend, but the site made fun of a certain vision of femininity: it was designed in various shades of pink, decorated with red hearts and smiley faces and offered funny psychological surveys and virtual greeting cards. The top banner featured mascots of different free software projects, which are usually shown single—but, on the banner, each mascot was kissing, holding hands or looking at a counterpart of its kind. Less obvious to a casual eye is that the women designed the website using free software programmes only. Furthermore, the site's content was licensed through a FS-style licence which indicated, 'this document can be reproduced by any means if it is not modified and if this note is attached' (copinedegeek.com 2002a).

The specifics of time and place matter for understanding how these caricatures became a key Francophone site for understanding geeks at the turn of twenty-first century. Many French Internet professionals at the time eagerly read books by communication theorists, curious about how FS might contribute to realizing what they saw as the revolutionary social potential of the Internet (Karanović 2008). Annabelle's sources of inspiration included funny and often offensive French online forums—comparable to today's 4chan—that made fun of Internet enthusiasts.

Most French FS developers, advocates and enthusiasts were organized through voluntary associations. In contrast to copinedegeek.com, FS associations in France had very few women members and abstained from geek imagery. The term that most FS advocates preferred for their engagement was *militant* (advocate). Within a broader constellation of terms that are used in France to denote public engagement, *militant* implied enthusiasm, abstaining from radicalism and active engagement with people who were unfamiliar with FS issues. Aiming to broaden the range of people interested in free software, FS advocates emphasized a sense of social purpose in contrast to imagery of geeks as asocial technophiles or gadget consumers. Some advocates readily affirmed that they were not geeks, that their organizations were not limited to technical specialists and that free software should be accessible to anyone, democratically. When preparing public presentations or staffing booths at public events, FS associations' members were instructed to avoid using computer jargon, being glued to the computer screen and, above all, showing the command window or source code to newcomers. Displaying these specific traits was reputed to scare away the non–computer-savvy visitors.

The visibility of copinedegeek.com caricatures catalyzed discussions about desirable engagements that advocates aimed to foster around free software. Several FS advocates criticized the gendered caricatures on which copinedegeek.com stories thrived. Mireille, one of the most outspoken critics, found that the site discouraged women technical workers, because it positioned women in the role of assistants to men, who were technicians. Mireille faced these stereotypes in her daily work as technical assistant in an FS company: whenever she picked up the phone, the client assumed that she was a secretary. Mireille adopted the (grammatically masculine) title of *technicien* (rather than *technicienne*, a neologism that would be visibly marked as feminine) in an attempt to fight harmful stereotypes of gender and technology. The texts on copinedegeek.com, she found, also stereotyped men FS developers as inept social beings.

I have faced a similar set of stereotypes regarding gender and technical skills in negotiating my participant observation. For example, my presence at public events increased the number of women, which defied stereotypes of free software being a men's domain but often reinforced other stereotypes, notably those about gender and technical mastery. This became clear during the European IT Week fair, when I spent three days at the free software booth wearing a badge that identified me as 'exhibitor'. When someone asked me a question and I could not answer it, in embarrassment, I tried to switch my badge to one that said 'visitor'. Mario, an FS advocate who was at the booth with me, said I didn't have to worry about it too much; if I did not know the answer, I could just ask someone. But I did not want to reinforce the impression that women were at the booth solely in order to attract visitors and that the knowledgeable people were men. Despite feeling uncomfortable, I decided to stay at the booth in the interest of my research. On another occasion, I asked the organizing board of the local Parisian FS voluntary association whether I could join its mailing list. In response, the association invited me to join the board. A board member explained that the association was considering applying for some public funds, and the presence of at least one woman on the organizing board would increase its chances of obtaining the funding. Again, in the interest of my research, I accepted the role. (The association did not submit the application for funding.)

An anonymous article on copinedegeek.com addressed some criticisms. The article stated that the creators of the site were interested in creative uses of computers; they installed FS operating systems on their computers and used them for daily work; they understood and could engage many debates about the benefits and drawbacks of specific FS programmes. The conclusion was, 'If the words "software," "hard disk," "motherboard" give you nausea… it's not obvious that you could be a geek girlfriend' (copinedegeek.com 2002b). In other words, the text suggested, copinedegeek.com offered one means of engagement around FS. But it did set a standard so that every man FS advocate had to decide whether he was a geek and every woman FS advocate whether she was a geek girlfriend.[6] Although many of my interviewees—men and women—grappled with the implications of endorsing gendered and heteronormative engagement with FS, all claimed that diverse engagements around FS, including copinedegeek.com, were welcome. Voluntary associations, after all, strove to advance a broad range of commitments.

Furthermore, the website did offer a means of engagement with FS for some women. In particular, some women FS advocates found that it offered them a presence in FS without the considerable investment of free time, which was necessary for work with voluntary associations. For example, Edith and her partner were trained as computer scientists and had been ardent supporters of FS in their twenties. I met Edith in her early thirties. At our first meeting, she adeptly drew logos of various FS projects (*animaux fétiches*) into my notebook and explained their symbolism, along with the principles of FS. She had recently given birth to her daughter, and both she and her partner had since stopped their advocacy activities, because most of their time was occupied by their work and family affairs. Copinedegeek.com offered a means for Edith to continue keeping in touch with her friends.

Still other FS advocates found copinedegeek.com to be an expression of the playful spirit of FS and a showcase for an increased presence of women in advocacy. Véra, a financial consultant and former president of a local FS organization, loved arriving at professional IT conventions and seeing the copinedegeek.com booth, which she saw as 'full of women interested in FS'.

Finally, at least one copinedegeek.com contributor saw the website in a more expansive light, as a platform for talking about women's firsthand experiences with FS. Irène contributed a text that adopted the viewpoint of her daughter. The text narrated how a girl watched her mother type and, afterwards, started pressing the keyboard keys herself and made an astonishing mess that occupied her mother for a long time afterwards. Irène was very proud of her contribution, which portrayed computers in an all-women context and reclaimed copinedegeek.com as the prime platform for women's writing about free software.

Copinedegeek.com was simultaneously marginal and central to FS advocacy in France. The women who embraced the moniker geek girlfriend were, to a great extent, interested and skilled in FS, but on the website they chose to claim an involvement in the community mainly through their relationships with men. While their gendered stereotypes undermined the ideals of meritocracy dear to FS advocates, they also provided one way of addressing the knotty questions of where, how and for whom gender matters in FS. The peculiar gendering of the term geek challenges the idea of a seamless global conversation across continents—even when the platforms, practices and some of the assumptions are shared.

Conclusion

By creating sophisticated media platforms and an unconventional but robust legal regime of circulation, FS activists recast media change in terms of choices, which are often tied to political and social conjunctures. My discussion of the hacker ethic and expansive sociality of FS suggests two ways in which legal, ethical and political confrontations around software are carried forward in daily life. Hackers' commitments to freedom of speech and sharing of information are oriented towards maintaining a community of peer developers which requires individuals to embark on a pedagogical, ethical and legal apprenticeship. I have argued that this kind of sociality is a central but not the only way of participating in free software. Actors and practices that are only incidentally related to coding, such as the copinedegeek.com team, nevertheless shape the social meanings of free software, even as they reframe the participation in FS in ways that elicit ambivalence among FS contributors. More broadly, copinedegeek.com suggests that there are multiple ways to be involved in free software. The acceptance of this diversity, as I have illustrated, invites a debate about the goals of FS projects as forms of public engagement.

FS is also an effective reminder that utopian ideals and formal dichotomies (e.g. free/proprietary, copyleft/copyright) are only a starting point for an investigation of the changing practices of media production, consumption and distribution. While FS licences uphold users' rights to share and modify software, much of the sharing practised on YouTube, Flickr and various social networking sites takes place in direct contradiction of their terms of use that reserve pervasive rights for infrastructure owners. FS principles then suggest one approach to sharing in a much more pluralistic landscape. Furthermore, various contingencies emerge when analysing how practices of online sharing combine with the rules of the marketplace and novel forms of publicity. For example commercial media producers have employed strikingly different strategies towards fans' distribution of media in the case of music sharing, anime fandom and viral marketing (Varnelis 2008). Although many goods are shared without charge, it is the diversity of commitments and relationships that are pursued through these activities that is striking (Rodman and Vanderdonckt 2006). For this reason, I hesitate to subsume various projects of no-cost digital media sharing under a common umbrella and instead suggest that 'entailments and containments' in these projects may be one rich area for further empirical study (Strathern 1996: 525). Not only may further studies shed light on the rationales of inclusion and exclusion around intellectual property claims in specific social contexts, as Strathern (1996) has suggested, but also on the previously neglected emotional, social and ethical considerations that guide individual choices in the proliferation of digital media (Gershon 2010; Miller and Horst in the introduction to this volume). These ethnographic investigations, in realms beyond free software, reassert the importance of what FS activists routinely (and indiscriminately) call 'users' or the 'rights of the public' in the making of new normativities in digital media. By highlighting diverse commitments pursued under the aegis of sharing, further anthropological studies may add a new twist to the debate about minding the legal and technical possibilities in repurposing digital media—which may be a promising contribution that the study of FS offers to thinking about a much broader variety of digital media practices.

Notes

1. Coombe and Herman argue that the opposition of corporations against individual consumers—key to FS and commons advocates—rests on imagining both consumers and corporations as sovereign entities and obscures other actors

whose cultural properties are also entangled in the constellation of intellectual property laws and business in intangible properties.

2. Open-source activist Eric Raymond provided a catchy analogy by arguing that the open-source model of software development is similar to 'a great babbling bazaar of differing agendas and approaches', which he contrasted with a top-down, 'cathedral-style' approach of corporate software development (Raymond 2001: 21, 223).
3. Through participant observation in Creative Commons and the open-source textbook project Connexions, Kelty (2008) has analyzed how the principle of modifiability is extended to science and other domains of cultural production. He took part in several conversations about publishing, scholarly societies and open access to anthropology research (Kelty et al. 2008), made his book accessible online free of charge and contributes to public anthropology via the blog Savage Minds.
4. In-line skating was a major socializing activity among Parisian software activists at the time, so an in-line-skating penguin is a mascot of the Parisian software association Parinux.
5. There were no public comments on this site; readers sent their feedback via e-mail.
6. When confronted with the option of being a geek girlfriend, a number of women FS developers and advocates adopted the moniker 'geekette'—that is a woman skilled and passionately interested in free software. Despite their often having geek boyfriends or husbands, geekettes felt very strongly about their autonomous commitment to the FS movement.

References

Benkler, Y. 2006. *The Wealth of Networks: How Social Production Transforms Markets and Freedom.* New Haven, CT: Yale University Press.

Born, G. 1996. (Im)materiality and Sociality: The Dynamics of Intellectual Property in a Computer Software Research Culture. *Social Anthropology* 4(2): 101–16.

Bowker, G., and S. L. Star. 1999. *Sorting Things Out: Classification and Its Consequences.* Cambridge, MA: MIT Press.

Boyle, J. 1996. *Shamans, Software, and Spleens? Law and the Construction of the Information Society.* Cambridge, MA: Harvard University Press.

Burgess, J. 2008. All Your Chocolate Rain Are Belong to Us? In *Video Vortex Reader: Responses to YouTube*, ed. G. Lovink and S. Niederer, 101–10. Amsterdam: Institute of Network Cultures.

Burgess, J., and J. Green. 2009. *YouTube: Online Video and Participatory Culture.* Cambridge: Polity Press.

Chan, A. 2004. Coding Free Software, Coding Free States: Free Software Legislation and the Politics of Code in Peru. *Anthropological Quarterly* 77(3): 531–45.

Coleman, E. G. Forthcoming. *Coding Freedom: The Ethics and Aesthetics of Hacking*. Princeton, NJ: Princeton University Press.

Coleman, E. G. 2004. The Political Agnosticism of Free and Open Source Software and the Inadvertent Politics of Contrast. *Anthropological Quarterly* 77(3): 507–19.

Coleman, E. G. 2009. Code Is Speech: Legal Tinkering, Expertise, and Protest among Free and Open Source Software Developers. *Cultural Anthropology* 24(3): 420–54.

Coleman, E. G. 2010a. Ethnographic Approaches to Digital Media. *Annual Review of Anthropology* 39: 487–505.

Coleman, E. G. 2010b. The Hacker Conference: A Ritual Condensation and Celebration of a Lifeworld. *Anthropological Quarterly* 83(1): 47–72.

Coleman, E. G. 2012. Phreaks, Hackers, and Trolls and the Politics of Transgression and Spectacle. In *The Social Media Reader*, ed. M. Mandiberg, 99–119. New York: New York University Press.

Coleman, E. G., and A. Golub. 2008. Hacker Practice: Moral Genres and the Cultural Articulation of Liberalism. *Anthropological Theory* 8(3): 255–77.

Coleman, E. G., and M. Hill. 2004. The Social Production of Ethics in Debian and Free Software Communities. In *Free and Open Source Software Development*, ed. S. Koch, 273–95. Hershey, PA: IGI Global.

Coombe, R. J., and A. Herman. 2004. Rhetorical Virtues: Property, Speech, and the Commons on the World-Wide Web. *Anthropological Quarterly* 77(3): 559–74.

copinedegeek.com. 2002a. A propos du site. http://copinedegeek.com/article_simple.php3?id_article = 9.

copinedegeek.com. 2002b. En chaque CDG sommeille une geekette… http://copinedegeek.com/article.php3?id_article = 109.

Future of Music Coalition. 2007. New Business Models…and How Musicians, Labels and Songwriters Are Compensated. http://futureofmusic.org/article/article/new-business-models.

Gershon, I. 2010. *The Breakup 2.0: Disconnecting over New Media.* Ithaca, NY: Cornell University Press.

Ghosh, R. A. 1998. Cooking Pot Markets: An Economic Model for the Trade in Free Goods and Services on the Internet. *First Monday* 3(2). http://firstmonday.org/htbin/cgiwrap/bin/ojs/index.php/fm/article/view/580/501.

Ghosh, R. A., ed. 2005. *CODE: Collaborative Ownership and the Digital Economy.* Cambridge, MA: MIT Press.

Ghosh, R. A., R. Glott, B. Krieger and G. Robles. 2002. *Free/Libre and Open Source Software: Survey and Study. Part IV: Survey of Developers.* Maastricht: International Institute of Infonomics. http://www.flosspols.org/.

Gillespie, T. 2010. The Politics of 'Platforms'. *New Media and Society* 12(3): 347–64.

Ginsburg, F. 2008. Rethinking the Digital Age. In *The Media and Social Theory*, ed. D. Hesmondhalgh and J. Toynbee, 127–44. New York: Routledge.

Ginsburg, F., L. Abu-Lughod and B. Larkin, eds. 2002. *Media Worlds: Anthropology on New Terrain.* Berkeley: University of California Press.

Himanen, P. 2001. *The Hacker Ethic and the Spirit of the Information Age.* New York: Random House.

Jenkins, H. 2006. *Convergence Culture: Where Old and New Media Collide.* New York: New York University Press.

Jordan, T., and P. Taylor. 2004. *Hacktivism and Cyberwars: Rebels with a Cause?* London: Routledge.

Juhasz, A. 2011. *Learning from YouTube.* Cambridge, MA: MIT Press. http://vectors.usc.edu/projects/learningfromyoutube/.

Juris, J. S. 2005. The New Digital Media and Activist Networking within Anti-Corporate Globalization Movements. *Annals of the American Academy of Political and Social Science* 597: 189–208.

Karanović, J. 2008. Sharing Publics: Democracy, Cooperation, and Free Software Advocacy in France. PhD dissertation, New York University.

Karanović, J. 2010. Contentious Europeanization: The Paradox of Becoming European through Anti-Patent Activism. *Ethnos* 75(3): 252–74.

Kelty, C. M. 2008. *Two Bits: The Cultural Significance of Free Software.* Durham, NC: Duke University Press.

Kelty, C. M., M. M. J. Fischer, A. Golub, J. B. Jackson, K. Christen, M. F. Brown and T. Boellstorff. 2008. Anthropology In/of Circulation: The Future of Open Access and Scholarly Societies. *Cultural Anthropology* 23(3): 559–88.

Lange, P. 2008. (Mis)Conceptions about YouTube. In *Video Vortex Reader: Responses to YouTube*, ed. G. Lovink and S. Niederer, 87–100. Amsterdam: Institute of Network Cultures.

Leach, J., D. Nafus and B. Krieger. 2009. Freedom Imagined: Morality and Aesthetics in Open Source Software Design. *Ethnos* 74(1): 51–71.

Lessig, L. 1999. *Code and Other Laws of Cyberspace.* New York: Basic Books.

Levy, S. 1984. *Hackers: Heroes of the Computer Revolution.* New York: Delta.

Lin, Y.-W. 2005. Gender Dimensions of FLOSS Development. *Mute* 2(1). http://www.metamute.org/en/Gender-Dimensions-of-Floss-Development.

Lin, Y.-W. 2007. Hacker Culture and the FLOSS Innovation. In *Handbook of Research on Open Source Software*, ed. K. St. Amant and B. Still, 34–46. Hershey, PA: IGI Global.

Lovink, G. 2003. *My First Recession: Critical Internet Culture in Transition.* Rotterdam: V2/NAi Publishers.

Malinowski, B. 1922. *Argonauts of the Western Pacific: An Account of Native Enterprise and Adventure in the Archipelagos of Melanesian New Guinea.* London: Routledge.

Marcus, G. E. 1996. *Connected? Engagements with Media.* Vol. 3. Chicago: University of Chicago Press.

Miller, T., N. Govil, J. McMurria, R. Maxwell and W. Ting. 2005. *Global Hollywood 2.* London: British Film Institute.

Moreau, A. 2005. Le copyleft appliqué à la création artistique. Le collectif Copyleft Attitude et la Licence Art Libre. Master's thesis (DEA), University of Paris 8. http://antomoro.free.fr/left/dea/DEA_copyleft.html.

Noyes, D. 2009. Hardscrabble Academies: Toward a Social Economy of Vernacular Invention. *Ethnologia Europaea* 39(2): 41–53.

Raymond, E. S. 2001. *The Cathedral and the Bazaar: Musings on Linux and Open Source by an Accidental Revolutionary.* Sebastopol, CA: O'Reilly Media.

Rodman, G. B., and C. Vanderdonckt. 2006. Music for Nothing or, I Want My MP3: The Regulation and Recirculation of Affect. *Cultural Studies* 20(2): 245–61.

Scholz, T. 2008. Market Ideology and the Myths of Web 2.0. *First Monday* 13(3). http://firstmonday.org/htbin/cgiwrap/bin/ojs/index.php/fm/article/view/2138/1945.

Shaw, A. 2011. Insurgent Expertise: The Politics of Free/Livre and Open Source Software in Brazil. *Journal of Information Technology and Politics* 8: 253–72.

Stalder, F., and C. Mayer. 2009. The Second Index: Search Engines, Personalization and Surveillance. In *Deep Search: The Politics of Search beyond Google*, ed. K. Becker and F. Stalder, 98–116. Innsbruck: Studienverlag.

Strathern, M. 1996. Cutting the Network. *Journal of the Royal Anthropological Institute* 2(3): 517–35.

Takhteyev, Y. 2009. Coding Places: Uneven Globalization of Software Work in Rio de Janeiro, Brazil. PhD diss., University of California, Berkeley.

Tirole, J., and J. Lerner. 2002. Some Simple Economics of Open Source. *Journal of Industrial Economics* 50(2): 197–234.

Turkle, S. 1984. *The Second Self: Computers and the Human Spirit.* New York: Simon & Schuster.

Turner, F. 2006. *From Counterculture to Cyberculture: Stewart Brand, the Whole Earth Network, and the Rise of Digital Utopianism.* Chicago: University of Chicago Press.

Varnelis, K., ed. 2008. *Networked Publics.* Cambridge, MA: MIT Press.

Von Hippel, E. 2005. *Democratizing Innovation.* Cambridge, MA: MIT Press.

Weber, S. 2004. *The Success of Open Source.* Cambridge, MA: Harvard University Press.

Zittrain, J. 2008. *The Future of the Internet—And How to Stop It.* New Haven, CT: Yale University Press.

–10–

Diverse Digital Worlds

Bart Barendregt

Digital Futures and Its Discontent

Book titles such as *How the Digital Age Is Changing Our Minds*, *The Future of the Past in the Digital Age* or, for that matter, *The Future of the Internet* suggest how our future is not only wide open but increasingly deemed to be digital. Yet, surprisingly little anthropological research is done on how people envisage these digital futures, nor has there been much attention devoted to the cross-cultural diversity of such imaginations. This chapter, then, will focus on how the idea and ideal of the information society and other modern myths, such as that of the digital revolution, have impacted digital practices around the world and how this sheer diversity will feed back into one of the main narratives of our time.

Join the Future (But Whose?)

For over four decades the ideal of the information society has been a battleground for ideologists, a struggle whose origins can be traced to the early Cold War era. Although in those days the United States outwitted the Soviets on most terrains, the latter could resort to the powerful rhetoric of tomorrow's communist paradise. Hence, a much-needed counterfuture was needed and was eventually to be found in McLuhan's *Understanding Media* (1964). While Soviet intelligentsia propagated a future of cybernetic communism, US think tanks appropriated McLuhan's technology in their drive for progress, above all his notion of the Global Village, eventually producing what is now known as the Net (see Barbrook 2007). Today our future is even more technologically driven, encouraging blind faith in digital technologies and bringing in its wake the rise of a global economy in which e-commerce and e-governance are not yet standard but, nevertheless, are much-sought-after ideals by states and the private sector. However, the very dominance of idealized digital futures has always led to at least a marginal dissident fringe in both the digital hinterlands and in the very heart of the information society. In these heartlands, dissidents point to the information society's shortcomings, creating counterideals of 'slow' life—with retro symbols of previous technologies such as knitting and black-and-white TV—while taking cult books such as the *Cloudspotter's Guide* (Pretor-Pinney and Cloud Appreciation Society 2006) to be their Bible. Many claim that the technology that is meant to connect actually disconnects, and those complaining are to regain control over their own lives. Even future-orientated magazines, such as *Wired*, seem to have a soft spot for cults for the Information Age, such as the 2005 Hipster PDA, or the Getting-Things-Done movement (after David Allen's 2001 book). Dissidents have thus tried to envisage an alternative future which ensures that such technologies adhere to, rather than destroy, wider spiritual values. In fact, this was an important element even in the original conception of digital futures in California's Silicon Valley. Both Turner (2006) and Zandbergen (2011) have described a spiritual undercurrent in San Francisco Bay Area geekdom, running all the way from Stewart Brand's journal, *Whole Earth Catalog*, to today's New Edge movement. Others write on cyber gnosis's blending of secular technology and a quest for a spiritual experience of ultimate reality (Aupers, Houtman and Pels 2008). Anthropologists may bear witness to another significant downside to the information society as both new technologies and their associated practices from the start seem Westerly dominated.

Globalizing the Digital

Hassan (2008) recounts how the ideal of an informational society that is cheap, efficient and clean ignores the hidden costs elsewhere. One only has to look at the electronic dumps of southern China (Basel Action Network 2002) or the civil war fought in Congo over much-needed minerals to help those in richer nations produce phones and game consoles, along with more general disputes over rare resources, to see the very material consequences of the digital. Answers to how to avoid such hidden costs have been sought in awareness campaigns such as the recent Fair IT approach, and major players involved in the digital revolution—the Microsofts, HPs and Sonys of this world—have special funds set aside for developing environmentally friendly green computing, lest it won't prove to be a failed revolution. If we put this evidence for the incorporation of digital technologies in fostering global inequalities within the larger political economy, together with the more traditional critique of the West that is associated with much of the developing world, it is not surprising that one of the main responses to the rise of digital technologies is a conceptualization of them as just the latest version of Western domination. Does this mean that what Barbrook and Cameron (1996) refer to as the 'Californian ideology'—a contradictory mix of the left's liberal society and the right's liberal marketplace—has become the dominant dictum in the information society?

The fear of the information society being yet another extension of global liberal capitalism reduces globalization processes to just that—its economic dimension. It is the globalization described by the likes of Friedman, Fukuyama and other hyperglobalists, who argue that we are currently witnessing an era of unprecedented acceleration and disembedding processes that will result in one single homogeneous marketplace (or, in a slightly milder form, that media capitalism will Westernize other cultures). However, the economy cannot be that easily separated from cultural, social or political issues. While recognizing the unique possibilities offered by transport and especially new communication technologies, many have also been keen to stress that globalization is hardly a new phenomenon. Indeed, it can be said (depending on one's interest) to have started as early as the fifteenth century intercontinental sea trade or that it began with the late-nineteenth-century era of electronic inventions. Those starting from such a historical perspective argue that an exclusive focus on the novelty of new media technology closes our eyes to the fact that many technologies coined as 'new' have actually been around for quite a while (for examples, see Goggin [2006: 23], on 1893 experiments with radio-by-phone in Budapest, or Standage [1998], on what he dubs 'the Victorian Internet'—telegraph and pneumatic tubes) and that most users are sometimes still happily living with old creolized technologies (Edgerton 2007).

Similarly, anthropological critique has targeted the supposed reach of globalization processes. Focusing on the digital, one may argue that what many theorists have described as globalization actually refers to transnational processes fed by interconnecting state-sponsored high-tech industries in California and in Asian hubs such as Singapore or South Korea, leaving out huge parts of the world—especially the less-well-developed world. More so, much of what passes as global Western culture is, as far as digital technology is concerned, increasingly a product of East Asian companies, leading some (in the West) to fear a highly techno-orientalist future (Morley and Robins 1995: 6). Others describe globalization as, at best, patchy. In his *Network Society* trilogy, Castells (1997) refers to 'the black holes' of informational capitalism, as even within the very same centres of the digital, possibilities tend to be unevenly distributed. With the digital haves better connected than the digital have-nots, gated communities have found their online equivalents with the like-minded and the well positioned increasingly talking amongst themselves and traditionally vulnerable groups such as immigrants, the lower classes or senior citizens simply dropping off the digital map. Digital technologies facilitate the outsourcing of simple and unpleasant work to cheap-labour countries such as Mexico, Suriname or the Philippines (see Shome 2006, for what she calls the 'crisis of logic of race' brought about by Indian call centre work) or 'body shopping' some of India's brightest engineers (Xiang 2007), leading to a brain drain, alienation and adding to already existing inequalities. 'Where do you want to go today?' was one of Microsoft's famous taglines hailing the pros of the information era; however, the consequence of the current 'materiality of the global' is that some are more mobile and much easier to connect than others (Inda and Rosaldo 2008: 29). Accordingly, anthropologists such as Tsing (2005) and Ferguson (1999) call upon their colleagues to not just focus on globalization's increased interconnectedness but on how it may actually disconnect and to focus not only on the privileged centres, cutting-edge technology or the hip informational avant-garde but also on those awkwardly connected places and people that are now simply ignored in globalization processes and, thus, left to themselves in formulating a digital future in which to participate.

Responses from the Digital Hinterlands

Studies of diverse digital worlds could thus benefit from work that shows how global cultural dynamics are far from the exclusive Western project so often imagined. Such work offers important correctives to the cultural imperialism thesis that was popular in the late 1970s and 1980s and that is still adhered to by informational critics such as Barbrook. Undeniably, ours is an era that sees Western cultural commodities and ideas flowing from the centre to be replicated in all outlying areas of the world. Take the sole dominance of word processing software such as Microsoft Word and its impact on the 'logic of script' in many vernacular languages (Dor 2004). However, this West is increasingly detached from the physical West, not least because of non-Western information technology specialists increasingly being responsible for the main share of programming and design in traditional Western digital centres such as Silicon Valley.

Inda and Rosaldo (2008) summarize three other critiques of the still-current cultural imperialism thesis which can be easily illustrated with examples from recent digital studies. A first critique is that, despite a dominant flow of all things cultural from the rich North to the poor South, recipients at the other end are never just passive. Many studies prove how consumers of Western digital technologies bring their own cultural impositions, reinterpreting and customizing such practices. Heeks (2008) illustrates how role-playing games such as World of Warcraft offer not just online entertainment but financial benefits and even educational skills to young Chinese players. Whereas their Western peers stick to the credo of fair play, Chinese gold farmers (named for their massive commodity production and sales on online fan sites) are hated for 'kill-stealing', 'ninja looting' and overt advertising. The Chinese, in turn, face threats and abuse and are (in games) massacred by Western players, who, ventilating negative homogeneous images of electronic sweatshops, clearly echo racial stereotypes of the first US gold rush (Yi-Shan-Guan 2006). The point here is that a Western online game in a Chinese setting is reinterpreted as a tool for production rather than consumption.

A second critique pertains to the supposed one-directional view of globalization, with anthropologists highlighting reverse cultural flows and processes of mutual imbrications. A case in point is the successful and much-awarded Village Pay Phone programme initiated by Grameen, which helped Bangladeshi 'phone ladies' to start their own pay-phone services to otherwise disconnected villagers (Sullivan 2007). Once successful, the programme was transferred and adapted to a Ugandan context with neighbouring African countries following suit. The huge popularity of village phone projects triggered offshoots such as Kenya's M-Pesa mobile banking project, using mobile phones to move money cheaply and quickly without the intervention of a bank (Hughes and Lonie 2007). The success of M-Pesa eventually resulted in the Vodafone Company experimenting with international remittances being sent by mobiles from the United Kingdom to Kenya.

Lastly, adherents of the cultural imperialism thesis have traditionally paid little attention to global circuits of exchange outside the West, neglecting for example increasingly intense South-to-South contacts. A good example of this is the international free and open-source software (FOSS) movement, examples of which can be viewed in the BBC World documentary *The Code Breakers* (2006).

Examples such as those mentioned show the unforeseen ways that globalization may trigger local responses and how those who are seemingly not in charge look for alternatives to what is posited as a homogeneous worldwide information society. In studying the sheer diversity of the digital, scholars can clearly profit from previous work done by anthropologists of the global, who traditionally have highlighted such processes by paying attention to customization practices in places away from the (digital) centres of the world (see the later section on 'Comparing Digital Worlds'). As a further illustration, the case study for this chapter is devoted to a particular instance in which the Western neoliberal origins of the information society—and their contribution to digital anthropology more generally—have been increasingly contested.

Extended Case Study: Indonesia

Today, a majority of people worldwide, with most users situated in the poor South, access the Internet and other electronic information not through a personal computer but through their cell phones. A burgeoning literature on mobile phones (for overviews see Castells et al. 2007; Katz 2008; Ling and Donner 2009) shows how the use of mobile phones in various cultural contexts away from the West has led not only to genuine customization of cell phone technology and its associated practices but also to a plurality of expectations about what it is to be mobile and connected in the near future. Indonesian cell phone use provides a good illustration of both. This section offers a brief introduction to the digital revolution in an Indonesian context, paying attention to the question of why mobile phone practices have found fertile ground here. However, even within this one country, a plurality of digital worlds coexist. Three different cell phone practices illustrate not only how some of these practices have been genuinely Indonesianized but also how they serve as multiple imaginations of an Indonesian digital future.

Digital (R)evolution in an Indonesian Context

From the outset, nation-building in developing South East Asian states such as Indonesia has been characterized by an obsession with things modern, foremost iconic information technologies. Anderson (1983) argues that print technology is instrumental in raising national awareness (the nation literally being 'consumed' in reading newspapers or national-language novels). His thesis asks others to focus on the formative role of yet newer technologies, describing how nationalist aspirations have been expressed through the fight over post-and-radio communication in Indonesia's 1945 independence struggle, but also with the newly independent nation investing in an archipelago-wide radio and television network. A home-grown satellite system launched in 1976 was the first of its kind in the global South and eventually proved to be instrumental in creating a modern-day variant of Anderson's national audience (Barker 2005). It also resulted in a dynamic media landscape that was soon to be beyond the regime's control. In May 1998, foreshadowing the now much-celebrated Arab Spring, Indonesian students who had become familiar with information and communication technology (ICT) from their education abroad occupied the Indonesian parliament using laptops and other communication devices, calling for democracy and freedom (Hill and Sen 2005). This 'Revolution of Small Media'—with equivalent electronic uprisings in democratizing societies such as the Philippines (Rafael 2003), South Korea (Castells et al. 2007) and the Arab world (Ibahrine 2008)—initiated an era of reform and a rise of civic initiatives. Given the early use of digital technology for political causes in the late 1990s and throughout the early 2000s, it is no surprise that in the subsequent years many important Indonesian Internet studies focused on issues of civil society, activism and the political potential of the web (Lim 2003; Nugroho 2011). However, in post-1998 Indonesia, as elsewhere (see Goggin 2006: chap. 3, on the 'cool phone') the Internet was predominantly used to embrace consumer fads, often imported from abroad and increasingly promoted by local lifestyle gurus, online Indonesian magazines and a blossoming creative industry based in Jakarta and other centres of hip. Since the early 2000s, a variety of social media has come and gone in rapid succession, but today mobile phones, preferably secondhand and reconditioned BlackBerry smartphones (other brands are simply too expensive), have become the ultimate Internet platform. Embracing their newly regained freedoms, Indonesians have transformed chatting, (micro)blogging and other forms of self-publishing into a national act, and within the space of only a few years, Facebook has become so popular that in early 2011 Indonesians form one of the largest Facebook nations (online users that are citizens from one particular nation state) worldwide.

Cultural Practices

Hitherto, few in-depth case studies have been published on the localization of mobile and new practices in cultural contexts away from the West. Works such as Horst and

Miller's (2006) on Jamaican phone practices and Pertierra's (2010) on new media use in the Philippines are among the exceptions. Two instances may help address the obvious question of how and in what way these new technologies can be described as distinctly Indonesian.

One of these practices is the prominence of social chatting software. Chatting in different forms remains by far the most popular use of digital media in Indonesia. Slama (2010) describes how chatting became part of an urban youth culture shortly after its introduction in the mid-1990s. The anonymity and other advantages offered by communication software such as mIRC or successful dating sites such as match.com and later Friendster allowed young Indonesians to safely experiment with romance in a society that otherwise disapproves of intimate public contact between the sexes. While seemingly unprecedented, and providing especially teenage girls with exciting new opportunities, the performative style of such amorous chit-chat can be traced to earlier Indonesian phenomena such as responsorial singing in the field, forest or during festivities, when prefab constructions were instrumental in creating an atmosphere of (t)ease and flirtation. Quite a few of the texts being sent by Indonesian mobile phone users or some of the more intimate exchanges in chat sessions seem to echo these older traditions. Over the years, compilations of text messages and Twitter poetry have been published, both online and as small booklets, spiced up with emoticons, English abbreviations and other forms of digital communication for the hip.

If the new private possibilities afforded by chat rooms and networking sites build upon certain Indonesian traditions, so do the more public uses of Indonesia's Internet. Much of the public discussion taking place on mailing lists or posted on YouTube, Facebook and other sites resembles earlier forms of *warung* (street stall) talk; the humorous, often engaged but otherwise very everyday conversations one can listen to in small, side-street shops, half-jokingly referred to as the 'people's parliament'. These conversations form a mixed modality with stories that are meant to communicate something but which are increasingly meant to be overheard (see Baym 2010: 63). New media language—including an increasing number of Indonesian blogs and Facebook sites using modern languages such as English—is part of the wider funky lifestyle now commonly glossed as *gaul*, meaning to socialize and talking about the right things often through word play.

Digital Nightmares and Possible Ways Out

To move from these initial questions of how technologies are appropriated within the country to the larger question of new imaginations of an Indonesian digital future, we need to bear three contextual issues in mind. First, strategically positioned between the West and the East, Indonesia contains the world's largest Muslim population. Ever since the Islamic revival of the early 1970s, various groups and spokespeople have used Islamic tenets as an antidote to Western colonial values and backwardness and have called for a genuine renaissance of the Muslim world. Alongside plans for Islamic science, economy and environmental care, information technology has been instrumental in revitalizing religion and making it ready for the twenty-first century. Second, we have to consider the sheer speed with which a country hardly penetrated by information technology infrastructure has become one of the fastest-growing markets in the region, where new and mobile media are sometimes plugged for the first time. Nonetheless, the spread of and access to the latest technologies is very uneven. Third, this initial use of digital media in the context of political action may have led to a wider conceptualization of the idea and ideal of a digital revolution. Despite these often unrealistic hopes, people's fears of the more sinister side of the digital revolution have also grown, with new media in Indonesia now commonly associated with political violence, piracy and pornography. Such fears of new technology are of all times and all places, an overview of which can be found in works such as Katz (2006) and Burgess (2004). Mobile phones are used to organize protests, but also possibly to trigger bombs, as was the case in the notorious Bali bombings of 2002. The rise of new and mobile media has led to and expressed new forms of public intimacy among Indonesian youth and a willingness to experiment with the new possibilities of cyber-ad phone sex. Skype in Internet cafés is used to circulate photos of girls, even veiled ones, displaying private parts of their bodies. Such practices are definitely not restricted to an Indonesian context, as proven by the work of Mathews (2010) on Filipina cam girls or Miller's (2011) treatment of the subject in Trinidad. But in Indonesia, new media, and especially the new anonymous sharing mechanisms it offers, have become associated with the rise of pornography as a Western perversity. New technology upsets existing configurations and forces people to take positions. In a country that has just freed itself from thirty-two years of authoritarian rule, censorship seems the least popular solution; as such, people have, more optimistically, thought about ways to facilitate, participate and actively stir and reorient the Indonesian information society. The fears outlined above, in tandem with the three aforementioned contextual issues—the country's position within the Islamic world, uneven access to information technologies and the coinciding of social and technical revolutions—lead to a plurality of visions about what the Indonesian information society may look like a few decades from now. To illustrate some of the more dominant, yet not mutually exclusive, future scenarios briefly, I refer to three mobile devices that have caught the public's attention over the last ten years, two of which can be seen as efforts to come to terms with an increasingly globalized information society by Indonesianizing such practices and the third being more postnational(ist) in character.

Indonesianizing the Mobile Phone

9949, the Presidential Hotline Early 2005 saw the rise of a daily column in the Indonesian national newspapers, which were often called 'open letters to the president'. These columns gave people the opportunity to send Indonesian president,

Susilo Bambang Yudhoyono (or SBY for short), a text message commenting on his first 100 days in office. Later that year, the president declared that citizens could now text him directly, and so he made public his private mobile phone number, 0811109949. He said at a public event that this number, the last four digits of which referred to his date of birth, 9 September 1949, had been a present from Telkomsel, the national telecommunication provider.

Stories in the national newspapers of the mid-2000s of presidential phone calls and text messages ride the waves of optimism triggered by the 1998 regime change and typify governmental hopes to facilitate and nationalize the global digital revolution. Such hopes include well-developed e-citizenship as an important token of countries being able to make it into the digital era and innovative e-governance applications, which have become a hallmark of nationalist modernity.

In practice, these official attempts to promote digital citizenship have been complemented by others probably not envisioned by the government. There is an overall rise in citizen journalism, and both Facebook and YouTube have been used passionately by Indonesians to fight injustice. With many quick to point out the new media's somewhat dubious reputation of 'one-click-activism', the organizational potential of blogs and network sites received an additional push when, in October 2009, a 'one million Facebookers' support movement was launched to petition against the arrest of two senior members of the national Corruption Eradication Commission. The latest case showing how digital citizenship may very well turn its back on its creator involves President SBY filing charges against a former ally, now suspected of bribery. In a much-forwarded text message, the man threatens revenge by uncovering a number of scandals, including election data manipulation. While acknowledging that the law allows media to move against the government, SBY urged the media to be responsible when publishing news discrediting the government ('After SMS Rumor' 2011); so much for openness and transparency.

The Cannibalized Phone The December 2004 issue of *Tren Digital* magazine describes how camera phones rapidly evolve in terms of authenticity of colours, number of pixels and improved zoom functions. Now, however, there is something that even phone companies have not dared to think about: a camera phone with X-ray function. Ryan Filbert, an independent cell phone technician from Jakarta, managed to build the X-ray phone camera using two Nokia 6600 phones and a chip with infrared/night-vision functions taken from a Sony Handycam. The article includes some pictures showing the camera's ability to see through people's clothes and concludes with a quotation from a Nokia spokesman saying there were no legal measures the company could take against its phones being cannibalized 'as Indonesia at present still lacks a law covering such activities'.

The cannibal phone is just one among many tactics enabling Indonesian geeks and the digitally less well-off to participate in a future that was not theirs in the first place. Other practices may include the worldwide practice of strategic miscalls or 'beeping' as described by Donner (2007), Filipino cost-saving strategies such as exclusively using text messaging (Pertierra et al. 2002) or what Qiu (2009) dubs Chinese 'working class ICTs'. All these manipulated technologies may digitally benefit the lower echelons of society and facilitate the exchange of information at affordable rates. In the Indonesian context, this information-for-all credo is less of a political stance taken through hacker spaces, phreakers collectives or, for that matter, the immense popularity of open-source programming in the country. Rather, it has to do with gaining access to the digital media's promise of a glamorous mobile lifestyle. In the last two decades, Indonesia's rapidly growing middle class has been among the most fervent users of new and mobile media. While this middle class still counts for only a small portion of the country's population of 260 million people, its members' lifestyles, and their social and physical mobility, serve as role models for Indonesians more generally. This much-aspired-to mobile lifestyle is also pronounced in the cell phone craze that has swept the country since the late 1990s. Nonetheless, this only could be realized by addressing each of the social classes in distinct ways. While Jakarta's upper class prides itself on being able to afford the latest fashionable Nokia or (more recently) BlackBerry models, the defining feature of the Indonesian mobile phone market is actually its division into various submarkets, with the less well-off habitually buying an affordable phone in the semilegal circuit. The trade in black market phones is, thus far, one of the most genuine local practices. Black market phones come in all guises, ranging from stolen and secondhand phones to imported electronic waste given a new lease of life on the Indonesian market and so-called reconditioned phones. The latter are fabricated by amateur technicians such as the above mentioned Ryan Filbert. These autodidacts, who have often followed two-week commercial crash courses in cell phone technology, use parts of broken phones; the better, more prestigious phone 'eating' the other, inferior one. Similar practices are known in other parts of the world, and Bar, Pisani and Weber (2007) and Molony (2008) give examples of creolization of mobile technology for, respectively, Latin America and the world's 'least wired region', East Africa. While often despised by the authorities and official hardware vendors (all of whom are rumoured to have a share in this lucrative business), estimates suggest that up to 80 per cent of all phones on the Indonesian market have some sort of connection to the semilegal market. There is also an associated literature with titles such as *Quick Lessons on the Most Hip Social Network Sites (Plus Some Tricks)* (Hartoko 2010), or *Cool Sites Are Not Just for Cheating (Tips to Make Money or Find a Partner)* (Magdalena 2009), which not only give Indonesians a quick fix on the dos and don'ts of the Internet, Twitter and social networking sites, but also teach them to use both hardware and software in creative, unpredictable and often semilegal ways.

Between the Global and the Local, There Is Transnational Religion Today's use of new media clearly shows how Indonesians are no longer exclusively lured by the appeal of nationalizing technologies; nor do they automatically fall for the global fancies promoted in and from the digital centres, although many continue to partake

Figure 10.1. Moses Street, Yogyakarta, Indonesia. Author's photo.

by resorting to creolization. Other affiliations are at hand, the emerging popularity of Islamic software and hardware being a case in point.

As was evident in the case of the Amish (Wetmore 2007), the resistance to technologies by staunch religious practitioners has tended to be more a case of selecting which technologies are appropriate rather than a blanket rejection of all new technologies. In practice, more formal religions have been very successful in using the new digital affordances to their own advantage (see Lim 2009). But while there is plenty of research on how new media technologies have impacted and extended traditional religiosity, relatively few publications focus on what religion does to dominant ideas of the digital revolution or, for that matter, how religion has sought to intervene in what we know to be the information society. Also in Indonesia, new media technologies have been used to show not only how modern Islam can be, but also to trigger discussions on which direction such Muslim modernities should take if the digital era is to be embraced, as the following case attests.

The Pocket Muslim A 2007 folder shows a young Muslim woman with a digital device in her hands. Hidden under her veil is a pair of earplugs, and hanging from the device is a small prayer compass. The device, sold as the 'first Muslim iPod', was among the first to target young Muslim hipsters nationwide, with other 'pocket

Muslims', often with or focusing on phone functionality soon following suit. These pocket Muslims are handhelds with all sorts of Islamic multimedia features. Among the functions are an authorized digital Koran (in various languages, one of which is Indonesian or Malay) by al Sharif al Azhar—the late mufti of Egypt—various Islamic books in electronic format and an animation preparing for the annual pilgrimage to Mecca. The handhelds are mostly produced abroad, sometimes proudly bearing the certificate 'Made in Mecca'.

Indonesia has seen a considerable growth in its wealthy middle class and—contra many secularization theorists—this middle class increasingly prefers a modern, but otherwise very orthodox, lifestyle. The growth of this Muslim middle class in Indonesia and neighbouring countries such as Malaysia coincides with the shift from a previous Islamic revival in the early 1970s, in which religion was largely seen as the antidote to Western colonial values, towards what Göle (2000) has come to define as post-Islamism—religion covering the nitty-gritty of the everyday and penetrating all domains of life. Post-Islamist lifestyles simultaneously challenge the orthodox, as it is 'contaminated' by Western consumerism and the secular modern, with public expressions of religiosity, obviously borrowing the imagery of its opponents. New media are prominent tools in emphasizing the notion of such a modern Muslim lifestyle (for a more general account, see Eickelman and Anderson 2003). New media have regularly been subject to fatwa, with Islamic hardliners quick to call for bans on, for example, bets placed via text and condemning excerpts from the Koran being used as ring tones. Others, more pragmatically, have categorized technology as *sunnatulah*—God-given—blaming not technology but its users when things go wrong. However, the import of Western technology has led many modern Muslims to lament the fact that, even in the postcolonial era, Muslim countries are still colonized by Western technologies and that these technologies, superior though they may be, lack a spiritual component. Clearly, the challenge here is how to constantly remind Muslims using (modern information) technology of Allah's greatness and to encourage them to abide by his laws.

So far, two different, though not mutually exclusive, scenarios have emerged in response. The first relates to exploiting ICTs' outwardly (hyper)modern appearance for the process of Islamizing modernity. The result is a shaping of new media technologies according to existing preferences and, preferably, giving them a conspicuously Islamic feel. The second scenario is potentially more revolutionary in character, focusing on how Islamic practices can truly benefit from new technological advances and, thus, modernize Islam.

Categorized under the first approach are those new media practices that have been shaped according to Islamic taste. Following Campbell's (2006) description of the kosher phone or Ellwood-Clayton's (2003) Catholic texting practices in the Philippines (see Bell 2006 for a comparative study of technospiritual practices), most of these practices have their equivalents in other world religions. Some, however, are more uniquely used by Muslims, such as Mobile Syariah Banking or validated added text services such as the Al Quran Seluler, initiated in 2002 by televangelist Aa Gym. But one can also include the various Muslim phones that have targeted South East Asian markets. One of the most interesting efforts to create software that is conspicuously Islamic (although not exclusively Indonesian) has been an open-source project named Sabily. According to its website, Sabily is a free, open-source operating system 'designed by and for Muslims' (following others, such as a Christian and even a Satanic version). It is based on an Ubuntu Linux distribution system, and new versions, with Islamic names like Gaza or Badr, appear every ten months. Sabily provides 'Muslim users with out of the box Islamic software and tools', such as a prayer times app and a Koran viewer. Sabily is growing in popularity, and, considering the preference for open-source software among Indonesians, it is likely to gather a huge following.

All of the Islamic hardware and software described here is subject to the rules of religion and to rapidly changing (commercial) tastes and users' allegiances and ages (for example attitudinal differences between Muslims aligned with Salafi, liberal, traditional or extremist positions). It may, therefore, be more fruitful to look at the actual use and what, according to Muslims, is won or lost when using religiously inspired technologies—which brings me to the second approach.

Figure 10.2. Free open-source Sabily software sleeve. Courtesy of brother Muslih, from the Sabily team.

The second possible scenario is not so much an Islamization of the modern, but rather a modernization of Islam. Seen from this perspective, and stressing function rather than form, many Indonesian Muslims do not disapprove of the outward appearance of Muslim mobiles or other religious software and hardware, but they fail to see much of the added value. Why buy a digital Koran if one has hard copies at home? Why pay for an expensive phone with call-to-prayer functionality if one lives in a country where mosques are omnipresent? Whereas in the first approach, new media practices are conspicuously shaped by religious preferences, in other instances, Islamic practice has been clearly extended by the new technological advantages. One is reminded of how new media have changed the annual Islamic holiday that comes at the end of the fasting month of Ramadan. Traditionally, people all over Indonesia return home at this time to restore social relations with their relatives and ask forgiveness for slights and misunderstandings. Today, however, this is increasingly being done by sending text messages or by contacting friends and family through social networking sites. Perhaps more exciting is how new media in an Indonesian context have started to change contacts between Muslims of the opposite sex. It appears that Salafist girls, largely restricted in their daily conversations with boys, are among the most fervent users of texting, because it allows them to engage more freely with male friends. Moreover, Internet mailing lists offer new public spaces for women Muslims to reflect on women's interests, including health, sexual reproduction and women's rights.

Comparing Digital Worlds

How, then, should we study the idea and ideal of the information society? This last section uses the Indonesian materials to offer some clues on how a digital anthropologist may conduct further research on plural digital worlds. This is done with reference to studies of globalization, media and material culture, especially those that deal with customization and other localizing practices. Second, a close reading of the Indonesian digital, especially its transnational religious aspirations, is used to further scrutinize how digital technologies themselves are increasingly used to imagine specific futures, hopes and aspirations that could be central to our understanding of other people's digital worlds.

Cultural Ideas: Style, Mixing and Indigenous Poetics

The presidential hotline and cannibal phone, respectively, representing a top-down neoliberal formulation of what an information society should look like, and those trying to participate in a digital future not theirs clearly show how some scenarios for the near future are mutually interrelated.

Again, much is to be learned here from students of the global or the work done in the field of multiple modernities. Such works show how it is not just a matter of adjusting form or recoding the practice to soften the impact of (global) modernity, but how the digital and other domains of life increasingly penetrated by processes of globalization are sites where a people are not externally made modern, but make themselves modern, thus providing themselves with an identity and a destiny (Gaonkar 1999). Much of the anthropological study of the global focuses on processes of localization, vernacularization, creolization or, more generally, customization, referring to processes in which formerly separate (but not necessarily pure) cultural traditions—here the Western digital and local readings of it—to a different extent can be mixed, often resulting in new, third forms.

In the field of media and material studies there are plenty of clues on how to study creative appropriations of dominant digital culture away from its centre. In an early study on Yoruba (analogue) photography, Sprague (1978) speaks of the ways African people may or may not use modern technology to visually shape their own (figurative) traditions, leading him to conclude how 'photographs are actually coded in Yoruba'. Sprague's and others' findings are taken up by those studying new media's 'indigenous poetics', referring to a culturally recognizable style and the ways distinctive cultural ideals, logic and knowledge are organized and expressed (Wilson and Stewart 2008).

Examples of such poetics include Hjorth (2009), who describes how, in many Asian societies, cell phone cameras have initiated 'techno-cute practices': 'feminine' customization ranging from pink casings or characters hanging from one's phone to the cute aesthetics of holding the cell phone camera in such a way that eyes look big and bodies small. Writing on the media use of first people groups, Ginsburg (2002: 220) describes the Tanami Network, an early video-conferencing network that was established by the Warlpiri communities of the Northern Territory, Australia. Tanami was intentionally designed to break with 'white people's' use of information technology, now prioritizing decentralization and interactivity. In a similar vein, Christie (2008) calls for a more indigenous-friendly approach to digital technologies, especially where digital rights management is concerned. In a fascinating account, Deirdre Brown (2007) describes how such an approach may respect local cultural values towards the digital. In an experiment at a New Zealand museum, Maori heirlooms are digitized for exhibition, taking into account ownership and possible issues of desacralization. It may be such and other creative appropriations that very much hold the key to further anthropological ventures into the digital.

Technological Drama

In certain respects, the Indonesian case in the previous section echoes a long-standing tradition in the anthropology of technology in which, following Bryan Pfaffenberger (1992), the emphasis is on the sociality of human technological activity. Today's information society forms part of much wider systems which incorporate issues of regularization, adjustment and reconstitution. South East Asian governments, including that of Indonesia, are eager to regularize, hoping to actively engage their citizens in a digital era and providing them with technologies and infrastructure. However, technological features mostly embody a larger political aim. Early satellite technology, as Barker (2005) illustrates, was mostly used to spread dominant Javanese values to the outer Indonesian islands and strengthened a nationalist-military vision of the thousand-island archipelago. And while the Internet now enables Indonesians to partake in a global world of capitalism, fashion and consumerism, the success of new, mobile and social media continues to be measured by their contribution to the national and international economical growth—all much in line with what critics such as Barbrook and Cameron (1996) argue to be 'the Californian ideology'. Our second scenario for which the cannibal phone stood as a model illustrates Pfaffenberger's notion of 'adjustment', or strategies to compensate 'the loss of self-esteem, social prestige, and social power caused by the technology' (1992: 506). In the Indonesian setting, the use of creole technology, piracy and other forms of cheap globalization are means to gain access to the dominant system otherwise impenetrable by the digitally less well-off. This leaves us with reconstitution, the third process mentioned by Pfaffenberger (1992: 506) and said to consist of the fabrication of counterartefacts, 'believed to negate or reverse the political implications of the dominant system'. Islamic software and hardware may have a different feel to its users, but in functionality it hardly differs from its secular counterparts. Indonesian Muslims are fully partaking in today's information society, and while there is plenty of discussion on what and what not to do with some of the new technologies, this is done without ever radically breaking away from what other peers are doing around the world—or is it?

Cultural Ideals: The Islamic Information Society

One interesting aspect of the use of Indonesian Muslim ICTs is their increasing transnational reach. This is not just a question of techno-savvy radical groups propagating the ideal of the cyber caliphate. More progressive thinkers promote the concept of tomorrow's ummah, first referred to by people as Muslim intellectual Sardar and embraced by Malaysian opposition leader Anwar Ibrahim (1991), which can compete with the crowd-pulling power of cyber-fundamentalism or, for that matter, the more Western-style liberal information society. Such futures of a post-postmodern Muslim society are, in an Indonesian context, never that far off. One can think of initiatives from the private sector, including transnational telecommunications services, which allow Indonesian pilgrims to use their own phones and subscriptions while in the Holy Land, or a digital growth centre with Malaysian money and expertise being built in Medina—not coincidentally, the holy city that saw the beginning of the Islamic acquisition of knowledge and which is now chosen to transform Muslims and bring about a true revival in the digital era. Similarly, Facebook and other social networking sites have contributed to religious exchange between Indonesian youth and their Muslim peers elsewhere. The above-mentioned Sabily is one such project.

Initially launched by a Tunisian programmer living in Paris and hosted by a Kuwaiti server, it is now particularly popular in Malaysia and Indonesia. Sabily is not only a good example of the transnational, rather than global, character of much of today's ICT use, it also stands for the recent urge for so-called South-to-South software as expressed by participants of the 2000 Tunis Forum on ICTs and Development in the Islamic World and the Organization of the Islamic Conference (OIC). In 2003, at its biennial congress in Malaysia, the OIC unfolded its Vision 1441 (2020 in the Western calendar). It urged its fifty-six member-countries to focus on strengthening the knowledge-based 'K-economy' and to fight the deepening divides that threaten much of the Islamic world. Many international Muslim academics are fully involved in this movement, which has now been widely dubbed information and communication technology for the Muslim world, or ICT4M. A few years ago, Islamic-world.net, the site of the Malaysia-based Khalifah Institute, came up with a 'Web Plan' to realize a number-one Islamic web portal providing positive information about Islam and giving daily commentary on international news events from an Islamic perspective. Other strategies in much the same vein as the present Web 2.0 hype include polls to assess the opinion of Muslims worldwide on various issues important to Islam. There is also the promise of developmentalism as cheaply photocopied materials are provided in areas of the world still with limited access to electronic information technology. However, most interesting is the proposal to develop the 'Islamic Net', separate from the Internet as we know it and with the provision of at least one computer terminal in every mosque in the world being linked to it. Turning to new media, the worldwide ummah seems to have awakened and has become increasingly aware of itself. With one out of five world citizens—the majority of which, as Bunt (2009) warns, is still not online—new technological dreams are dreamt that may very well influence the course of what we understand to be today's information society.

How, Then, to Read the Digital Future?

Why should we care about tomorrow's digital dreams? And why focus on the discontents of today's information society? The simple answer is because that is what anthropologists do; they show that there are always various ways to address a problem and that, apparently, the problem can even differ from one society to another. Studies of digital culture have hitherto focused on the powerful centres of the information society, zooming in on research labs, geeks and youth cultures in the West and East Asia's metropoles, leaving the rest of the world to be digitally developed and thus the focus of information and communication technology for development (ICT4D) studies. If the interest in information technology in the Islamic South shows one thing, it is how digital technologies are used to imagine specific futures and cultural styles. Increasingly the digital itself is a prominent building block in shaping people's futures. One important task for anthropologists of the digital may be to compare such digital futurities, or forms of the future; the digital revolution and Western information society are but two of such possible metanarratives.

There have been no ethnographic equivalents to popular books on those places where the digital future is actually shaped: the local boardrooms of multinational players such as Google, Nokia or Samsung; on everyday life in digital growth centres such as Porto Digital, a high-tech development park in Brazil; Korea's Guro Digital Industrial Complex; the Medina Knowledge Economic City and many others involved in formulating the future digital. Again this is only half of the picture, and anthropologists of the digital would do well to incorporate those places more awkwardly connected. The essay of Watts (2008) on Scottish Orkney, a site for high-tech future-making in a 'far off place', serves as a good example, as does the study on the downsides of informational futures for women working in the information technology industry in Barbados by Freeman (2000) and Lindquist's (2009) similar account of the digitally deprived on the Indonesian island of Batam. Not everyone will be interested in doing fieldwork among policymakers, think tanks, futurists or trend watchers, but these are not the only ones to make a future. Anthropological fieldwork has shown that it is one thing to have an affluent dream about tomorrow's possibilities, but an entirely different thing to consider how such dreams act upon the present and upon those who seem to be left voiceless in such matters. Possible trajectories toward the future may start from small acts of resistance, such as a Muslim version of Facebook or a self-(re)styled hip phone for the poor. With other parts of the world vastly adopting, appropriating and reconstituting information technologies, embedding digital practices in a culture of their own, an exciting new era for anthropologists is about to dawn. It is up to us to show how technologies once picked up in those parts of the world we have traditionally been interested in may lead to a reconfiguration of our sociotechnical systems and how other people's use may shape our own dreams for tomorrow's technologies.

References

After SMS Rumor, SBY Asks Media to be Cautious. 2011. *Jakarta Post Online*, 5 June. http://www.thejakartapost.com/news/2011/05/30/after-sms-rumor-sby-asks-media-be-cautious.html.

Allen, D. 2001. *Getting Things Done: The Art of Stress-free Productivity.* London: Penguin Books.

Anderson, B.R O'G. 1983. *Imagined Communities: Reflections on the Origin and Spread of Nationalism.* London: Verso.

Aupers, S., D. Houtman and P. Pels. 2008. Cybergnosis: Technology, Religion and the Secular. In *Religion: Beyond a Concept*, ed. H. De Vries, 687–703. New York: Fordham University Press.

Bar, F., F. Pisani and M. Weber. 2007. Mobile Technology Appropriation in a Distant Mirror: Baroque Infiltration, Creolization and Cannibalism. Paper presented at Seminario sobre Desarrollo Económico, Desarrollo Social y Comunicaciones Móviles en América Latina, 20–1 April. http://citeseerx.ist.psu.edu/viewdoc/download?doi=10.1.1.184.5809&rep=rep1&type=pdf.

Barbrook, R. 2007. *Imaginary Futures: From Thinking Machines to the Global Village.* London: Pluto.

Barbrook, R., and A. Cameron. 1996. The Californian Ideology. *Science as Culture* 6(1): 44–72.

Barker, J. 2005. Engineers and Political Dreams: Indonesia in the Satellite Age. *Current Anthropology* 46(5): 703–27.

Basel Action Network. 2002. *Exporting Harm: The High-tech Trashing of Asia.* Basel: BAN.

Baym, N. K. 2010. *Personal Connections in the Digital Age.* Cambridge, UK: Polity.

Bell, G. 2006. No More SMS from Jesus: Ubicomp, Religion and Techno-spiritual Practices. *Lecture Notes in Computer Science* 4206: 141–58.

Brown, D. 2007. Te Ahu Hiko: Digital Cultural Heritage and Indigenous Objects, People, and Environments. In *Theorizing Digital Cultural Heritage: A Critical Discourse*, ed. F. Cameron and S. Kenderdine, 78–91. Cambridge, MA: MIT Press.

Bunt, G. R. 2009. *IMuslims: Rewiring the House of Islam.* Chapel Hill: University of North Carolina Press.

Burgess, A. 2004. *Cellular Phones, Public Fears, and a Culture of Precaution.* New York: Cambridge University Press.

Campbell, H. 2006. Texting the Faith: Religious Users and Cell Phone Culture. In *The Cell Phone Reader: Essays in Social Transformation*, ed. A. P. Kavoori and N. Arceneaux, 139–54. New York: Peter Lang.

Castells, M. 1997. *The Information Age: Economy, Society and Culture.* Malden, MA: Blackwell.

Castells, M., M. Fernández-Ardèvol, J. Linchuan Qiu and A. Sey. 2007. *Mobile Communication and Society: A Global Perspective: A Project of the Annenberg Research Network on International Communication.* Cambridge, MA: MIT Press.

Christie, M. 2008. Digital Tools and the Management of Australian Aboriginal Desert Knowledge. In *Global Indigenous Media: Cultures, Poetics, and Politics*, ed. P. Wilson and M. Stewart, 270–86. Durham, NC: Duke University Press.

Code Breakers. 2006. Asia Pacific Development Information Programme. DVD documentary. London: One Planet Pictures. http://www.archive.org/details/The-Codebreakers.

Donner, J. 2007. The Rules of Beeping: Exchanging Messages via Intentional 'Missed Calls' on Mobile Phones. *Journal of Computer-Mediated Communication* 13(1): 1–22.

Dor, D. 2004. From Englishization to Imposed Multilingualism: Globalization, the Internet, and the Political Economy of the Linguistic Code. *Public Culture* 16(1): 97–118.

Edgerton, D. 2007. *The Shock of the Old: Technology and Global History since 1900*. Oxford: Oxford University Press.

Eickelman, D. F., and J. W. Anderson. 2003. *New Media in the Muslim World: The Emerging Public Sphere*. Bloomington: Indiana University Press.

Ellwood-Clayton, B. 2003. Texting and God. The Lord Is My Textmate—Folk Catholicism in the Cyber Philippines. In *Mobile Democracy: Essays on Society, Self and Politics*, ed. K. Nyíri. Vienna: Passagen. http://www.socialscience.t-mobile.hu/dok/8_Ellwood.pdf.

Ferguson, J. 1999. *Expectations of Modernity: Myths and Meanings of Urban Life on the Zambian Copperbelt*. Berkeley: University of California Press.

Freeman, C. 2000. *High Tech and High Heels in the Global Economy: Women, Work, and Pink-collar Identities in the Caribbean*. Durham, NC: Duke University Press.

Gaonkar, D. P. 1999. Alter/Native Modernities—On Alternative Modernities. *Public Culture: Bulletin of the Project for Transnational Cultural Studies* 11(1): 1.

Ginsburg, F. 2002. Mediating Culture: Indigenous Media, Ethnographic Film, and the Production of Identity. In *The Anthropology of Media: A Reader*, ed. K. M. Askew and R. R. Wilk, 210–31. Malden, MA: Blackwell.

Goggin, G. 2006. *Cell Phone Culture*. London: Routledge.

Göle, N. 2000. Snapshots of Islamic Modernities. *Daedalus: Proceedings of the American Academy of Arts and Sciences* 129(1): 91.

Hartoko, A. 2010. *Belajar cepat situs pertemanan paling gaul, plus tips & tricks* [*Quick Lessons on the Most Hip Social Network Sites (Plus Some Tricks)*]. Jakarta: Buku Kita.

Hassan, R. 2008. *The Information Society*. Cambridge: Polity Press.

Heeks, R. 2008. Current Analysis and Future Research Agenda on 'Gold Farming': Real-World Production in Developing Countries. IDPM Working Papers, University of Manchester. http://www.sed.manchester.ac.uk/idpm/research/publications/wp/di/di_wp32.htm.

Hill, D. T., and K. Sen. 2005. *The Internet in Indonesia's New Democracy*. London: Routledge.

Hjorth, L. 2008. *Mobile Media in the Asia Pacific: The Art of Being Mobile*. London: Routledge.

Horst, H. A., and D. Miller. 2006. *The Cell Phone: An Anthropology of Communication*. Oxford: Berg.

Hughes, N., and S. Lonie. 2007. M-Pesa: Mobile Money for the 'Unbanked'; Turning Cell Phones into 24-hour Tellers in Kenya. *Innovations* (Winter–Spring): 63–81.

Ibahrine, M. 2008. Mobile Communication and Sociopolitical Change in the Arab World. In *Handbook of Mobile Communication Studies*, ed. J. E. Katz, 257–72. Cambridge, MA: MIT Press.

Ibrahim, A. 1991. The Ummah and Tomorrow's World. *Futures* 23: 302–10.

Inda, J. X., and R. I. Rosaldo. 2008. *Anthropology of Globalisation: A Reader.* Malden, MA: Blackwell.

Katz, J. E. 2006. *Magic in the Air: Mobile Communication and the Transformation of Social Life.* New Brunswick, NJ: Transaction.

Katz, J. E. 2008. *Handbook of Mobile Communication Studies.* Cambridge, MA: MIT Press.

Lim, F.K.G. 2009. *Mediating Piety: Technology and Religion in Contemporary Asia.* Leiden: Brill.

Lim, M. 2003. From War-net to Net-war: The Internet and Resistance Identities in Indonesia. *International Information and Library Review* 35: 233–48.

Lindquist, J. 2009 *The Anxieties of Mobility. Development and Migration in the Indonesian Borderlands.* Honolulu: University of Hawaii Press.

Ling, R. S., and J. Donner. 2009. *Mobile Communication.* Cambridge: Polity Press.

Magdalena, M. 2009. *Situs Gaul, Gak Cuma buat ngibul (tips lengkap cari duit, cari jodoh & cari dukungan)* [*Cool Sites Are Not Just for Cheating (Tips to Make Money or Find a Partner)*]. Jakarta: Gramedia.

Mathews, P. W. 2010. *Asian Cam Models. Digital Virtual Virgin Prostitutes.* Quezon City: Giraffe Books.

McLuhan, M. 1964. *Understanding Media: The Extensions of Man.* New York: McGraw-Hill.

Miller, D. 2011. *Tales from Facebook.* Cambridge: Polity Press.

Molony, T. 2008. Nondevelopmental Uses of Mobile Communication in Tanzania. In *Handbook of Mobile Communication Studies*, ed. J. E. Katz, 339–52. Cambridge, MA: MIT Press.

Morley, D., and K. Robins. 1995. *Spaces of Identity: Global Media, Electronic Landscapes, and Cultural Boundaries.* London: Routledge.

Nugroho, Y. 2011. *Citizens in @ction: Collaboration, Participatory Democracy and Freedom of Information Mapping Contemporary Civic Activism and the Use of New Social Media in Indonesia.* Manchester Institute of Innovation Research and HIVOS Regional Office Southeast Asia Report. http://www.cdi.manchester.ac.uk/newsandevents/documents/Citizensinaction-MIOIR-HIVOSFinal_Report.pdf.

Pertierra, R. 2010. *The Anthropology of New Media in the Philippines.* IPC Culture and Development Series no. 7. Quezon City: Institute of Philippine Culture, Atone de Manila University.

Pertierra, R., et al. 2002. *Txt-ing Selves: Cellphones and Philippine Modernity.* Malate, Philippines: De La Salle University Press.

Pfaffenberger, B. 1992. Social Anthropology of Technology. *Annual Review of Anthropology* 21: 491–516.

Pretor-Pinney, G., and Cloud Appreciation Society. 2006. *The Cloudspotter's Guide.* London: Sceptre.

Qiu, J. L. 2009. *Working-class Network Society: Communication Technology and the Information Have-less in Urban China.* Cambridge, MA: MIT Press.

Rafael, V. L. 2003. The Cell Phone and the Crowd: Messianic Politics in the Contemporary Philippines. *Public Culture* 15(3): 399–425.

Shome, R. 2006. Thinking through the Diaspora. *International Journal of Cultural Studies* 9(1): 105–24.

Slama, M. 2010. The Agency of the Heart: Internet Chatting as Youth Culture in Indonesia. *Social Anthropology* 18(3): 316–30.

Sprague, S. 1978. Yoruba Photography: How the Yoruba See Themselves. *African Arts* 12: 52–9.

Standage, T. 1998. *The Victorian Internet: The Remarkable Story of the Telegraph and the Nineteenth Century's On-line Pioneers.* New York: Walker.

Sullivan, N. P. 2007. *You Can Hear Me Now: How Microloans and Cell Phones Are Connecting the World's Poor to the Global Economy.* San Francisco: Jossey-Bass.

Tsing, A. L. 2005. *Friction: An Ethnography of Global Connection.* Princeton, NJ: Princeton University Press.

Turner, F. 2006. *From Counterculture to Cyberculture: Stewart Brand, the Whole Earth Network, and the Rise of Digital Utopianism.* Chicago: University of Chicago Press.

Watts, L. 2008. Orkney: Landscapes of Future Resistance. Paper presented at 4S/EASST 2008, Erasmus University Rotterdam, August. http://eprints.lancs.ac.uk/11452/.

Wetmore, J. 2007. Amish Technology: Reinforcing Values and Building Community. *IEEE Technology and Society Magazine* 26(2): 10–21.

Wilson, P., and M. Stewart. 2008. *Global Indigenous Media: Cultures, Poetics, and Politics.* Durham, NC: Duke University Press.

Xiang, B. 2007. *Global 'Body Shopping': An Indian Labor System in the Information Technology Industry.* Princeton, NJ: Princeton University Press.

Yi-Shan-Guan. 2006. Nick Yee's Daedalus Project: The Psychology of MMORPGs. Untitled entry. http://www.nickyee.com/daedalus/archives/001493.

Zandbergen, D. 2011. New Edge, Technology and Spirituality in the San Francisco Bay Area. PhD thesis, Leiden University.

–11–

Digital Engagement: Voice and Participation in Development

Jo Tacchi

Across the world, what constitutes democratic participation is being debated (Gaventa 2006). Democracy is the language of militarily imposed change, neoliberal market forces and international development agendas (Appadurai 2002; Gaventa 2006). Participation is considered to be a cornerstone of democracy and of international development—a building block of reform and progress. While democracy speaks to formal political participation, central to this notion of participation are issues that can be encompassed by the idea of 'voice'. Voice is about the agency to represent oneself and the right to express an opinion. The promise of voice—the opportunity to speak, be heard and have some influence over decisions that affect one's life—is central to the institutional legitimacy of contemporary democracies (Couldry 2010). It is also core to a rights-based approach to international development (Sen 1999, 2002) and to discourses and policies around social and digital inclusion and exclusion. Voice and participation are highly charged and promoted concepts in development that point to a tension between an imperative to engage closely with the local situations and needs of aid recipient communities, and the modernization paradigm that continues to underpin development policies and practices. While attention is given to the issues of voice and participation—for instance through the World Bank's Voices of the Poor programme—far less attention is given to ideas around 'listening' in the broad field of development.

As James Ferguson (1994) demonstrates in *The Anti-Politics Machine*, development is a central organizing concept of our time that frames our thinking about much of the world. It is a political project and has also become an interpretive grid, providing meaning for a range of observations. This is not to suggest that 'development' is an uncontested concept, but that it is a contemporary problematic that imposes questions rather than answers. This chapter will focus upon two distinctive subfields of development—communication for development (C4D) and information and communication technology for development (ICT4D)—through two case studies of recent research on the relationship between media, technology and development. This chapter explores differences between the two subfields within anthropology's broader critique of development, taking us from digital divide agendas to notions of a participatory culture. The first study is an experiment in participatory content creation with a focus on issues of voice, conducted in South Asia. The second case study involves a project in Nepal that explores issues around the valuing or recognition of voice—what we might think of in terms of listening. The case studies will be used to illustrate some key challenges for C4D, ICT4D and the ideals of participation, with implications for development more broadly, and the ways in which digital anthropology can inform these development agendas. Following Ferguson (1994), I am less concerned here with how and why development became such a central concept and problematic and more interested in what its effects are on the world through development practice. While appreciating and critiquing development discourse and rhetoric as often performing a form of Western hegemony, I am equally concerned with the complexities of how this is translated, embraced, resisted and experienced through practice. In this way the chapter aims to avoid an overly populist and deconstructionist approach to development (Olivier de Sardan 2005) in favour of exploring particularities of development through practice.

Development, Media, Communication and the Digital

Emerging in the wake of World War II, notions of development often incorporated modernization theory frameworks wherein Third World countries had not yet reached the stage of development of First World countries situated largely in the West (Crewe and Harrison 1998; Escobar 1995). Efforts to move different societies forward on the pathway to development involved, among other things, the introduction of modern technologies (Waisbord 2001). From the introduction of production technologies and industries for farmers, medical technologies and family planning to mass media programming and the recording of metrics of media infrastructure such as a free press, radio and (most recently) Internet and mobile phone penetration rates, notions of technology transfer as a way to shape and change the current socioeconomic situation remain central to development agendas (Gardner and Lewis 1996).

Within this broader context, C4D has emerged as a field of knowledge and of practice (Waisbord 2008; Wilkins 2000; Wilkins and Mody 2001). Servaes (2008) suggests that while the words used to define C4D might have changed over time, since the mid-1970s definitions contain reasonably constant themes. These revolve around communication techniques and media as participatory processes for social change and dialogue as key to socially inclusive processes (for example Fraser and Villet 1994; Rogers 1976; United Nations 1997; World Congress on Communication for Development 2006). The underlying theories of development communication have shifted quite significantly over time towards participatory communication paradigms. Ideas of communication as exchange, meanings and processes rather than about the transmission of messages have concretized, even if this is yet to be as widely or fully practised as generally thought (Fraser and Restrepo-Estrada 1998;

Inagaki 2007). A participatory communication approach is highly complementary to new digital communication environments, because it promotes horizontal and participatory models of development rather than vertical, one-way, top-down or trickle-down models more suited to modernization and economic growth approaches to development (Servaes 2008; Waisbord 2001). Yet while modernization and diffusion models of development and of development communication are generally considered to be outdated (Waisbord 2001, 2008), they still appear to guide policy and practice (Inagaki 2007; Mansell 2011).

When it comes to the field of ICT4D, the effort and focus tends to be on innovative applications of information and communication technology towards economic growth and on efficient dissemination of information, thus placing most of the agency on the technology and its developers rather than on poor and marginalized populations (Unwin 2009). ICT is seen by some proponents in this field as having made a progressive contribution to development, largely missing its inherent promise for transformation—disruptive technologies, according to Heeks (2010), can deliver resources from North to South and can transform development itself. Such a focus on the transformational qualities of ICT as a universal good and universal concept tend to obscure particularities of poor and marginalized populations, reinforce normative modernizing models of development (Unwin 2009) and maintain a notion of technology as a solution to the problem of development which can be addressed through increased efficiency in production (Heeks 2005). The human development goal of expanding people's freedoms and capabilities (Sen 1999) is often unconnected to technologically focused interventions which are informed more by studies of information systems than development studies (Heeks 2010). On the one hand, the promotion of new ICTs for development, based as much on their promise as practical demonstrations of effectiveness, has undoubtedly led to many innovative experiments but equally to a rapid evolution and expansion of technological determinist responses from development agencies (Article19 2005: 3).

ICTs have been promoted as transformative technologies creating new 'knowledge economies' and 'networked societies' (Castells 1996; Selwyn 2004). The term 'digital divide' emerged as a stark indicator of those who are part of, and those who are not part of, these new developments, but the term has recently been questioned and has largely fallen out of use except by those who are focused mainly on technologies and infrastructure. The concept has been considered less useful than 'digital inequality' or 'digital inclusion' (DiMaggio and Hargittai 2001; Selwyn 2004) as ways to describe the relationships between ICTs and development to those who are more focused on development itself. There are complex interrelationships between social and technological networks and issues of access versus effective use or engagement (Warschauer 2003). While the term 'digital divide' was useful in highlighting gaps in infrastructure as well as more fine-grained issues of social and economic status and access, a major problem was the way digital divide policy debates focused almost exclusively on macro issues, assuming that digital technologies are beneficial to all citizens and the only barrier to closing the gap is lack of access. As Robin Mansell (2002) pointed out, interpretations of the causes and consequences of the divide were inadequate, and because of this, so were actions to bridge the divide or to understand its consequences. The disadvantages of being on the wrong side of the divide were seen as stemming from the ways in which social and technical relationships were understood at a position removed from actual practices rather than how they were lived.

As anthropologists have highlighted, Mansell (2011) calls our attention to the way that development's preference for a 'one knowledge system' fails to appreciate the political nature of knowledge and the importance of multiple knowledges. Local knowledges are complex cultural constructions, often with different modes of operation and relations to social and cultural fields (Escobar 1995). Development attempts to recodify local knowledge to make it useable for development activities, with a goal of enhancing expert knowledge and increasing the chances of success for development brokers. While certain forms of universal knowledge—especially concerning scientific or health-related knowledge—are seen as fixed, it is the particularity of local knowledge that makes it valuable in a human development or participatory approach, but often because it might provide insights about how to implement external development interventions or change local knowledge and practice rather than to inform and change development agendas. Here is a central issue for development as practice: how do we account for and respond to 'worlds and knowledges otherwise' (Escobar 2007)? A digital anthropology might emphasize the existence and importance of multiple knowledges as a means to understand what it is that makes us human.

In light of these perspectives on the relationship between communication, knowledge, ICT and development, two concepts are particularly useful in conceptualizing the current moment: voice and listening. Drawing upon collaborative research, the two case studies explore notions of voice and listening further. We learned through a research project called Finding a Voice that finding ways to give voice to a range of people through traditional and new media technologies does not necessarily mean that the listening end of the equation will simply fall into place even if engaging content is produced. We learned through a project called Assessing Communication for Social Change (AC4SC) that while it is possible to set up local processes for listening, the knowledge produced is not necessarily in a format that development agencies are predisposed to listen to.

Case Study One: Voice—Finding a Voice

Voice is about the agency to represent oneself and the right to express an opinion. These are literal meanings of the word, in common understanding. Following Couldry (2010), voice is both a process and a value. By voice as a process, he means the process of giving an account of one's life and its conditions. By voice as a value, he means the act of valuing, and choosing to value, those frameworks for organizing human life and resources that themselves value voice (as a process). We might learn important lessons from studying examples of valuing voice in development. Through directly examining voice in development activities we are able to understand whether and how voice is valued in a range of contexts; we can explore the role of traditional and digital media and communication technologies and uncover the implications for development. Voice has been linked to participatory development, but this is often with specific reference to voice as process, so that the valuing of voice receives far less attention.

The project Finding a Voice took an ethnographic approach to a multisited study of and experiment in digital content creation.[1] The project was made up of a research network of fifteen local media and ICT initiatives in India, Nepal, Sri Lanka and Indonesia. Some of the sites were community radio stations, some were video projects and others were computer and resource centres or community libraries. All had or were provided access to computers and the Internet. The goals of Finding a Voice were to increase understanding of how ICT can be both effective and empowering in each local context, to investigate the most effective ways of articulating information and communication networks (both social and technological) to empower poor people to communicate their voices within and beyond marginalized communities. This involved researching opportunities and constraints for local content created by and for specific local communities for the development and communication of ideas, information and perspectives appropriate to those communities. It took place at a time when many development agencies were investing in ICT4D initiatives and were keenly interested in better understanding the development potential of new digital technologies.

The project began with a broad definition of voice—essentially referring to ideas around self-expression, inclusion and participation in social, political and economic processes. There was a specific focus on ICT and development at the community level and the significance of voice in terms of poverty—'voice poverty'—understood as the inability of people to influence the decisions that affect their lives and the right to participate in that decision making (Lister 2004). According to Appadurai (2004: 63) one of the poor's 'gravest lacks' is 'the lack of resources with which to give "voice"'. This is about the poor being able to express themselves in order to influence political debates around wealth and welfare so that their own welfare is given due attention. Voice in ICT4D implies access and skills to use technologies and platforms. However, access is a complicated and complex notion that is multidimensional, dependent upon a range of conditions, and not simply about the physical. It embraces cognitive, affective, political, economic and cultural domains (Rice and Atkin 2001).

The project had three distinct components. The first component was capacity development. We worked with members of the local media initiatives to develop capacity in local research and in digital content creation. Each local initiative employed a local researcher who we trained in an approach called ethnographic action research

(Tacchi et al. 2007). They formed a network of local researchers and shared data and experiences through a specially designed website. They researched local communities and their engagements with the media initiative, including the use of digital technologies. We also trained these local researchers and other staff from the local sites in new content creation techniques and formats through a series of workshops based on a training-of-trainers approach. Participants then adapted the techniques and processes we introduced according to their own local strategies and conditions. One particularly useful format we introduced, which was taken up, adapted and applied in a variety of ways across the sites, was digital storytelling. Digital stories are generally three- to five-minute multimedia creations using digital images and voiceovers, told in the first person (Hartley and McWilliam 2009). Across the sites, digital storytelling was found to be an interesting way to encourage participation and engage the voices of people who otherwise have no access to the media. Through this approach they were able to express their concerns about various social or personal issues. The stories produced were distributed in a variety of formats such as DVD, video, and streaming or downloadable formats on the web, television, radio (minus images) and community screenings.

The second component was to follow the local development of participatory content creation activities in each site. Each site is different, has access to different facilities and media, and faces different local circumstances. The range of stories emerging and the varied strategies for participatory content creation employed by each site were captured through the accounts of the local researchers or site visits by the academic researchers. In all sites the process of engaging people in participatory content creation activities was challenging for a range of reasons. Consequently, a variety of strategies emerged (Watkins and Tacchi 2008). Examining the varied experiences across the sites, we found that as a development activity, participatory content creation through digital (often combined with traditional) media and communication technologies is a useful mechanism for achieving levels of participation that are hard to achieve in wider development practices (Tacchi 2009). Digital technologies and participatory content creation can contribute to wider development agendas when they are taken up and adapted to local social and cultural contexts, presenting an interesting and tangible mechanism for ensuring levels of participation in wider development initiatives. For example, in an Indian ICT centre for women located in a Delhi slum, local researcher Aseem Asha Usman developed a vocational media course for young women. Digital storytelling was one of the main components in the three-month media course he developed, which also covered web design and multimedia production. He developed the course to fill a gap in the local employment market for creative design skills.

It became very clear that the most marginalized or excluded groups needed to be actively and creatively engaged in ways that suited their needs and circumstances. Simply providing the technologies and opportunities to participate was not enough. The use of a mobile telecentre in Sri Lanka as a means to engage with Tamil youth provided a good example of why and how special effort is required to achieve participation from the most excluded (Tacchi and Grubb 2007). The young people lived in settlements very close to a community media centre, but their engagement was minimal. Access was not limited because of geographical distance, since the young people lived very close. Rather, their access was limited because of ethnic and linguistic marginalization and other burdens of extreme poverty and disadvantage. A three-wheeled motorized vehicle fitted with a radio outside broadcast unit, laptop, mobile Internet connection, loudspeakers and projector, called the eTuktuk, travelled to their houses in an effort to engage them in participatory content creation. The young people's content was screened to their families and friends using the projector in the eTuktuk. This relates to the third component of the project, which was concerned with what happened with content and how it contributed to ideas about development.

This third component was less well developed through the project, as most of our effort was directed towards encouraging new and inclusive forms of content creation. However, we did spend some time working with local researchers, staff and participants to think through strategies for distribution, developed by and geared towards the overall aims of each centre. The bulk of the content produced across the sites was circulated to local audiences. For digital stories this was often through local screenings to small gatherings to generate discussion about the issues raised. The screenings were an effective mechanism for raising awareness, sharing perspectives and encouraging others to make their own content and have a voice to the extent that this kind of activity allows. Some of the content created in the early phase of this project was subtitled in English and circulated by UNESCO on a DVD with the idea of sharing different perspectives on development themes. This is both interesting and useful, but in terms of day-to-day activities at the various centres, preparing their content for wider audiences, even given the existence of digital distribution platforms, is often not a feasible regular activity or useful for their purposes, which are focused on locally appropriate development.

Among the strategic requirements specified in the Rome Consensus developed by the World Congress on Communication for Development (2006) are access to communication tools so that people can communicate amongst themselves and with decision makers, recognition of the need for different approaches depending on different cultures and support to those most affected by development issues to have a say. Finding a Voice found that many people want to use media to highlight social issues or demonstrate how one might challenge adversity, often through the device of providing an inspirational example. We also found that other kinds of engagements with media that are about self-expression were popular. Ultimately, Finding a Voice was interested in the ways in which practices of voice (through ICT) might be articulated into wider practices of social and political action and change, but our efforts focused largely on setting up processes for voice with far less opportunity to examine or promote the valuing of voice. Even given the apparent affordances and accessibility of new digital media, a huge amount of effort was required for the local initiatives to develop processes for voice that included the most marginalized populations. This highlights the deeply questionable notions around new media and social media as themselves a form of participatory culture. It also indicates the need to think beyond this, to what Couldry (2010) calls 'voice that matters'. Finding a Voice revealed some interesting and promising opportunities for developing processes for voice. However, we need to think carefully about how to encourage active listening. Debate and dialogue, which are considered central to participatory development, clearly happened in many of our research sites, and this proved important in many ways at the local level, but how this translated into action to influence wider social change, and by whom, calls for further research.

Case Study Two: Listening—Assessing Communication for Social Change

In both C4D and ICT4D there is an emphasis on the delivery of information from development agencies and experts to poor populations. The focus in impact assessment is most often on whether those poor populations are listening effectively and therefore on whether their lives and behaviours change as a result. This is to place the emphasis in terms of listening on poor people and is based on the assumption that knowledge resides with the developers. Ideas around voice challenge this relationship and have given rise to a broadening of ideas about what constitutes poverty (Narayan et al. 2000) as well as new ways of engaging with poor people through participatory assessments of their experiences based on dialogue (Chambers 1997). These approaches introduce alternative ways of thinking about the speaker–listener relationship. It is through the process of listening that the value of voice is mutually registered. Susan Bickford's writing on politics, conflict and citizenship (1996) points out how political theory has consistently focused on the politics of speaking but has paid scant attention to listening. Attention to listening foregrounds questions of recognition (Honneth 1995), receptivity and responsiveness. In its many formulations, the politics of recognition centres on the esteem, value and attention given to social and cultural difference as questions of justice, on attention and response as questions of communicative justice.

In the context of media and communication, justice becomes a question not simply of access to production but also of the quality of relationships between speakers and listeners, mediated by institutions. To put it another way, the politics of recognition suggests that a redistribution of material resources for speaking or voice is inadequate unless there is also a shift in the hierarchies of value and attention accorded different actors and communities. While the participatory development paradigm places dialogue at the centre of development, we still fundamentally lack an understanding of the information and communication needs and aspirations of people who are marginalized or socially excluded. We need to more effectively listen across difference and inequality (Dreher 2009). We learned through Finding a Voice that in assisting people to create content and express themselves through digital media, one cannot assume there is anyone listening. The very institutions that excluded communities might usefully try to engage with through ICT are often structurally unsuited for listening. Even through their monitoring and evaluation activities, development agencies are often only looking for and able to identify (or listening to and able to hear) predetermined indicators that are readily measurable (Lennie and Tacchi 2012). Development generally positions poor populations as listeners rather than people whom they should be listening to. To present this challenge in concrete terms, we can explore an example from Nepal—a project called Assessing Communication for Social Change: A New Agenda in Impact Assessment (AC4SC).[2]

Underpinning AC4SC was recognition of the importance of listening and responding to different knowledges. AC4SC was a collaboration with Equal Access Nepal (EAN), a local development communication organization that makes and distributes radio programmes with development goals. A range of radio programmes are produced, and EAN works with local radio stations and government and nongovernment bodies and groups to communicate with communities across Nepal. Since Nepal is an ethnically and linguistically diverse country, and geographically challenging in terms of travel, local partners are crucial to EAN's operations. Some programmes, or programme segments, are repackaged by local radio stations into local languages. EAN also supports a network of local listener groups, ranging from young people who listen to the youth-oriented programme *Chatting to My Best Friend* to broader groups who listen to programmes with a wider audience in mind, such as *New Nepal*, which focuses on raising awareness of new governance structures, justice and security issues and constitutional reforms.

AC4SC was a project that developed and implemented a participatory methodology for evaluating the impacts of the radio programs produced by EAN. It grew out of an interest from EAN to learn how to improve its programmes and demonstrate its impact. It offered a team of Australian researchers (including three anthropologists)[3] a chance to work with EAN over four years, and help it develop monitoring and evaluation system that enabled it to listen to the people the programmes are trying to reach. The impact assessment methodology that was developed and implemented informed EAN's programming, its funding applications and its reports to donors. The methodology incorporates ethnographic principles of long-term engagement and immersion with communities and combines them with many of the features of participatory action research (Tacchi, Lennie and Wilmore 2010).

Essentially the research was about assessing the impact of EAN's work by producing data through qualitative engagements with local communities. The bulk of the data were generated by eight community researchers, who were people from those communities trained in appropriate data collection methods. This produced qualitative data in a way that aimed to not only prove impact to EAN's donor organizations but also to allow the organization to improve its practices (Lennie, Tacchi and Wilmore 2012). However, in attempting to move away from an information delivery (top-down) model of communication for development and to work closer to the ground in terms of generating research data, EAN met with a level of complexity and uncertainty in its data, which made it difficult to tick the required donor boxes and often challenged the evaluation approach of donors and their indicators for impact.

While AC4SC clearly increased EAN's capacity to be responsive and develop more nuanced understandings of its audiences, the data generated through this kind of listening are not easily translatable into donor reports. Now that AC4SC has finished as a discrete project, the processes developed continue to be used and adjusted to suit EAN's needs, and the organization has changed in how it considers its relationship to communities and donors. The challenge remains that donors continue to maintain their position and remain unsuited to listening to different kinds of evaluations. Chambers and Pettit (2004: 137) capture this situation when they write about the way that development rhetoric has changed in recent years, to include new words like *partnership*, *participation* and *transparency*, which imply 'changes in power and relationships, but [which] have not been matched in practice'; rather, power and relationships are governing dynamics that in practice 'prevent the inclusion of weaker actors and voices in decision-making'. Development rules and procedures are a part of what needs to be changed, to open up to different ways of operating, to allow for different voices and prevent this structural stifling of meaningful participation. To this end, AC4SC highlights the kinds of relationships that development agencies encourage and allow despite their rhetoric, and the project demonstrates a push for change, providing both detailed alternative approaches and examples and alternative indicators of success. Development might be far more effective if listening happened with people on the ground, building relationships at that level. The Listening Project (2009) has talked to development workers and communities across a range of countries globally and has found a consistent story whereby 'systems of international assistance bias the ways that agencies and aid workers listen and do not listen, what they listen to, where and when they listen, and to whom they listen'. This is about acknowledging and respecting alternative forms of knowledge; something which perhaps presents us with one of our biggest challenges. Being prepared to accept and respect alternative knowledge and knowledge practices, which may be contradictory to dominant knowledge practices and beliefs, is challenging, especially to development.

Conclusions

There are many studies of the affordances and potential of new and traditional media technologies for participation, voice and development (cf. Currie 2007; Deane 2004; International Telecommunication Union 2005; World Congress on Communication for Development 2006) and political transformation made possible through networked social production (Benkler 2006; Castells 2009). The idea of affordances (Norman 2002) relates to the constraining and enabling material possibilities of media. The new communication environment made up of digital technologies appears to change the possibilities for development to enable far more horizontal processes, possibilities for exchange and multiple information sources, providing the perfect communication environment for participatory development to thrive. As Table 11.1 illustrates, new possibilities emerge for communication for development. One way is to replace message delivery with networks, so that information from multiple sources might be available in response to questions rather than preempting or predetermining what those questions should be.

However, claims about the transformative potential of digital technologies for development are not necessarily consistent with human development aspirations, but rather with Western-centric models of development and economic growth (Mansell 2011). While such technologies are 'accompanied by major structural, cultural, social and economic transformations' (Mansell 2011: 2) that hold potential for participation, development, political transformation and networking, underlying notions of development follow a modernization agenda. Analysing a sample of texts published between 1998 and 2009 from United Nations agencies and the World Bank, Mansell reveals the predominant exogenous model of development, even when alternative and participatory or endogenous models of development are considered to have influenced the policies and practices of these agencies. Many have critiqued the digital divide agenda preferring to think about digital inclusion and engagement, yet the activities and policies of major development agencies remain wedded to ideas resonant with digital divide discourse.

Development complicates a straightforward consideration of the inherent affordances of technologies and the ways they are used. Over the past five to ten years, mobile phones have become a key example of this. Whereas economics (Jensen

Table 11.1. The New Communication Environment

Traditional media	*New and social media*
Vertical patterns of communication—from government to people	Horizontal patterns of communication—from people to people
Unipolar communication systems	Communication networks
Few information sources	Many information sources
Easy to control—for good (generating accurate information to large numbers of people) and ill (government control and censorship)	Difficult to control—for good (more debate, increased voice, increased trust) and ill (more complex, issues of accuracy)
Send a message	Ask a question

Source: Adapted from Deane (2004).

2007), business (Prahalad 2006) and other disciplines and public conversations stress the potential of mobile phones for economic growth, ethnographic and other work on mobile phones in these contexts has led to more complex insights. Archambault's (2011) study in rural Mozambique reveals how mobiles simultaneously operate as part of the informal economy, creating economic opportunities for some individuals, but Archambault also notes that 'the ways in which mobile communication participates in the circulation of and access to information: not necessarily the kind of "useful information" referred to by endorsers of the "ICT for Development" perspective, but rather information that is meant to remain secret' (2011: 444). Horst and Miller (2006) found that while mobiles play a role in economic growth among low-income Jamaicans, mobile phones were valued primarily for their role in the redistribution rather than accumulation of money. Savings and accumulation represent one of the key features of economic development. Wallis's (2011) recent work on the use of mobile phones among young, low-wage women migrants in Beijing also reveals the ambivalent and often contradictory relationships young women have with communication technologies like the mobile. Introducing the concept of 'immobile mobility' defined as 'a socio-techno means of overcoming spatial, temporal, physical, and structural boundaries', Wallis argues that young migrants' positionality creates 'particular constraints on their capacity for various forms of agency, thus rendering them relatively immobile in the labor sphere' (2011: 474).

With respect to other forms of digital media, Gabriella Coleman (2010) points out that media cannot be discussed as a universal experience. The ethnographic evidence is at best unconvincing that digital media are solely or even primarily responsible for producing 'shared subjectivity' or a new sensorium, and even less a life world that can be used to characterize whole populations (Coleman 2010). On the contrary, while digital media are shown to play an important role in social, linguistic, political and economic processes as well as in perceptions and representations of self, the particular details of how they are experienced in the everyday argues against universal and uniform human experience. Yet development agencies and policies tend to assign characteristics and affordances for digital technologies that converge with the focus on economic growth as the key indicator of poverty reduction as development. This results in a normative consensus about how technologies lead to development and subsequent strategies for technological diffusion. On the ground, in the particular moments of development interventions, such straightforward and normative agendas struggle to succeed.

This touches on Amartya Sen's discussion of how culture matters in development (Sen 2004). He suggests that the neglect of considerations of culture by economists have influenced the outlook and approaches of development agencies and that 'the cultural dimension of development requires closer scrutiny in development analysis' (2004: 37). For one thing, culture is implicated in political participation. Public discussions, interactions and participation are central to democratic practices, and such participation and political activity is influenced by cultural conditions. Since political participation is a critical component in ideas of development—certainly human development and capability approaches to development—culture becomes an important influence and setting for development analysis (Sen 2004: 40–1). While it is important to avoid cultural determinism, culture must be an important part of how we understand social and economic development. Yet culture is not homogeneous, not static; it is interactive and porous. The issue for Sen is not *whether* culture matters, but *how.*

Arjun Appadurai considers *why* culture matters in development. The tendency within development has been to understand culture as a matter of the past, as tradition or custom, while development's orientation is to the future (Appadurai 2004). Economics has become 'the science of the future, and when human beings are seen as having a future, the keywords such as wants, needs, expectations, calculations, have become hardwired into the discourse of economics' (Appadurai 2004: 60). This results in the association of cultural actors with the past, and economic actors with the future, and the opposing of culture to development. Appadurai argues that while some of the blame might be laid at the economists' door for their neglect of culture, anthropologists must bring the future back into economists' cultural frames. The future, and people's aspirations, are cultural capacities. Appadurai (2004) argues that, within a development context, culture can be seen as a capacity worth strengthening, linked to aspirations of the future (plans, hopes and goals) as much as it is rooted in the past (habit, custom, tradition). Culture, then, is important, along with relationships, since it is only in relationships that values are ascribed and positions defined—norms, values, beliefs and aspirations are all relational. What role do media and technology and the processes for valuing voice and listening play in this? How might media and technology, when valuing principles such as voice and listening, enhance forms of ethnographic practice? This idea of culture—its orientation to the future and roots in tradition—and the central role of relationships in ascribing values mean that ethnographic study is well suited to capture and describe the processes that matter. These are embedded and only accessible through close engagement with each context.

Digital anthropology as represented in this volume has an important contribution to make. Given the highly generalized discussions of development, these can easily become abstract goals oriented to the requirements of agencies and policy discussions and distant from practice. By contrast, digital anthropology examines multiple forms of digital technology, recognizing that the impact of a mobile phone might be entirely different from the spread of local radio or the use of Internet-based communication, and each in turn may have complex often contradictory impacts on any given population. As this chapter has shown, the debates on C4D and ICT4D must retain a level of concrete engagement and a sense of contradiction and complex consequences which earlier discussions of digital divide tended to gloss over. On the other hand, what the development discussions add to digital anthropology is a clear agenda oriented towards welfare and various forms of capability such as participation and voice, which can be lacking in some of the academic discussions within more parochial anthropology. Given the sheer power and influence of development agendas and practices, it seems of immediate importance that digital anthropologists participate in such discussions and applications.

Notes

1. The full title of the project is Finding a Voice: Making Technological Change Socially Effective and Culturally Empowering (www.findingavoice.org). The project was funded by the Australian Research Council (www.arc.gov.au) through its Linkage grant scheme (LP0561848), with strong collaboration and further funds and in-kind support from the United Nations Educational, Scientific and Cultural Organization (UNESCO) and the United Nations Development Programme. The project ran from 2006 to 2009.
2. Assessing Communication for Social Change: A New Agenda in Impact Assessment was funded by an Australian Research Council Linkage grant (LP0775252) and Equal Access. The project ran for four years, from 2007 to 2011.
3. The three anthropologists were Jo Tacchi, Andrew Skuse and Michael Wilmore. Also on the team was June Lennie, an evaluation expert.

References

Appadurai, A. 2002. Deep Democracy: Urban Governmentality and the Horizon of Politics. *Public Culture* 14(1): 21–47.

Appadurai, A. 2004. The Capacity to Aspire: Culture and the Terms of Recognition. In *Culture and Public Action*, ed. V. Rao and M. Walton, 59–84. Stanford, CA: Stanford University Press.

Archambault, J. S. 2011. Breaking Up 'Because of the Phone' and the Transformative Potential of Information in Southern Mozambique. *New Media and Society* 13: 444–56.

Article 19. 2005. *Experiencing Technical Difficulties: The Urgent Need to Rewire and Reeboot the ICT-Development Machine.* Thematic Reports 45. London: Article 19.

Benkler, Y. 2006. *The Wealth of Networks.* New Haven, CT: Yale University Press.

Bickford, S. 1996. *The Dissonance of Democracy: Listening, Conflict, and Citizenship.* Ithaca, NY: Cornell University Press.

Castells, M. 1996. *The Rise of the Network Society.* Cambridge, MA: Blackwell.

Castells, M. 2009. *Communication Power.* Oxford: Oxford University Press.

Chambers, R. 1997. *Whose Reality Counts? Putting the First Last.* London: Intermediate Technology Publications.

Chambers, R., and J. Pettit. 2004. Shifting Power to Make a Difference. In *Inclusive Aid: Changing Power and Relationships in International Development*, ed. L. Groves and R. Hinton, 137–62. London: Earthscan.

Coleman, G. E. 2010. Ethnographic Approaches to Digital Media. *Annual Review of Anthropology* 39: 487–505.

Couldry, N. 2010. *Why Voice Matters: Culture and Politics after Neoliberalism.* London: Sage.

Crewe, E., and E. Harrison. 1998. *Whose Development? An Ethnography of Aid.* New York: Zed Books.

Currie, W. 2007. Post WSIS Spaces for Building a Global Information Society. In *Global Information Society Watch 2007: Focus on Participation*, 16–22. Association for Progressive Communications and Third World Institute.

Deane, J. 2004. The Context of Communication for Development, 2004. Paper prepared for the Ninth United Nations Roundtable on Communication for Development, 6–9 September. Food and Agriculture Organization of the United Nations (FAO), Rome.

DiMaggio, P., and E. Hargittai. 2001. From the Digital Divide to Digital Inequality. Working paper, Center for Arts and Cultural Policy Studies, Princeton University.

Dreher, T. 2009. Listening across Difference: Media and Multiculturalism beyond the Politics of Voice. *Continuum: Journal of Media and Cultural Studies* 23(4): 445–58.

Escobar, A. 1995. *Encountering Development: The Making and Unmaking of the Third World.* Princeton, NJ: Princeton University Press.

Escobar, A. 2007. 'World and Knowledges Otherwise': The Latin American Modernity/Coloniality Research Program. *Cultural Studies* 21(2–3): 179–210.

Ferguson, J. 1994. *The Anti-politics Machine: 'Development', Depoliticization, and Bureaucratic Power in Lesotho.* Cambridge: Cambridge University Press.

Fraser, C., and S. Restrepo-Estrada. 1998. *Communicating for Development: Human Change for Survival.* London: I. B. Tauris.

Fraser, C., and J. Villett. 1994. *Communication: A Key to Human Development.* Rome: Food and Agriculture Organization of the United Nations (FAO). http://www.fao.org/sd/cddirect/cdpub/sdrepub.htm.

Gardner, K., and D. Lewis. 1996. *Anthropology, Development and the Post-Modern Challenge.* London: Pluto Press.

Gaventa, J. 2006. Triumph, Deficit or Contestation? Deepening the 'Deepening Democracy' Debate. IDS Working Paper 264. Brighton: Institute of Development Studies (IDS).

Hartley, J., and K. McWilliam, eds. 2009. *Story Circle: Digital Storytelling Around the World.* Oxford: Wiley-Blackwell.

Heeks, R. 2005. ICTs and the MDGs: On the Wrong Track? I4D online.net. http://i4donline.net/feb05/perspective.pdf.

Heeks, R. 2010. Do Information and Communication Technologies (ICTs) Contribute to Development? *Journal of International Development* 22(5): 625–40.

Honneth, A. 1995. *The Struggle for Recognition: The Moral Grammar of Social Conflicts*. Cambridge: Polity Press.

Horst, H., and D. Miller. 2006. *The Cell Phone: An Anthropology of Communication*. New York: Berg.

Inagaki, N. 2007. Communicating the Impact of Communication for Development: Recent Trends in Empirical Research. Working paper. New York: World Bank, Development Communication Division. http://wwwwds.worldbank.org/external/default/WDSContentServer/WDSP/IB/2007/08/10/000310607_20070810123306/Rendered/PDF/405430Communic18082137167101PUBLIC1.pdf.

International Telecommunication Union. 2005. Tunis Agenda for the Information Society. World Summit on the Information Society, 18 November. http://itu.int/wsis/docs2/tunis/off/6rev1.pdf.

Jensen, R. 2007. The Digital Provide: Information (Technology), Market Performance, and Welfare in the South Indian Fisheries Sector. *Quarterly Journal of Economics* 122(3): 879–924.

Lennie, J., and J. Tacchi. 2012. *Evaluating Communication for Development: A Framework for Social Change*. Oxford: Earthscan, Routledge.

Lennie, J., J. Tacchi and M. Wilmore. 2012. Meta-Evaluation to Improve Learning, Evaluation Capacity Development and Sustainability: Findings from a Participatory Evaluation Project in Nepal. *South Asian Journal of Evaluation in Practice* 1(1): 13–28.

The Listening Project. 2009. *LP Factsheet and Timeline*. http://www.cdainc.com/cdawww/pdf/other/lp_factsheet_20091105_Pdf.pdf.

Lister, R. 2004. *Poverty*. Cambridge: Polity Press.

Mansell, R. 2002. From Digital Divides to Digital Entitlements in Knowledge Societies. *Current Sociology* 50(3): 407–26.

Mansell, R. 2011. Power and Interests in Information and Communication and Development: Exogenous and Endogenous Discourses in Contention. *Journal of International Development* (10 July). doi: 10.1002/jid.1805.

Narayan, D., R. Chambers, M. Kaul Shah and P. Petesch. 2000. *Crying Out for Change*. Voices of the Poor series. Oxford: Oxford University Press, World Bank.

Norman, D. 2002. *The Design of Everyday Things*. New York: Basic Books.

Olivier de Sardan, J.-P. 2005. *Anthropology and Development: Understanding Contemporary Social Change*. London: Zed Books.

Prahalad, C. K. 2006. *The Fortune at the Bottom of the Pyramid: Eradicating Poverty through Profits*. Upper Saddle River, NJ: Wharton School Publishing.

Rice, R. E., and C. K. Atkin, eds. 2001. *Public Communication Campaigns*. 3rd ed. Thousand Oaks, CA: Sage.

Rogers, E., ed. 1976. *Communication and Development: Critical Perspectives*. Thousand Oaks, CA: Sage.

Selwyn, N. 2004. Reconsidering Political and Popular Understandings of the 'Digital Divide'. *New Media and Society* 6(3): 341–62.

Sen, A. 1999. *Development as Freedom.* New York: Anchor Books.

Sen, A. 2002. *Rationality and Freedom.* Cambridge, MA: Belknap Press.

Sen, A. 2004. How Does Culture Matter? In *Culture and Public Action*, ed. V. Rao and M. Walton, 37–57. Stanford, CA: Stanford University Press.

Servaes, J., ed. 2008. *Communication for Development and Social Change.* London: Sage.

Tacchi, J. 2009. Finding a Voice: Digital Storytelling as Participatory Development. In *Story Circle: Digital Storytelling Around the World*, ed. J. Hartley and K. McWilliam, 167–75. Oxford: Wiley-Blackwell.

Tacchi, J., J. Fildes, K. Martin, K. Mulenahalli, E. Baulch and A. Skuse. 2007. *Ethnographic Action Research: Trainers Handbook.* Delhi: UNESCO. http://ear.findingavoice.org.

Tacchi, J., and B. Grubb. 2007. The Case of the e-Tuktuk. *Media International Australia Incorporating Culture and Policy* 125: 71–82.

Tacchi, J., J. Lennie and M. Willmore. 2010. Critical Reflections on the Use of Participatory Methodologies to Build Evaluation Capacities in International Development Organisations. Presented at the ALARA World Congress, Melbourne, 6–9 September. http://wc2010.alara.net.au/html/papers_t.html.

United Nations. 1997. *UN Resolution 51/172.* http://www.undemocracy.com/A-RES-51–172.pdf.

Unwin, T. 2009. Information and Communication in Development Practices. In *ICT4D: Information and Communication Technology for Development*, ed. T. Unwin, 39–75. Cambridge: Cambridge University Press.

Waisbord, S. 2001. *Family Tree of Theories, Methodologies and Strategies in Development Communication.* South Orange, NJ: Communication for Social Change.

Waisbord, S. 2008. The Institutional Challenges of Participatory Communication in International Aid. *Social Identities* 14(4): 505.

Wallis, C. 2011. Mobile Phones without Guarantees: The Promises of Technology and the Contingencies of Culture. *New Media and Society* 13: 471–85.

Warschauer, M. 2003. *Technology and Social Inclusion: Rethinking the Digital Divide.* Cambridge, MA: MIT Press.

Watkins, J., and J. Tacchi, eds. 2008. *Participatory Content Creation for Development: Principles and Practices.* New Delhi: UNESCO.

Wilkins, K., ed. 2000. *Redeveloping Communication for Social Change: Theory, Practice and Power.* Boulder, CO: Rowman & Littlefield.

Wilkins, K., and B. Mody. 2001. Reshaping Development Communication: Developing Communication and Communicating Development. *Communication Theory* 11(4): 385–96.

World Congress on Communication for Development. 2006. *Rome Consensus.* http://www.uneca.org/africanmedia/documents/Recommendations_Rome_Consensus.pdf.

Part V
Designing Digital Anthropology

–12–

Design Anthropology: Working on, with and for Digital Technologies

Adam Drazin

Many of the digital technologies which we take for granted have been designed with the critical input of anthropological work and thinking: the personal computer, e-mail, windows-type interfaces and smartphones are all examples of things which since the 1970s anthropologists have helped to shape. The things and the lives which digital anthropologists work on are in small part products of anthropology as well as study objects, but you will not always find this acknowledged in books and articles. I outline in this chapter how the subfield now known as design anthropology has developed hand-in-hand with the study of the digital and with digital ways of working—one of many parallel fields concerned with computing—and I evaluate some of the contributions to emerge. My main argument is that the digital artefacts which are created and used (often convergently) in design anthropology amount to what Harraway (1991: 191) calls 'situated knowledges', or, more specifically, 'partial, locatable, critical knowledges'. In design work, digital artefacts are used when abstractions of physical forms and contexts are required (for example a digital model of a putative product which does not yet exist), and these fit collaborative thinking work in a team. My secondary aim is to provide an introduction to the history and terminology of our work with digital design and engineering. The chapter is predicated on the idea that every anthropologist needs to know more about this area, not only because we are all potentially implicated in it, but because we need to think about how it may or may not be productive for us and for others.

The politics of the digital arena has changed, and our discipline has been one of the participants. The anthropologist's role as a translator has catalyzed—and, in some cases, comprised—conversations between the producers and consumers of technologies. Design work's focus has gradually shifted away from points of view which are entirely driven by building technologies towards also exploring ideas of need, local values, relationships and identities. This parallel social science work informs, critiques and inspires engineering and design.

How has this occurred? By what kind of process? Anthropological engagements with design have particular qualities. They are often *demonstrative.* Design anthropology frequently presents itself not as a text but as a knowledge artefact—an object, video clip, or image—which is trying to do some kind of anthropological *work*. Consider for example the difference between talking with a digital designer to write up an interpretation of design or talking with the designer *for* a design project, probably while constantly taking notes or drafting PowerPoint slides. Both exercises can be culturally critical and interpretive, but the latter has an engaged immediacy where the actors are embedded in the exercise. Although anthropological products (e.g. an ethnography) differ from design's products (e.g. a design), an anthropological dialogue may happen as a part of the work process towards both. And the dialogue, in an increasingly digitalized world, is often itself a knowledge artefact of a digital kind.

The influence of anthropology in design has not always been beneficial or even effective. Actively or through missed opportunities, anthropology has played a part in some poor design, inadequate technologies and exploitative products and services, as well as admirable ones. The experience of many anthropologists moving into this area has been confusing, frustrating and disillusioning. Design anthropology work happens in places dominated by other disciplines, by other approaches, and by other ways of talking. What design anthropological practice comprises then is not a privileged position or well-defined project but the experience of immersion into complicated multilateral conversations where the anthropological voice is present but dissolved.

Lucy Suchman, one of the most prominent anthropological voices in design, points out that her own work in commerce has been fundamentally misunderstood in many news articles over the years: 'These articles announce the emergence of anthropology itself as commercially valuable. Or rather, not anthropology, if by that we mean all of the contested modes of theorizing and practice that characterize the field, but anthropology figured…as a novel form of market research' (Suchman 2007: 4). Her many cultural commentaries and social critiques have often been misreported and misunderstood as the *production of value*, of products and of services. Her anthropological work has been confused with other kinds of work.

Since 2000, an increasing number of people present themselves as design anthropologists, more confident that they and their work are less likely to be misunderstood. This chapter is, then, largely a description and illustration of the interdisciplinary dialogues which design anthropologists are involved in. My hope is that this introduction to these dialogues can be illuminating and disillusioning. I continue by outlining the historical roots of the field and explaining some of the main terminologies and subdisciplinary areas. This is a kind of literature overview, focusing on key moments and contributions for anthropology. I then provide two illustrations of the kinds of things design anthropology can do, drawing from my own work with digital artefacts in commercial design projects. I finish the chapter by looking at some of what I consider key questions emerging for the future.

Human–Computer Interaction: A Brief History

Human–computer interaction (HCI) is, generally speaking, the broadest term for the research field which has led, over some decades, to a self-aware design anthropology. As the name suggests, HCI does not define itself by a specific disciplinary approach, but by its subject—effectively, computing. HCI therefore implies a putatively universal human moment as the lens through which to understand how all sorts of actual people (humans) engage with all sorts of high-tech machines (computers) in all sorts of ways (interactions). Histories of the development of this area have been written by different authors (Bannon 2010, 2011; Dourish 2001b; Grudin 2005, 2007; Harrison, Tatar and Sengers 2007; Pew 2003), and a condensed pastiche of these follows.

In the early days of computing, interaction meant physical engineering. To reprogram the early computers, going back to the 1960s and before, you did not necessarily have a keyboard, or a screen, or software. To reprogram a computer could mean rewiring and resoldering the physical parts by hand. This meant that the understanding of the person who used a computer was highly physical. There was an interest in posture, in how an arm or hand for example might interact with the machine. Over time, keyboards and screens were introduced. Early models of computing processing (flows of information) considered just the machine, with people featuring outside its informational system, initiating information processing but not being a part of it.

The HCI field grew with the realization that there was a need to include humans in the understanding of informational systems, a research interest initially called human factors. As research began to include the active intentions, thoughts, calculations and wishes of people, there was then a move 'from factors to actors' (Bannon 1991). When HCI turned to psychology (Card, Moran and Newell 1983; Norman 1988) to find answers to its new questions, multidisciplinary research teams resulted, which could also incorporate anthropologists and sociologists. It has been suggested that a 'second paradigm' of HCI originated at this time, 'organised around a central metaphor of mind and computer as symmetric, coupled information processors' (Harrison et al. 2007: 5).

In the 1970s, one foremost multidisciplinary research centre was Xerox PARC in Palo Alto, California, 'the birthplace of many radical ideas that affected the world of technology, including the laser printer, the desktop graphical user interface and the Ethernet, the technology that connected it all' (Sellen and Harper 2002: 2–3). At PARC, the Work Practice and Technology Group, headed by Lucy Suchman, had a major impact, definitively convincing many HCI researchers that researching computing involved researching entire social ecosystems around computers. This meant questions such as 'how were computers embedded within the complex social framework of daily activity, and how did they interplay with the rest of our densely woven environment (also known as "the real world")?' (Weiser, Gold and Brown 1999: 693).

At the same time, across the Atlantic, in Sweden and Denmark, another very different design revolution was happening. The social democratic political establishment introduced legislation which required 'consultation with workers' (Crabtree 2003: 132) over any new workplace technologies, to avoid 'de-skilling' (Braverman 1974). A series of design projects rose to this challenge through the late 1970s and 1980s, using this engagement with workers as a driving force to devise new systems, or 'design by doing' (Bødker 1987; Bjerknes, Ehn and Kyng 1987). This was the beginning of participatory design.

By the mid-1980s, 'social computing' (Dourish 2001b: 55) was more important: the term implies new research foci 'from product to process' (Grønbæk et al. 1993), more social science and a more socially aware design politics. However, with the PC still embryonic, HCI was still very focused on workplaces, not homes. Social life was seen, in large part, as built on work and on what people *do*.

The 1990s saw the rise of domestic computing, with the PC and Internet, and a renewed need for companies to explore mass markets convergently with design. This opened the door for another anthropological impact on HCI, particularly by anthropologists at Intel's People and Practices Group, among them Genevieve Bell. The art of cultural critique (not just social observation) was brought to bear more effectively than ever before on employer organizations and colleagues. Senior directors in major computing companies recognized that computing varied and was cultural, as evidenced in important emerging markets such as India, China and Europe, and that gendering could be a factor. You could no longer justify building computers in a uniform way, in the expectation that people would shape themselves to a device built by and tested on white, male, middle-class Californians. The big companies' research facilities expanded into Europe, India (especially Bangalore) and China, significantly changing ideas of what and who those companies comprise. Perhaps these shifts seem obvious, but anthropology catalyzed them.

The recent phase of HCI development and change has been more cultural than social. More attention is paid to meanings, identities and relationships; exploring practice has grown into experience (practices plus meanings). There had always been voices arguing for the importance of these things, but they only recently gained wider recognition. Harrison et al. (2007) characterize a 'third paradigm' in HCI as 'phenomenological': it is about embodied interaction, meaning, a focus on values in design and the centrality of context (2007: 7–9). Importantly, those who practise this paradigm in HCI can frame multiple questions along very different lines. Questions such as 'how fast should a mobile phone interface be?' can be asked alongside ones such as 'what does a mobile phone interface speed mean?' Technological change has accompanied this shift, moving from what is done at a desktop to what is experienced while carrying personal mobile devices.

What the story of anthropology within HCI shows is two of the points I started with. First, anthropological work has stimulated political shifts in high-tech digital design and around corporations. Second, the design of digital products and services has occurred in parallel with anthropological work and thinking. This does not mean that you can point to the 'anthropological' bit in your smartphone. But if you ask questions about what kinds of 'experience' happen around a mobile device, you should recognize that experience has been intended in the product design because of anthropology. The question is implicated in the product, and the study of digital anthropology is implicated within design anthropology. To understand how this has happened, we need to examine some of the terms and subfields current in HCI to see how design anthropology locates itself and what it comprises. We have allies and collaborators—fields where the questions are useful for understanding society and culture and fields where that is subsidiary to other aims.

Main Subfields of HCI and Applied Design Movements

Computer-Supported Cooperative Work (CSCW)

Computer-supported cooperative (or collaborative) work describes the intensive contextual study of group work to help design systems which support it. Its core ideas and its sense of a coherent identity were set out in the 1980s (Greif 1988). Its contributions over the years have created key bridges between HCI and anthropological concerns. It has established unequivocally the social nature of 'work' (see Blomberg and McLaughlin 1993; Blomberg, Suchman and Trigg 1997; Hakken 2000; Rosner 2010). Work is seen as a social process or flow, beyond the labour individuals do. As an example, academic study work is both individual (e.g. library or desk work) and group-based (e.g. seminars, lectures, exams). It is the alternation of the two phases, and the carriage of information between phases and people, which is often the engine by which any work moves forward: individual study happens for group events and vice versa. CSCW's understanding of work as social has also examined anthropological or ethnographic work (Forsythe 2001).

CSCW also changed ideas of what the designed or technological object actually is, by perceiving the importance of its cultural dimensions. For example one could evaluate a design by outlining the needs of a user and then seeing how a device or system meets them, but this is inadequate for CSCW without considering how people characterize, and know, their own work relationships and workflow (Grønbæk et al. 1993). Returning to the example of studying, can you say what makes a good book? A book is not important just because you can read it; it makes sense within the purposes of study. How do you *know* it is a good book, and what or who asserts this? So there is a complicated set of common knowledges affirming what the work is and the roles of artefacts. Many CSCW studies, including many of workplaces (Luff et al. 2000), are not so much the testing of a system, but more a cultural critique. The corpus of work has served to justify the importance and value of observational and descriptive work, especially participant observation.

At the same time, despite these contributions, CSCW research is not necessarily anthropological even when it is ethnographic. The ethnography conducted in CSCW has been of a particular 'ethnomethodological' kind—useful for some kinds of anthropological work but not always reflecting mainstream practice.

Participatory Design

Participatory design (Schuler and Namioka 1993; Bødker 1987; Bødker and Kensing 2004), as we have already seen, refers to a broad set of social initiatives and policies, and even to particular national histories. It has become a broad term which can be used to emphasize the political acts which legitimize design, technology and change, and when design work is supposed to proceed from participation more than from a particular technology. Darrouzet, Wild and Wilkinson (2009) write about conducting a 'participatory ethnography' in a hospital context. The conduct of group work during research stimulated conversations and communications across the hospital, such that the research itself began to address some of the problems for which a new technological system had been envisaged. Participation does not necessarily require design, but it does inform it.

Participatory design as a broad movement has made several contributions to anthropology. It offers ways of informing design that is driven not only by science but by traditional social science concerns (Sanoff 2008). It is a design tradition whose roots are *not* in commerce and the private sector, and so many anthropologists based in universities may find it attractive. But it can also be difficult to separate out its aims from the culture and politics of Scandinavia (and a specific social democratic historical era at that).

User-Centred Design (UxD)

User-centred design (or UxD) refers to a set of design methodologies which start with potential users or communities of users. UxD is not mainly about understanding social lives (like a lot of CSCW), but rather is about creating a design. Its methods can be participatory, but a lot of UxD preserves a separation between studio design work and fieldwork. Often there is a work process which alternates between studio or lab and field sites involving repeated iterations of design revisiting design needs, concepts, demos and prototypes. UxD grew into a serious, mainstream approach in the 1980s, when sets of principles were debated and proposed (Norman and Draper 1986). From the late 1990s, many user-centred designers began to take an interest in designing for user experience (or DUX).

The UxD movement and community have especially increased our understanding of experience as variable and social (Heath et al. 2002; Picard 1997; Zelkha and

Epstein 1998), not just commonsensical. It has especially begun to question the balance between when experience is about 'meaning', which suggests people want to understand things, and when it is about emotional concerns, which brings in a more sentimental and affective interest (Caspi and Gorsky 2006; Gaver 2009; Hutchins 1995; Norman 2005).

Although it has been argued that it is not nearly as good at producing new innovations as traditional scientific lab work (Norman 2010), UxD has had an impact in many corporations. UxD is quite capable of coming up with a list of specific design requirements which engineers can act on, unlike some ethnographic observational work. It is more about design and psychological (often cognitive) understandings than cultural or social ones.

Ubiquitous Computing (UbiCom) and Pervasive Computing

Through the 1990s, an increasing number of people in HCI moved into the study of ubiquitous computing (or UbiCom) and pervasive computing, which are essentially computer science's responses to the blending of computing into telecommunications. UbiCom is partly a project, not only the study of a social environment or technology but the attempt to implement something. Mark Weiser and others set out a vision for computing in the early 1990s (Weiser et al. 1999), directly informed by what ethnography had done for Xerox PARC. This combination of an empirical pragmatism with the seeds of an implied idealism is common to many areas of computing (Dourish and Bell 2011), giving direction to research.

This field has produced work which critically discusses exactly what ubiquity or pervasiveness may mean, while computing spreads far beyond desktop PCs. Studies have looked at computing as abstract process or information and as material thing (Rodden et al. 2004). One example is the idea of the 'disappearing computer' (Streitz, Kameas and Mavrommati 2007; Tolmie et al. 2001). More usefully to anthropology, others have probed a concept which anthropologists have often depended on overmuch: context (Dilley 1999). Paul Dourish's (2001a, 2004) work on contextual computing as ideal and/or thing illustrates the possibility of a critical grasp of constructions of context.

Movements within Design

Outside of HCI, but overlapping with it, a lot of important approaches have been germinated by people who are strictly design practitioners rather than engineers or computer scientists. As a field in its own right, design varies from graphic designers to fashion and textiles to product designers, systems designers and some artists. Design skills vary, but there is a lot of common ground, too. Design is one of the skill sets which have intruded into HCI in parallel with anthropology. Designers are especially good at bridging technical innovations and contexts of use, which makes their skills crucial for successfully acting on social and ethnographic research.

Design approaches and terminologies include contextual design (Holzblatt 1993, 2003; Holzblatt, Burns Wendell and Wood 2005), which is a set of ways of designing from an exploration of context. The firm IDEO has created some of the best-known examples of contextual design. CoDesign, meanwhile, refers to ways of doing design brainstorming with informants themselves—for example through design games (Brandt and Messeter 2004).

The field of interaction design has also become important in recent years, combining computer science and graphic design skills. An interaction designer basically designs interfaces, which could be anything from a refrigerator door to a bus stop. Seen in its broadest terms, interaction design is a perspective on the world which reconfigures almost every material and immaterial element as a potential interface, and hence potential relationship.

One of the most important design ideas for anthropologists is critical design. Critical design implies that design work is a cultural commentary, not necessarily functional work. So a design prototype, for example, can be presented not only as something which is being tested to see if it works, but as an artistic provocation which asks questions. Critical design is more about provoking new questions than producing answers. Design noir (Dunne 1999, 2008; Dunne and Raby 2001) is an example of critical design.

As a discipline, design offers immense anthropological potential in collaborative work, because it demands sets of informed sociocultural ideas. While a new *technology* can exist without thinking much about people, a new *design* must think about people.

Design Anthropology

These various HCI and design movements show us how design anthropology locates itself. The story behind these approaches and movements is politically loaded; different practitioners set out their stalls proactively and reactively to bring the broad agenda back to the questions they want to ask, to certain methods or to certain end aims. CSCW and UxD might appear to be asking similar questions, but one intends a sociological analysis and the other a design. While their methods sound the same, you will often see clear differences in the way they are implemented and witness debates between collaborators on a project.

Unlike some of these fields, design anthropology has no manifesto or set of principles—there are plenty of perfectly good definitions of anthropology. But from the 1990s, it became increasingly clear that more people with an anthropological background were working in HCI and that their work looked different from other peoples'.

Rather belatedly, the term 'design anthropologist' became current. Anthropological consultancy in Silicon Valley was highly significant in making this idea of the design anthropologist explicit, for example by Doblin Group, then eLab (see Robinson and Hackett 1997). The groundswell of consultancy (the part which pays the bills) has been marketing and branding. Yet ethnographic work has often led to unexpectedly deeper understandings and a need to redesign (Squires and Byrne 2002), not just rebrand. These consultancies established ethnography (and anthropology) as a recognizable, distinct practice and skill set, one not hidden within multidisciplinary teams.

In the jostle of HCI approaches, anthropologists are able to draw on those elements emphasizing ethnography (like CSCW, see Shapiro 1994) to bring in varied stakeholders in a participatory way (participatory design) and feed into questions about context and experience (UbiCom, CSCW). The digital artefacts used in their work at times embody field data, but at other times critical designs treat concept testing or prototyping as a potential cultural commentary. Design anthropology then comprises a group of anthropologists who do anthropological work, producing critical cultural commentaries alongside design and in ways that aspire to be constructive for design. Their aim is cultural commentary more than design or marketing, but their work is only justifiable when it engages with those aims in some sense. They are to be found in companies, universities, nongovernmental organizations and public-sector environments.

Apart from being a way of working, a space of ideas has begun to be carved out, as in the Internet group anthrodesign and the EPIC Conference (Ethnographic Praxis in Industry) established in 2005. Notable contributions are being made to thinking about the boundaries and core of anthropological work and thinking (see Ingold 2007). Detailed autobiographical reflections of anthropological practice proliferate (e.g. Cefkin 2009; Kaplan and Mack 2010; Moed 2010; Solomon 2010) which detail procedures, relationships, politics, value and values. Flynn (2009) outlines for example how the ways people in corporations identify with anthropological knowledge and representations—by having an iconic image of a 'user' specific to their team—can hinder as well as illuminate design.

I use two examples from my own work to illustrate how the particular kinds of digital artefacts used in design anthropology present questions for our understandings of anthropology and anthropological praxis. Digital artefacts are reflexive commentaries on what anthropological work is, and they constitute dialogues with informants as well as about informants.

Audiophotography Research at Hewlett-Packard Labs

The audiophotography project, conducted at and by HP Labs, by myself and David Frohlich, explored 'remembering' with digital media (Drazin and Frohlich 2007). In the United Kingdom, the year 2002 was a moment of uncertainty, experimentation and speculation about photography. Some people were shifting from analogue to digital cameras, and a few mobile phones contained cameras, but what might be done with a digital image was unclear. In companies like Hewlett-Packard (HP), some argued that all still and paper photos would soon disappear, replaced everywhere by video clips; others thought that printing would proliferate. Would remembering practices change or persist? Few anthropologists can be explicit about speculative social futures and how informants' lives may suddenly and utterly change—except anthropologists in corporations, who have to be. What research method we used was crucial. It had to both reflect on current remembering (to support it via design) and evoke new remembering and technical possibilities. We had to get information about remembering in context and create digital memory artefacts which would look convincing, even enchanting, to our engineering colleagues.

Drawing on the long-term work of David Frohlich (Frohlich 2004), a project was proposed on audiophotography—that is, still images with sound. Sound could be contextual (recorded when the photo was taken), a retrospective narration, music or nothing (silence is also a sound in digital media terms). A standard way to do this might be to invite a structured sample of people into the lab to create audiophotos. This would mean you could compare photos A and B, or informants X and Y, directly and keep technical standards high (this is important to engineers). You could also interview people about their thoughts and rationales behind audiophotos, producing user profiles. However, we rejected this proposal and argued for an anthropological approach, spending time with people at home to talk about remembering, photos, music and social life generally, before we even mentioned audiophotographs. We understood the project as being about remembering in its variety, and audiophotos as just a device. We wanted to look at remembering within relationships, not by asocial individuals. So we started networking in two hobby groups to find pairs or chains of people who probably already shared photos and/or music.

That first stage of the research, spending time with people, was evidently anthropologically the most valuable, but it was regarded by some colleagues as no method at all. We had to justify it. The justification was that we would learn real-world instances of sharing photos, music and memories, so as to create audiophotos envisaging actual relationships, audiences and motivations. So in the second stage, we asked people to envisage one such instance and make up two audiophoto albums—one with their narration and the other one matching photo and music collections. A mother who was in the habit of sending mini photo albums of her children to her mother in the United States made an audiophoto album for her mother. She also collated photos for her different children, each of whom had their own album sitting on the living room shelf—and so she narrated a story album for her daughter about their trip to Disneyland. Meanwhile, a widower who went through his photos to remember his late wife created a musical album with her in mind.

In a third stage of research, we invited people into the lab to show them how their audiophoto albums looked on different platforms (for example desktop screens, digital frames, digital paper, booklike forms and some new devices labelled 'patent applied for').

What we managed to uncover was something of the wide range of ways of remembering that can be found even within one home. The variety revealed the cultural, not biological, nature of remembering. Consider how remembering works differently with music or with a photo, for example. A Christmas photo can evoke a particular Christmas moment, while a piece of Christmas music more often brings habitual memories of 'Christmases when I was young'. When we looked specifically at the range of photos, we noticed recurring patterns in how they were placed and framed in the home, and we described these patterns in terms of four broad groups. First, there were lots of loose photographs kept somewhere—sometimes literally in a shoebox—jumbled, unsorted, almost deliberately messy. These were just 'memories'. Second, there were pinboards or displays in the hall or on the refrigerator door—the 'rogues' gallery' according to one family. Here were images of friends—people like you. While some of the photos here were deliberately placed there, others seemed to just find their own way. They arrived in an envelope, they really were not supposed to be thrown away, but ought somehow to be visible, at least for a bit; and there they landed, onto the fridge door. The third kind of presentation was in photo albums, some loose and some organized with handwriting and captions. Unlike the iconic images of rogues' galleries, albums remember events and are historicized, marking the turning and passing of the years. As a rule, albumed memories are household memories; other peoples' images, sent to you, rarely make it inside the album covers. The last kind of photo was the framed photo, reserved for family. Putting a school friend on your wall in a big, substantial frame would be risky. The framed pictures sit alongside paintings, landscapes, posters, art and decorative pieces. They sit there for a long time, possibly years, and age very slowly. A framed picture of a person as they looked ten years ago is still fitting now; if it were in a rogues' gallery, it wouldn't be.

The treatment of photographs in the home could be used to interpret, even model, remembering as an informational system. But that would not fully appreciate the culture of remembering, which was important for us. When imagining digital memory artefacts, we could begin to envisage sound as a kind of framing. The audio part of audiophotos might do similar kinds of things to frames, albums and rogues' galleries: for example make them appropriate for certain relationships, ascribe temporal qualities to them or designate the borders of the home.

Making audiophotos revealed something of the emotional burdens, and difficult responsibilities, of remembering and of memory artefacts. Music might transform a pedestrian image into a repository of nostalgia. Many images chosen had deeply emotional stories connected to them—a friend who has been ill, children who had recently left home. Our informants wrestled with how to treat their memories in an appropriate way. They were haunted by the vague sense that they should sort, frame and album those memories. There was often a palpable sense of obligation in going through other peoples' images: to sit with someone and go through their holiday or wedding album may be nice, but the fact is you are obliged to do it whatever. Likewise, to receive a framed portrait or audiophoto of a partner, boyfriend or girlfriend implies moral responsibilities around that image.

Perhaps our most important observation was that a lot of remembering is actually more about the future than the past, which may seem counterintuitive. For example a framed photo on your wall implies planning to remember that person every day. Placing photos on the fridge door indicates that the memory will be there for a while, but not forever. So memory artefacts in context are also about the future intention to remember. In fact it's not always clear which is most important. This means acts of remembering—holding artefacts, narrating, where you put them down—are simultaneously remembering and remembering ahead in the same action.

This project illustrates something about digital artefacts in design anthropology work. In a lot of anthropological work, you would avoid the second and third stages (making audiophotos) altogether, because it has an imaginary element. Audiophotographs did not exist in these peoples' homes, and might never exist. And yet the framework of remembering did, and we tried to fit into this framework 'from inside', so to speak. Making audiophotographs was a creative act in which a new artefact, a plausible artefact, was made which might fit that relationship. The artefact would attempt to demonstrate an imagination of what sort of relationship that was, without the fixity of words. Strangely, this suggests that anthropological work which draws on digital design methods to pay explicit attention to material forms can be very good at abstract imagination of sociality. Conversely, anthropological work which pays less attention to material forms, which is unquestioning of them, may remain bound by current and past material conditions. It follows that the right methods must be used for the right kinds of question.

But if some might say this was not traditional anthropological practice, it's not traditional HCI either. Our albums were, from a scientific point of view, all over the place: no consistency, no comparability, no technical specifications; all audio qualities, and none. One is a standalone art piece for a gallery by a semiprofessional photographer, another a botched sequence on a risky teenage booze-up. They do not make it possible to derive technical specifications for an engineer to use; and yet, anthropologically, the contrasts and comparisons evoke the families, relationships and backgrounds they came from. So for us, they were entry points into stories we could tell about what remembering is, and was, for different people.

I've talked a lot about how and why we did what we did, our methodology. This is important, because reflexivity is a common part of design anthropology fieldwork. The homes we worked with all used digital technologies that were designed, manufactured and promoted by companies such as HP. Companies are a part of remembering processes, and the corporate side of the conversation is the part which is missing in a lot of anthropological work. We learned how a lot of HP colleagues would equate 'good remembering' with technical excellence—a higher spec of camera or more crystal-clear sound. Understanding this engineering culture of remembering threw a lot of what we saw in peoples' homes into sharp relief, but it also helped explain a lot of the technology of remembering. So we could use the debates, the multidisciplinarity, the multiple stakeholders and the design process to feed into the anthropological learning process. The digitalized audiophotos in the later part of our research were the focus for this kind of learning process, so digital working helped provide perspectives distinctive to design anthropology.

Irish Rural Transport Research at Intel Digital Health Group

A second example, one without a very specific technological remit, will show some different sides to digital design and what digital artefacts do in design anthropology. The rural transport research conducted in 2007–8 by Intel Digital Health Group in Ireland was tasked to understand and design for global ageing. Our aim was to understand experiences of isolation and mobility in rural Ireland among older people and initiate an ongoing iterative design process.

The gatekeeper for the research was the Rural Transport Network, a group of organizations across the counties of Ireland. Most of the organizations run weekly minibuses which go door-to-door across the countryside, bringing elderly passengers to a local town or a community centre. The aim could be to collect weekly pensions, shop, attend a community group or fulfil health appointments. We approached five very different organizations: from large to small, in mountainous and flat areas, desolate and commuter belt. One was a profit-making company, another voluntary, another based on state-funded services. Some only provided transport, others provided community groups or meals-on-wheels. Three anthropologists (myself, Simon Roberts and Tina Basi) spent at least a week on one or two projects. We spent a lot of time on the buses, and we also met and interviewed a range of community and project stakeholders (passengers, drivers, district nurses, office organizers, post office staff, priests and so forth). We were loaded down with technology—camcorders to make shaky clips of country lanes, voice recorders which were almost permanently on and GPS locators tracking our routes by satellite.

What we really wanted to do was to (1) gather as much rich information as possible on the experience of the transport and place and (2) look at the contrasts and dialogues between stakeholders, not to understand the system but to draw out the contrasts.

Back at Intel, we gathered in groups with one another and with designers and engineers. We looked over everything we had—a mass of video clips, themes, different analyses, quotations, user profiles and still photographs—and began to produce sets of ideas of problems, opportunities and potential responses. To take a simple example, we might contrast the views of passengers and office staff on how the transport is organized to see if a design space existed to help them work smoothly together.

Many of our informants were very suspicious, certainly at first, and clearly many suspected that we were there to test the rural transport, perhaps to cut or withdraw it. In the past, anthropology has had a mixed record in rural Ireland. Several anthropologists have been (rightly, I think) accused of misunderstanding or misrepresenting Irish life, especially about isolation (see Peace 1989). To consider therefore someone living alone, with severe mobility difficulties, in a house distant from any other, in terms of isolation is problematic in more ways than I can elaborate on here. What was very clear, however, was that in our work, isolation was evident in its negation by the buses. The rural transport has transformed lives. People gain regular social contact, better shopping opportunities, better diets and more physical activity. Social networks open up, the local news grapevine is intensified and emotions and spirits rise. The rural transport is not a utopia, because it often happens against a background of growing inequality, poverty, changing gender and generational relationships and rural economic decline. Ireland has been changing immeasurably in the past two decades. Yet a single, short minibus ride each week makes a difference, and the tangible experience is important in this. To be on the buses can be intimidating, full of banter, jokes, gossip and laughter. Men in particular can find this difficult, as most passengers are women. Commonly, men join the bus in pairs: two quiet, elderly farmers waiting at a crossroads, who climb in and sit modestly at the back.

We began to appreciate transport as a social event, by contrast with some transport design approaches. Transport is not always an undesirable asocial moment happening between two desirable social places or events. To be on the rural transport is to be a member, and people often travel weekly even without anything to do at the other end. The bus is another node in the network, and weekly routine, of rural life—alongside the church, the pub, the Gaelic sports match and the livestock market, where on different days of the week news is handed on. The informational needs of the rural transport organization are also routinized: on any one trip, the driver has to know who is *not* joining the bus, not who *is* coming. In effect, people 'book' non-attendance, often by calling one key passenger who will sit up the front and tell the driver what to do—or what not to do.

After fieldwork, we then spent some months developing concepts, in short bursts of brainstorming, and narrowing them down to a few which might be workable. A professionally trained designer drafted these conceptual services or devices as on-screen simulations, flash programmes which you could click on. In the main, the concepts adapted and redeployed elements of the ethnographic research, using images and instances from the fieldwork which had been digitally recorded.

These digital demos were brought back to the rural transport projects, not to test but to try to advance them constructively, in a participatory way. So we tended to ask not 'would you use this or not?' but rather envisage specific elements about them. Where might an interface be located? Who uses them? Who has responsibility for personal information? Specific suggestions were also invited about the concepts, how the screen looks, touch screens, split screens, different kinds of devices and so on.

The moment when we presented these concepts to people, to try to engage them in the design process, marked a shift in the relationship. The previous suspicion of being tested fell away, so conversations were less optimistic and more balanced, and these shy and respectful people were not afraid to criticize either our demos or rural life.

> *Our village is dead* (Nan and Ettie, rural transport passengers in Sligo, reacting to product concepts)

> *Not one person in our club would use that* (Kate, Westmeath)

> *I'm happy enough with a phone call* (Anthea, Sligo)

The presentation of digital demos was no longer primarily an interpretive act, but a demonstrative one. This was the moment people realized we were serious about engaging, and the digital artefacts were the calling card of our intentions. They facilitated the imagination of benefits (or detriments) in actual, immanent social terms.

> *You wouldn't feel under a compliment* (Dorothea, Sligo—poetically expressing the burdens of community life and responsibility)

> *It should have a 'funeral' button, to automatically invite people to a funeral* (Julia, Sligo—funerals are key social events in the West of Ireland)

So the digitalized concepts began to illuminate problems and tensions and unpack the appearance of unity and uniformity in the rural transport. Such tensions were important for us to consider as we thought about what isolation and mobility mean and how they are articulated. What they also helped us negotiate in this work was the balance between an exercise in learning and in being taught. A simple idea of the research might have been that it was to understand social problems, which anthropology interprets and models to inform a design response. However, the fact is that a response to a complex set of problems of ageing and rural life is already there—the rural transport minibuses work, and they require support.

But the way that the rural transport is an answer as well as question is not just about what the rural transport is like. It is also this way because of the framework of design anthropology, which is an engaged one. In design anthropology work, many aspects of life can appear as either phenomena or responses to phenomena, and you can choose to privilege either aspect. So, for example, you might observe the fact of men joining the (female-dominated) bus in pairs and perform an analysis of how this constructs gender in rural Ireland, how it makes men and women. In our project, we could see it as a response, one solution which people have devised to the issues of how gender is. One way you might talk about this is that there is a shift from 'matters of fact' to 'matters of concern' (Heidegger 1967; Latour 2004). It is one of the ways that, as an anthropologist, you can choose to frame your work—are you producing interpretations or responses?

Conclusions and Future Questions

When you get down to specific instances of lived lives, work in digital design can be exciting and refreshing. Anthropological contributions frequently bring a provoking freshness and illumination to the occlusion which computing design (as with any social group or project) is at risk of falling into. But I do not want to address here what anthropology can do for digital design, or even how it studies digital technologies. More important are the two questions I started with: what can this engagement do for us as anthropologists in the work of producing sociocultural interpretations, and how has design anthropology work operated within the political field of digital technologies?

Digital knowledge artefacts are at the heart of both questions. Design anthropology as a practice is strongly dialogic and 'situated' (Harraway 1991), in the sense that if you encounter it, you are probably already implicated in it. The use of digital artefacts and media comes to be especially important in order to adequately negotiate the web of relationships within which design anthropology research is inevitably conducted. They constitute the dialogues by which the work progresses. They are deployed in some sense as agents, as things which *do* work, as well as purporting to be partial interpretations of social forms. The stance of design anthropology encourages, even necessitates, a questioning attention to physical and material contexts, as a route into examining contemporary conceptions of social trajectories and attitudes towards social change. Such a stance involves a serious reorientation as regards informants. What we do with digital prototypes and concepts can *affect* informants. The digital is here not an act of mutual consumption, but a sharing and acknowledgement of responsibility and intent (Grudin and Grinter 1995).

There are several unfolding contributions here which are being made to digital anthropology. Design anthropology is evidently in a privileged position when it comes to seeing inside corporations. Companies, especially multinationals, are very influential, but they patrol their boundaries very carefully; ethnographic work is very difficult, and definitively extricating yourself from the field (i.e. the corporation) with participant observation data intact is positively gymnastic. Design consultancy provides an entry point for the anthropological discipline. However, this is not only about corporations per se, but understanding their changing significance. As new information technologies infuse objects, the skills to deal with them do as well, and so consumption changes. Nowadays you do not just buy and listen to music, you also have sets of skills, software and tools by which you work with the media. A person who buys a digital product is no longer a consumer in the same sense, but is also a producer and a craftsperson (Gauntlett 2011). Design, then, is becoming a popular, public activity, and it potentially signifies shifts in the balance of power and expertise between companies and publics. The question is, as the skills to make and work with products become popularized, is this an empowerment of publics in relation to corporations or a neutralization as they align themselves closer to corporate thinking?

A range of anthropologists and design thinkers are unpacking the idea of 'craft' to look at the two above points. Craft can describe the ways we work with our material environments, compounding the things surrounding us with the skills we have (Sennett 2008). Craft also has a history of political and protest movements, reacting to and resisting the advance of anonymous industry and commodities (see Dormer 1997). It is like a popularization of design without the high-class and exclusive overtones of that word. To talk of craft is to talk of the work we put into things (Suchman 1995)—the difference between the gift of a cake from the shop and a cake we have made to our own recipe. As digital skills become popularized, and material things more digitized, more of our world could become like the cakes we have baked than those we have bought.

Perhaps the most important area which design anthropology can help us with is the question of trying to specify and critique what anthropologists do. One of the points which really hits anthropologists hard when working in design is having to put into words and justify what they *do*, not only what they know. Design anthropological writing (Cefkin 2009) addresses these concerns: the praxis of anthropology and the heuristics; what the debates are; where processes fail and where they work; when they are anthropological and when they are not. The majority of design anthropology writing is reflexive work on what anthropologists themselves have done, laid out almost in a spirit which invites critique. The kinds of knowledge artefacts resulting from anthropological work in this area are like designs or craft objects insofar as they incorporate a sense of social justification in their form and use.

What should be clear from the examples given is that in anthropological work, digital media can actually have a lot of political and ethical implications. Digital artefacts are not just data. They can change the basis of anthropological relationships. They have social traction, not just informational content. Digital media are good for some kinds of work but are poor for others. What is crucial in anthropology is to learn from our engagements with digital design and, in a sense, to tame the digital and harness it to the kinds of work we wish to do.

References

Bannon, L. 1991. From Human Factors to Human Actors: The Role of Psychology and Human-Computer Interaction in Systems Design. In *Design at Work: Co-operative Design of Computer Systems*, ed. J.G.M. Kyng, 25–44. Hillsdale, NJ: Lawrence Erlbaum.

Bannon, L. 2010. On (the) Doing (of) Things. Paper presented at the European Association for the Study of Science and Technology (EASST) conference, Trento, Italy, 3 September.

Bannon, L. 2011. Reimagining HCI: Toward a More Human-Centred Perspective. *Interactions* (July–August): 50–7.

Bjerknes, G., P. Ehn and M. Kyng, eds. 1987. *Computers and Democracy: A Scandinavian Challenge.* Aldershot: Avebury.

Blomberg, J., D. McLaughlin and L. Suchman. 1993. Work-Oriented Design at Xerox. *Communications of the ACM* 36(6): 91.

Blomberg, J., L. Suchman and R. Trigg. 1997. Back to Work: Renewing Old Agendas for Cooperative Design. In *Computers and Design in Context*, ed. M.L.M. Kyng, 267–87. Cambridge, MA: MIT Press.

Bødker, S. 1987. A Utopian Experience: On the Design of Powerful Computer-based Tools for Skilled Graphical Workers. In *Computers and Democracy: A Scandinavian Challenge*, ed. G. Bjerknes, P. Ehn and M. Kyng, 251–78. Aldershot: Avebury.

Bødker, K., and F. Kensing. 2004. *Participatory IT Design: Designing for Business and Workplace Realities.* Cambridge, MA: MIT Press.

Brandt, E., and J. Messeter. 2004. Facilitating Collaboration through Design Games. In *Proceedings of the Eighth Conference on Participatory Design*, 212–31. New York: Association for Computing Machinery.

Braverman, H. 1974. *Labour and Monopoly Capital: The Degredation of Work in the Twentieth Century.* London: Monthly Review Press.

Card, S., T. Moran and A. Newell. 1983. *The Psychology of Human-Computer Interaction.* Hillsdale, NJ: Lawrence Erlbaum.

Caspi, A., and P. Gorsky. 2006. Online Deception: Prevalence, Motivation and Emotion. *Cyberpsychology and Behaviour* 9(1): 54–9.

Cefkin, M. 2009. *Ethnography and the Corporate Encounter: Reflections on Research in and of Corporations.* Oxford: Berghahn Books.

Crabtree, A. 2003. *Designing Collaborative Systems: A Practical Guide to Ethnography.* New York: Springer.

Darrouzet, C., H. Wild and S. Wilkinson. 2009. Participatory Ethnography at Work: Practicing in the Puzzle Palaces of a Large, Complex Healthcare Organization. In *Ethnography and the Corporate Encounter*, ed. M. Cefkin, 61–94. Oxford: Berghahn Books.

Dilley, R. 1999. *The Problem of Context.* Oxford: Berghahn Books.

Dormer, P., ed. 1997. *The Culture of Craft: Status and Future.* Manchester: Manchester University Press.

Dourish, P. 2001a. Seeking a Foundation for Context-aware Computing. *Human-Computer Interaction* 16(2–4): 229–41.

Dourish, P. 2001b. *Where the Action Is: The Foundations of Embodied Interaction.* Cambridge, MA: MIT Press.

Dourish, P. 2004. What We Talk about When We Talk about Context. *Personal and Ubiquitous Computing* 8(1): 19–30.

Dourish, P., and G. Bell. 2011. *Divining a Digital Future: Mess and Mythology in Ubiquitous Computing.* Cambridge, MA: MIT Press.

Drazin, A., and D. Frohlich. 2007. Good Intentions: Remembering through Framing Photographs in English Homes. *Ethnos* 72(1): 51–76.

Dunne, A. 1999. *Hertzian Tales: Electronic Products, Aesthetic Experience and Critical Design.* London: RCA CRD Research Publications.

Dunne, A. 2008. Design for Debate. *Architectural Design* 196: 90–3.

Dunne, A., and F. Raby. 2001. *Design Noir: The Secret Life of Electronic Objects.* London: August/Birkhauser.

Flynn, D. 2009. 'My Customers Are Different!' Identity, Difference and the Political Economy of Design. In *Ethnography and the Corporate Encounter*, ed. M. Cefkin, 41–60. Oxford: Berghahn Books.

Forsythe, D. 2001. *Studying Those Who Study Us: An Anthropologist in the World of Artificial Intelligence.* Stanford, CA: Stanford University Press.

Frohlich, D. M. 2004. *Audiophotography: Bringing Photos to Life with Sounds.* Dordrecht: Kluwer Academic.

Gauntlett, D. 2011. *Making Is Connecting.* Cambridge: Polity Press.

Gaver, W. 2009. Designing for Emotion (Among Other Things). *Philosophical Transactions of the Royal Society B-Biological Sciences* 364(1535): 3597–604.

Greif, I., ed. 1988. *Computer-Supported Cooperative Work: A Book of Readings.* San Mateo, CA: Morgan Kaufman.

Grønbæk, K., J. Grudin, S. Bødker and L. Bannon. 1993. Achieving Cooperative Systems Design: Shifting from a Product to a Process Focus. In *Participatory Design: Perspectives on Systems Design*, ed. D.S.A. Namioka, 79–97. Hillsdale, NJ: Lawrence Erlbaum.

Grudin, J. 2005. Three Faces of Human-Computer Interaction. *IEEE Annals of the History of Computing* 27(4): 46–62.

Grudin, J. 2007. A Moving Target: The Evolution of HCI. In *The Human-Computer Interaction Handbook*, 2nd ed., ed. A.S.J. Jacko. Abingdon, UK: CRC Press.

Grudin, J., and R. Grinter. 1995. Ethnography and Design. *Computer-Supported Cooperative Work* 3(1): 55–9.

Hakken, D. 2000. Resocialing Work? Anticipatory Anthropology of the Labor Process. *Futures* 32(8): 767–75.

Haraway, D. J. 1991. *Simians, Cyborgs and Women: The Reinvention of Nature.* London: Free Association.

Harrison, S., D. Tatar and P. Sengers. 2007. The Three Paradigms of HCI. Paper presented at ALT:CHI 2007, 28 April–3 May, San Jose, California.

Heath, C., P. Luff, D. vom Lehm, J. Hindmarsh and J. Clerverly. 2002. Crafting Participation: Designing Ecologies, Configuring Experience. *Visual Communication* 1(1): 9–33.

Heidegger, M. 1967. *What Is a Thing?* Washington, DC: Gateway.

Holtzblatt, K.S.J. 1993. Contextual Inquiry: A Participatory Technique for Systems Design. In *Participatory Design*, ed. D.A.N. Schuler. Hillsdale, NJ: Lawrence Erlbaum.

Holtzblatt, K. 2003. Contexual Design. In *The Human-Computer Interaction Handbook*, ed. J.A.S. Jacko. London: Lawrence Erlbaum.

Holtzblatt, K., J. Burns Wendell and S. Wood. 2005. *Rapid Contextual Design: A How-to Guide to Key Techniques for User-centred Design.* London: Morgan Kaufman, Elsevier.

Hutchins, E. 1995. *Cognition in the Wild.* Cambridge, MA: MIT Press.

Ingold, T. 2007. Anthropology Is Not Ethnography. *Proceedings of the British Academy* 154: 69–92.

Kaplan, J., and A. Mack. 2010. 'Ethnography of Ethnographers' and Qualitative Meta-Analysis for Business. In *Proceedings of the Ethnographic Praxis in Industry Conference (EPIC) 2010*, 110–12. American Anthropological Association.

Latour, B. 2004. Why Has Critique Run Out of Steam? From Matters of Fact to Matters of Concern. *Critical Inquiry* 30(2): 225–48.

Luff, P., et al. 2000. *Workplace Studies: Recovering Work Practice and Informing System Design.* Cambridge: Cambridge University Press.

Moed, A. 2010. Back to the Future of Ethnography: Internal User Research at a Consumer Internet Company. In *Proceedings of the Ethnographic Praxis in Industry Conference (EPIC) 2010*, 14–25. American Anthropological Association.

Norman, D. A. 1988. *The Design of Everyday Things.* New York: Basic Books.

Norman, D. A. 2005. *Emotional Design: Why We Love (or Hate) Everyday Things.* New York: Basic Books.

Norman, D. 2010. The Research-Practice Gap: The Need for Translational Developers. *Interactions* 17(4): 9–12.

Norman, D., and S. Draper, eds. 1986. *User-Centered Systems Design: New Perspectives on Human-Computer Interaction.* Abingdon: CRC Press.

Peace, A. 1989. From Arcadia to Anomie: Critical Notes on the Constitution of Irish Society as an Anthropological Object. *Critique of Anthropology* 9(1): 89–111.

Pew, R. 2003. Evolution of Human-Computer Interaction: From Memex to Bluetooth and Beyond. In *the Human-Computer Interaction Handbook*, 1st ed., ed. J. Jacko and A. Sears, 1–15. Hillsdale, NJ: Lawrence Erlbaum.

Picard, R. 1997. *Affective Computing.* Cambridge, MA: MIT Press.

Robinson, R., and J. Hackett. 1997. Creating the Conditions of Creativity. *Design Management Journal* 8(4): 9–16.

Rodden, T., A. Crabtree, T. Hemmings, B. Koleva, J. Humble, K.-P. Akesson and P. Hansson. 2004. Between the Dazzle of a New Building and Its Eventual Corpse: Assembling the Ubiquitous Home. In *Proceedings of the Fifth International Conference on Designing Interactive Systems*, 71–80. New York: Association for Computing Machinery (ACM).

Rosner, D., and K. Ryokai. 2010. Spyn: Augmenting the Creative and Communicative Potential of Craft. In *Proceedings of the 28th International Conference on Human Factors in Computing Systems*, 2407–16. New York: Association for Computing Machinery (ACM).

Sanoff, H. 2008. Multiple Views of Participatory Design. *ArchNet: International Journal of Architectural Research* 2(1): 57–69.

Schuler, D. E., and A. E. Namioka. 1993. *Participatory Design: Principles and Practices: 1st Participatory Design Conference: Papers*. Hillsdale, NJ: Lawrence Erlbaum.

Sellen, A. J., and R. Harper. 2002. *The Myth of the Paperless Office*. Cambridge, MA: MIT Press.

Sennett, R. 2008. *The Craftsman*. London: Allen Lane.

Shapiro, D. 1994. The Limits of Ethnography: Combining Social Sciences for CSCW. In *Proceedings of the Conference on Computer Supported Cooperative Work (CSCW) 1994*. New York: Association for Computing Machinery (ACM).

Solomon, K. 2010. A Comparison of Ethnographic and Autoethnographic Data for New Product Development. In *Proceedings of Ethnographic Praxis in Industry Conference (EPIC) 2010*, 66–78. American Anthropological Association.

Squires, S., and B. Byrne. 2002. *Creating Breakthrough Ideas: The Collaboration of Anthropologists and Designers in the Product Development Industry*. Westport, CT: Bergin & Garvey.

Streitz, N., A. Kameas and I. Mavrommati, eds. 2007. *The Disappearing Computer: Interaction Design, System Infrastructures and Applications for Smart Environments*. Berlin: Springer-Verlag.

Suchman, L. 1995. Making Work Visible. *Communications of the ACM* 38(9): 56–64.

Suchman, L. 2007. Anthropology as 'Brand': Reflections on Corporate Anthropology. Paper presented at Colloquium on Interdisciplinarity and Society, Oxford University, 24 February. Earlier draft (2000) available at: www.lancs.ac.uk/fass/sociology/research/publications/papers_alpha.htm.

Tolmie, P., J. Pycock, T. Diggins, A. MacLean and A. Karsenty. 2001. Unremarkable Computing. In *Proceedings of the CHI 2001 Human Factors in Computing Conference*, 399–406. New York: Association for Computing Machinery.

Weiser, M., R. Gold and J. Brown. 1999. Origins of Ubiquitous Computing Research at PARC in the Late 1980s. *IBM Systems Journal* 38(4): 693–6.

Zelkha, E., and B. Epstein. 1998. From Devices to 'Ambient Intelligence'. Paper presented at the Digital Living Room conference, Laguna Niguel, California, June.

–13–

Museum + Digital = ?

Haidy Geismar

As is common within many discussions of digital technologies, 'digital' is used as a catchall term, uniting many different forms and practices. This is particularly the case in museums, where digital technologies are increasingly integrated into diverse practices of collection and collections management, information management, curating, exhibiting and educating. Here, I draw on Miller and Horst's definition of the digital in the introduction to this volume, identifying the digital by the technical process of translation into binary register (and back again), and the standardization, transformation and mediated experience this technological shift effects. In this essay I discuss and describe the effects of this kind of technological mediation on museum practice and experience, focusing on the remediation of collections online and in the space of the museum catalogue and storeroom. In the case studies that follow, I focus on how digital projects 'encode' theories of digital sociality and how the digital coproduces not only representations of objects and social relations, but collections and sociality in museum worlds.

As representational forms, analysts have long drawn analogies between the drawing together of objects for collection and exhibition and the constitution of society *through* the representation of these objects within the museum (see Bennett 1995). How do digital technologies participate in the representational and creative habitus of the museum? How does binary code fit into a continuum of knowledge management and presentation? How does the digital enhance the sensory power and affectivity of exhibitions? In the case studies that follow, I reevaluate the broad claim, common across digital studies, that the digital is a completely new domain of form and practice that creates social and material encounters that are radically different from its antecedents.[1] The emergence of digital technologies in museums is in fact part of a long-standing trajectory of networking, classifying and forging representations of relationships between people and things.

An Overview of the Anthropology of Digital Technologies in Museums

Accounts of the digital as a new genre of museum practice are largely celebratory, applauding the democratic expansion of a commons of cultural information and objects to greater numbers of people. The discursive tropes of access and accountability are also hallmarks of a continually emergent 'New Museology' that has documented a shift of interest in museums away from objects and toward people, society and experience (see Hein 2000; Hooper Greenhill 2000; Vergo 1989).

Broadly speaking, accounts of digital practices in museums recognize the digitization of museums in the catalogue, the website, online exhibitions, social media and the technological interfaces that act as communicative and structuring mechanisms that simultaneously interpret and provide greater access to museum work (collecting, exhibiting, educating, socializing and researching). Many analysts focus on the ways in which these digital museum practices challenge conventional understandings of museum collections, perceptions of authenticity, replication and the visitor experience (see Bayne, Ross and Williamson 2009; Conn 2010; Isaac 2008).[2]

Much of the relevant literature focuses on the ways in which museums use digital technologies to generate new social relations and to create new epistemologies and classificatory systems, emancipating museums from a variety of constraints: budgetary, spatiotemporal, political and institutional (see, for instance, the extensive online reports from the annual Museums and the Web conferences, and see Parry 2010).[3] The digital museum is the ultimate 'museum without walls' (Malraux 1967). There is an emphasis on the ways in which the digital enhances mutability and polyphony and can make connections in time and space that transcend the possibility of other kinds of museum matter (Henning 2007), effecting a kind of 'figurative repatriation' (Kramer 2004) and reconnection between museum collections, communities and individuals.[4] In turn, the creation of new digital collections has expanded the possibilities of how the ownership of collections may be imagined (Geismar 2008), and has forged a new genre of collection: digital cultural heritage (Brown 2007; Cameron and Kenderdine 2007) as well as new forms of return referred to as 'digital repatriation' (Christen 2011; Hennessy 2009).[5]

The digital has become the leitmotif of a broader field of museum practice in which museum objects may no longer be understood in and of themselves, but as part of broader fields of representation, mediation and communication. As I have argued elsewhere (Geismar 2010), stimulated by Conn's polemical question, *Do Museums Still Need Objects?* (2010), much museum studies literature uses a specific template for understanding museum objects, exemplified by nineteenth-century collections of material culture. This view of objects does not understand digital technologies (computer monitors, video installations, sound) as new objects in collections, but rather sees them as re-mediations of the authentic stuff. Recent anthropological work on digital collections provides a corrective to this perspective: Isaac's work on technology in the National Museum of the American Indian (2008) and Kirschenblatt-Gimblett's work at the Museum of the History of the Polish Jews in Warsaw (2009) sensitively take into account the nature of digital materiality and digital collections and their implication for new museum projects. For instance writing of the National Museum of the American Indian's 'purposeful and philosophical move away from what the director perceived to be the object-centric museum model' (2008: 291),

Isaac discusses how touch screens and other digital media in the exhibitions are often more accessible and visually compelling than the other objects on display. She argues that 'the media technology itself becomes a museum object, requiring an ideological shift in how we situate new configurations of these means of communicating or interpreting knowledges' (2008: 306; see Frey and Kirschenblatt-Gimblett 2002). For Isaac, digital technologies form part of new museological strategies of display that negotiate and try to distance themselves from colonial legacies of objectification and that provide new aesthetics for visual experience and sensory engagement in museums.

Similarly, Deirdre Brown (2007, 2008) describes the Virtual Patu project in Canterbury, New Zealand (in which an unprovenanced *wahaika* or cleaver in the Canterbury Museum was digitized and apprehended by visitors wearing user-worn devices via the Magic Book augmented reality interface), and *Te Āhua Hiko*/The Digital Form (an experimental project in which Māori performers were digitized three-dimensionally, then electronically inserted into a Māori animated environment, to be played to visitors to the Canterbury Museum). She argues that digital technologies are able to activate the objects' true meaning and purpose in ways that more static, and less immersive, traditional ways of displaying indigenous objects cannot (see also Taylor 2010). These digital objects are fully understood as authentic and traditional, and they are treasured by indigenous people.

Alongside these accounts of what is both new *and* traditional about digital collections is a growing body of work that analyses the digital as a zone for reordering knowledge systems and museum epistemologies. The trope of 'relationality', inspired by the mapping of social and material fields using actor network theory as well as anthropological material culture studies, is increasingly used as a guiding discursive tool for understanding how complex material engagements in museums may be translated into digital form (see Glass and Keramidas 2011; Zeitlyn, Larson and Petch 2007).[6] The relational knowledge fields converted into binary and remediated by digital technologies are not fixed, but rather are continually emergent out of preexisting fields, power relations and modes of social engagement, ranging from staff to software, which in turn create the habitus within which people make sense of digital technologies in the museum space.

Manovich observes that the (museum) database is not just a structure for storing information, it is a symbolic form in which the interface and the object are the same thing ([1999] 2010: 69). For a digital anthropology, this draws attention to the complex ways in which social transformation is mediated by processes of representation—in the case of digital technologies, predominantly visual representations mediated by binary code. In this sense we can map an anthropology of the conversion of information about museum collections into digital form onto something like the anthropology of kinship, in which the map (or kinship diagram/family tree) brings its subject into being as much as it represents it (see Bouquet 1996). In analysing many digital museum projects, it soon becomes apparent that the digital domain functions simultaneously as a representation of other sites and practices and as a site and practice in itself. This perpetual 'doubling' needs to be unpacked since it is one of the key ways in which the digital works. Such doubling maps onto many tensions at the heart of anthropological investigation that for many, from material culture theorists (e.g. Gell [1992] 1999; Miller 2005; Strathern 1990) to proponents of multiple ontologies (e.g. Henare, Holbraad and Wastell 2007), takes questions of representation as central not just to the form of the enquiry but to its content.

In the rest of this chapter, I emphasize that the digital is a specific form of museum object that moulds in particular ways, as any other artefact does, the classificatory systems and epistemological frameworks that in turn structure museums and the practice of collecting and exhibiting artefacts. In other words, the digital in museums creates an epistemology for understanding the relation between objects, knowledge, people and the environment. In the following case studies, I survey the ways in which digital technologies both encode existing relations and impose new forms and orders on existing museum practices.

Case One: Digital Forms as Encoding Sociality—Tagging, Folksonomy and Crowd Curation

As is typical of the kind of recursion common to the ways in which the digital is understood to both evoke and respond to sociality (see Kelty 2008), digital technologies in museums presume a theory of the social and often represent not only objects and collections but the social relations that collections and knowledge systems are active participants within. This is why digital museum tools are often described in terms of their social effects—access, accessibility, availability, democratization, community, constituency and their alter egos secrecy, restriction, protocols and hierarchy.

The digital is a continual process of translation and apprehension (the creation of an interface) by which data is converted into binary information that is converted back into multiple representations that are both codifications as well as instantiations of sociality. Sociality in this form is modelled in terms of networks, access and openness. What, however, is achieved through access to this kind of social encounter? How do these codes transform social relations, if at all? What do they really describe? The emergence of social tagging, and the representational theory of folksonomy (collaborative forms of classification), in relation to museum information management systems is a good place to think these questions through. In 2005 the Steve.museum project was founded in the United States to address concerns by art museums regarding the expansion of access through digitization and placing their collections online. One of many similar museum projects at this time interested in harnessing the power of Web 2.0 in the museum, Steve attempted to create and investigate the potential for tagging, or user-generated taxonomies, in describing collections. As its website describes, the Steve project 'formed a collaboration, open to anyone interested in thinking about social tagging and its value to museums, and began to develop a set of open source tools for collecting, managing, and analyzing user-contributed descriptions'.[7]

The notion of open-access via digitization of collections and their accessibility on the Internet and the kinds of participation that this both presumes and promotes has been a central theme to many museum engagements with the digital. Tagging, objectwikis, folksonomies and crowd curation have all become frames for articulating and promoting the democratization of the museum, often described in glowingly utopic terms.[8] For example, Cameron, framing the work of the Powerhouse Museum in Sydney's investigations of a more open classificatory system comments:

> Google-mediated searches are enabling the 'networked object' to play a role in political interventions in public culture...This highlights the fluidity, complexity, contested and political nature of cultural interactions and exchanges around what an object might mean. It also demonstrates how the divide between so-called high culture and popular culture, museum culture and public culture can spontaneously dissolve, and how easily people can combine museum collections with other cultural forms. (Cameron and Mengler 2009: 192)

Srinivasan et al. (2009a, 2009b) challenge such celebratory discussions of tagging and folksonomy. They are sceptical of the kinds of expert knowledge that are required not only to make sense of collections but of the digital interface, and they question the assumption that tagging and other online additions to catalogue information permit a deeper, more sustained engagement with collections. A certain kind of curatorial process is needed for projects that potentially engage masses of people, which in some ways replicates the same structures of authority that the utopian visions of open access and folksonomy are trying to leave behind. In a February 2011 search on the Steve project website intended to locate examples of interesting tags, most of the links to participating museums were broken, and of the images of artworks linked in the section 'Steve in Action', almost all of them remained untagged. There is increasing recognition by museum professionals, and by the Steve project, that in order to be useful, tagging needs to be moderated and standardized, with constituencies organized into communities of 'trust'.[9] Access to the democratic republic of tagging works best with smaller communities of like-minded people who share knowledge bases, interests and skill sets.[10]

Tagging and folksonomies are perhaps better understood as representations of users as well as collections, reflecting the intent of the museum to represent itself as open and non-hierarchical on the one hand and reflecting the opinions and knowledge of the public on the other. They are recursive in that they create a form of openness (and a perception of the public) that in turn alters the public's perception of the museum as an open space. Many projects are successful in these terms and genuinely inflect a sense of participation even if the actual form of participation in formalizing knowledge around collections remains limited. For instance, White (2009) argues that the new digital gallery and database *Our Space* at the Museum of New Zealand Te Papa Tongarewa, ensures that the museum lives up to its objective to present itself as a 'forum' for the nation. *Our Space* comprises an online component in which users can upload their own images to the central server, defining 'their' New Zealand through both image and associated documentation (see http://ourspace.tepapa.com/).[11] These images are then activated in the museum on a digital wall, upon which other visitors may choose from the archive, create new images and content and create their own cultural map of New Zealand, which they can save on a memory stick to take away with them.

My own contribution to the archive, two photographs tagged 'cheese' and 'road trip', have been used on the wall four times (as of March 2011). However, a scan of the interactive wall that is photographed and archived online shows mainly the grinning faces of museum visitors as they play with the touch-screen technology.

The most common use of the wall is therefore in the project of self-representation. Users work on their own self-image and literally emplace themselves in the museum, but little real dialogue about the nature of collections, the democratization of conceptual categories or classificatory systems emerges. The new digital space has been exploited for purposes of self-presentation that becomes the objective of entering into a relationship with the museum's digital collections.

In the successfully crowd-curated exhibition *Click!* held at the Brooklyn Museum in 2008, anyone with Internet access was invited to participate in the selection of images online.[12] An open call to artists invited electronic submissions on the theme 'The Changing Face of Brooklyn'. Visitors to the website were then invited to go through the image bank and anonymously jury the exhibition. The final selection included images 'democratically' preferred by the majority of visitors. The supplementary information on the website broke down jurists by location, allowed access to comment and discussion around the images and other facts and figures about the exhibition were collected. However, as one of the invited commentators (a curator at the Brooklyn Museum of Art) noted, highlighting the recursivity of these digital initiatives:

> So if the crowd juried the images, how was it curated? And what was the idea curated? The theme of the photographs submitted was 'The Changing Faces of Brooklyn,' but that is not the theme of the installation that is presented in our galleries. Although the changing faces of Brooklyn is an idea that underlies each of the works of art in the exhibition, the exhibition itself is about the notion of selection, and, specifically, selection by the crowd.[13]

Case Two: Radical Archives and the Limits of Openness

My first example of the ways in which digital technologies have been used to open up the process of knowledge production, interpretation and curation to different, nontraditional constituents highlights briefly how digital museum practices encode social theories and work to produce an image of a public and, by extension, the museum-visiting public itself. These new museum subjects inevitably add a layer of (self-)representational effect to digital objects. In this second case study, I move behind the scenes to look at the ways digital archives constitute an alternative imaginary of access and public access that similarly critiques the representational authority of the museum and archive. Unlike the crowd curation and tagging projects, which open up collections promiscuously, these radical archives resist and subvert the model of open access. They frequently critique the authority of museum collecting practices—speaking back to histories of privileged access and exclusion. Projects focused on indigenous peoples and collections exemplify this trend. For many indigenous peoples, especially those in settler colonies with vibrant museum cultures (e.g. Australia, Canada and New Zealand), this is a question of sovereignty as much as protocol. Access to archives becomes a political act where control over the visibility of information is hoped to facilitate the devolution of other kinds of power and authority. As Field points out, connections to museum collections reflect crucial interpretive issues around 'recognized status and . . . the sovereignty over their cultural identities' (2008: 25).

The potential for openness evoked by digital technologies makes them fertile grounds for expressing this critique. The project Digital Futures by anthropologist Elizabeth Povinelli, who has worked for many years in Aboriginal Australia, interrogates the resonance of archiving practices for Aboriginal Australians and 'asks what a postcolonial digital archive becomes if, instead of information, circulation, and access, we interrogate it from the perspective of socialities of obligation, responsibility and attachment'.[14] Upon entering the project and clicking on a map location, text on screen informs us that:

> You are about to participate in a form of circulation, the circulation of information, persons and socialities. This form of circulation has a metaform, a sociality, a way of anticipating, addressing, and incorporating the things that move through it, including you. The government wishes to help.

The site then presents a series of filmed narratives, mediated by a digital cartography, that fundamentally destabilizes the viewer. The narratives are elliptical, like the footage, off-subject, challenging our expectation of the kinds of information that should be archived or the ways in which cultural knowledge might be visually and discursively embodied. As digital catalogues move outside of the space of the museum or archive (via web technologies), the context in which these relationships are viewed becomes infinite, as the terminals on which the catalogues are viewed will vary as well as the physical environments in which they are located, challenging the boundaries of how the museum itself frames this material and holds authority over it. Povinelli's archive will ultimately be based in handheld units (like smartphones), in which geographic information system technologies will link stories, photos, videos and other data in ways that can only be accessed when people are in specific places. Another text that scrolls over the screen as you navigate the site states: 'Even as I address you as *you* this is an impersonal you, a third person form of the second person. We have programmed *you* into this site without knowing who you are.'

Many discussions of the process of digitizing in museums take for granted, particularly in the context of museums and archives, that collections are supposed to be seen (see Brown 1998). This is part of our own, often unexamined, cultural perspective that insists on visibility as one of the prime modes of acquiring knowledge (seeing is believing). Our own cultural assumption is that digitization equals access and broad circulation, even though governments and corporations are desperately encoding restrictions in law.[15] However, the open circulation of images and objects and information may, in fact, work against local understandings of the appropriate use of museum collections. For Aboriginal Australians, for instance, only initiated cultural insiders are traditionally supposed to fully apprehend the true meaning and stories contained within locally produced images, even as they circulate in wider and wider contexts (see Myers 2002, 2004). Indigenous protocols that hinge around the idea of invisibility (or holding back) are carried through into other contexts; for example historically in many communities, when someone died, all mention of the person would cease and his or her belongings would be destroyed. The person was no longer referred to, represented or seen—provoking an anxiety regarding the unauthorized presence of photographs in print, on display or in archives.

These traditional protocols are being institutionalized in new ways, despite an on-the-ground fluidity in the ways in which Aboriginal Australians themselves use photographs and other media images (see Deger 2006). In Australia, it is increasingly the custom to preface publications, exhibitions, websites and films with a warning to Aboriginal people that they may see images of people now deceased in order to limit the cultural harm that this visibility may render. However, the proliferation of technology works in communities in different ways, and opening images up to different forms of mobility (particularly mobile telephones) has altered Aboriginal engagements with the materiality and visibility of digital images (see Christen 2005).

Digital technologies thus facilitate a sustained engagement with the power relations that surround the museum and archive. In Australia, there is a growing digital movement that rethinks the openness and accountability of digital archives. The Ara Iritija project is a database and archive housed in mobile units that service thirty-one Aboriginal communities in central Australia (see Christen 2006; Thorner 2010; http://www.irititja.com/). The mobile platform is an archive organized with community engagement and protocols in mind that is networked on a localized intranet. Thorner describes this process of 'indigenizing the internet', but comments that 'the potential of the new Ara Iritija (both the software package and its dynamic approach to archiving) is embedded in its optimized flexibility, and yet, there are limits to the ways in which digital technologies can be mobilized in the interests of Anangu cultural production' (Thorner 2010: 138; see also Christie 2005). Indigenous database projects are continually negotiating between different domains: community expectation and experience, local knowledge systems, previous methods of collecting and organizing collections and the constraints of digital technology (with its attendant expectation of form, content and access).

Another example of how these protocols can be expressed (and effected) digitally can be found in the Mukurtu Wumpurrarni-kari Archive, a browser-based digital archive created initially for the Warumungu community in Tennant Creek, Northern Territory, Australia, in collaboration with Kim Christen, Chris Cooney and other researchers from the United States and Australia. Mukurtu has now been launched as open-source software aimed specifically to provide archiving solutions for indigenous peoples and other communities with nonhegemonic archival needs and desires.[16] Initially, the project's goal was to develop a local archive that was sensitive to indigenous concerns regarding the handling of cultural materials that belonged to specific communities, families and individuals. But the project also aims to provide a more universal platform for indigenous people, an alternative archival structure to the conventional museum catalogue that presumes open access and a particular model of proprietorship over cultural knowledge and objects. In this way, the specificity of Aboriginal Australian negotiations with their own traditions of image management and the settler-colonial culture of museum collection is made generic and extended to other cultural and colonial contexts.

A demonstration of the archive (also as a contribution to the journal *Vectors* entitled 'Digital Dynamics Across Cultures', http://vectorsjournal.org/projects/index.php?project=67) illustrates a number of ways to deal with the combination of Aboriginal protocols and the reproduction of images in the archive: photographs are obscured by pieces of tape or made entirely unavailable; videos cut out or fade halfway through and warnings are given about the gendered nature of knowledge. In addition, each of these protocols is explained carefully on the site to give the non-indigenous viewer a chance to rethink the viewing restrictions that are embedded within Aboriginal engagements with images in the archive.[17] The commons—a public-domain resource open to all to appropriate both visually and in other operational ways—has been indigenized, re-presented within a frame of very different values around access, visibility and entitlement.

It is becoming clear that in some places the upshot of community collaboration and consultation around collections may in fact be the end of public access to certain collections and the emergence of what I term an 'indigenous commons'—archives regulated in relation to very different kinds of protocols to those that have developed within the colonial or modern museum (Geismar forthcoming: chap. 5; c.f. Brown 2003). Rather than being tools of enlightenment, in which the world is neatly packaged and displayed for a general public, democratically defined (see Bennett 1995), the sensibility of 'radical archives' suggests an understanding of knowledge as constructed through power-inflected and specific relations between object, institution and

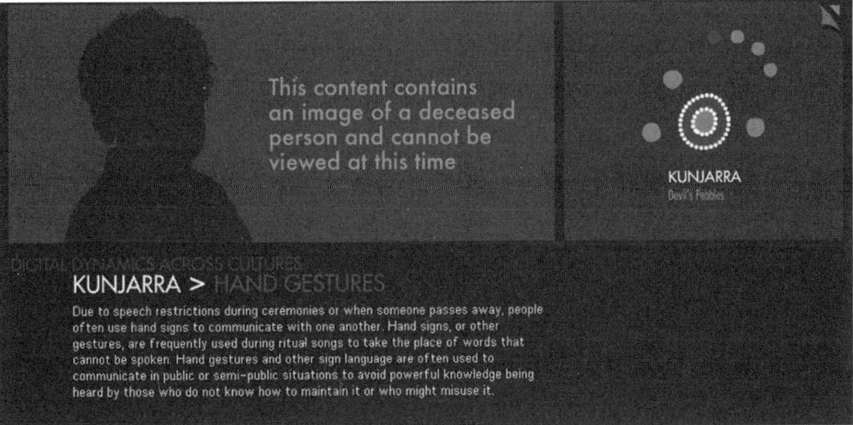

Figure 13.1 Screen shot from the Digital Dynamics Across Cultures project.

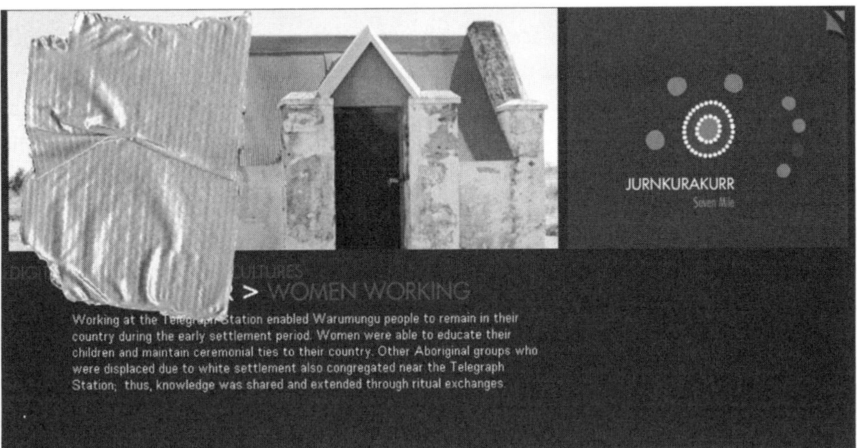

Figure 13.2 Screen shot from the Digital Dynamics Across Cultures project.

visitor, and in which visibility is not the only way in which this relationship may be configured.

The end space and after-effect of many of these projects is, like the Steve. museum, representational as well as political. The representations of these archives draw attention to the basic assumptions of access and availability and the presence of other epistemological and ordering protocols. A debate has arisen between commentators such as Michael Brown (1998, 2003), who think it inappropriate and impractical to translate the diversity of indigenous values and entitlement into generic or national cultural/museum policy, and those who think that this view perpetuates the very hierarchies and elitisms that recoding and re-signifying projects aim to address (e.g. Simpson 2007). I argue that digital projects need to be understood not only as representational projects but also as real-world sites of engagement and experience.

Case Three: New Database, New Epistemology? The Digital Practices of the Vanuatu Cultural Centre

In my final example, I turn to the digitizing practices of the Vanuatu Cultural Centre and National Museum (VCC), which aim to constitute a synthetic archive that unites many different kinds of collections: audio, photographic, video, objects, archaeological site research and languages. In this example, I argue that we need to understand the emergence of digital practices in cultural context and with historical specificity. Two key tropes within contemporary accounts of the digital are rupture and novelty: the digital is presumed to herald unprecedented radical structural and social transformation. Yet accounts of the development of the telegraph (Standage 1998) or of eighteenth-century wetware (Riskin 2003) demonstrate a lengthy history of technological (re)mediation of our very understanding of the object world. In practice, catalogue systems have long been precedents for the digital mediation of collections. Despite the multiplicity of digital projects and uses, almost all digital museum forms have their roots in a relatively limited number of programmed forms (e.g. the relational database) and algorithms (see Manovich 2002: chap. 1), which in turn use binary code to create secondary representations which themselves are apprehended as primary cultural representations (exhibition displays, text, image, sound and film and so forth).[18] This raises the question of what precisely is new or novel within digital museum forms and what indeed is culturally specific? Does the digital museum forge new kinds of social relationships and practices or does it replicate, or encode, preexisting ones? A further set of questions revolve around the social and political implications of these replications and transformations. For example, is digital repatriation a genuinely new condition of ownership for new and renewed forms of cultural heritage/museum collections? Or does it reinforce centuries-old imperial hierarchies of access and ownership of collections, offering the olive branch of digital access without actually sharing power or ownership of the original objects that remain in the museum, perhaps even recreating a colonial museology? In the case of Vanuatu, we may also ask what indigenous forms are being encoded within the space of the database. This discussion is taken from a longer account of the database at the Vanuatu Cultural Centre (Geismar and Mohns 2011).

Analysts understand digital code to not only signify but reorder knowledge at a profound level. Srinivasan and Huang (2005) develop the notion of 'fluid ontologies', in which database encodings may be used to alter the hierarchies emplaced within classificatory systems in museums by privileging different fields, concepts and terminologies. Christie describes how his project to create a Yolngu database worked with 'friendly and fuzzy search systems' (2005: 57), which could incorporate alternate spellings, pronunciations and levels of literacy as appropriate for a privileged aboriginal user. He notes, 'Databases are said to have ontologies insofar as they bear assumptions about the fundamental nature of what they contain' (Christie 2005: 60).

We are made aware throughout our searches within a digitized museum catalogue that the end result—a series of catalogue records—has emerged not only because of our own inputting of terms of enquiry, but because of a complex—and to us, the user, invisible—process of classification and organization. The end-view itself, generated by our idiosyncratic engagement with the available search criteria, is also what draws some relationships into view and obscures others. This is the problem with many understandings of digital relationality that assume relationships and visibility to be one and the same. It is also a problem with the visualization and metaphor of the network promoted within actor network theory that presumes to map sociality as a form of visible connectivity. The ever-invisible (to all but the programmers) domain of the digital (the binary code itself) itself instantiates a critique of the visible network.

As many of the articles in this volume demonstrate, the digital is not something that is brought to culture, facilitating or changing it. It is a cultural object and a cultural process. In this way, we need to develop a perspective on digital technologies in museums that sees these forms as structure *and* effect, an intrinsic part of the dialectic of cultural production (Miller 1987). Even the most innocuous classificatory system emerges from classifications that in turn reflect local values, local understanding of connectivity and local framings of knowledge. The magnification of thousands of local museum catalogues into increasingly global databases in fact magnifies their provincialism rather than reducing it. For instance, Table 13.1 shows a list of the keywords starting with the letter C for the catalogue of the Vanuatu National Museum—the words that organize and categorize the collections. They could only be generated in Vanuatu and of course speak to the history and concerns of this Pacific archipelago. At the same time, the words (in English, the language of one of Vanuatu's colonial administrations) represent generifications of local experience that map onto lexicons of anthropology, museum classification and other typological systems. These keywords organize the collection, determine the outcome of research and regulate access to objects and information. They both structure the collection and give substance to it.

The digital collections of the Vanuatu Cultural Centre can now be catalogued in relation to a number of different viewing restrictions (currently the system relies on sixteen different levels of restriction based on gender, family, village, descent group and island). Any one of these categories/restrictions has the power to remove the record entirely from visibility. An entry archived in relation to these restrictions will not be made available in a search until a user with the appropriate privileges logs in.

Table 13.1 Keywords to the Vanuatu Cultural Centre Database

Canoes	Chief	Coffee	Cotton
Carvings and Sculptures	Children	Colonial	Crab
Cattle	Church	Commerce	Cultural Centre
Caves	Circumcision	Communication	Culture
Census	Clay	Condominium	Custom
Ceremony	Cocoa	Conservation	Custom Calendar
Chicken	Coconut	Copra	Cyclone

Hard copies of photographs are hidden in the 'real' archive in manila envelopes that must not be opened, and even curators are excluded from accessing these images. Viewing collections in relation to local protocols is an important intervention and challenge to the authority of any museum to speak for, order and present cultural materials. Developed using open-source software, the database has been coded by committee (a team comprising technical staff and cultural experts). This committee extends the remit of the VCC to bring local knowledge into the museum, to respect grassroots and newly national hierarchies of entitlement and authority and to engage with this through museum practices from collecting to exhibiting and programming. This coding practice unites very local concerns for knowledge management with more global templates.

The template for the database's model of secrecy is not only the affordances of new digital technologies but a number of geophysical locations: the sacred men's houses within local *nasara* (dancing grounds) *and* a room within the inner sanctum of the VCC archive known as the Tabu Room (where the photographs are quietly filed away). This room, with locked door, was constructed to reassure those permitting sensitive or restricted material to be recorded and collected that the material would not be freely available for viewing by those who were not entitled, and as a safe house to protect such material from the potential threat of hurricanes, tropical rain and erosion. Since its inception, villagers have been encouraged to use the room as a bank for *kastom*, to protect valued artefacts and documentation and to preserve them for future generations, safe in the knowledge that the archives can be restricted along *kastom* guidelines defined mainly by connections of persons to places, to families, and by traditional status. The collections in the Tabu Room thus constitute a pre-digital archive drawn out of traditional practice by the idiosyncratic appropriation of international museum technologies and principles by the VCC: audiovisual recording, archiving and conservation (see Geismar and Tilley 2003; Sam 1996).

Such newly made museum objects include documentations of personal testimonies, stories, myths, music, ceremonies, national political and cultural events, ritual paraphernalia and artefacts recorded in a variety of media: written texts, audio tapes, film, slides and photographs. As the Tabu Room is in the process of being incorporated, and indeed transformed, into the database, all material, including digital material, is subject to the same restrictions as any other artefact, and a copy of every recording is left with the people with whom it was made, both assuaging people's concerns about the removal of local *kastom* from the islands and creating further anxiety about the possibility of endless circulation or mishandling.

At the time of writing (2011), the VCC database is only available via a local intranet—it is primarily accessed by the curatorial team in the VCC and is used by members of individual sections to upload and organize data, to perform searches for internal use and on behalf of the general public and visiting researchers. The most synthetic use of the catalogue is in the National Library. Visited every day by local ni-Vanuatu and schoolchildren, the two librarians use the catalogue to do thematic searches for any visitor, and the list of associated music, sound, films, documents and books are printed out and given to visitors to assist them with their research. What is really impairing the usability of the database is a lack of hardware, not software limitations. There are no networked computers available for public access currently in the VCC and limited resources for the maintenance and upgrade of network infrastructure to facilitate both internal and public access.

Despite these limitations, the database has created a template for restructuring the ways VCC staff and users interact with the collection and archives. Staff will still control the level of accessibility of information stored in the archives, but once the appropriate staff member assigns a level of accessibility, then anyone who is granted that level of access can potentially access that information without the knowledge or assistance of that staff member. In short, while VCC staff control the parameters for access to individual objects, some of the role of keeper and gatekeeper of knowledge is transferred from the staff member to the database system as the user interacts with the system to retrieve cultural information rather than the staff of VCC.

Through discussing how to deal with the issue of place in cataloguing these images in the database, it was clear that for the database committee the form of the database was mapped directly onto the handling of the material in question. There was no distinction made between the virtual information within the database and any other object: masks, cassettes, photographs, videos and other documents and documentation. The reference and referent are one and the same. This conflation is supported by the pragmatic decision of the VCC to use the hard drive, or very substance of the database, as its fundamental unit of storage. Increasingly, these gigabytes of storage are the very form of the collection, particularly as the VCC focuses its work on audiovisual documentation. Therefore, when browsing the image or music files of the newly digitized collection of oral traditions or of photographs, one is able to connect directly with the source of the reference—to download the museum-quality image or to listen to the recording itself. The difference between an idea of the original object and any other copies is therefore not really an issue in this digital space, and this pragmatic view maps onto an ontological view of authenticity that has been described by many anthropologists as very Melanesian (see Leach 2003). This is in keeping with local understandings of objects, in which it is the reference point or knowledge behind the form that is the essential object rather than the momentary form in which it might be manifested.[19]

Unlike most databases, which are perceived to be almost shadows or partial representations of the collection (itself housed elsewhere), the VCC database increasingly configures the digital collection *as* the work of the VCC. Object collection has always been a subsidiary occupation of the VCC, with photography being perhaps the archetypal material collected. The principles of photography, with its basis in evidential and objective recording and the potential for multiple reproduction and circulation, is much more suited to the main interests of the VCC in cultural regeneration and activation than the more object-led model of salvaging material which is supposed to stand in for disappearing or diminished cultural practice. Instead, museum objects (photographs, video, film and audio recordings) are very much viewed as momentary manifestations of cultural practices, the recording of which, as a process, contributes to the perpetuation of practice, both within and without the museum walls (see Geismar 2006; Geismar and Herle 2010). Focusing on the ways in which the database participates in creating networks focused on place, secrecy and restriction and language demonstrates how digital spaces don't just represent other spaces, but are part of the processes by which these spaces, and relationships, are forged. We see how the importing of certain technologies (and the attendant importing of flexibility and cultural sensitivity they permit) engenders a dialogue that is made visible via the aesthetic of the database itself. Its users are not abstract citizens, or the public, but people with specific investments in the networks of connection that lie within.

Conclusion

In the case studies presented in this chapter, I have emphasized the ways in which digital technologies encode different forms of sociality, in very different places around the world. Whilst it might seem that I am promoting a reification of cultural difference along borders very familiar to anthropologists in which Melanesians, or Aboriginal Australians, are somehow radically different to non-indigenous Brooklynites or New Zealanders, in fact I am highlighting the ways in which all digital technology is bound up within the same epistemologies of cultural representation as other kinds of museum artefact and practice and should be scrutinized with the same level of comparative attention and cultural sensitivity. However, it is also true that digital technologies have provided an important forum for indigenous people to raise a series or critiques of mainstream museum practices and issues regarding access, accessibility and the public—to levy a critique of cultural relativism itself. I am suggesting here that digital technologies do *not*, contra many accounts, merely engender new forms of sociality, at least not in the way that they are usually described. Rather, digital technologies facilitate the emergence and development of existing social concerns through the one quality that they have that differs to other formal mechanisms for engendering social connectivity or managing access and accountability. That quality is that of recursivity, or reflexivity. It is a quality in which sociality is reflected through the forms that both produce and represent it. This recursive effect creates a compressed zone in which technology and sociality seem to, in fact, be the same thing. The recursive effect of the digital in museum is to foreground and make visible a kind of sociality that was historically obscured by museums in the ways in which collections were made, organized and displayed. Now Aboriginal Australians and ni-Vanuatu are also making their own cultural protocols visible (and, indeed, deciding what to render invisible). Visitors to Te Papa make themselves and their own photographs visible in the formal halls of the institution. These are true challenges to the authority of the museum, but they are made using tools provided and structured by that very institution. In turn, and somewhat paradoxically, digital encodings of collections can also challenge this very visibility, and they have the potential to restructure display and access.

Accounts of digital practice and form in museums that can be called truly anthropological are still few and far between. Studies of digital technology in museums tend to be over-determined by the form of the digital and less descriptive of the intricate ways in which the digital can be embedded in pre-existing frames of being: of classification, epistemology and sociality (but see Isaac 2011). However, many of these accounts draw out the ways in which these digital projects are themselves inherently anthropological: in that they are de facto representations of emergent theories of sociality, and which in fact function *through* these representations of social interconnection. The forms of sociality that are presumed by the relational database and the way in which it may be extended into a hypersociality of the World Wide Web or made to conform to more exclusive sets of indigenous protocols suggest that the work of digital anthropology is itself encoded in the digital platform. This is not to suggest that the task of the analyst is merely to expose an endless recursivity between objects, data, cultural systems and digital systems, but rather to highlight the ways in which all of these digital projects continue the foundational work of museums more generally—to create a sense of public, to draw in community and engage community with broader educative, expressive and experiential ideas about knowing things through things. The digital is yet another object through which these knowledge practices are channelled within museums.

As museums and galleries move into digital environments such as Second Life, as we increasingly experience objects first and foremost in digital form, as the strategy of the hyperlink both defines and expands the ways in which different forms of knowledge can be connected to collections, it is important that we have accounts of digital practice that are ethnographic, that focus on the decisions, structures, assumptions and imaginaries that themselves encode code.

Notes

1. Here I'm thinking of the brash talk of the 'Twitter Revolution' and the certainty that a disembodied social media could foment political transformation to an unprecedented degree.
2. See, for example, the Virtual Museum of Canada initiative (http://www.musee-virtuel-virtualmuseum.ca/index-eng.jsp). The US Holocaust Memorial Museum states that its online exhibitions 'present new subjects and also extend the reach of Museum public programs and special exhibitions' (see http://www.ushmm.org/museum/exhibit/online/). Equally, the British Library uses its specially devised 'turning the pages' software to enable online visitors to access virtual books (http://www.bl.uk/onlinegallery/virtualbooks/index.html). The soon-to-open Museum of the History of Polish Jews in Warsaw will have a virtual shtetl and use three-dimensional technologies to evoke the lost lifestyle of nineteenth-century Jews (http://www.jewishmuseum.org.pl/). All of these projects create cultural representations that are radically new and different from previous representational strategies. However, none of them draws attention to the history and particularity of digital form and its role in cultural representation.
3. The conference proceedings are published and archived each year: http://www.archimuse.com/conferences/mw.html.
4. See, for instance, the digital re-creation of Barnum's museum, which was destroyed by fire in 1865 in the Lost Museum project (http://lostmuseum.cuny.edu/), or the interventions of Art Mob—creating unofficial podcasts for New York's Museum of Modern Art (http://mod.blogs.com/art_mobs/).
5. Digital repatriation may refer to projects that share digital resources or return historic collections in digital form. More critical discussion is required with reference to the complex evaluation and politics of repatriation and its diverse cultures in different places. For a more nuanced discussion, see Bell (2003) on the implications and effects of the circulation of historic photographic collections and see Geismar (2005, 2009a, 2009b, 2010) and Geismar and Herle (2010).
6. The Pitt Rivers Museum's project, Rethinking Pitt Rivers, analyses the collector as a centralizing force within complex networks that drew together objects, information and the nascent discipline of anthropology (http://web.prm.ox.ac.uk/rpr/).
7. See http://steve.museum/index.php?option=com_content&task=blogsection&id=6&Itemid=15.
8. See, for example, http://tagger.steve.museum/, and http://objectwiki.sciencemuseum.org.uk/wiki/Home. In 2006, the Powerhouse Museum launched OPAC 2 (Open Public Access to Collections; http://www.powerhousemuseum.com/collection/database/), an online public-access catalogue aimed at making the museum's collection more usable through Google-enabled initiatives and, through a sustained research project, Reconceptualizing Heritage Collections,

evaluated the use and utility of this initiative (see Cameron and Mengler 2009 and http://www.powerhousemuseum.com/dmsblog/index.php/category/folksonomies for some museum commentary on this). See, for example, http://www.brooklynmuseum.org/exhibitions/click/.

9. The latest project of the Steve team is a collaboration with the University of Maryland and the Indianapolis Museum of Art. Called T3 (text terms trust), the project 'combines text mining, social tagging and trust inferencing techniques to enrich the metadata and personalize retrieval' (http://steve.museum/index.php?option=com_content&task=blogsection&id=1&Itemid=2).
10. Another project that rethinks and indigenizes the commons can be found in the Reciprocal Research Network (http://www.moa.ubc.ca/RRN/about_overview.html), an international network that aims to unite communities from the northwest coast of Canada to museums and other repositories all around the world. Managed out of the University of British Columbia's Museum of Anthropology, the network has developed a digital platform that links catalogue information and collections databases from all of the partner institutions to communities via research hubs, to which access must be gained by collaboration and partnership. The network allows for discussion, comment, critique and information sharing in a safe and sensitive way, utilizing the digital to create a different kind of openness—not a public, but a more restricted community that would not normally be able to access the collections in situ (see Phillips 2011).
11. I was unable to acquire screen grabs for many of these digital projects that are of high enough resolution to print and hope that interested readers will seek out the images to accompany these texts on the sites cited in the discussion.
12. In the exhibition, 389 photographs were submitted, and 344 evaluators cast 410,089 evaluations. On average, each evaluator looked at 135 works. The top 20 per cent of ranked images were displayed in the final exhibition (http://www.brooklynmuseum.org/exhibitions/click/quick_facts.php).
13. See Kevin Stayton, http://www.brooklynmuseum.org/community/blogosphere/2008/07/23/crowd-curated-or-crowd-juried/.
14. See Elizabeth Povinelli, Digital Futures project, http://vectors.usc.edu/projects/index.php?project=90&thread=ProjectCredits.
15. See the highly contentious Digital Economy Act of 2010, which aims to crack down on peer-to-peer file sharing and which advocates the ability for Internet access to be denied to file-sharing perpetrators. See also the conflict, Joywar, between artist Joy Garnett and Magnum photojournalist Susan Meiselas over Garnett's appropriation, from the Internet, of Meiselas's photo of a Sandanista, the subsequent legal battle (which Garnett lost) and continued reproduction by artist activists of the image. The entire debate is surveyed and commented on at http://www.firstpulseprojects.com/joywar.html.
16. See http://www.mukurtuarchive.org/.
17. See http://www.vectorsjournal.org/issues/3/digitaldynamics/.

18. Ramesh Srinivasan comments:

> The growing excitement around ethnography relates to the increased understanding (finally) that visualizations may provide explanation but embedded within each visualization is a certain ontological perspective around how that information is to be counted, mapped, and coded, and thus visualized! Instead ethnography which starts with raw, unbridled observations, and attempts to be explicit about the bias of the researcher and present as much information as possible from the ground-up, can be seen as more respectful and at least at first puts bias aside to present data in less structured forms. (http://rameshsrinivasan.org/2010/12/28/code-and-culture/)

Srinivasan's work aims to develops what he terms 'fluid ontologies' and alternative paradigms in the development of software tools for community archiving and other digital projects.

19. This is a common philosophy behind many different objects in the Pacific, notably Malanggan; see Geismar (2009a) and Bell and Geismar (2009).

References

Bayne, S., J. Ross and Z. Williamson. 2009. Objects, Subjects, Bits and Bytes: Learning from the Digital Collections of the National Museums. *Museum and Society* 7(2): 110–24.

Bell, J. A. 2003. Looking to See: Reflections on Visual Repatriation in the Purari Delta, Gulf Province, Papua New Guinea. In *Museums and Source Communities: A Routledge Reader*, ed. L. Peers and A. K. Brown, 111–22. London: Routledge.

Bell, J. A., and H. Geismar. 2009. Materialising Oceania: New Ethnographies of Things in Melanesia and Polynesia. *Australian Journal of Anthropology* 20: 3–27.

Bennett, T. 1995. *The Birth of the Museum: History, Theory, Politics.* London: Routledge.

Bouquet, M. 1996. Family Trees and Their Affinities: The Visual Imperative of the Genealogical Diagram. *Journal of the Royal Anthropological Institute* 2: 43–66.

Brown, D. 2007. Te Ahu Hiko: Digital Cultural Heritage and Indigenous Objects, People and Environments. In *Theorizing Digital Cultural Heritage: A Critical Discourse*, ed. F. Cameron and S. Kenderdine, 77–93. Cambridge, MA: MIT Press.

Brown, D. 2008. '*Ko to ringa ki nga rakau a te Pakeha*'—Virtual *taonga* Māori and Museums. *Visual Resources* 24(1): 59–75.

Brown, M. 1998. Can Culture Be Copyrighted? *Current Anthropology* 39(2): 193–222.

Brown, M. 2003. *Who Owns Native Culture.* Cambridge, MA: Harvard University Press.

Cameron, F., and S. Kenderdine. 2007. *Theorizing Digital Cultural Heritage: A Critical Discourse.* Cambridge, MA: MIT Press.

Cameron, F., and S. Mengler. 2009. Complexity, Transdisciplinarity and Museum Collections Documentation: Emergent Metaphors for a Complex World. *Journal of Material Culture* 14: 189–218.

Christen, K. 2005. Gone Digital: Aboriginal Remix and the Cultural Commons. *International Journal of Cultural Property* 12: 315.

Christen, K. 2006. Ara Iritija: Protecting the Past, Accessing the Future—Indigenous Memories in a Digital Age. *Museum Anthropology* 29: 59–60.

Christen, K. 2011. Opening Archives: Respectful Repatriation. *American Archivist* 74: 185–210.

Christie, M. 2005. Words, Ontologies and Aboriginal Databases. *Media International Australia: Digital Anthropology* 116: 52–63.

Conn, S. 2010. *Do Museums Still Need Objects?* Philadelphia: University of Pennsylvania Press.

Deger, J. 2006. *Shimmering Screens: Making Media in an Aboriginal Community.* Minneapolis: University of Minnesota Press.

Field, L. W. 2008. *Abalone Tales: Collaborative Explorations of Sovereignty and Identity in Native California.* Durham, NC: Duke University Press.

Frey, B. S., and B. Kirschenblatt-Gimblett. 2002. The Current Debate: The Dematerialization of Culture and the De-accessioning of Museum Collections. *Museum International* 54(4): 58–63.

Geismar, H. Forthcoming. *Treasured Possessions: Culture, Property and Indigeneity in the Pacific.* Durham, NC: Duke University Press.

Geismar, H. 2005. Footsteps on Malakula: A Report on a Photographic Research Project. *Journal of Museum Ethnography* 17: 191–207.

Geismar, H. 2006. Malakula: A Photographic Collection. *Comparative Studies in Society and History* 48: 520–63.

Geismar, H. 2008. Cultural Property, Museums, and the Pacific: Reframing the Debates. *International Journal of Cultural Property* 15: 109.

Geismar, H. 2009a. The Photograph and the Malanggan: Rethinking Images on Malakula, Vanuatu. *Australian Journal of Anthropology* 20: 48–73.

Geismar, H. 2009b. Stone Men of Malekula on Malakula: An Ethnography of an Ethnography. *Ethnos: Journal of Anthropology* 74: 199.

Geismar, H. 2010. Review of *Do Museums Still Need Objects?* by S. Conn. 4 March. http://www.materialworldblog.com.

Geismar, H., and A. Herle. 2010. *Moving Images: John Layard, Photography and Fieldwork on Malakula since 1914.* Honolulu: University of Hawaii Press.

Geismar, H., and W. Mohns. 2011. Database Relations: Rethinking the Database in the Vanuatu Cultural Centre and National Museum. *Journal of the Royal Anthropological Institute* 17(s1): S126–48.

Geismar, H., and C. Tilley. 2003. Negotiating Materiality: International and Local Museum Practices at the Vanuatu Cultural Centre and National Museum. *Oceania* 73(3): 170–88.

Gell, A. [1992] 1999. The Enchantment of Technology. In *The Art of Anthropology: Essays and Diagrams*, ed. E. Hirsch, 159–86. Oxford: Berg.

Glass, A., and K. Keramidas. 2011. On the Relational Exhibition in Analog and Digital Media. In *Objects of Exchange: Social and Material Transformation on the Late Nineteenth-Century Northwest Coast*, ed. A. Glass, 217–27. New York: BCG Focus Gallery/Yale University Press.

Hein, H. S. 2000. *The Museum in Transition: A Philosophical Perspective.* Washington, DC: Smithsonian Institution Press.

Henare, A., M. Holbraad and S. Wastell. 2007. *Thinking through Things: Theorising Artefacts Ethnographically.* London: Routledge

Hennessy, K. 2009. Virtual Repatriation and Digital Cultural Heritage: The Ethics of Managing Online Collections. *Anthropology News* (April): 5–6.

Henning, M. 2007. Legibility and Affect: Museums as New Media. In *Exhibition Experiments*, ed. P. Basu and S. Macdonald, 25–47. Oxford: Blackwell.

Hooper-Greenhill, E. 2000. *Museums and the Interpretation of Visual Culture.* London: Routledge.

Isaac, G. 2008. Technology Becomes the Object: The Use of Electronic Media at the National Museum of the American Indian. *Journal of Material Culture* 13: 287–310.

Isaac, G. 2011. Whose Idea Was This? *Current Anthropology* 52(2): 211–33.

Kelty, C. M. 2008. *Two Bits: The Cultural Significance of Free Software.* Durham, NC: Duke University Press.

Kirschenblatt-Gimblett, B. 2009. Materiality and Digitization in the Museum of the History of Polish Jews. 25 July. http://www.materialworldblog.com.

Kramer, J. 2004. Figurative Repatriation. *Journal of Material Culture* 9: 161–82.

Leach, J. 2003. Owning Creativity: Cultural Property and the Efficacy of Custom. *Journal of Material Culture* 8(2): 123–43.

Malraux, A. 1967. *Museum without Walls.* London: Secker & Warburg.

Manovich, L. 2002. *The Language of New Media.* Cambridge, MA: MIT Press.

Manovich, L. [1999] 2010. Database as Symbolic Form. In *Museums in a Digital Age*, ed. R. Parry, 64–71. New York: Routledge.

Miller, D. 1987. *Material Culture and Mass Consumption.* Oxford: Blackwell.

Miller, D. 2005. Materiality: An Introduction. In *Materiality*, ed. D. Miller, 1–50. Durham, NC: Duke University Press.

Myers, F. R. 2002. *Painting Culture: The Making of an Aboriginal High Art.* Durham, NC: Duke University Press.

Myers, F. R. 2004. Ontologies of the Image and Economies of Exchange. *American Ethnologist* 31: 5–21.

Parry, R., ed. 2010. *Museums in a Digital Age.* New York: Routledge.

Phillips, R. 2011. The Digital (R)Evolution of Museum-Based Research. In *Museum Pieces: Toward the Indigenization of Canadian Museums*, ed. R. Phillips. Montreal, Canada: McGill University Press.

Riskin, J. 2003. Eighteenth-Century Wetware. *Representations* 83: 97–124.

Sam, J. K. 1996. Audiovisual Documentation of Living Cultures as a Major Task for the Vanuatu Cultural Centre. In *Arts of Vanuatu*, ed. J. Bonnemaison, K. Huffman, C. Kaufmann and D. Tryon, 288–90. Bathurst, Australia: Crawford House Publishing.

Simpson, A. 2007. On the Logic of Discernment. *American Quarterly* 60: 251–7.

Srinivasan, R., R. Boast, K. Becvar and J. Furner. 2009a. Blobgects: Digital Museum Catalogues and Diverse User Communities. *Journal of the American Society for Information Science and Technology* 60(3): 1–13.

Srinivasan, R. S., R. Boast, J. Furner and K. M. Becvar. 2009b. Digital Museums and Diverse Cultural Knowledges: Moving Past the Traditional Catalog. *The Information Society* 25(4): 265–78.

Srinivasan, R., and J. Huang. 2005. Fluid Ontologies for Digital Museums. *International Journal of Digital Libraries* 5: 193–204.

Standage, T. 1998. *The Victorian Internet: The Remarkable Story of the Telegraph and the Nineteenth Centurys On-line Pioneers.* New York: Walker.

Strathern, M. 1990. Artefacts of History: Events and the Interpretation of Images. In *Culture and History in the Pacific*, ed. J. Siikala, 25–44. Helsinki: Finnish Anthropological Society.

Taylor, B. L. 2010. Reconsidering Digital Surrogates: Towards a Viewer-Orientated Model of the Gallery Experience. In *Museum Materialities: Objects, Engagements, Interpretations*, ed. S. Dudley. London: Routledge.

Thorner, S. 2010. Imagining an Indigital Interface: Ara Iritija Indigenizes the Technologies of Knowledge Management. *Collections: A Journal for Museums and Archives Professionals* 6: 125–47.

Vergo, P. 1989. *The New Museology.* London: Reaktion Books.

White, G. 2009. Our Space: A Forum for the Nation. Unpublished Master's Thesis, Program in Museum Studies, New York University.

Zeitlyn, D., F. Larson and A. Petch. 2007. Social Networks in the Relational Museum: The Case of the Pitt Rivers Museum. *Journal of Material Culture* 12(3): 211–39.

–14–

Digital Gaming, Game Design and Its Precursors

Thomas M. Malaby

With the arrival and expansiveness of digital gaming a new contingent of anthropologists has appeared, giving fresh attention both at the general level to the cultural form of the game itself and specifically to the way the situated practices of gaming trouble our understandings of governance, institutions, immersion, creativity and other issues. This new anthropological work is pushing productively against treatments of gaming that tend to get caught up in their own normative positions on gaming as positive or negative (a problem that bedevils treatments of the digital more generally). It has also gone further to highlight the designed quality of digital gaming experience and the ways in which this material dimension should prompt us to consider the projects of their designers and sponsoring institutions. This work furthermore shows us how institutions are beginning to deploy the principles of game design beyond digital games explicitly presented as such; that is we can see game design at work in arenas such as Amazon's Mechanical Turk, or in new forms of corporate management (see Malaby 2009a).

The opening up of territory for inquiry that is the aim of digital anthropology is a project that occurs amidst broader and long-standing anthropological hesitations about high technology and the interactions mediated by it. Compounding this are further hesitations about the 'studying up' that understanding the digital must also entail. When our focus narrows to digital games, anthropologists encounter an additional hurdle, and that is the rather limited and sporadic treatment of games over the course of our disciplinary history (especially striking when considered against the voluminous and exceptional work on a comparable cultural form, that of ritual; see Malaby 2009b). As such, the notable work on digital games in our discipline constitutes a still small set, although interest in the subject, especially at the graduate student level, is growing very rapidly.

In one sense the trajectory of the study of games in anthropology over the course of the twentieth century is a familiar one: it falls more or less neatly into a divide between those following a primarily materialist approach and those following one that is primarily representationalist. The first treated games and their assumed supercategory, play, as defined by their lack of productivity—that is by their status as not-work. This presumed lack of stakes in play was reflected in its relatively meager treatment in the anthropological literature, dwarfed in scale by treatments of work.

Around the same time, however, there was a discipline-shaking answer to all materialist treatments of culture, in the form of the writings of Clifford Geertz. Geertz's Weberian-influenced approach treated meaning-making as something other than epiphenomenal. Strikingly for the subject at hand, one of his essays, and perhaps the one most well known beyond anthropology, was about a game and about play: 'Deep Play: Notes on a Balinese Cockfight' (reprinted in Geertz 1997). In the essay, Geertz imbued the occasion of a cockfight with the highest stakes of all—that of a culture's meaning in a grand sense; the cockfight becomes the portrait of the Balinese culture that it paints for itself. But these grand stakes coexist with a strange blunting of more proximate consequences, and with an explicit rejection of the contingency of games as at all relevant for our understanding of them. As Geertz wrote (1997: 433): 'Much more is at stake than material gain: namely, esteem, honor, dignity, respect—in a word, though in Bali a profoundly freighted word, status. It is at stake symbolically, for (a few cases of ruined addict gamblers aside) no one's status is actually altered by the outcome of a cockfight.'

In his zeal to trump whatever material stakes were in play with the stakes of meaning-making, Geertz eliminated from consideration any consequentiality beyond the affirmation of meaning. On this view, games became static appraisals of an unchanging social order, and an element of games that is vital for any understanding of the experience of play was lost. That element is the distinctive and contrived indeterminacy of games and the way in which, by being contingent in their outcomes, they encapsulate (albeit in this contrived fashion) the open-endedness of everyday life (see Malaby 2007). Viewed this way, games stand as having a powerful relationship to human practice and social process. What is more, this allows us to see how games may be related to a particular mode of experience, a dispositional stance toward the indeterminate. This is an aspect of experience which is lost if practice is left out in favour of materiality or representation.

More recently, anthropological work on games demonstrates the distinct strengths of an anthropological perspective that has left representationalist and materialist monisms behind. For the most part these works have criticized the work/play distinction or abandoned it entirely, and instead have concentrated on situating the cultural form of games in specific cultural historical moments. (In this they resemble those anthropologists throughout the twentieth century who examined the cultural form of ritual without subjecting it in every case to a litmus test of whether it brought about transcendent experience.) Ellen Oxfeld explored how the playing of mah-jong by expatriate Hakka Chinese in Calcutta shed light on their distinctive entrepreneurial ethic (Oxfeld 1993). Rather than contradicting their capitalist efforts, gambling at mah-jong reflected their commitment to the uncertainties of the market itself. My own study of game-playing in a Greek city was offered in a similar vein (Malaby 2003). Paul Festa (2007), in his study of mah-jong in Taiwan, showed how game practice was intimately connected to the position of young Taiwanese men in a nation-state characterized by martiality.

In the realm of digital games, Alex Golub (2010) has pursued an understanding of massively multiplayer online games that is deeply mindful of our past pitfalls, including our tendency to reify this form of social action into distinct 'places', exceptional to the other parts of our lives. This is perhaps particularly dangerous in the context of online games and virtual worlds, he suggests, because of our tendency to make sense of players' commitment to these spaces in terms of their sensorial immersion. By showing that players become committed to these spaces in ways that lead them to make their experience of the game *less* sensorially rich, and connected more and more to activities outside of the game proper, Golub directs our attention to the reality of games based on players' involvement with wider collective projects that they care about—projects which largely ignore a distinction between being in a 'world' and being out of it. Golub compares this with the way anthropologists have come recently and productively to theorize Oceania (Golub 2010: 20). Thereby, Golub neatly and ironically makes the case for understanding digital games as both familiar and exotic in ways that should help us make sense of the field.

Golub's attention to the rise of collective projects directs our attention to the role of institutions as increasingly interested in games as a cultural form now that they are networked and digital (and therefore centrally and swiftly manipulable as well as potentially gigantic in reach). Historically, the relationship between political institutions and games has been marked by famous miscalculations and unintended consequences. While the Olympic Games were the subject of a Nazi project to garner political and ideological legitimacy, the open-endedness of the games themselves provided the opportunity for Jesse Owens's conjunctural agency, subverting those intentions in stunning fashion (Sahlins 2004). In historian Amy Chazkel's remarkable treatment of Brazil's clandestine lottery, the *jogo do bicho*, we see what originated as a raffle at a Rio de Janeiro zoo in 1892 become a national phenomenon, go underground in the face of government attempts to control it and ultimately provide a model for informal, gray-market trade throughout urban Latin America (Chazkel 2011).

Today things appear to be different, as the encounter between games and digital technology makes the contrivance of contingent experience within limits a safer bet for institutions. Nothing demonstrates the extent and stakes of these institutional projects of control as effectively as Natasha Dow Schüll's work on the production of digital slot machines, designed with enormous effort to hit the sweet spot of 'perfect contingency' that commands the attention (and quarters) of its users (Schüll forthcoming). Schüll recognizes how we need to see the disposition of play that games aim to prompt as analogous to the sentiments of belonging that ritual seeks to elicit, and furthermore to recognize how both are used by institutions (see also Malaby 2009b).

The use of digital games to accomplish institutional projects makes the position of their makers particularly important to understand, while recognizing that this group itself is actually a complex mix of programmers of various specialties, game designers, 'community managers' (for online games), marketing staff, system administrators and others. But access to the inside of game and virtual world development companies has been extremely difficult for many researchers across the social sciences. My access to Linden Lab could be understood partly as a result of sheer luck, combined with Linden Lab's own peculiar desire to have its (to it, exceptionalist) story told (Malaby 2009a). Another digital anthropologist with access to high-profile game design studios is Casey O'Donnell, who has done ethnographic research within game development companies for the past several years and whose work is just starting to appear. O'Donnell is pursuing vital questions about how the coproduction of games by their users is importantly shaped by the tension between openness and closure on many fronts, including access to the 'tools' of development (O'Donnell 2009), engaging further an issue perhaps first flagged by the insightful journalist of technology, Julian Dibbell (1998), in his memoir about the virtual world LambdaMoo: the fraught distinction between the world creators and users engaged in making 'content' given their differential access to what is 'under the hood' (Malaby 2009a: 111).

Across this work there is a sensitivity to the cultural status of disorder, an attitude that reflects its distinguished, if underrecognized, role in social theory (see Malaby 2007). For much of modernity's reign, the classic nation-state of the West, and many of its other modernist institutions, pursued the promise of control through order. Order, Michael Herzfeld has written, is 'one of the most tenacious of "absolutes" posited by the exponents of Western rationality' (1988: 69), and the strategic essentialism of the bureaucratic claim to order was exposed by the messy practicalities of the everyday. Nation-states and other large-scale institutions, such as corporations, hoped that efficiency and productivity were to be found at a final, ordered destination of perfectly organized and controlled people, systems of classification and technologies.

But perhaps not meaning. Meaning, as Weber suggested, was not rationality's strong suit. Ritual, in all its ordered spectacle, became the cultural form through which meaningful belonging could be cultivated. Now, however, many such institutions have found and are perfecting a different cultural form—that of the game. If any game is in important respects understandable as a domain of contrived contingency that, if done well, is both compelling and has the potential to generate (rather than simply affirm) meaningful outcomes, then the creators and sponsors of games have the opportunity to architect contingent experiences for us that can generate meanings and subjectivities as well as do work for capitalism. The most interesting thinking in this vein is by Julian Dibbell (2006). His work suggests that the ludification of daily life (in our media consumption or in our engagement with everything from tax software to ATM interfaces) is the way it is beginning to be presented as gamelike, providing performative challenges for the user.

Google is an institution taking such steps to enlist participation and work through postbureaucratic techniques. It has created a game to accomplish an enormously valuable task that would otherwise be cost-prohibitive to undertake: the labelling of its vast corpus of billions of images, culled from its scouring of the web and cached on its servers. The images by their nature cannot be searched by text (except, poorly, by their file names and related text-based information). But they become effectively searchable once they are tagged with descriptors—keywords that describe the image—and such tags must be added by humans who can make sense of the often complex images. To have employees or contractors do the work of labelling these images would be extremely expensive, so Google developed a game (the Google Image Labeler Game) which gets the images labelled by its players, people all over the world who do it for free. Two players are anonymously paired for each game; the players are shown the same image for two minutes and must tag the image with as many descriptors as they can. If both players type in the same descriptor, they receive points in the game. The players can record and compare their high scores (if they are registered users), but otherwise the points have no value; Google has succeeded in leveraging the contrivance of contingency to command the attention of thousands of users who collectively perform work for the company.

Another example is TopCoder.com, which hosts a programming contest where winners receive cash prizes but lose the commercial rights to the code they produce. The contests are weekly, with a larger one biannually, and the competitors code (i.e. write software for) solutions to complex real-world problems. Here game design forms the incentive to participation, specifically the application of effort and cultural capital (competence) to perform in a compellingly contrived, indeterminate system—a game. The success of the enterprise depends on TopCoder's ability to tap into this playful competitive mode or disposition, while the entire game activity is extrinsically governed by an ulterior profit motive geared to practical applications of the winning solutions after the fact.

Presaging some of O'Donnell's concerns, Kalman Applbaum (2004), in his work on marketing, found an emerging distinction between the lower-level, and dismissively labelled 'creatives', and the higher levels of management which had successfully found ways to exploit their creativity. This suggests that, along with the use of games to attempt to colonize creativity, we should also notice the implicit distinction here between players and the sponsoring institutions which create the conditions for such play. World of Warcraft, a massively multiplayer online game created by Blizzard Entertainment, is played by more than twelve million participants worldwide, and Blizzard has taken steps not only to cultivate its players' attention through the production of a compelling game, but also to extract creativity from its users through its opening up of the game's interface to third-party development of modifications ('mods' or 'add-ons'), but under strict conditions. As Bonnie Nardi has discussed, this managed creativity depends upon a reimagining of users in a way that enlists their participation in the production of the game without sacrificing Blizzard's control over a proprietary creation (Nardi 2010).

In a related way, Tom Boellstorff's *Coming of Age in Second Life* charts the experience of that virtual world from the users' many points of view, showing how its extensively marketed vision of 'creationist capitalism' hits home for users who have made a deep investment of their selves into this virtual environment (Boellstorff 2008). Boelstorff argues persuasively and provocatively for the many ways in which human lives have always already been virtual through his careful engagement with Second Life as an ethnographic site on its own terms. In many respects, Boellstorff's ethnographic research within Second Life has provided the model for bringing our field's distinctive methodology into such (often game or gamelike) spaces.

But the use of games is not limited to the exploitation of creativity. Take Back Illinois was a game created by Ian Bogost for the Illinois House Republican Campaign in 2004. The game was Flash-based, meaning it could be played within a web browser, and it was prominently available on the campaign's website. In the small window for the game, players saw a small section of a city from an angle slightly above (what game designers call two and a half D [dimensions]). The game included several sub-games and called upon the player to make adjustments to policies (such as, in one of the games, caps on medical malpractice damages) in order for public life to flourish over the course of one year (time ticked away steadily within the game). Success in each game was implicitly (in the software) coded to align with Republican policies.

Similarly, and also in 2004, Kuma Games created John Kerry's Silver Star, a game created to contribute to the debate over John Kerry's Vietnam War experiences. In the game, the player played as John Kerry, piloting a swift boat up the Mekong Delta. The claim of the makers was that playing such a game would help the player decide for themselves what must have happened. Games such as these make knowledge claims in new ways, implicitly in the code itself, and they persuade (Bogost 2007) the player in new ways as well. Rather than a performative representational claim about politics and reality, the game involves the player's practice and seeks to cultivate a normatively charged disposition about the subject at hand. Again we witness the human capacity to reimpose normativity in the context of digital technologies (Miller and Horst, this volume).

In all such cases, the successful game must also provide the proper balance between routine and surprise, between pattern and novelty, to be compelling and command the attention of players. But these new efforts by technological institutions evince a further and specific set of assumptions—they put forth an ideal of individual mastery of complex systems, and this ideal has a specific history, one linked to the post–World War II era of technology and programming and which I have termed 'technoliberalism' (Malaby 2009a). In it, there is an overriding faith in technology, a suspicion of conventional modernist (top-down) institutions and a conviction that the aggregate effects of individual engagement of technology will generate social goods.

Technoliberalism is the attitude found amongst the programmers and hackers currently being examined so fruitfully in the work of anthropologists Gabriella Coleman (2004) and Christopher Kelty (2005), who show how the practical nature of these programmers leads them to architect certain ideals into their creations while denying their participation in political discourse. In a similar way, Schüll's work shows how the contrivance of compelling, open-ended experience has reached unprecedented scope and effectiveness with the advent of digital technology. In virtual worlds like Second Life (see Malaby 2009a), and in the examples above, the digital architecture evinces a picture of the human/user as individual (rather than social), seeking mastery and eager to be provided domains within which to gain and display this mastery.

To explore these issues in the digital anthropology of games, I here give deeper consideration to two cases. The first is that of Linden Lab, maker of the virtual world Second Life, who has deployed gaming to govern and to realize a specific cultural logic—one that places enormous faith in the combination of games and technology to provide the means to generate, in an almost marketlike fashion, social goods. Second Life began from the desire to use digital networks to generate a gamelike, self-sustaining society, and therefore specifically to realize a peculiar yet universalizing technoliberal dream. The second case explores a precursor to such technoliberal digital gaming: Greece's first (and hugely successful) state-sponsored gambling game, Pro-Po, a football pool begun in the 1950s. Initially run analogically (now it is almost entirely digital, at least in its administration), it relied heavily on both centralized institutional statistical expertise and the cultivation of a distinctive subjectivity of individuated performance on the part of its users. I conclude by looking ahead to the potential of future work on gaming in digital anthropology, noting that such work will flourish to the extent that it both examines the efforts to use games as part of institutional projects (and the broader ideological commitments which often lie behind them) while at the same time using the tools of anthropology to understand the specific dimensions of gaming as it plays out on the ground.

First Case, Second Life

Second Life (SL) was built in fundamental ways on the basis of a distinctly asocial imagining of the human, one grounded in a technoliberal sensibility. On this view, humans are resolutely individuals, at root motivated by the challenge to act within and gain mastery of complex and open-ended systems (it is not entirely coincidental that this is also a construction of a specific kind of gamer). Correspondingly, social effects (the creation of exclusionary groups, lobbying and other political activity and others) are ideally at best minimized or at worst excluded by system design, an issue that I have explored at length in the context of Linden Lab's internal decision making (Malaby 2009a). The imagined user of SL was in many respects not supposed to be social except in a very narrow sense, and this raised a number of challenges for users of SL as well as for the employees of Linden Lab ('Lindens'), who struggled to support the emergent uses of the world that challenged their expectations. These design decisions had enormous implications for the kinds of social action that were architecturally recognized within SL, even if in practice users could, to a certain extent, transcend these.

The research that forms the basis for the ideas in this chapter consisted of more than a year of ethnographic fieldwork at Linden Lab from 2004 to 2006, during which time I engaged in extensive observations of Linden Lab's work practice, interviewed dozens of present and past employees at length, and performed work tasks for the company to understand how it used a variety of technological affordances to build, maintain and add new features to Second Life. In collaboration with Wagner James Au, a journalist also working at Linden Lab at the time, in 2005 I created an online wiki for Lindens, inviting them to contribute to their own history of the company. It became clear from this wiki, and from many of my interviews, that while the idea for the company sprang specifically from the mind of Philip Rosedale, founder of Linden Lab, his inspiration was itself rooted in ideas about technology, humanity and creativity that are part of a specific history in the United States, one that found fertile ground in the San Francisco Bay area. It is a set of primarily practical (rather than discursive; see Kelty 2005) assumptions and ideological commitments which continues to shape the dispositions of those that architect our increasingly digital lives.

In technoliberalism there is an emphasis on the positive social effects that can emerge from a multitude of individual acts, but technoliberalism extends liberalism's ideas beyond the market and also places technology centre stage (Malaby 2009a: 16, 59–61, 133). Technoliberalism entails an intense suspicion of vertical authority, a commitment to making technology universally accessible and beyond institutional control and a deep faith in the positive aggregate effects that follow from individual use of this technology for the purposes of creative expression. Game design comes to occupy a central position in technoliberalist projects because of the possibility and promise it presents of *contriving* the complex systems within which this individual expressive mastery can take place. We can recognize this interest in turning to game mechanics to solve social problems not only in Linden Lab, but in other projects that shape our digital lives (such as Amazon's Mechanical Turk), and we can see it promulgated in recent high-profile trade books (McGonigal 2011).

Rosedale was fascinated by complexity after encountering the ideas of Stephen Wolfram concerning single-cell simulations. Wolfram sought to demonstrate how complexity could evolve in nature through the reproduction of a single-cell organism following a small set of simple rules. Rosedale successfully produced a version of this simulation that he coded himself on an Apple computer in 1982 when he was fourteen years old (see Au 2008: 15–16). He was again inspired ten years later by Neal Stephenson's *Snow Crash* (1992) to create a similarly complex, networked simulation of a world, with evolving flora and fauna. After becoming chief technology officer of Real Networks in the mid-1990s, he left the company toward the end of the decade to create the early version of SL called Linden World.

Linden World is worth taking some time to describe, because in important ways it both reflects these early inspirations and stands in marked contrast to what Second Life came to be. As Au characterizes it,

> Rosedale saw this as an Eden that he and Linden Lab would shape, and only then allow users to interact in. '[Y]ou would wander around in it as an avatar,' Rosedale recalls imagining, 'and you'd come across animals—maybe they'd try to eat you or something—that no one had ever seen.' (2008: 23–9)

Creating first (in true demiurgic fashion) an ocean that flowed across two servers, the Lindens added land and creatures to create a complex, evolving, networked system on a massive scale. Their imagined users' relationship with it would be essentially adventurous, whether in the opportunity to observe an accurate astronomical simulation above or in battling the world's denizens and each other in virtual battle-capable robots.

All of this changed in the midst of a presentation to Linden Lab's investors shortly thereafter. It is a moment I heard referred to repeatedly around Linden Lab, although I could not specify the exact time frame (the best guess would be early 2001). During the demonstration, a live feed of Linden World included Lindens using the in-world tools—that had been coded into the programme specifically for Linden developer use—to create objects. This caught the attention of Mitch Kapor and others around the table, who pushed Linden Lab to make those tools available to users, to shift the world fundamentally from a complex system the Lindens created themselves, and which users explored, to one in which the users would themselves create the content (in video game industry terms) that would fill the world and potentially attract new users.

Much followed from this change in approach, including the abandonment of battle-bots and the development of avatars, and the focus shifted from users encountering a complex world to enlisting the actions of users to generate something like the same kind of complexity that had interested Rosedale for so long. The users were assumed to be motivated by a desire to express themselves individually, using the content creation tools provided in the client software to make things in the world. In these early years of SL, the content creation tools, not surprisingly, perfectly mirrored the same tools that a more conventional gaming company would use internally. These three basic tools are three-dimensional modelling, scripting (programming objects so that they can be interactive and perform actions in the world) and texture-mapping (the wrapping of objects in textures to create a sense of different materials and surfaces in SL). Lindens tended to imagine, even through 2005, that the content created by users was *only* that which was modelled, scripted or texture-mapped (see Malaby 2006b), and this practical (not necessarily intentional) bias reflected a limited view of creativity, understandable given the computer gaming development backgrounds of many of Linden Lab's developers.

The demiurgic quality of world creation that complex computer game development engenders, especially within the context of three-dimensional, graphically intensive 'first-person shooters' (such as Halo), follows from the creation of not only a world, but the very physics that operate within it. Game development typically splits these two in-house processes into the development of the game engine (which defines such deep characteristics as the physics of the world and how calculations for its objects and their movement or collision will be handled and rendered) and the development of the game content (the specific look of the world, its narrative or backstory—if any—and the topography, objects and avatars that fill the space). As this distinction unfolded in Linden Lab, the Lab effectively assumed responsibility only for the game engine—the physics of SL itself—and for the hosting and maintenance of a giant world, with continents and islands and some infrastructure but left to a great extent otherwise undefined. For SL, Linden Lab controls the engine, and the users are effectively the content team.

A representation of the demiurgic, even magical, quality of the creation of this content was intentionally architected into SL. Every time a resident works with the tools of Second Life, whether doing something as common and simple as engaging in text-based chat or changing clothes or appearance, but most obviously and grandly when scripting or building, the resident's activity is represented in gestures and actions of the avatar itself. What is more, if an object is being worked on, the changes to that object are observable by others in the world in real time, even down to click-to-click changes in, say, the object's colour as the user tries different points on the building tool's colour wheel. This publicly visible creation was an intentional decision by the developers of Second Life, and, according to one engineer who had direct responsibility for coding this part of the client, it ran counter to a number of users' preferences. It was, however, consistent with, as he put it, the promotion of 'shared experience'—the idea that while 'in world', the users would be able to be in touch with what others were doing.

But the emphasis, deeply inscribed in Second Life's code, is on representing *individual* content creation activity to others, and again with a conception of content that gives pride of place to the technical activities of content creation, especially building and scripting. Sociality here is the restricted sociality of appreciating or experiencing the content someone else has made. In this way, the cultural capital of effective building performance is valorized, while the social capital mediated through deeper social exchanges is strongly deemphasized. The contribution of many other kinds of content to Second Life, such as the organization of a regular meeting group for victims of domestic abuse or establishing oneself as a charismatic socialite in dance clubs, are not distinctively represented in one's avatar's actions; mastery of these kinds of social creation finds little purchase on SL's architecture. The social in SL's architecture over its first years was, to the extent it existed at all, architecturally restricted to an expressive individualism, where what one creates is not only conceived as content in a specific sense, but furthermore as the realization of an individual user's creative desires.

Rosedale's approach to SL, and that of many of the developers at the company, was one characterized by a technoliberal sensibility; they were interested in aggregate effects of individual actions when access to technology was unconstrained (though within a system the company created and ultimately controlled). This meant that, once the shift to a networked space for user creation happened in 2001, Rosedale imagined SL (the Linden World) as needing many, many people, but he still did not see making SL as making a society, with all that would entail. It was not enough that users have individual desires waiting to be expressed. To create this content in SL, especially the impressive content creation of crafting a dinosaur in real time, requires *mastery* of those content tools. Mastery is an important concept for understanding the ideological underpinnings of SL's architecture, because it points in another way to the status of the individual, and furthermore helps us to identify what kind of learning SL architecturally prompts, and what kind it ignores.

But such new institutional attempts to colonize the human encounter with open-ended experience do not occur in a vacuum. In many respects they collide with existing cultural logics of engaging the indeterminate, and such has been the case in Greece. There we can witness the rise of state-sponsored gambling, which in important respects promoted a normatively charged subjectivity concerning chance and institutions that presaged the efforts we can see around us today. There we can recognize an encounter between an established Greek cultural disposition toward the indeterminate—what I have called 'instrumental nonchalance' (for which most illegal gambling provided a context)—and the relatively recent institutional project wherein young men are called upon to demonstrate their individual mastery of football (soccer), but as mediated by the state.

Instrumental Nonchalance and the Case of Pro-Po

In Greece the state has sought to raise revenue through the sponsorship of gambling for some time. OPAP, founded in 1958, is the exclusive operator of lotteries and sports betting games in Greece. This monopoly accounts for its status as the largest betting firm in Europe, and it has in recent years come under increasing scrutiny and pressure from the European Union, which wants Greece to open up its gambling market to competitors. Some may recall the riots in Greece in December 2008, which were sparked by the murder of a fifteen-year-old boy protester by an Athens police officer. One of the issues that figured prominently in the riots was political corruption, and the most immediate and specific example the protesters pointed to was the state's then-recent action (illegally, under EU law) to shut down the offices of competitors to OPAP's monopoly on Greek citizens' legal gambling.

When one considers OPAP as a state-sponsored gambling company (the Greek state now owns 34 per cent of OPAP—it previously was its sole owner), it is quite easy to look first to its lotteries and scratch-ticket games, which, after all, are in many respects identical to those common in other nation-states. But what is less often commented upon with regard to OPAP is where it began—how it started in its efforts to colonize Greeks' engagement with chance. Instructively, its name translates as the

Greek Organization of Football Prognostics. It began in 1958 as the operator of its first game, Pro-Po, a game very much unlike a traditional lottery.

What is Pro-Po? While it has undergone several minor revampings over the course of its more than fifty-year existence, its major features have remained unchanged. Players fill out a form that is printed anew each week. On it are thirteen upcoming football matches to occur over the next seven days (most on the weekend). Players must pick, for each match, which team will win (1 means the home team, 2 the visiting team) or predict a tie (designated by an X). After the week's matches are played, any players with all matches selected correctly split a jackpot. The matches selected are always a mixture of familiar ones from leagues in Europe and more far-flung matches in obscure leagues from around the world. At the time of my research, each week there were games from eight different football leagues worldwide. Jackpots were exceedingly rare, and often shared when they did occur; in the mid-1990s, jackpots usually totalled roughly between several hundred thousand and one million drachmas (between about US$1,000 and US$4,000).

But in the course of my research in 1994 to 1995, I did not pick up on what made Pro-Po so distinct and what kind of relationship between players, institutions and chance it suggested. I was drawn instead to the very widespread illegal and informal gambling that takes place in coffee houses, clubs and homes and to the scratch-ticket and conventional lotteries that were OPAP's other offerings (Malaby 2003). Through them I came to understand a widespread and distinctive disposition toward the indeterminate, one that characterized in particular (although not exclusively) Greek men. This attitude I came to refer to as 'instrumental nonchalance', and it bespeaks not only a player's approach to the flow of indeterminate outcomes one encounters in Greece within games such as poker, backgammon or dice, but more broadly how many Greeks (particularly men) seek to demonstrate how they engage the vagaries of experience in whatever domain they are found. As I described it (2003: 20–1):

> Instead of concerning oneself with squaring the outcomes in a gambling situation with one's place amidst them through the use of one trope of accountability or another, many gamblers prefer to present themselves as completely unconcerned about these outcomes, placing themselves above the fray, as it were. This 'instrumental nonchalance' is a difficult pose to put into practice, as it is the presentation of a subtle but unbreakable manifest conviction that neither favorable nor unfavorable results are important, a seamless unflappability. In a way, this is a kind of performance of non-performance, as it is a resolute refusal to play along, so to speak, but one which is paradoxically effective in bringing about preferable results.

In the course of my research, this disposition and the cultural logic about contingent circumstances it displays arose time and again as I came to see a number of Greeks act across several domains of their experience (including one who faced the certainty of imminent death but also its indeterminate timing). Contained within it is not only a recognition of the indeterminate unfolding of social experience, but also an ethos about one's own actions amidst that uncertainty—how one's own agency can be brought to bear on such outcomes, and potentially influence them in one's favour. The result is a performative challenge that leads not to omnipotence, but rather to a constant testing of oneself against each outcome as it appears. The good and the bad, each must not matter, and if they do not, only then do the fruitful results multiply.

The segment of the Greek population that played Pro-Po, however, through it evinced a very different approach to contingency and their own agency amidst it. These were typically young men between the ages of about eighteen and thirty. They were, in every case I encountered (I spoke to more than thirty Pro-Po players over the course of my research), very dedicated football fans and extremely knowledgeable about not only the Greek teams, but also the premier league teams throughout Europe and the major national teams throughout the world. Unlike most state-sponsored game players, who usually purchased lottery or scratch-ticket games quickly on their way from one errand in Chania to another, Pro-Po players would typically get the ticket for the week's matches, take it with them to a café and begin researching that week's teams, using football and sports-focused newspapers and magazines. As I note in my earlier work, they would take my presence as an opportunity to do yet more research, asking my opinion about the US national team, if it was on the list that week, or other national or league teams from North and Central America. These were players who were eager to master the complex system of international football and to demonstrate their prowess in predicting the week's matches as selected and provided by OPAP, thereby hopefully beating not only other players (by ideally having the only winning ticket), but OPAP itself, which of course sought to limit their chances severely through its considered inclusion of the obscure.

In Pro-Po, one can see a distinctive set of promises about individual players' performative competence and an architected array of carefully selected games, and it is one that speaks to a player subjectivity that is entirely different from instrumental nonchalance in a number of respects. First, players do not hesitate to publicly display their active interest in maximizing their chances through research, and they correspondingly do not seek to show any strategic nonchalance about the outcome. They stand out against other Greek players of games in their eagerness to show their mastery. Second, the players do not voice a problematic relationship with the Greek state as the mediator of this game playing. Whereas for other games (as I discussed extensively in the original work), the Greek state is the capricious and corrupt enemy (something to hide from or to cheat through tax evasion), for Pro-Po players, the state seemed, to put it simply, unproblematic. The state's legitimacy as the operator of this game was unquestioned—instead, it simply provided a context in which individual player skill could be tested.

The government-owned gambling agency through Pro-Po cultivated a different relationship between individuals, chance and institutions than that which prevailed in most Greek gambling. Players were called upon to engage the complex and indeterminate outcomes of global football matches as mediated by the state's selection of them. A promise of reward for skilful performance drew players into a relationship with the state that was marked by something other than the typically Greek antagonism toward it. Instead, the state provided a legitimate context in which individual football fans (almost exclusively young men) sought to display their individual mastery of a global hierarchy of football teams and leagues in a tantalizing but virtually impossible project.

We can recognize here a disposition that, in certain respects, is strikingly similar to that found in Google's TopCoder competition and in Second Life's infinite landscape of programmer possibilities. It is (like other Greek state gambling games) resolutely individual, putting the player in an individual relationship with the state as opposed to setting a group of players against the state. But unlike its sponsor's other, purely stochastic offerings, it calls for the mastery of a complex and global system, challenging players about just how knowledgeable and smart about football they are. Second, the player's relationship to the institution that sponsors the game is not antagonistic. Instead, and interestingly, it seems to mark a subjectivity where the players' aim is to align themselves with the institution's selections. That is their successful mastery as displayed through a completely correct ticket speaks more powerfully than anything else (even more than their own knowledge of football) to how OPAP's mastery of football 'prognostication' and their own are one. Finally, it uses technology to architect this chanceful enterprise, not only in the actual submission of players' tickets (read by machines), but in OPAP's gathering of information about possible matches and its own incentive to use statistical reasoning for its own purposes.

The contrast in Greece between instrumental nonchalance and technomediated individual mastery strikes me now as presaging the kind of collisions between digitally architected gamelike domains and existing cultural logics of the indeterminate happening now. To round off these cases, then, I would like to suggest, cheekily perhaps, a parallel between the kind of alignment that Pro-Po players aspire to through their successful performance and the simple and largely unremarked-upon second button on that most famous of web home pages, google.com.

Google's famously Spartan home page has long been home to three elements beyond the colourful logo. These are the search bar, the search button and a second button with the label 'I'm Feeling Lucky'. Upon entering search terms and clicking the search button, the familiar listing of results is returned, ranked according to Google's complex search algorithms. Those rankings reflect, in a way that has vast economic consequences (given the interest in commercial and other websites in increasing their page rank), an alignment between the user's capacity to conceive of and type in search terms that index their goals and Google's own complex assessment and organization of the information available across the web. One can immediately notice the 'global hierarchy of value' of which Michael Herzfeld wrote in the context of Greek artisans at work (Herzfeld 2004). This is a global hierarchy of value with which millions of people contend every day in a gamelike fashion. Will the user type in terms that are effective? Will Google return effective results? The link between action and event is open-ended and relates individual mastery of the complex semiotic realm of possible search terms with Google's digitally architected regime.

When a user chooses instead to select the I'm Feeling Lucky button (and it matters little that the button is rarely used—its presence reflects Google's commitment to this kind of practical logic), the stakes of alignment between searcher and Google become even more magnified, because the user is taken immediately to the first webpage that would have been listed had the conventional search button been pressed. We may usefully ask of this encounter to what extent a successful arrival at just the page the user wanted could carry with it something like the magical or divinatory associations which anthropology has long recognized as particularly rich aspects of social life. Google's labelling of the button only heightens the association, turning the meeting point of individual searcher, seeking to display mastery, and the architected value of Google's organization of the web into the occasion for luck. Like the players of Pro-Po, I would suggest, a bringing together of individual, institution and contingent outcomes is on display in a way that highlights a particular kind of subjectivity. This strange kind of luck in the context of digitally mediated experience points toward an engagement with the contingent unfolding of experience that foregrounds individual mastery, eschews certain kinds of sociality and backgrounds institutionally shaped digital architecture.

Digital Anthropology and Gaming—Future Directions

The extent to which such a parallel is instructive signifies, I suggest, the vital place that the study of digital games has for digital anthropology. Work to date in the area is marked by a particularly promising eschewal of past assumptions surrounding games, play and technology as well as a rejection of an exclusive focus on the subaltern. To the extent that anthropology has always interrogated the power-laden relationships between individuals, social groups and institutions with a certain readiness to make use of the ethnographic and other research methods wherever they can be applied, digital anthropology in its study of games is a distinctively worthy inheritor of that disciplinary ethic. Moving forward, the examination of the role of digital games in the projects of institutions will continue to be a site of vitality for digital anthropology.

In a related fashion, digital anthropology's study of games must also work to confront the relationship between this cultural form and the subjective experience it is contrived to elicit. Anthropologists are well placed to move beyond hackneyed understandings of the nature of play (as normatively charged, without stakes and separate from everyday life) and thereby give ethnographic, experience-near accounts of the always culturally shaped experience of that mode of experience we so often label 'play'.

The parallel with the study of ritual is again constructive. William James's (1902) contributions on religious experience enabled us to see religious experience as distinct from ritual as a cultural form. This is a vital insight going forward, because it allows us to decouple playful experience from a determinate relationship with games, just as our discipline recognized ritual as a cultural form irrespective of whether it brings about religious experience. Thus we may say that a game may prompt a playful disposition, but then again it may not. Playful experience is not irrelevant to games, on this view, of course. All the same, and just as with ritual, it is the power of the mode of experience associated with it that makes the deployment of the cultural form a tempting project for individuals and institutions. This way of thinking about digital games and play opens a powerful line of inquiry for digital anthropology that situates them amid institutional interests and cultural experience without stumbling over, or getting fixated on, any particular game's ability to bring about play.

And finally, in addition to pursuing questions about the use of digital games and gamelike experiences, vast in scope, by institutions and about the culturally shaped human experience of them, digital anthropologists focusing on games must delve into the deep and complex relationship between them and the flow of social change/social reproduction itself. Games make performative demands upon their players in ways that highlight the tension between what Marshall Sahlins termed systemic and conjunctural agency present throughout the unfolding of social life (Sahlins 2004). As he showed, there is a world of difference, in anthropological and historical terms, between the Yankees' 1939 season of seemingly inevitable domination and the Giants' 1951 season, culminating in one of the most dramatic events in baseball history (Sahlins 2004: 127–38). For Sahlins (and for Moore 1978), keeping clearly in view the always open-ended, gamelike quality of social life is the only way to avoid the typical mistakes of what he calls 'leviathanism' and 'subjectology' (138–54). Speaking of the Fijian case, in which Ratu Cakobau narrowly evaded assassination, Sahlins writes:

> From the perspective of the cultural order, what happened was arbitrary, but what followed was reasonable. The culture did not make the contingency as such, only the difference it made
>
> Of course, the structural coherence of a contingent outcome gives the strong impression of cultural continuity, or even cultural determinism—as if the system were impervious to the event. But one need not be thus misled. (2004: 291)

What this means for digital anthropologists of games is that our work is not only uniquely situated to illuminate the systemic and conjunctural transformations that mark a world increasingly saturated by the digital, but also to examine the distinctive characteristics of games as a cultural form as they are disseminated through these often-vast digital structures. The meeting point of interest, following the principles outlined at the start of this volume, is between the materiality of digital games, including the way in which they extend quantitative logics architecturally, the normativity that adheres in such systems from design to use and the different degrees and dimensions of openness and closeness for those engaged with them.

We are beginning to see the contrivance of compellingly contingent experience—the hallmark of good games—developed by institutions and distributed on a massive scale, and not only in games nominally designated as such. As institutions are coming to deploy games in their governance and in their engagement with a computer-mediated public, we may be well advised to see their efforts as similar to the age-old and ongoing attempts to employ ritual to prompt sentiments for nations or other groupings. The disposition of play is, in many ways, the latest sentiment to have been turned into the object of institutional desire, and digital games have become the primary technique through which institutions reach toward that disposition. Digital anthropology is well placed to help us understand what this means for a humanity increasingly engaged in gamelike digital experience.

References

Applbaum, K. 2004. *The Marketing Era: From Professional Practice to Global Provisioning.* New York: Routledge.

Au, W. J. 2008. *The Making of Second Life.* New York: HarperCollins.

Boelsltorff, T. 2008. *Coming of Age in Second Life: An Anthropologist Explores the Virtually Human.* Princeton, NJ: Princeton University Press.

Bogost, I. 2007. *Persuasive Games: The Expressive Power of Video Games.* Cambridge, MA: MIT Press.

Chazkel, A. 2011. *Laws of Chance: Brazil's Clandestine Lottery and the Marking of Urban Public Life.* Durham, NC: Duke University Press.

Coleman, G. 2004. The Political Agnosticism of Free and Open Source Software and the Inadvertent Politics of Contrast. *Anthropological Quarterly* 77(3): 507–19.

Dibbell, J. 1998. *My Tiny Life: Crime and Passion in a Virtual World.* New York: Holt.

Dibbell, J. 2006. *Play Money: Or, How I Quit My Day Job and Made Millions Trading Virtual Loot.* New York: Basic Books.

Festa, P. 2007. Mahjong Agonistics and the Political Public in Taiwan: Fate, Mimesis, and the Martial Imaginary. *Anthropological Quarterly* 80(1): 93–125.

Geertz, C. 1997. *The Interpretation of Cultures.* New York: Basic Books.

Golub, A. 2010. Being in the World (of Warcraft): Raiding, Realism, and Knowledge Production in a Massively Multiplayer Online Game. *Anthropological Quarterly* 83(1): 17–45.

Herzfeld, M. 1988. *The Poetics of Manhood: Contest and Identity in a Cretan Mountain Village.* Princeton, NJ: Princeton University Press.

Herzfeld, M. 2004. *The Body Impolitic: Artisans and Artifice in the Global Hierarchy of Value.* Chicago: University of Chicago Press.

James, W. 1902. *The Varieties of Religious Experience: A Study in Human Nature.* New York: Modern Library.

Kelty, C. 2005. Geeks, Social Imaginaries, and Recursive Publics. *Cultural Anthropology* 20(2): 185–214.

Malaby, T. M. 2003. *Gambling Life: Dealing in Contingency in a Greek City.* Urbana: University of Illinois Press.

Malaby, T. M. 2007. Beyond Play: A New Approach to Games. *Games and Culture* 2(2): 95–113.

Malaby, T. M. 2009a. *Making Virtual Worlds: Linden Lab and Second Life.* Ithaca, NY: Cornell University Press.

Malaby, T. M. 2009b. Anthropology and Play: The Contours of Playful Experience. *New Literary History* 40(1): 205–18.

McGonigal, J. 2011. *Reality Is Broken.* New York: Penguin Press.

Moore, S. F. 1978. *Law as Process: An Anthropological Approach.* Boston: Routledge & Kegan Paul.

Nardi, B. 2010. *My Life as a Night Elf Priest: An Anthropological Account of World of Warcraft.* Ann Arbor: University of Michigan Press.

O'Donnell, C. 2009. The Everyday Worlds of Videogame Developers: Experimentally Understanding Underlying Systems/Structures. *Transformative Works and Cultures* 2. http://journal.transformativeworks.org/index.php/twc/article/view/73.

Oxfeld, E. 1993. *Blood, Sweat, and Mahjong: Family and Enterprise in an Overseas Chinese Community.* Ithaca, NY: Cornell University Press.

Sahlins, M. D. 2004. *Apologies to Thucydides: Understanding History as Culture and Vice Versa.* Chicago: University of Chicago Press.

Schüll, N. Forthcoming. *Addiction by Design: Machine Gambling in Las Vegas.* Princeton, NJ: Princeton University Press.

Stephenson, N. 1992. *Snow Crash.* New York: Bantam Books.

Index